1 MONTH OF
FREE
READING

at
www.ForgottenBooks.com

By purchasing this book you are eligible for one month membership to ForgottenBooks.com, giving you unlimited access to our entire collection of over 1,000,000 titles via our web site and mobile apps.

To claim your free month visit:
www.forgottenbooks.com/free226276

ISBN 978-0-265-21676-7
PIBN 10226276

THE
SCOTTISH REVIEW.

JULY AND OCTOBER,

1896.

VOL. XXVIII.

ALEXANDER GARDNER,

Publisher to Her Majesty the Queen,

PAISLEY; AND 26 PATERNOSTER SQUARE, LONDON.

MDCCCXCVI.

INDEX TO VOLUME XXVIII.

THE
SCOTTISH REVIEW.

JULY, 1896.

Art. I.—HJALTLAND.

'And wake the gales on Foula's steep
Or lull wild Sumburgh's waves to sleep.'
—*The Pirate.*

IN a former number of this *Review* * I endeavoured to summarise for the reader certain main characteristics of the Orkney Isles in respect of their natural scenery, early history, antiquities, etc. In the present paper I propose to treat on the same lines the more remote twin-group of our Northern British archipelago, the Isles of Shetland, or, to give them their Norse appellation, Hjaltland.

If the tourist finds it a far cry to the Orkneys, much more will he account it so to the Shetlands. For, whereas the Pentland Firth is but a span of some six or seven miles across, reckoning from the Caithness shore to the nearest of the Orcadian islands, —the northernmost land of Orkney and [excluding Fair Isle] the most southerly point of Zetland, Sumburgh Head, are separated by a fifty miles' interval of as turbulent Atlantic water as can be found over the wide world. But this distance by no means measures the length of the sea journey the British voyager to Hjaltland must perforce take. For, the shortest possible unbroken spell of shipboard is by steamer between Kirkwall and

* *Scottish Review*, April, 1896.—'The Orkney Isles.'

Lerwick, a passage of 9 or 10 hours, sometimes more, according to weather.

Thus, it might be inferred that the divergences from the normal typical conditioning of the Scottish mainland, which I noted in discussing Orkney, would be still more marked in the isolated region of Zetland. And in regard of place-names, speech, history, traditions, manners, and customs, even to the aspects of the landscape of Hjaltland, this is so. The dullest observer could hardly fail to notice it. When it is remembered that the extreme northern point of the Shetland Isles is not much farther distant from the Norwegian coast than it is from the Caledonian mainland, it seems less strange to think of those isles as having once belonged to Norway as completely as do now the adjoining Faröes and Iceland to the sovereignty of Denmark.

As in Orkney, vestiges of early Christian settlements are strewn thick through the Shetlands. But the actual remains of the ancient church buildings are scanty and fragmentary; nor has Shetland anything to show like the noble Minster of Kirkwall. As for the Pictish Towers (brughs or brochs), they also, as we shall see hereafter, abound in the outer cluster of the Nordreys. Of incidents of domestic life, or those dramatic personal adventures which tinge with such vivid colour the Saga-story of Orcady, we have comparatively few concerning the homesteads and notables of Hjaltland. Still, there are ample to demonstrate the frequent visits of the Nordreyan Jarls and the kings of Norway to Zetland, and the constant intercourse which was maintained between the Scandinavian motherland and its dependencies in this northern *Aegean* of Britain. Substantially, the Norse history of Orkney is the Norse history of Zetland. The same suzerainty exercised from Bergen; the same dynasty of rival Jarls contending one with another for supremacy. Betwixt the two insular groups fleets of galleys were continually sailing, bent on plunder or vengeful errand. Orkneyman and Hjaltlander had a like zest for wassail or war: the island homes of both were never secure from the foraying of swashbucklers. The clash and clang of arms were perennial: and, in the deadly sea-fights where ship engaged ship at close quarters, assuredly 'every battle of the warriors' was 'with confused noise and garments rolled in blood!'

From the artist's standpoint Shetland, if we except the highly picturesque isle of Hoy, stands head and shoulders above Orkney for interest. Cultivated fields and vegetable patches are far less in evidence : for the most part the Zetland isles present wilder wastes of heath, more barren soil, duskier peatbogs interspersed with innumerable small lakes in the moorland hollows. But, above all, it is beyond question the desolate grandeur of the massive cliffs along the coastline, torn and shattered into shapes fantastic of stack, skerry, arch, and vaulted cavern, which in Shetland appeal so to the lover of seascape scenery.

In the domain of romance, again, Hjaltland must ever take a special place as having been made to captivate for all time the imagination of reading men and women in the pages of *The Pirate.* For myself, if the egoism may be excused, I may say it was the dream and aspiration of my life, ever since on the verge of my teens I read that fascinating book, to see with my own eyes the rugged rifted precipices of Sumburgh and Fitful Head, to tramp the mosses of Dunrossness with Mordaunt Mertoun, to explore the ancient mansion of the convivial old Udaller, and to track the footsteps of the Sybil Norna through the principal scenes of her wanderings. And this, after long waiting, it was recently given me during two summers in some sort to do.

With these preliminary observations, I will ask the reader to make a start with me from Kirkwall by steamboat *en route* to the chief town of the Shetlands, Lerwick. Let us suppose it may be near about midsummertide, and not the typical British weather described by the Latin historian 'foul with frequent storms and mists,' though we may pray for his qualification as to the temperature.* In this extremity of Britain at that season we shall be able to endorse the further observation of Tacitus that one may distinguish but little interval between the end and the beginning of daylight. And if, wrapped up in an adequate overcoat you prefer sitting out on deck and can keep your eyes

---

* 'Cœlum crebris imbribus nebulisque fœdum : asperitas frigorum abest.'—Tacitus, *Agric. Vit.*, XII.

open, there is much to recompense you. Exquisite indescribable tints of sea and firmament, amber, opaline, roseate, cerulean; with perhaps a passing vessel or fishing lugger encountered dark and shadowy in the twilight. Then, over yonder, about midway in the great Sound which separates the two insular clusters, where we discern a brilliant light, is Fridarey (Fair Isle), its western face all cleft into lofty stacks and *gios* by the tremendous ocean-surge.

Fair Isle (isle of sheep) has quite a little history of its own. From its peculiar situation—an elevated holm lying in mid-sea between the Orkneys and Shetlands—its manifest advantages as a signal station were called into play near eight hundred years back. For it was one of the chain of beacon-lights erected by Jarl Páll Hakonsson, the fires whereof were to be lit on the approach of foes from Hjaltland. Directly the Fair Isle beacon was kindled and visible, the fire-signal was repeated from Rinansay in Orkney, and so on in succession through other Orcadian isles. The first lightkeeper on Fridarey, so the Orkneyinga Saga tells us, was one Dagfinn Hlödverson, who on one occasion was tricked into lighting up his beacon by a false alarm, the result of which was to pass the alarm on to the Orkneys and so collect a great band of Jarl Páll's fighting men. Soon thereafter, a certain Eirik took Dagfinn's place in charge of the Fridarey beacon, and he in his turn was outwitted by Uni (of Earl Rögnvald's following), who, under false pretences, got temporary custody of the beacon, and when no one was near drenched the fuel-pile with water. Whereupon it fell out that, on the coming south of Jarl Rögnvald and his warrior-band from Hjaltland, it was impossible to light the beacon; and so they were got to Westray or ever Earl Paul could be given timely warning of their movements. It was to Fridarey, also, that the renowned rover, Swein Asleifson, once had to betake himself for shelter in stress of weather with twelve of his galleys.

Coming down the centuries, we may picture to ourselves a scene of different complexion in these waters and upon our little lone islet. When Drake and Howard, in that memorable August of 1588, had crippled and discomfited the Spaniard in the chops of the English Channel, and when even the stars in their courses

had begun to fight against him, the great Armada, still numbering 120 vessels, was driven by the elements to steer for the
Orkneys, and try to work back to Spain by way of the Pentland
Strait and outside Ireland. With the pen of a pastmaster in
graphic description, James Anthony Froude at this point in the
drama reveals to us the situation :—

With 'a sea growing wilder as they passed the shelter of the Scotch
coast,' the ships 'lost sight of each other for nearly a week. On the 9th-
19th (August) the sky lifted, and Calderon found himself with the Almir-
ante of Don Martinez de Recalde, the galleon of Don Alonzo, the San
Marcos, and twelve other vessels. Sick signals were flying all round, and
the sea was so high that it was scarcely possible to lower a boat. The large
ships were rolling heavily, their wounded sails had been split by the gusts,
and masts and yards carried away. That night it again blew hard. The
fog closed in once more, and the next morning Calderon was alone on the
open sea without a sail in sight, having passed between the Orkneys and
the Shetlands. Recalde and da Leyva had disappeared with their consorts, having, as Calderon conjectured, gone north.'

Calderon luckily was able to catch up Medina Sidonia and the
main body of the fleet miles outside Cape Wrath, but Recalde
and Alonzo da Leyva, with five and twenty ships, steered north-
west after passing the Orkneys. 'They went on,' says Froude,
'to latitude 62°,' shaping course for Iceland, but 'the wild west
wind came down once more.' What a wild wester or nor'wester
here must have meant to the hapless crews of Andalusians,
Catalans, and Castilians, only those who have been out in such
gales can realise.

'One galleon was driven on the Faröe Isles ; the rest turned about, and
made for the Shannon or Galway. . . . A second was lost on the
Orkneys.'

Though Fair Isle, as a matter of fact, is classed among the
Shetlands, it was doubtless to the wreck of a galleon or transport
on this desolate spot that the historian was referring. The ship
was *El Gran Grifon*, belonging to the squadron [8th division of
the fleet] commanded by Don Juan Gomez de Medina. Two
hundred or more of the crew [soldiers and sailors] managed to get
ashore, of whom—for we know many of the galleons were desper-
ately short of victual and without fresh water—some died of star-
vation, thirst, or both ; and some were thrown over the cliffs or

otherwise despatched by the islesmen. A circumstantial and highly interesting narrative of the Spaniards' reception and doings during their five or six weeks' stay in the island is supplied by James Melvill, who fell in with the strangers, and extracted from them a recital of their adventures. The Zetlanders appear to have regarded the unfortunate foreigners with horror and apprehension as bringers of famine to the island: nay worse, as emissaries of the Prince of Darkness sent to eat them up.* Ultimately, the shipwrecked aliens got over to Dunrossness, and from thence to Dunkerque, calling in at Anstruther on the voyage south. These Spaniards, says Melvill, were, 'for the maist part young beardless men, sillie, trauchled, (worn out), and hungered.' The minister and bailies of the ancient Fife town, compassionating their sorry case, fed them for a day or two on 'kail, porridge, and fish.' On reaching France, Gomez de Medina showed his grateful sense of this kindness by making interest for the release of an Anstruther ship then detained in arrest at Calais.

The current story is that the remnant of the castaway Spaniards beguiled their enforced leisure in Fair Isle by teaching the natives how to dye and weave, after the fashions of Cadiz and Malaga, the quaint patterns in woolwork for which the island is still famed. Likewise, it has been supposed that in the physiognomies and complexions of some of the islanders one may still see traces of the consorting of the swarthy Spaniard with the Zetland women. As to the Spaniard's supposed weaving lessons, the tradition or common idea has certainly obtained large acceptance, and figures in many published works. On the other hand, an eminent archæologist has represented to me with much force that, considering the brief stay of the Iberians in Fair Isle and the determined hostility shown to them by the islanders, the popular notion hardly holds water. Moreover, there is the fact that the dyes used in the Fair Isle worsted work are produced from the lichens and peaty matter indigenous to the islands, while both dyes and patterns of the yarns appear to be much

---

* See the *Diary of Mr. James Melvill* (Bannatyne Club), p. 174 ; and an Account by Monteith of Egilsay, written in 1633.

the same as those generally met with throughout the Scottish Isles.

My first introduction to Hjaltland proper was in one of those dense sea-fogs which, evolved from the warm currents of the Gulf Stream, are so common in Shetland waters, especially during the months of July and August. We had been steaming alternately half-speed or dead slow for some hours, swaying about in the long swell of the Roost of Sumburgh, and ceaselessly sounding our fog whistle. We had crept unawares into some spot in the Dunrossness peninsula near enough to make out for a moment a grim beetling precipice, when the mist closed again. Thereafter nothing whatever was visible till, all in an instant, a gap opened in the dense vapour, and there abreast of the steamer loomed up a huge rampart of dark rock fissured and caverned, with a glimpse of a grand natural archway at its extremity, and above it the white walls and buildings of a lighthouse. The array of stern-faced cliffs turned out to be the southern shore of the isle of Bressay, and the point surmounted by the lighthouse was Kirkabister Ness. Here rounding the corner of the coast-line we pass a cluster of houses and the site of the ancient chapel of St. John, which evidently gave the Ness its name. A couple of miles onward the steamer enters Bressay Sound [Breideyarsund], and, curving in sharply to westward, unfolds to us a very striking and picturesque view of the town, shipping, and fine sheltered harbour, of Lerwick, the Zetland capital. Half-an-hour later we are alongside the quay and ashore on the main isle of Hjaltland.

No visitor should leave Lerwick without if possible making a day's excursion to the island of Noss lying outside Bressay; for its eastern cliffs are undoubtedly a marvel of wild and desolate grandeur hardly to be matched in the circuit of Great Britain. From Lerwick quay we can boat or ferry across to the western side of Bressay, landing near about the old church by the Voe or creek of Leiraness. Or, again, one can land at the jetty below Maryfield, where I believe it is customary to apply for permission to visit Noss. From here it is a pleasant walk of some 2½ to 3 miles over the hill [that is, the dorsal ridge of the island] past two lochs to Brough. As one mounts the hill-slope and looks

back toward the stone-built town across the Strait, one can
fancy the stirring and picturesque scene on the waters of
Breideyarsund during that memorable summer of 1263.   For
here it was that, after two days' sail from Bergen, King Hakon's
great armada first dropped their anchors, and stayed a month ere
they pushed on southward to the Orkneys.   In the euphuistic
diction of the Hakon Saga 'no scarer of dragons saw ever
together more numerous hosts' than those of 'the puissant far-
renowned monarch,' 'the wise and glorious prince,' who had
brought with him in his 'sea-borne wooden coursers' priests,
chamberlains, and fighting men 'breakers of tempered metals,' to
settle once for all who should be permanent sovereign of the
Western Isles.*   And three centuries later Kirkcaldy of Grange,
who with Murray of Tullibardine after Carberry fight made
sail for the Orkneys in hot pursuit of the fugitive Bothwell, was
wrecked in the ship *Unicorn* on a reef outside Bressay Sound.†
French and Spanish vessels, too, have been in these waters upon
hostile errands against the Hollander, either fighting his warships
or damaging his fishing craft.

From the eastern shore of Bressay one may have to signal for
the ferry-boat to come over from the Noss side, sometimes—
especially if it be a sea-fog as on the day I was there—by shouting a hail at the top of one's voice across the Sound of Noss, a
narrow strait only a couple of hundred yards or more in width,
but a veritable roost (röst) for the rapidity of its current.
Having landed and passed the ruin of a little ancient chapel
overlooking Nesti Voe, and the adjoining farm-stead, the best
route, if we want thoroughly to explore the majestic cliffs, is to
make their entire circuit or nearly so, a walk of perhaps four
miles.   Skirting the Voe of Mels and holding to the right along
the cliff edge, we find ourselves mounting and mounting ; the
crags growing ever higher and higher, caverns and rock crannies
gloomier and wilder, screams of sea-fowl shriller in chorus, boom

---

* In the pages of this *Review* [See Art. 'The Orkney Isles,' April 1896],
I traced the further progress of this Norwegian expedition.

† See Schiern's *Life of James Hepburn, Earl of Bothwell*, translated by
D. Berry.   Edinburgh : Douglas, 1880.

of the breakers albeit in remoter depths below yet more thunderous in its rumbling echoes.

For, the island is a sort of down or sloping heathy plain tilted up towards the east or seaward side, where the cliffs attain their highest altitude, and drop abruptly and almost vertically into the sea. When the extreme southern point of the island, Fladda Ness, is reached, the line of precipices takes a sharp turn to the left, and we find ourselves on the verge of a sheer and profound chasm over against the Holm of Noss. This holm is a tiny rock-islet, walled all round with a precipitous face, but flattened atop into a small area or plot of scant herbage, which in the breeding-season is a perfect aviary of sea-birds, chiefly gulls of sorts, swartbacks and kittiwakes, and puffin. Here they swarm, nest, and rear their broods, and across the narrow but tremendous abysm one sees them crowded together over the guano-bleached flat in serried rows, sitting or standing, and filling the air with their alarmed and discordant shrieks. Yet, notwithstanding one's presence in full view, with the instinct of wild creatures they seem to realise the assurance of safety for themselves, their eggs, or their young, afforded by the isolation of their nesting-place.

At one time a frail rope and cradle-bridge spanned the inter-vening chasm, by which the few sheep the islet could pasture were wont to be conveyed over to it season by season. This rude sling-bridge was first put in use about the middle of the 17th century, the cradle or conveyance-car being a box large enough to carry a man holding a sheep between his legs.

From the Holm, all the way up the ascent of Setter to the Noup or Head of Noss, is one succession of recessed *gios*, under-scarped with caves and perpendicular cliffs, with vantage-points here and there whence to look ahead round the sweep of Rum-ble Wick (the rumbling bay) to the majestic culminating steep of the Noup, a plumb-drop of close on 600 feet. Then, if one has a good head, and will peer down over the edge of the great precipices, an extraordinary concourse of birds may be seen perched, rank below rank, along the ledges and projections far down in the dark gulfs below ; those on the lowermost shelves, mostly cormorants, craning out their long scraggy necks over the

ceaseless surf and dashed with its spray, while the swartback
gulls sit higher up motionless, brooding stolidly out over the
water, some of them (the younger birds) so close under your
nose that you could almost touch them with a long stick. Then
drop a stone or two among the conclave, and out from the walls
of the Rumbling amphitheatre the birds will flash and flurry in
the wildest pell-mell confusion, with an indescribable din of
screeches, and alight at length, a legion of minute black and
white specks far out in the dark heaving cauldron of waters
below. One more note I made was that, seen from the brink
of the highest acclivities, the gulls, as they flew about near the
cliff-base, looked so diminutive as to suggest the idea of white,
fluttering butterflies.

Such, then, are the wild aspects of nature to be had in a day's
walk round the rock-ramparts of outlying Noss.

Facing inland from the Noup, one sees nought but a sloping
plain of rough pasturage descending to the point we started
from. Traversing this plain, my companion and I came across
mushrooms in great abundance and fine condition, but, curiously,
these do not appear to be prized in Shetland, for the tenant of
the island-farmhouse by the chapel told us he had never heard
or thought of making any use of them. When we told him the
price these mushrooms would fetch per lb. in an English market,
he and his wife seemed utterly astonished.

Bressay Island deserves a day's exploration to itself. The
gios, stacks, caverns, and cliff-arches along the rifted stretch of
shore, which converges wedge-like to the promontory of Bard,
are something to be remembered. Then, besides Kirkabister,
already mentioned, there are the ruins of two other ancient
churches—St. Olaf's, at the north end of the island, overlooking
Aith Voe, and St. Mary's on the shores of the Voe of Culbinsburgh. It was near the Culbinsburgh church that a memorial-
slab was found bearing rude Christian emblems, plait-work
patterns of the so-called Runic style, and an inscription in
Ogham characters. To these we may add some archaic tumuli,
and the indications of the Brough or Picts' Tower which has
fastened its *cachet* upon a neighbouring loch and farmstead.
And there are many lakes in the island, one of them named from

a solitary monolith or *menhir* near by, 'Loch of the Standing
Stone.' Here, too, as throughout Hjaltland, a glance at the
maps of the National Survey suffices to locate us at once in old
Norseland, for the Icelandic topographical nomenclature abounds;
such place-names as Grimsetter, Wadbister, Sweyn Ness, Gun-
nista, along with the *garths, holms, ayres, taings,* and *gios,*
repeated from our Orkney experiences, but with the foreign
smack in yet greater measure. Nor must I forget the diminutive, shaggy Shetland ponies, herds of which, mares and foals,
run wild on Bressay, and are a ruling feature of the landscape.
'Long-backed and short-legged,' says Sir Walter Scott, 'more
resembling wild bears than anything of the horse tribe. The
stallions are, I believe, or were, segregated on Noss Island. The
object is to reduce to the utmost the size of this breed of ponies
in order to fit them for draught service in the mines. It is
almost sad to think of the fate of these poor little shelties, for
the most part destined to be transported from the free, fresh air
of their native moors and buried underground away from the
daylight, never to re-ascend the dismal shaft for a glint of sunshine or a sniff of pure atmosphere.

Lerwick, the chief town of the County of Zetland, has in
great measure the primitive aspects of Orcadian Kirkwall and
Stromness, especially of the latter; yet it has withal certain
distinct characteristics of its own. Its main street has the same
narrow and tortuous peculiarities we noted in the Orkney towns,
and is paved like them with large flagstones, but without the
central carriage track. A feature of the shops of Lerwick is
the exquisite knitting in shawls, neckerchiefs, etc., almost
rivalling lace work in fineness, and as soft as the Indian muslins
of our younger days. The best specimens fetch high prices.
Then, there are the comely and picturesquely clad Hjaltland
women to be admired, ruddy and weather-tanned, brisk and
bright-eyed. Of Sunday evenings, one notices the curious
separation of the sexes. The male-folk would be seen either
marching about in groups or seated in rows by themselves on
suburban walls and palings; while the girls and women in knots
of three or four together would be strolling up and down the

streets with linked arms, very much as is the wont of the *paysannes* in Brittany.

Naturally, all peasant-women in Shetland can row; and wherever one meets them along the country roads or on the moorlands, it is generally with an enormous peat creel on their backs, and incessantly knit-knitting as they walk. I was much struck with this: so also with the delightfully frank sympathetic manners and kindly aspect of the Zetland women-folk everywhere. Their comeliness, too, as I have said, is quite noticeable. Frames shapely and well-grown, and this notwithstanding their prevailing poverty and necessarily spare diet: light-brown hair, dark blue or violet eyes with well-marked lashes. An Iberian brunette strain is to be traced here and there among them, revealing itself in dark hazel eyes, black tresses, and slightly swarthy or olive complexion; but these are the exception. Their manner of salutation, too, accent, and colloquial phrases, have something of foreign flavour; different from the Orkney speech, different from the accost and intonation of the mainland Scots. In converse with them, a common expression of assent with your views of things in general will be 'that's true,' or 'Ay indeed and that's exactly true,' or 'Weel and that's right too.' Another quaint way of expressing surprise at something said, was 'I hear you.' These and such like characteristics give a dash of genuine salt to one's intercourse with these Hjaltland folk: a spice of piquancy refreshing indeed at this fag-end of our *siècle,* when the smart and the superfine and the 'up-to-date' have well-nigh played out every possible sensation of humanity.

Lerwick is still a great centre of the Shetland herring fishery; but its halcyon days, when the Dutch Mynheers used to swarm over with an immense fleet of smacks, and almost crowd out the Zetlanders from their own chief town, are long gone by. Yet even in these days some hundreds of the Hollanders' boats find their way across the North Sea to Bressay Sound during the annual fishing season: and doubtless still achieve in miniature a little of the smuggling of Schnapps and Schiedam, tobacco, and other miscellanea, which once gave a flourishing contraband trade to the great Netherlands fleet fishing year by year in Zetland waters.

Most of the writers of topical treatises on Shetland have hitherto assumed it to be the *Thule* of the ancient geographers. The great Sir Walter, with a romancist's license, gives expression to the same idea all through *The Pirate*. And when recently the town of Lerwick was granted municipal armorial bearings, the motto adopted in the coat was taken from Tacitus—'dispecta est Thule.' Ctesias of Cnidios, Diogenes Antonius, and Pytheas of Massilia, the Humboldt of his day, who in the course of his explorations penetrated far north into Scandinavian waters, wrote about Thule. The name was familiar to Strabo: it was known to Pliny and Juvenal: and Virgil in one of his poetic flights sings of 'ultima Thule.' Modern compilations of the 'Orbis veteribus notus,' based upon the geography of Claudius Ptolemaeus, label Shetland as Thule. Tacitus, moreover, when making mention of the circumnavigation of Duncansby Head by Agricola's fleet and the discovery of the Orkneys, proceeds to tell us that 'Thule, till now obscured by snow and winter, was descried.' And, to make the prevalent theory square with this passage, it has been inferred that the rocky outlying isle of Foula with its lofty heights and precipices may have been the part of Shetland alluded to as visible from the Roman ships.

The most recent discussion, however, on this vexed question seems to bring to light in the older designation of the name of Iceland the true Thule. 'Houl-i' (Celtice, 'Isle of the Sun'), suggesting the classic 'sol' and 'helios,' passes easily into the 'Thyle' of the venerable Bede; into Thile, and the Thule no less of the Irish monk Dicuil than of the ancients; all signifying that in that vast sombre volcanic yet glacial island, the sun at about the summer solstice stayed above the horizon for days together. 'No other island' [than Iceland], says Mr. Benediktsson, 'corresponding with the earliest descriptions, could have been known to the ancient Greek writers in which the sun for days never set.' *

---

* See an interesting paper read before the 'Viking Club' by Einar Benediktsson entitled 'The ancient Thule or the Isle of Sun,' 21st February, 1896. The President of this learned Society, in closing the discussion, told the meeting that 'he had come there as a Shetlander prepared to resent any attempt to locate Thule elsewhere than in Shetland, but he was bound to say the lecturer had converted him.'

This may seem rather a long dissertation about the meaning of a place-name. But, in view of the persistency with which modern writers upon Shetland have claimed for it identity with the classical *Thule*, what I have said may not be out of place.

And now I must take the reader with me to explore the long narrow peninsula which stretches away five and twenty miles nearly due south from Lerwick, and terminates in Dunrossness [Dynröstarnes, promontory of the Roost or tide-race]. From the circumstance of its being the main arena in which the characters of Scott's *Pirate* play their parts, this tract of country acquires an especial interest. Here one can trace out many of the scenes and localities presented to us by the great novelist, breathe his romantic atmosphere, and verify for oneself the remarkable fidelity of his colouring and delineations.

The peninsula is by no means accessible. That is, to say, there is one road along its eastern side from Lerwick to the region of Sumburgh and Fitful Heads, but no practicable public conveyance, so that the visitor is driven to hire a pair-horsed carriage if he wants to transport himself and his baggage to those parts. We will suppose the reader thus provided for, and on his way, if he has bespoken them, to the only habitable tourists' lodgings thereaway, namely, the house near Spiggie, belonging to the estimable brothers Henderson, fishery agents, farmers, universal providers—and one of them a notable 'master in Israel' to boot.

About a mile out of the Zetland capital, the road passes a most picturesque little lake, the Loch of Clickhimin, from the shore of which a spit or neck of land runs out into its waters. At the point of this spit is a remarkable example of one of those defensive circular towers, variously styled 'Pictish towers,' 'brochs,' 'broughs,' 'borgs,' 'burghs,' to which we were introduced in Orkney. All over our northern archipelago these objects of antiquity cluster thick. They are numerous also in Caithness, Sutherland, and some of the Hebridean isles; and a few isolated specimens are met with elsewhere on the Scottish mainland. They were built without cement, with no windows or apertures in the external walls except usually a small contracted doorway. The walls were enormously thick, and contained galleries or chambered spaces sometimes with ascending spiral stairways. From three to four score of these towers have been traced in the Shetlands; about an equal number in Orkney; a like number in Caithness, Sutherland, and the Western Isles respectively, bringing up the total to over 350. The invading Norsemen, we know from the Sagas, found many a 'borg' standing when they established themselves in these northern parts of Albyn. But we have no written record of the people or race who built the towers: the only clue to what manner of folk they were is to be sought in the relics found within the .buildings. The borg-dwellers used rude pottery, and 'there is abundant evidence,' says Anderson, 'that they were not only expert hunters and fishers, but that they kept flocks and herds, grew grain and ground it by bandmill, practised the arts of spinning and weaving, had ornaments of gold of curious workmanship and were not unskilled workers in bronze and iron.' * It has been usual to conjecture them as the aboriginal Picts or Celts of the country, for lack of any certain information.

Leaving Clickhimin, we pass first the head of the Voe of Sound, a tidal water famous for its autumnal sea-trout fishing, and next two lonely lochs buried in dark peat mosses. Then at the ' Hollander's Knowe' the road leaves the highway to Scalloway, making a sharp turn, and in another mile or so we are abreast of the Bay of Gulberwick. Some spot in or near this picturesque inlet was the scene in the twelfth century of one of those stirring incidents—in this case a shipwreck—which the old Sagas are given to record with such vividness and circumstantiality. In our Orkney excursions, it will be remembered, the personality of a mighty Jarl of the Nordreys, Rögnvald Kali, came conspicuously to the front. He it was who brought over a crusading band from Norway, and spent a winter in the Orkneys *en route* to Jórsalaland.

It was while this expedition was being organised in Norway that Earl Rögnvald set out thence homeward bound for the Orkneys, intending to pass two winters there. The Norwegian King, Ingi, to speed him on his voyage, gave Rögnvald two

---

* *Orkney Saga*, Introd., p. cx.

longships, small but swift and very beautiful. Of these one named *Fifa* was assigned to the Earl's young kinsman, Jarl Harald: the other, the *Hjálp*, Earl Rögnvald reserved for himself. In these vessels on a certain Tuesday night the two Earls put to sea, holding westward with a fair wind. 'But on the day following,' says the Saga, 'there was a great storm, and in the evening they saw land.' It was very dark, and breakers beset them on all sides; insomuch that there was no choice but to run the ships ashore, which they did on a narrow and strong beach engirt with crags. All hands on board were saved, but great part of their stores were lost, though some afterwards washed up as wreckage. Through all the turmoil and peril Earl Rögnvald was very blithe, and heartened up his crews by singing snatches of Scaldic song. The Earl sent off a dozen of his men to Einar of Gulberwick to crave shelter, and meanwhile the shipwrecked Norsemen distributed themselves among the neighbouring farmsteads. Rögnvald lived a long time in Hjaltland after this untoward mishap, and then fared on to his Orkney dominions, whence he returned to Norway to make his final preparations at Bergen for the crusading voyage to the East.

A little further along our route are two more Pictish Towers, one on the lonely lake of Brindister, the other on a projecting cape known as the Brough of Burland: and next we descend on the church and hamlet of Quarff. Here the peninsula of Dunrossness narrows to less than two miles' width, and a valley runs across it from sea to sea, connecting the East and West Voes of the parish. The advantages of this natural hollow traversing the isthmus suggest themselves in the place-name Quarff, which I believe is in Norse 'Hvarp' (Warp), the equivalent of the *Tarbert*, or *Tarbet*, of Celtic Scotland; where boats and small vessels could be *warped*, towed, or dragged along overland upon rollers between the shores of two separate waters. The Norsemen were well up to this kind of work. King Magnus Berfœttr accomplished it at Tarbert [*Tara-bart*, draw-boat] in Loch Fyne eight centuries back. So did royal Hakon in 1263, when, transporting some of his fleet from the ocean at Arrochar in Loch Long, he re-launched them at Tarbet in Loch Lomond, and was able to ravage its beautiful shores and to scourge the

Colquhoun country with impunity. Here at Quarff, for vessels hailing from Lerwick on the eastern side of Hjaltland and bound for Scalloway or the havens on the western side, the short-cut across Quarff isthmus would not only save some fifty miles of coasting, but also avoid the risks and rampage of the tides of the terrible Dynröst.

Proceeding—with magnificent vistas of cliff, headland and ocean expanse both near and far, notably the southern crags of Bressay,—we pass Fladdabister, and reach the tract of Cunningsburgh, whose native habitants are said to be of ancient British descent—Pictish or Celtic rather than Norse—and to have lacked the islanders' customary virtue of hospitality. The long promontory of Helli Ness, screening its *taing, holm,* and skerry, stretches away to our left; and, passing another ruined *brough* at Mail and the site of an ancient Celtic church of St. Columba, we sight at the far-end of the deep bay abreast of us the island of Mousa, and the ruin of its famed tower standing dark and solitary by the water's edge. Soon we round a little rocky inlet (Wick of Sandsayre), and drop down upon a cluster of cottages and a pier, near to which is Sand Lodge, the residence of a member of the present ruling family in Dunrossness. Here it is necessary to obtain permission to visit the isle of Mousa, a permission given as a matter of course to any respectable stranger, and accompanied in my own case with much courtesy, assistance, and friendly hospitality. The Sound of Mousa, the passage betwixt the island and mainland, is perhaps three quarters of a mile wide; but if one takes boat across from Sand Lodge pier as I did, and makes straight for the 'Castle of Mousa,' the distance comes to near about two miles.

The *borg*, or 'Castle' (so-called) of Mousa, is perhaps the most perfect and typical example of its class extant. There is one among a small group of these Picts' Towers surviving in a valley of Glenelg, Inverness-shire, which for completeness and preservation [when I saw it three or four and twenty years ago] would rank as a good second to Mousa.* But Mousa has the

---

* See a detailed account of the Glenelg *brochs* with woodcut in I think the third of a series of illustrated articles contributed by the present writer to *Good Words* (May to September, 1874,), entitled 'On the West Coast.'

superior reputation, and, frcm its having more than once figured in historic times, has secured an interest such as to make it the premier antiquity of Shetland, or very much what Maeshowe among the chambered tumuli is in relation to the Orkney Isles.

The tower of Mousa stands over 40 feet high, and consists of a ring or circular wall of masonry enclosing a small internal area or court of about 10 yards diameter. The ring-wall is of immense thickness, and is hollowed inside into a number of galleries built one over the other in tiers by means of horizontal cross-slabs, these slabs serving also to bond the masonry of the wall. A rude stone stairway ascending spirally within the wall connects the galleries, and there are openings here and there from the galleries into the court, doubtless to provide light and ventilation. On the ground level three small oval-shaped and domed cells or chambers are built in the thickness of the wall next the court, and are entered from it. Whether the tower was originally roofed in or not is uncertain; the court is now open to the sky. Altogether, this structure has a singular and primeval aspect, and its tapering yet partially bulging profile, as seen from the outside, with no external aperture except the entrance doorway, heighten the impression of its strangeness and antiquity. And then the utter desolateness of the spot, situated as the tower is on the very verge of the fissured and surf-lashed rocks of this tiny islet.

The tower or 'Castle' of Mousa (Moseyjar-borg) figures twice in the Norse Sagas; and, curiously, in both cases, the incidents related in connection with it are the old, old story—elopements. The earlier record occurs in the Saga of Egill Skalagrimson, the warrior-poet, and refers to a period about A.D. 900.* A certain Bjorn Brynulfson cast eyes on the daughter of Thora Roald, and, for that his sire was obdurate and refused sanction to their marriage, the lovers fled away from Norway oversea, and were shipwrecked on Mousa Isle. Bjorn managed to get his cargo safe to land, and in this forlorn tower he and his love celebrated their union, passing the winter here; thereafter they escaped to Iceland. Thus, even at this early date of Bjorn's coming to Mousa the *borg* was apparently deserted.

---

* *Orkney Saga* (Anderson), Introd., p. cxi.

The other Saga-story associated with Mousa sets forth how Jarl Harald (Maddadson), wroth with Erlend Ungi for daring to woo his (Harald's) widowed mother Margaret, sought to slay Erlend: how Erlend collected men and carried off Margaret from Orkney to Hjaltland, making for Mousa: how he, the lady, and his followers, ensconced themselves in the *borg;* how he made preparations for its defence. Earl Harald pursued the fugitives and blockaded Moseyjar-borg, but found it a tough nut to crack. Then followed negotiations which ended in a reconciliation, and Erlend Ungi was allowed to wed the Earl's mother and become his man.*

Just opposite Mousa, on the mainland, at the point of Hoga in Burra-land, another *burgh* can be traced; and beyond this juts out the curious peninsula of 'No Ness,' caverned, and at one spot tunnelled through by a subterranean passage, and having a Liliputian lake at its extremity.

Returning to Sandwick, we have a singularly wild bit of country to traverse *en route* to Spiggie. A narrow road winds about till we reach the Bay of Channerwick, and here two ways part, one route keeping to the east side of the long dorsal ridge of the peninsula from Gord Hill to Ward of Scousburgh, the other crossing the ridge and skirting its western slopes. The latter was the route I took, and it has the advantage of opening up a perfect panorama of the majestic western cliffs of Dunross-ness, and bringing into view below you the fine crags and green downs of St. Ninian's Isle, a spot of very remote and saintly traditions. A narrow elongated mole or spit of seabeach connects this little isle with the mainland. Vestiges of the ancient church with its burial-ground and Holy Well are still visible, and a walk round the island reveals along its sea-marge a wonderful series of detatched holms, rock-stacks, caverns, and a fine natural archway.

A whole chapter of *The Pirate* is devoted to this highly venerated ruin—'the haunted kirk of St. Ringan' as Swertha styled it—which in Scott's time was evidently half-buried in sand-drift. Here, he tells us, 'the rude and ignorant fishermen

---

* *Orkney Saga,* Chap., xcii.

of Dunrossness' were wont to come with offerings they had
vowed to the saint, and drop them in at the little lancet window.
Within the sacred walls passing seafarers at times would see by
night phantom lights foreboding wrecks and disaster. And to
this weird spot came the elder Mertoun to consult Norna, and
inside the old churchyard he found 'the dame of doubt and
dread' chanting incantations over the tomb of an ancestral
warrior.

It is something of a surprise to meet with the renowned her-
mit-saint of Whithorn and 'Candida Casa' in this boreal outpost
of the British Isles. Yet that the halo of his name spread to
these remote northern parts of Alban is evidenced by dedications
to St. Ninian or Ringan, at Rinansey and South Ronaldsay in
Orkney, in Sutherland, in Caithness, and here in Zetland.
Traces, too, of other Scoto-Irish missionary apostles are still
found in religious sites scattered throughout the Orkney-Shetland
archipelago : and there were probably many more such sites now
lost to us. For, from the notices of former writers as Jo Ben,
Hibbert, Low, Brand, Sibbald, and others, it is certain that
ancient Christian foundations abounded in Hjaltland. As late
as the last century, the three northernmost of the Zetland isles,
Unst, Yell, and Fetlar, possessed among them no less than five
and fifty recognisable remnants of churches or chapels.* The
conclusion generally accepted respecting these commemorative
Catholic sites is that we are to recognise in the Nordreys two
distinct strains or national currents : (1) the Celtic element in
the plantations of the Scoto-Hibernian anchorites, these probably
being the earlier in date, and (2) the Scandinavian element with
an after-tinge from the crusading fervour as seen in votive
ascriptions of churches to St. Olaf, St. Magnus, St. Peter, St.
John, Holy Cross, etc., etc.

A couple of miles beyond St. Ninian's Isle bring us to the
beautiful Bay of Scousburgh. Then, passing the little cluster
of cottages similarly named, we mount the final hill of the
journey, and, descending a by-road, arrive at our destination ;—
a long low range of buildings with shop and farm-steading

---

* See *Ork. Saga* (Anderson)—Introd., p. xv.

attached, looking out over the fine Loch of Spiggie and away across it to the uplands of Fitful Head.

'How refreshing,' wrote Edward Fitzgerald to Fanny Kemble of one of Scott's novels, 'is the leisurely easy movement of the story, with its true and well harmonised variety of scene and character.' Much the same may be said of *The Pirate*, but perhaps what one notes most in that romantic story is the singular fidelity with which the great master has caught and limned for us the sombre colouring, fantastic forms, changeful moods, and strange underlying mystery withal, of Nature's architecture in Hjaltland. What, for example, could better bring before us the impressive grandeur and twilight hyemal gloom of the seascape than this description of the scenery of Dunrossness, in which Mordaunt Mertoun passed his later boyhood. 'Precipices and headlands, many hundred feet in height—amid perilous straits and currents and eddies—long sunken reefs of rock, over which the vivid ocean foams and boils—dark caverns to whose extremities neither man nor skiff has ever ventured—lonely and often uninhabited isles—and occasionally the ruins of ancient northern fastnesses dimly seen by the feeble light of the Arctic winter.' Or, again, Minna Troil's weatherwise warnings to Mordaunt before the great storm. 'Oh, the morning mist lies heavy upon yonder chain of isles. . . . The fowl are winging their way to the shore and the sheldrake seems, through the mist, as large as the scart. See the very sheerwaters and bonxies (skua gulls) are making to the cliffs for shelter.' And how wonderfully in touch and harmony with the character of this peculiar scenery is the figure of Minna. She loved Hjaltland: her spirit rose to its inward charm: 'the love of natural objects was to her a passion.' In Sir Walter's time sentiment and romantic imaginings had not been killed out of the Minnas and Brendas of the social circle by the brusque deportment and tomboy diversions of the modern mannish matter-of-fact young woman, who has neither leisure nor palate for much else than the latest phases and crazes of fashionable excitement.

So, then, at Spiggie—with Sumburgh Cape and Fitful Head each within the compass of an easy day's walk—we seem to feel we have reached the main arena of the 'Great Unknown's' story, and can pursue our rambles round the cliffs with an intenser interest.

To reach Fitful Head from the Spiggie domicile, it is best to get down at once to the seashore and climb the slopes of Fora Ness, making for the edge of the cliffs, which are full of indentations, each revealing in succession a new picture. From one of the *gios* here there is an especially grand view, worth a day's walk for itself, looking towards the great rock-stack of Gray Noup and the 'Nev' of Fitful Head beyond. One immense slanting rock-shelf here with a fairly even surface was simply alive with disturbed gulls hovering and screaming in mid-air: and a curious thing I noticed was their shadows projected on the cliff-face in the bright sunshine, giving the effect of dark phantom duplicates of the birds flitting about. The whole way on is an ascent, round the Wick of Shanni, along the precipices of the 'Windy Stacks' and past 'Rushy Cups,' till the summit of the Head, a line of lofty clifted steeps two miles long, is attained, 928 feet above the sea. A spot frightfully exposed to all the winds of heaven, bare, stern-faced, desolate, and, meteorologically speaking, eminently *fitful*. Truly a congenial haunt for the 'Reim-kennar' and witch-seer, Norna. A long spur, Siggar Ness, garnished with stacks and skerries, sticks out from the southern extremity of Fitful Head, and another very bold scarped promontory, Garths Ness, interposes before we arrive at the fine sheltered Bay of Quendale.

It was to this bay that the shipwrecked Spaniards from Fair Isle were conveyed, and here they were lodged awhile and hospitality treated by a Zetland odaller till passage for France could be got for them. And into this inlet, we are told, some fifty years since, a prodigious shoal of whales numbering many hundreds was driven and captured in two or three hours. I remember a visit to this charmingly situated bay on a certain first of July. The day was one of brilliant sunshine, and a delicious little sandy nook, shut in by rock ledges baked hot under the solar rays, tempted one to bathe. But the sea-water was intensely cold, rather surprisingly so considering the air temperature and time of year. I had no towel, but was very soon sun-dried.

For Sumburgh Head another day should be reserved. The conformation of the peninsula of Dunrossness, it may here be observed, is not unlike that of Italy : a long boot with a toe and heel. The heel is Fitful Head with its backing of hill slopes. The toe is the cape of Sumburgh, with an offshooting spur or prong, Scatness.

From Spiggie, one's way to Sumburgh is to get round the Loch of Brow, and strike the highway near the parish church. The road then runs about due south two or three miles, crossing the Ward Hill, till the little inlet, Virkie Pool, where the toe narrows to an isthmus, is reached. Here the road forks, one branch conducting to Scatness, the other continuing across the ' Links of Sumburgh,' towards the bluff promontory which is the main objective of our walk. These ' links ' are a delightful breezy stretch of low heathy sandhills, clothed with short crisp turf of velvety verdure interspersed in the floweret season with king-cups and large patches of the golden sweet-scented cypripedium (lady's slipper). The exquisite green and aureate tints of this heath in early summer contrast charmingly with the grey background of Sumburgh Head and with the dun hues of the bare scrub wastes we have been hitherto traversing. The links draw in to a low flat neck enclosed between two sea-inlets. One is the creek named Grubness Voe, a great depot for fish-curing : the other on the western side is the Voe of Sumburgh.

It is on the shore of this latter bay that the old mansion-house of Jarlshof is situated, in which the moody misanthrope of Scott's romance, Basil Mertoun, took up his abode and led the life of a recluse, far away in sooth ' from the madding crowd.' The building is now a roofless and deserted ruin, but it may originally with adjunct offices have been a domicile of respectable size. It appears to have been erected by one of the later Orkney Earls. Close by is the fine modern residence, Sumburgh House, of the proprietor of a large tract of the adjoining country, its garden wall at one corner scarce half-a-dozen yards from the sea-beach.

For a description of the Sumburgh headland, it would be hard to better Sir Walter Scott's. ' A cliff of immense height, which presents its bare scalp and naked sides to the weight of a

tremendous surge. . . . This lofty promontory is constantly
exposed to the current of a strong and furious tide. . . .
On the land side the promontory is covered with short grass and
slopes steeply down to a little isthmus, upon which the sea has
encroached in creeks.' The isthmus and creeks are the heathy
neck and voes I have just referred to : and, as the great novelist
accurately observes, the encroachment of the sea on either side
at the neck will probably in the lapse of time altogether insulate
the rocky mount itself, ' when what is now a Cape will become a
lonely mountain islet severed from the mainland.' The eastern
side of the mount is composed of enormous smooth slabs or
layers of grey sandstone (called by Scott ' sand-flag ') sloping or
' dipping ' down to seaward ; and these slabs, crumbling away
and becoming detached, lie in loose masses along the hillside and
can be slid down with the foot :—a desolate chaos of rock-debris.

Here it was that the Mertouns, father and son, climbed the
day after the tempest, and stood contemplating the tumultuous
heaving waters of the Roost. How vividly the scene is borne in
upon us. The sighting of the dismantled vessel, the generous
impulse of the young Mordaunt to rush down the cliff and save
the wrecked mariner, the inrush and smash-up of the hulk on
the rocks, the rescue of the pirate, the approach of the merciless
wreckers, for, as the old harpy Swertha put it, in these isles a
ship ashore was ' a sight to wile the minister out of his very
pu'pit in the middle of his preaching, muckle mair a puir auld
ignorant wife frae her rock and her tow !'

More Pictish towers. Yonder, at the extreme point of Scatness was a *brough*, as we might infer from the designation of the
spot, ' Ness of Burgi.' Higher up the coast is another, which
has given its name to an adjacent islet ; and further on, near
Boddam, yet another of these strongholds, looking out upon
caves, and over a ' Stack of the Brough' on the seashore below.

On the extremity of Sumburgh Cape is a fine lighthouse,
which I shall ever remember as seen long while from steamer-
deck brilliantly flaming out on a certain dark autumnal night, in
a heavy gale, with the Roost running ' mountains high.'

Besides the large loch of Spiggie, there is another smaller one
quite close to it, the Loch of Brow (*Brough* again, evidently).

The trout-fishing in the former is disappointing. So demoralised have the fish in it become from the use of indiscriminate and unsportsmanlike lures, that now they can hardly be got to look at a fly, nor does the artificial minnow seem to be much good. A common practice is to bait with a lump of herring, and an old Spiggie man told me he once in autumn time impaled on his hook a mouse he had caught in a trap, and with this uncanny morsel captured a trout over a pound weight. The fisherman, however, so they said, may do better sometimes on the water of Brow, where the trout, though not running so large as on Spiggie lake, take the fly more readily.

Dunrossness is the haunt of many wild birds of comparative rarity in our islands. In the desolate cliffs of Fitful Head the peregrine falcon still nests and breeds : and an occasional pair as late as 1894 were known to frequent the cragged cape of Sumburgh. Merlin are occasionally shot in these parts. The owl—a long-eared greyish variety—is met with, of which I was shown a fine stuffed specimen shot not long since. On the loch of Spiggie the osprey has been seen on rare occasions, generally pursued and screeched at by innumerable seagulls. In the rock-scarped islet of Colsay the eider-duck breeds. And here too the raven has his habitat, more mischievous depredator even than his brother, the hooded crow, particularly at nesting time in spring when his young have to be fed. The inroads made by the ravens on the cottagers' poultry, is serious. Mr. H——told me of one that had actually pounced on a full-grown duck in his yard, and had made off with it some distance before he was shot.

The first time I visited Dunrossness, one of those Shetland sea-fogs already spoken of hung over everything

'Like the dun wimple of a new-made widow,'

and continued without break the two or three days I was able to remain at Spiggie. Thus I had to leave without even a glimpse of Fitful Head or the cliffs adjoining. Two years before a weather experience of a different kind though equally aggravating had befallen a German artist, who had come to Spiggie to paint a stormy sea for a picture of the Saviour in the tempest on the lake of Galilee. The poor man passed in fruitless expectancy three weeks of uninterrupted fair calm weather, and then departed in despair : the Spiggie fishermen declaring they would they could have him always with them !

A curious and distinctive feature of the Zetland landscape is the prevalence of the little walled enclosures, or 'plantie cruives,' along the hillsides. They are really small vegetable gardens or kailyards, which by Shetland custom any cottar may reclaim for himself from the bleak heathland wastes so common and extensive in Hjaltland. The dry-stone wall built round these plots is absolutely necessary to shelter them from the piercing winds which sweep over the bare wolds. You see them in all parts of the Shetland Isles ; and, looking across a wide stretch of country, the new-comer wonders what on earth these high-walled structures can be, scattered promiscuously about in such numbers.

Unless prevented by fogs or stress of weather, the steamer plying between Stromness and Scalloway calls in about bi-monthly off Spiggie going northward. This gives an alternative route whereby to get back to Lerwick, or proceed on to the further parts of Shetland. Going this way, one has fine views of the cliffs, fiords, and outlying isles along the western side of the mainland (Meginland). Among these latter, the two Burras which shut in Clift Sound are the largest and most interesting ; West Burra being generally accepted as the *locus* of Magnus Troil's mansion-house, Burgh Westra. From here Minna in the story could espy the distant heights of Fitful Head : and here in the old mansion we can picture Eric Scambester on convivial occasions launching his master's huge punch-bowl loaded with a full cargo of ' good Nantz, Jamaica sugar, and Portugal lemons.'

At the extreme north-end of Clift Sound is Scalloway (Skalavag, bay of the *skali*), a cluster of houses grouped round a little voe or inlet, which forms a sheltered harbour. As one steams up alongside the pier, the ruined old castle built by a dreaded and rapacious Earl of Orkney, Patrick Stewart, is seen close by rearing its head above the intervening town buildings. This castle is of the usual sixteenth century Scottish type and, though much plainer and smaller, is not unlike in style to the Palace at Kirkwall erected by the same noble. It has small projecting angle-

tourelles, finished off below with ornamental corbelling. Over the main doorway of the castle is a stone escutcheon with the inscription, 'Patricius Orcadiæ et Zetlandiæ comes,' and a Latin couplet; and high up in the wall flanking this doorway may be seen an iron ring attached to a pinnacle of the masonry. This ring served the purpose of a gallows, and is so placed that, when a man was hoisted up and hanged by a rope reeved through it, his body would dangle just in front of the doorway and window above it. On the other side of the building, also high up near the eaves, a small lancet aperture, almost invisible from below, is pointed out as the airlet to a secret chamber, in which Earl Patrick lay hid when under arraignment for sundry high crimes and misdemeanours. The story goes that a posse of the King's men who were in pursuit of the Earl had unsuccessfully searched the castle in quest of him, and were on the point of departure, when some one of the company, scanning the battlements from below, espied a faint curl of smoke escaping from the tiny aperture in the wall. The smoke came from the fugitive's tobacco pipe, and, the search being renewed, the obnoxious Earl was captured and afterwards executed.

There are a few oldish dwelling-houses in Scalloway. Above the entrance doorway of one I noted a scutcheon with the date 1755, and a quaint motto, 'Tace aut Face,' over the names James Scott and Katharine Sinclair.

As at Stromness in Orkney, an enormous herring fishery trade is done at Scalloway. During the season it is a sight to see the quays. The usual practice here is to assort the fish going to market into three classes, the rest of the herrings not good enough for classification being thrown aside for manure.

An ancient usage prevalent in the Faröe Isles is said to be still traceable as a survival in Hjaltland. This is the winter custom of what is called going 'hussamillie,' that is, between or among the houses. The term appears to be in frequent use throughout Zetland as well as in Faroe. 'After dinner and a thorough 'wash and brush-up they' [the Faroe folk] 'go hussa-millie. All the young people gather into a house or two, the women bring their knitting, and the men their wheels and cards.' Then they dance, etc., ' High and low are socially equal : all go hussamillie, and all mingle together on equal terms. In Shetland, it is said, there are two classes, an upper and a lower, but no middle class.'* After all, there is something commendable in the idea of this Arcadian simplicity, fraternity, or whatever we may style it. And from my own observation of the Zetland people, I should judge such a custom to be exactly in accord with their forthright sympathetic manners, which, especially when coming from women to men, are so attractive.

The limitations of space are such that I must hurry over what remains of the Shetlands with few words.

From Scalloway a charming trip may be made to the northwestern regions of Zetland, round by Papa Stour and across the spacious bay of St. Magnus to Hillswick. The whole journey is a vision of strange rock-shapes, fissured precipices, and wave-washed islets, grouped in such sort that, if Hjaltland is not the ' Ultima Thule,' it might well pass for it. The mere names of the coast features in themselves carry a suggestion of darksome sea-alleys and gloomy grots—vestibules, it might be, of Erebus —haunted by an under-world of hyperborean mermen and marine monsters; spots where, in the words of the classic singer, ' the seas dashed upon the rocks re-echo.'

Especially striking is the stretch of coast-line betwixt the Sounds of Vaila and Papa. On the islet of Vaila a great rock-stack stands up like a ruined castle-tower of old; and from Watsness to Quilva Taing is a majestic chaos of nature's battlements breached and riven into ragged buttresses and pinnacles by the never-ceasing assaults of the tremendous surge. The sea-margin of Papa Stour isle itself is a marvel of indented notches —creeks or voes where the furious tides have eaten their way far into the island core. Here, too, are caves, natural arches, subterraneous rock-tunnels, skerries in numbers. Then, rounding the corner of Sandness and holding north-east, we can just sight over yonder the deep-embayed inlet which terminates in West Burra Firth, or Borgarfiord [fiord of the Borg]. Near here stood the Pictish Tower whence the Norsemen gave its name to

* See an interesting account of this primitive custom in *The Scotsman* of 5th July, 1894.

the spot; and where, the Orkneyinga Saga tells us, Jarls Magnus and Hakon in their earlier days of amity slew a famous chieftain, Thorbiörn.

The approach to Hillswick, the tourist's portal to Northmaven, is characteristically Zetlandish. The steamer passes up Ura Fiord, a long, narrow, and perfectly sheltered haven : and brings to in the little off-shooting loop or *vik*, where a few houses, sheds, and fishing craft cluster together along a low isthmus. Behind and across this isthmus, a grand vista of lofty cliffs, the 'Heads of Grocken,' are seen looming up in retreating perspective. As for this strange outlying northern region of Northmaven—all but severed from the mainland isle, for the connecting ligature at Ellwick scarcely exceeds fifty yards in width—its broken coast-line is reckoned perhaps the wildest and most diversified in all Shetland, and that is indeed saying much. But to do these labyrinthine sea-shores justice would be to write another article : and so we must borrow a rhyme from the poet-fictionist, and say with Claud Halcro,

> ' Farewell to Northmaven,
> Grey Hillswicke farewell !
> To the calms of thy haven
> The storms on thy fell.'

As for Foula, solitary and remote, planted like Fair Isle leagues away from the main Zetland group, it is a spot hard to get at, but wondrous worth seeing. For are there not its sites of ancient church, Picts' House, and burial mounds; its lofty summit-ridge, 'the Sneug;' the adamantine fantastically-shaped wall of cliffs between the Hœvdi capes and on to the Wick of Helliberg, facing out to the golden sunset; and the marvel of superabundant bird-life which makes this island-fastness its home ?

It still remains to devote a word to the north group of the Hjaltland isles. Starting from Lerwick in a coasting steamer, one skirts the eastern shores of the mainland, passing many a voe, fiord, ness, and skerry, till Whalsey is reached—an isle which still retains vestiges of its three ancient churches, *brochs* two, a Pict's house, many lakelets, and a farmhouse which bears the unsavoury name of Sodom. Leaving Whalsey to our right, we

sail through Linga Sound, sighting the 'Out Skerries,' and their
lighthouse tower. Thence passing the Ness and Holm of **Lunna**,
and opening Yell Sound [Jalasund], we stand over to **Fetlar**, and
enter the Wick or Bay of Tresta, which, should a south-easter
be blowing, will not commend itself to us as a very sheltered har-
bourage. This island has some interesting antiquities both pre-
historic and mediæval. Of the three or four relics of the latter
class, the ruined ' kirk ' or chapel near the Free Church Manse
is said to have been dedicated to a patron saint, whose name I
cannot remember to have come across before in Scotland, though
it is well known to English lawyers, St. Hilary. Great things
were told me of the trout fishing in the little loch, 'Papil Water,'
which nestles behind the spit of beach at the head of the Tresta
Bay. And doubtless others like myself would gladly stay a few
days in this interesting island to explore its treasures, if one only
knew where to lodge and could make sure of catching a return
steamer after a reasonable interval.

Whoso has the chance—or *mis*-chance, some might hold it—
to take the voyage I have been describing in a pretty stiff half-
gale [as once happened to the present writer], will best realise
the ironbound character of the Shetland coast. For, as one
passes now and again the vast swart rock-piles and spires lashed
with white jets of sea foam, and the vessel plunges through the
narrows of the sounds, quite close to a Scylla on the one hand,
or a Charybdis on the other,—one begins to grasp the risks and
perils of this coasting service, carried on as it is all through the
long stormy darkness of the Zetland winter!

From Fetlar our steamer crosses over to the eastern shores
of Yell, the largest of the Shetland isles next after the main
island. As we have noted elsewhere in the Zetland archipelago, Yell island is all but cut in two at á central point where
two Voes have run up into the heart of the land to within a
mile of one another. It is into the eastern of these two Voes
that we wend our way, entering it by a narrow passage, and
passing within a stone-cast of its northern headland. Once
we are inside Mid Yell Voe, the view of inlet and valley is very
picturesque, not to say romantic, and conveys an absolute
sense of land-locked shelter. Yell is rich in sites or ruins of

quondam Catholic churches and Pictish towers. Of the latter, there is a fine example at Burra Ness, which we pass on the way to Unst. And here it may be observed that the place-name, 'Burra,' is continually recurring all through Shetland, tacked on to firths, capes, islands, or whatever it may be, and all pointing to the near vicinity of some one or other of these archaic burghs or broughs.

Of Yell Sound (Jalasund) we hear something in the Saga of the Orkneys. One summer, in the early years of the 12th century, came Jarl Rögnvald over to Hjaltland from Norway, bringing with him two noble chieftains, Sólmund Sigurdson and Jón Pétrsson, with a band of warriors and a few galleys. They reached Hjaltland about midsummer, but, strong and contrary winds springing up, they brought their ships to Jala-sund, and, being well received by the Bændr (landholders) of Yell, went feasting about the country.

Unst, the northernmost of the Shetland Isles, is separated from Yell by a narrow strait, half a mile to a mile in width. Shaping now our course north-eastward, we sight the islet of Uyea, interesting from its group of Picts' houses and its ruined chapel, which has the same special feature seen in some early Irish oratories, and in certain of the old Orkney churches. This is a doorway constructed without rebate for a door, thus suggesting, thought Sir Henry Dryden, the primitive method of closing an entrance to a building by a hide or curtain. Next we pass the Castle of Muness, of like style and date with the crumbling ruin at Scalloway, and not unlike Orkneyan Noltland. A few miles further the steamer runs in between the islands of Huney and Balta into the fine haven named after the latter, Balta Sound. Here one finds an excellent little hotel, and one or two comfortable 'pensions' to select from.

From Balta Sound, a walk of three or four miles across the intervening high ridge of Vailafield, brings you down to the western shore of Unst, overlooking the boundless Atlantic. At any point between Hevda Hill and Hagdales Nest a really marvellous panorama is obtained away round and across ocean to the far-away Gloups of Yell, but to the north, along the

Unst shore, the view is barred by the Brough of Valaberg. It is a walk and vista once seen never to be forgotten. Another delightful day's occupation is to walk or drive over to the hither extremity of the Loch of Cliff, take a boat for the day there, and row slowly over the three miles' length of this narrow and picturesque lake, with a fishing-line or two out astern. Then fish down the half-mile of rivulet which connects the loch with the sea at the head of Burra Firth. A farther walk past the site of the *brough*, which has given its name to the Firth, and on to the promontory of Hermaness, will be a good day's work. From the hill of Hermaness you look across the waters of the Burra Firth to the precipices of Saxavord. Then, to northward, the eye gazes down over the forlorn group of skerries, on one of which, Muckle Fladda, is a lighthouse, and travels on over a dark swirling surge of waters to the rocky ' Out Stack,' outmost skerry of them all, and interesting as the most northerly spot of land in the British Isles !

Saxavord, it may be noted, was a terminal station of the great meridional arc observed and computed by the staff of the Ordnance Survey of the United Kingdom. The southern terminal of the arc was at Dunnose in the Isle of Wight.

Balta Sound is associated with memories of two eminent men of science, who, in the early years of the present century, worked alongside of one another, though independently. One was M. Biot, a French *savant*, who was sent over here to make observations in connection with the length of the seconds pendulum in this latitude. The other was Captain Colby of the Royal Engineers, afterwards chief of the Ordnance Survey, who carried out work of a similar kind and with a similar object. The little island of Balta, which in ancient days had its Pictish tower and chapel, forms a natural and perfect breakwater to the sound, and here Colby and his surveyors took up their quarters.

Harolds Wick, the fine bay next-door to Balta isle, is, says tradition, the spot where in the ninth century the great Scandinavian king, Harald Harfagri, came ashore on his first expedition to Hjaltland to root out the unruly Vikings, and take the islands for himself.

'I do not,' says Virgil in one of his Georgics, 'hope to include all things in my verses, not if I had a hundred tongues, a hundred mouths, and a voice of iron.' Nor does the present writer pretend to have done more than offer here a representative selection from the abundant store of interesting material that appertains to Hjaltland. As the topmost boughs of a tree yield the finest blooms and fruit, so will the tourist often have to go afar for the scenes and regions best worth seeking. And if these few pages shall have satisfied the reader that there is treasure-trove in remote Hjaltland well worth searching for, they will have served their purpose.

T. PILKINGTON WHITE.

ART. II.—SERAPIS—A STUDY IN RELIGIONS.

'THE Egypt which you so praised to me, my dearest Servian!' wrote the Emperor Hadrian to his brother-in-law, 'I have learned to be thoroughly false, fickle, and swayed by every breath of rumour. Those who worship Serapis are Christians; and those who call themselves bishops of Christ are vowed to Serapis. There is there no ruler of the Jewish synagogue, no Samaritan, no priest of the Christians, who is not an astrologer, a diviner, and a charlatan. The very patriarch, when he comes to Egypt, is compelled by some to adore Serapis; by others, Christ. . . . . . .' The language of the Imperial writer was perhaps a little exaggerated, for the Alexandrians about whom he was writing had done their best to provoke a ruler even of his statesmanlike temper. As he tells us in the same letter, he had during his stay in their city renewed their privileges, granted them new ones, and showered benefits upon them, to be repaid as soon as his back was turned by lampoons upon himself, his adopted son Verus, and his favourite Antinous. Yet the Alexandrians probably knew with whom they were dealing. Had they shown as much levity towards his predecessor, Nero, it might have proved so congenial to that vain and hysterical nature as to confirm him in his desire to transfer his household, with its cruelties and intrigues, to the mouth of the Nile. Had they chosen one of his half-barbarian successors as the theme of their jests he might have massacred half the town, as the savage Caracalla afterwards did for much the same reason. But the *dilettante* Hadrian, though capable of awful severity when the interests of the State were in danger—as his extermination of the Jewish nation a few years later showed clearly enough—was, like our own Charles II., too cynical and perhaps too good-natured to take serious vengeance for merely verbal insults to himself. So, after declaring that the god which all the Alexandrians really worshipped was money, he concludes his letter by the wish that they may suffer no worse punishment than to be fed on their own chickens, whose incubation in a manure heap seems to have been very offensive to the Roman sense of delicacy.*

But who was this Serapis whom Hadrian found adored by Pagans and Christians alike? The answer to this question, though it takes us into some rather musty history, affords us a bird's eye view of the evolution of an ethical cult from the most primitive beginnings, which is, I believe, without parallel in the history of Religions.

To begin at the very beginning :—Some 6000 years before Christ the fertile plains between the Tigris and the Euphrates were inhabited by a people known to science as the Sumerians. They seem to have been of the Mongoloid stock, and to have resembled the modern Chinese, who are, according to writers of high authority,† to be counted among their direct heirs more closely than any other nation. Like the Chinese, they spoke an agglutinative language and shewed an amazing aptitude for the material side of civilisation; while even at the early

---

* The letter is given in the Saturninus of Fl. Vopiscus (*Hist. Aug. Scriptor*, VI., *Lugd. Bat.*, 1671, II. pp. 718-780). Its authenticity has been successfully defended by Bishop Lightfoot. (See *The Apostolic Fathers*, Lond. 1869, I., p. 481).

† See the review of recent works on Oriental Archaeology in the *Scottish Review* for October, 1894.

date of which we are speaking, their religion had developed from the rude Fetichism of all primitive peoples into a worship of ' great Fetiches,' or personifications of natural phenomena, presided over by a Triad consisting of the gods of the sky, the earth, and the intermediate atmosphere.* Their principal pursuit was agriculture, as was perhaps natural in a country where wheat grows wild, and from very early times they seem to have been pressed hard by the shepherd nomads of Semitic race, who poured in upon them from the neighbouring deserts. It is possible that a faint echo of this fact may be preserved in the Biblical legend of the strife between Cain, the tiller of the soil, and Abel, the keeper of sheep.†

The coming of the Semites into Mesopotamia naturally brought with it some modification of the national religion, but it is very unlikely that this involved any of the violence and bitterness with which the modern world is apt to receive any interference with its sharply-defined theologies. For, in Mesopotamia as elsewhere in the ancient world, religion was very much an affair of locality. As Apollo was worshipped at Delos, Athena at Athens, and Hera at Argos, so Anna the Sky-god was best adored at Erech, En-lilla the Air-god at Nipur, and Ea the Earth-god at Eridu.‡ Hence, on the formation of a new town, it was only necessary to raise a temple to some personification not previously possessing one, for a new god to be added to the Mesopotamian pantheon, without interfering with the privileges or exciting the jealousy of its former occupants. To such an extent was this system carried that, some seven centuries before our era, it was possible for a king of the

---

* For a fuller account of the Sumerian pantheon, see the article mentioned in last note.

† It was not until Semitic influence began to be felt that bloody sacrifices were offered to the gods of Mesopotamia. The earliest Sumerian inscriptions—those of the kings of Lagash—provide for offerings only ' the fruit of the ground.'

‡ All these places were situate in ancient Babylonia. Erech is the modern Warka ; Nipur is still called Niffer ; Eridu, once a seaport on the shores of the Persian Gulf, is now covered by the inland mounds of Abu Shahrein.

Mesopotamian country where the Semitic element was strongest to declare his belief in ' 65,000 great gods of heaven and earth.' *

It was no doubt in this way that a god originally came to be worshipped in the great city of Babylon, who was destined to figure more largely in the eyes of posterity than all the rest of the Mesopotamian divinities put together. This was the god Marduk or Merodach, the god of the Sun, who was worshipped there certainly as early as 4000 B.C. He was always known as the first-born of Ea, either because the Sun appears to primitive peoples to be born every day from the earth, or, as is more likely, because Babylon was itself peopled by a colony from Eridu, the seat of the earth-god's worship. It is possible, too, that the worship of Merodach may have first sprung up under Semitic influence, though this really rests upon no surer foundation than the marked fondness of the Semites for solar deities. But it was to his association with Ea that he owed his principal characteristic, which was his benevolence towards mankind. For Ea was the culture-god of the Sumerians, who had himself brought to them, according to their legends, the rudiments of all their arts and sciences. And when the air-god En-lilla tried to destroy mankind by a flood, Ea contrived to save a remnant, in exact correspondence with the story of Genesis, by shutting them up in an ark which floated over the waters.† Yet in these good offices he was far excelled by his son Merodach, 'the creator and redeemer of mankind,'‡ between whom and his father he eventually became the mediator.§ The clay tablets, inscribed with the hymns used in his worship,

---

* So Assur-natsir-pal. Prof. Sayce (*Hibbert Lectures for* 1887, p. 216), thinks that there was ' a little royal exaggeration ' in the number.

† A full translation of the legend is given in Sayce's *Higher Criticism*, Lond., 1894, Chap. III.

‡ For the creation of mankind by Merodach see T. G. Pinches' *New Version of the Creation-story*, (Trans. Ninth Intern. Congress of Orientalists, Lond., 1893, II. pp. 191-192). He is called their redeemer in a text translated by Mr. Boscawen in the *Babylonian and Oriental Record* (1889, IV. 11.) It seems to refer to the (Biblical) Fall of Man.

§ See Hommel's *Der babylonische Ursprung der ägyptischen Kultur*, München, 1892, p. 21.

a good number of which are now in the British Museum, are full of praises of his forethought for man. When Tiamat, the monster of chaos, seeks to wreck the ordered world of the gods, it is Merodach who, in spite of the horns, claws, and tail with which like the mediæval devil she is armed, overthrows and destroys her.* When the plague is in Babylon, it is Merodach who mourns over his city, and finally gets the curse transferred to Erech! And when the demons of disease or death assault any of his people, it is Merodach who, on the performance of the proper ceremonies, obtains leave from his father to pronounce the Great Name, at the sound of which all demons fly away.† Hence he is spoken of in the cuneiform texts as ' The merciful one among the gods, the merciful lord who loves to raise the dead to life.'‡ ' The establisher of the lowly and the supporter of the weak,'§ and by many other epithets of the same kind. Even his proper name is significant of the same qualities. It is in its extended form *Asari-uru-dugga*, 'The chief who does good to man,'‖ or, to take the last two syllables, *uru-dugga*, ' The benefactor,' in later Sumerian *Mirri-dugga*, from whence the still more modern name of Merodach.

From Babylon to Egypt may seem a long step, but it is one that the worship of Merodach can now be proved to have taken. The long struggle between the Mesopotamian king-doms and Egypt for the mastership of Western Asia must have begun before the dawn of history, and about the year 3800 B.C., we find Sargon of Accad, the hero king of Babylonia, forcing his way westward to the shores of the Mediterranean and planting his victorious standards in the island of Cyprus. So close a neighbourhood to Egypt implies some interchange of ideas, and we are therefore in some degree prepared for Professor Norman Lockyer's discovery of two years ago, that some of the Egyptian temples show considerable acquaintance on the part of their builders with the Mesopotamian calendar.

---

* Sayce's *Hibbert Lectures*, p. 102.

† The texts on this subject are well brought together by M. Laurent in *La Magie et la Divination chez les Chaldéo-Assyriens*, Paris, 1895.

‡ Sayce *Hibbert Lectures*, p. 99.　　§ *Ibid.* p. 100.　　‖ *Ibid.* p. 106.

But it is more surprising to learn that the best-known god worshipped by the Egyptians was but the Merodach of Babylon in a foreign dress. Yet this is the result of the researches of Professor Hommel of Munich and Mr. C. J. Ball. The name of the god whom the Egyptians called *Uasar* or *U'sir* and the Greeks Osiris has no meaning in Egyptian, but corresponds closely to *Asari*, which formed (as we have seen), the first part of the proper name of Merodach. Both have the bull as their symbol, and the resemblance is completed by the epithet *Un-nofer* or Onophris, which is almost invariably associated in Egyptian texts with the name of Osiris, this being, like *Mirri-dugga*, simply 'the benefactor.' While, as if to make all doubt impossible, it is now shown that at a date when the Sumerian script was still pictorial or ideographic instead of cuneiform, the sign for Merodach's name was identical with the hieroglyph afterwards used by the Egyptians to denote Osiris, namely, *a stool* and *an eye*. It seems, therefore, impossible to resist the conclusion that Osiris was not originally an Egyptian god at all, but that his worship was brought into Egypt from Babylon where he was known as Merodach.*

The worship of Osiris, however, became in Egyptian hands a very different affair from that of his Asiatic prototype. It is true that he was like Merodach, a solar deity, the son of the earth-god Seb, and the husband of his own sister Isis—two names which Dr. Hommel has identified on linguistic grounds with those of their Sumerian analogues, Ea and Istar. He was also the slayer of a serpent who seems to typify darkness. But here the parallel ends. For the national characteristics of the Egyptians differed *toto coelo* from those of the Babylonians among whom the idea of a solar god first took definite shape. The Sumerian, like the Chinese, was tenacious, practical, and ingenious; the Semite, then as now, was fierce, cruel, and greedy; but the Egyptian was, in the words of Herodotus, 'religious to excess, far beyond any other race of men.' Un-

---

* The Babylonian origin not only of the worship of Osiris, but also of the whole civilisation of Egypt is fully dealt with in the review mentioned in the note on p. 34.

like the Sumerian, who was by nature and inclination either an agriculturist or an artificer, or the Semite, who was a warrior or a trader, the Egyptian longed above all things to be a priest. Full of that melancholy ' which rejoiceth exceedingly and is glad when it can find the grave,' to live in a temple all day, to compose hymns to the gods, and to muse on the life to come seemed to the Egyptian the highest delight that this world had to offer.* Among such a people, the deity who in Babylon was the warrior of the gods, became a god not of the living but of the dead. The Egyptian priests taught that Osiris had once come down from heaven to rule over men, to whom he had taught all useful knowledge including the cultivation of corn and the vine; that he had been treacherously torn in pieces by his brother Set, his widow Isis wandering weeping over land and sea until she had collected and buried with pious care his mangled remains; and that his son Horus when arrived at man's estate had avenged his father, and now ruled over the world as the visible Sun, while Osiris retained the sovereignty of the underworld to which all men must go after death.† Henceforward, to the Egyptian, this life became more than ever a preparation for the next. If he could commit to memory the spells and formulas which would enable him to combat successfully the demons and monsters who would beset his path beyond the tomb; if he could ensure that after death his carefully embalmed body should be laid in a sepulchre enriched with the offerings of food and fruit, either in actual or in pictorial form, on which he might feed in the centuries to come; if he could be buried with all the ceremonies which attended the interment of the dead Osiris :—why then his double or phantom might hope to come forth from the tomb, to win its perilous way to the Hall of the Two Truths, there to make its denial of sin before Osiris as judge of the dead, and thereafter to become

* Compare the statement of Diodoros (A. 51) that the Egyptians ' called the dwelling-place of the living, guest-chambers, as we inhabit them but a short time, while the houses of the dead they name eternal mansions, because we abide in the house of Hades for a boundless age.'
† G. Maspero *The Dawn of Civilisation*, Lond. 1894, p. 174-176.

identified in some not very intelligible way, with Osiris himself. But such privileges were naturally within the power of the rich alone: to the poor was held out no hope beyond the grave save of a wretched existence for a few weeks, during which the soul might wander upon the earth feeding upon filth and refuse, until complete annihilation put an end to its sufferings. Those who praise the pure ethics and spiritual character of the Egyptian religion seem to forget that its promises, like its ceremonies, concerned none but a small part of the nation who professed it. *

Let us turn now from the creeds of Asiatics and Africans to that brilliant and wonderful people to whom we are directly indebted for our science, our art, our literature, and in fact for nearly all our intellectual possessions. The religion of the Greeks was not, in its origin, very unlike those of the barbarians just noticed. In the Iliad, the gods preserve epithets which show that they, like the deities of Babylon and Abydos, were once merely the *fetiches* or tutelary spirits of the little communities in which their worship grew up. Aphrodite is still Kypris ; Hera, Hera of Argos, and Apollo the god who watches over Tenedos. Even Zeus, the father of gods and men, has such local adjectives as Dodonaian appended to his august name. But these deities were, for the most part, the gods of the kings and warriors, that is to say, of the conquering Dorian race who played in Homeric Greece the part acted in England by the Normans. The rustics and peasants of Attica held fast to the worship of their native divinities, and foremost among these was Demeter, the goddess from whom they learned the art of agriculture.

The legend of Demeter has been made so familiar to us by both ancient and modern art that there can be no need to do more here than refer to it. Everyone has heard how Demeter, a personification of the earth in its smiling and beneficent aspect, bore a daughter, Persephone, whose beauty breathed desire into Hades the king of the lower regions ; how he carried

---

* See Jequier *Le Livre de ce qu'il y a dans l'Hadés.* Paris, 1894, pp. 9-10 : Maspero *Et. de Myth. and d'Arch. Egypt.* Paris, 1893, I., pp. 347-348.

her off to his gloomy abode; and how Demeter refused to allow the earth again to bring forth fruit until a treaty was arranged by which Persephone was to spend half the year with her mother above ground, and the rest with her new consort. This seems to have been in its origin a nature-myth setting forth the rude ideas of an agricultural people as to the mystery of the germination and growth of the corn sown in the earth, and it was originally portrayed in dramatic form at festivals held at particular times of the year, in the way that Mr. J. G. Frazer in *The Golden Bough* has shown to be common to tillers of the soil nearly all over the world. But about the year 600 B.C., a new element was introduced into these agricultural festivals of Attica by the addition of a new actor. This was the god of the vine, the Thracian Dionysos.

The first home of this god is not very clear. The old explanation of his name is that it meant ' the Zeus of Nysa,' but as nobody has been able to identify Nysa with any place known to the ancients, this does not take us much further. M. Langlois would make him out to be the Vedic god Agni-Soma, but although the myths of the two deities present many features in common, the parallel is not so close as to make it necessary to suppose any direct connection between the two. The most that we know about his origin with tolerable certainty is that the Thracian immigrants into Boeotia brought with them a god of this name, who seems to have been looked upon as the supreme god of vegetation and reproduction, from which, by a very natural association of ideas, he became the god of the underworld, and therefore the deity who presides over the life and death of man. Him Epimenides,—a wise man of Crete who had been sent for to purify Athens from the murder of Kylon and the plague which was supposed to be its consequence—introduced into the festivals of Demeter, and particularly into that prolonged one which culminated in a solemn procession from Athens to Eleusis. The secret rites celebrated on that occasion were probably already known as the Eleusinian Mysteries.

The agricultural side of these rites is fairly well known to us. They displayed the carrying-off of Persephone, the wanderings of Demeter in her pursuit, the gift of corn to Triptolemos, the fosterling whom Demeter had taken to console her in her affliction, and the departure of the same hero in his winged car drawn by serpents to spread the knowledge of agriculture throughout the world. The part at first played in them by Dionysos is not so clear, but in any case the wave of religious thought which swept over Greece about the middle of the sixth century before Christ must have completely transformed it. For, at about this period, a sect known to us as the Orphic Brotherhood sprang up in Greece. These sectaries—it is doubtful whether they were ever formed into a regular association or not—claimed to have an exclusive knowledge of such recondite matters as the creation of the world, the legends of the gods, and the future lot of man, special revelations as to which they professed to have found in the poems of the mythical Thracian singer Orpheus.* At first their ideas seem to have made little way but they were favoured by Peisistratos, then tyrant of Athens, and received a great accession of strength on the break up of the Pythagorean schools of Magna Graecia in B.C. 510. From that time forward, Orphic ideas permeated the whole teaching of the Mysteries, until at last Orpheus was looked upon as their founder. As Dionysos was the God whose worship formed the central point of the Orphic system, he naturally, under their influence, assumed a more important place at Eleusis. The form which his legend finally took was as follows :— Dionysos Zagreus, or 'the hunter,' was the son of the omnipotent Zeus by his virgin daughter Persephone. He was the favourite son of his father, who gave to him the kingdom of this world, and sent him upon earth to escape the jealousy of Hera. But the latter incited against him the Titans, who surprised him by a trick, tore him in pieces, and ate his flesh. The heart was saved by Athena, from which was born again the infant Dionysos, the mystic child whose birth formed one

---

* It is now generally admitted that the poems attributed to Orpheus were not the work of any person of that name. The earlier ones extant are nearly all by different members of the first Pythagorean school. See Abel's *Orphica*, Lips., 1885, pp. 139-140.

of the most impressive scenes of the Mysteries. Zeus destroyed the Titans with his thunderbolts, and out of their ashes men were born. But, as the Titans had swallowed the flesh of Dionysos, every man has within him a spark of the Divine nature, which is immortal. Its gradual purification is effected by successive incarnations, until at last the Dionysiac spark is free from the stains of Titanic matter, when it will again become united to the deity from whom it was violently severed. Such was the story set forth in the later form of the mystic rites, where the whole drama of the life and 'Passion' of Zagreus was enacted before the eyes of the initiate. He was also shown, as appears from many passages in the Attic dramatists, a representation of the torments of the wicked and the delights of the just in the underworld. How much of this was consciously borrowed from Egyptian teaching is very difficult to say, but it is worth while noticing that the worship of Osiris had early penetrated to Crete, from whence Epimenides the reformer of the Mysteries came, and that all Greek travellers from Herodotus to Diodoros assigned an Egyptian origin to the Eleusinian rites.*

Unfortunately for those who love a clear outline in such matters, the Orphics were not content with assigning to their own peculiar deity the most honoured place in the Greek worship. They—or at least such of them as had once been Pythagoreans—were above all things, philosophers, and had inherited much of the teaching of that Ionic School which first arrived at the truth that Nature proceeds only by fixed and immutable laws. Hence to them the stories told in the Mysteries were not historical facts, but allegories shadowing

---

* Theodoret, *Therapeutica*, IV. (Migne), p. 796, *sqq.*, says distinctly that the Eleusinia were brought to Greece from Egypt, and that the hierophant knew that the Passion of Zagreus referred to the murder of Osiris. In a memoir presented to the *Académie des Inscriptions* in 1893, M. Foucart, whose authority in such matters is very high, advances the same theory, and at any rate makes it clear that the Mysteries were not indigenous to Greece. Towards the end of last year the Greek Archaeological Society were said to have discovered at Eleusis proofs of the correctness of M. Foucart's theory. Details are still wanting.

forth the causes of natural phenomena.   Dionysos was not for
them, as for the ignorant multitude, a man who had taught his
fellows the art of wine-making and had been deified for his
pains: he was the Universal Soul or animating principle which
the Supreme Mind had breathed into his ordered world.   But
as this principle was necessarily one and not several, it followed that all the gods worshipped by the multitude were
but the same principle under different aspects.   Thus arose
the work of fusion or absorption of one god into another—
Theokrasia the Greeks called it—which in the early Christian
centuries made such wild work in the classical Olympus.
Herakleitos of Ephesus, whose date may be put at 505 B.C.,
proclaimed openly that Hades and Dionysos were the same
divinity, thus making the likeness of Dionysos, as a god of the
dead, to Osiris still closer.   Then Euripides identified him with
the Delphic Apollo, which, as Apollo had already swallowed
up the Homeric Sun-God Helios, gave to Dionysos as to
Osiris a solar character.*   And while Dionysos was thus iden-
tifying himself with the gods of the Homeric pantheon,
Demeter was doing the same with the goddesses.   The distinction between Demeter and Persephone—of the earth and
the seed which she receives in her bosom—never very marked,
began gradually to fade away.   Then came her fusion with
the mother-goddesses Rhea and Cybele on the one hand, and
with the daughters of Zeus, Athena, Artemis, and Aphrodite,
on the other.   Dionysos thus became at once the father, the
son, the brother, and the spouse of the goddess with whom
his legend was linked, and this in its turn hastened his own
identification with that omnipotent god of whom he was
originally merely the vicegerent.   Some writers even think
that there are signs of an eventual fusion between Dionysos
and Persephone as representing the active and passive forms of
the same energy.   It is not too much to say that at the time
of Alexander, the educated and initiated class in Greece,
among whom alone the Orphic theories had taken root, worshipped a *Deus Pantheus*, from whom all things came, and to

---

* Abel, *op. cit.*, pp. 148, 217.

whom all things must return. But they believed that this god manifested himself in three principal forms, which were these :—

(1) The architect and ruler of the Universe, who was called Zeus among the living and Hades among the dead.

(2) The female principle or receptive power of Nature, usually invoked as Aphrodite and Persephone.

(3) The son of the two preceding, the mediator between his father and mankind, known indifferently as the infant Dionysos, Eros or Apollo.

Now it is a commonly observed phenomenon in the history of religions that a creed which seems incapable of expansion in its native country will often meet with widespread acceptance so soon as it is transplanted to a slightly different soil ; and something of this kind seems to have taken place with the Orphic teaching. Its really distinctive feature—the transmigration of souls—never met with any great success in Greece. It might be sung about by poets like Pindar, or taught by philosophers like Plato ; but there is no reason to think that it ever became part of the popular beliefs, while most of the learned were formally opposed to it. The Mysteries must have been the only centre from which it could be spread, and these Mysteries were not only confined to a very limited number, but were protected against profanation by terrible sanctions. But when, on the division of Alexander's Empire, Ptolemy, the son of Lagos, received Egypt as his portion, the Orphic doctrines were given an impetus that sent them all over the civilised world. For Ptolemy, carrying out it may be one of his dead master's unfulfilled plans, set about establishing in his new capital Alexandria, a mixed worship which should form a link between his Egyptian subjects and the ruling class of Greeks and Macedonians who formed the support of his throne. With this purpose he sent for Timotheos, one of the sacred family from whom the hierophants of the Mysteries were chosen, and entrusted to him and Manetho, an Egyptian priest of high rank whom he had won over to his service, the task of devising a religion which should satisfy the spiritual aspirations of Greek and Egyptian alike.

The result, which, *more hellenico*, was sanctioned in due course by the oracle at Delphi, was pretty nearly what might have been expected from the relative position of the two nations. The gods of Eleusis passed into the new religion under Egyptian names; but, though they might thus be invested with a few Egyptian attributes, they yet lost none of their own. The child-god of the Mysteries became the child Horus —in Egyptian, *Har-pa-Khrat*, of which the Greeks made Harpocrates; Demeter was called by the name of Isis, which had, perhaps, been originally hers; while her spouse, Dionysos, took that of *Osor-hapi*, or Osiris in his earthly form as the Bull Apis —for he, like Merodach and Dionysos Zagreus, was a tauriform god—corrupted by the Greeks into Sarapis, of which Serapis is the Latin form. These identifications dated from the time of Herodotus, and the Egyptian legend of the tearing in pieces of Osiris, the wanderings of Isis, and the birth of Horus so closely corresponded with the Eleusinian stories that they can hardly have required much alteration. But in all other respects the worship of Serapis was but that of the Mysteries in another and rather simpler form. The neophyte had to undergo a long and gradual initiation before he was admitted to the full knowledge of the religion; he was taught the dogma of the reincarnation of souls, which was entirely foreign to the ideas of the native faith; * and he was most plainly given to understand that the new names given to his deities did not prevent him from worshipping them in their old guise if he were so minded. All the plastic representations of the Alexandrian Triad yet found are fashioned according to the rules not of Egyptian but of Greek art. Serapis is always portrayed in them not as a bull or a mummy, as was the Egyptian Osiris, but with the lofty brow and noble features of the Greek Zeus; and 'Serapis alone is Zeus' is a watchword which is repeated with wearisome frequency on most of the monuments of the cult. As has been well said, the new god was a Greek soul dwelling in an Egyptian body.

---

* Sir Peter Renouf (*Hibbert Lectures for* 1879, p. 182-183) has made it clear that the Egyptians of Pharaonic times were utterly ignorant of the Greek doctrine of metempsychosis.

At first, the innovation produced little practical result. Although a few Egyptians and even some temple-servants of the lower class may have given in their adherence to the new faith, the great native priesthoods held coldly aloof from it. The priests of Memphis, where there was a native temple of Osor-hapi, allowed the king to build a Serapeion close to their own, but it is significant that the two are separated by a long avenue of sphinxes and that the Greek votive inscriptions do not include a single Egyptian name. Like the Papacy, the Memphite priesthood had seen many dynasties come and go, and they no doubt felt that Ptolemy's best policy would have been not to set up a new religion but to have managed a conversion to theirs. The event proved them right; for Epiphanes, the 5th Ptolemy, was glad enough, after the suppression of a native revolt, to be crowned like the ancient Pharaohs as the incarnate Sun-God and the descendant of Ptah, with all the ancient ritual set out upon the Rosetta Stone.* Yet, though he thus failed in his immediate purpose, Ptolemy Soter was building better than he knew. The worship of the Alexandrian gods spread wherever the Alexandrian traders went: and under his politic rule, Alexandria soon became the trading centre of the Hellenist world. The novelty-loving Athenians were so pleased with it that they soon began to use the oaths ' By Isis ' and ' By Horus ' in ordinary conversation —to the great wrath of the dramatists of the New Comedy. A few years later we hear of it in the cities of Boeotia, then in the islands of the Aegaean and throughout Asia Minor. And a yet wider field was now opening to it. In the early part of the second century B.C., the Alexandrian gods had established themselves in the seaports of Southern Italy frequented by foreign merchants. From thence their worship proceeded with slow but certain step towards Rome until, 80 years before our Era, it gained a foothold in the Eternal City. Thenceforth its future was assured. As early as the days of the First Triumvirs, one of the proscribed could find no disguise so little likely to attract attention in the streets of Rome as

---

* See Revillout, *Révue Archéologique*, 1887, pp. 339-340.

the linen robe of a priest of Isis, and under Nero the worship
of Serapis and Isis was formally recognised by the State.
From that time, they marched with the Roman legions into
every corner of the Empire, and their monuments have been
found in France, Germany, Austria, and Switzerland, and even
in countries so far from the first seat of the cult as Morocco,
Spain, and Great Britain.   Ptolemy's gods, like Ptolemy's
master, might have boasted that they had conquered the whole
world.*

For some time, it must have seemed as if their kingdom
would have no end.   The philosophers who were once, perhaps, the worst enemies of the mystic rites, now gave them
their support. Stoicism, which for some centuries was fashionable at Rome, taught like the Orphics that all the gods were
interchangeable forms of the same energy.   The Pythagorean
school was also revived, and renewed the forgery of Orphic
verses, while they discovered hidden meanings in the Mys-
sterics which must have astonished no one so much as their
fellow-initiates.   Nor did the worship of the stranger gods
who during the first three centuries poured into Rome, do
much to damage the credit of the Alexandrian divinities.
True to the system of 'Theokrasia' which had given them
birth, they hastened to assimilate to themselves almost every
deity of the ever increasing pantheon. 'The Phrygians, first-
born of men,' says the goddess of Apuleius', romance to her
votary 'call me Pessinuntica, mother of the gods; the natives
of Attica, Cecropian Minerva; the wave-rocked Cyprians,
Paphian Venus; the arrow-bearing Cretans, Diana Dictynna;
the three-tongued Sicilians, Stygian Proserpine; the Eleusin-
ians, the ancient goddess Ceres; some Juno, some Bellona,
others Hecate, others again Rhamnusia; but those who are
lightened by the first rays of the nascent Sun-God, the
Ethiopians, the Arii, and the Egyptians skilled in the ancient
teaching, worshipping me with ceremonies peculiar to me
alone, call me by my true name, Queen Isis.'   And in this

* G. Lafaye *Les Divinités d'Alexandrie hors l'Egypte*, Paris, 1884, Chaps.
I., II., and VIII.

readiness to coalesce with other deities, Serapis was no whit behind his sister and spouse. The Syrian Adonis was confounded with him, and the Thessalian Esculapius, and even the half-Persian god Mithras. It seems as if the worship of any foreign divinity had only to become popular to find a place in his temple.

Does this explain Hadrian's statement that the Alexandrians worshipped at the same time Serapis and Christ? The thing is not at first sight impossible, for at Alexandria eclecticism was in the air. Even the Jews had so far yielded to the influence of the place that in Tiberius' time Philo, one of the most eminent among them, had put forth a compound of the Platonic philosophy and Judaism, which, if not very Greek, was at any rate as far removed as possible from the faith of the Hebrew Prophets. And the Christianity of Alexandria was never distinguished for its orthodoxy, but seems to have grown out of that strange faith which we call, for want of a better name, Gnosticism. Now one of the principal tenets of the Gnostics was that it was permissible for them to profess any outward religion that they pleased, so long as they held fast the knowledge of the magical formulas and ceremonies which were supposed to give them predominance in the next world. We know also from Hippolytus that some of the Gnostics were particularly fond of frequenting the Mysteries of Isis and her numerous analogues, of which Mysteries they declared that they alone were capable of penetrating the true meaning. Hence it is possible that Hadrian, who was extremely inquisitive in all matters relating to religion, may really have come across some heretical sect who did combine the worship of Serapis with the belief in the divine mission of Jesus. But against this there is one fact which seems fatal. Christianity was not like Judaism, a *religio licita* in the Roman Empire, and we may be quite sure that Hadrian would never have alluded to a Christian ' Patriarch,' or have known anything of the doings of such an officer had he been in existence. For the educated class at Rome were in complete real or affected ignorance of the true position of the Christians, whom they constantly confused with the Jews. It is therefore probable that the patriarch referred to is some Jewish functionary—perhaps the ethnarch himself —and that Hadrian, who is credited in the traditions of the Rabbis with a prolonged enquiry into their faith, had failed to grasp the distinction between the First and the Second Persons of the Trinity. If it be objected to this that the Jews were too constant to their creed to bow the knee in the temple of Serapis, I can only reply that the author of the treatise on Isis and Osiris which passes under the name of Plutarch, formally accuses them of trying to introduce Jewish history into the legend of these gods, that they attempted to identify Serapis with (of all people in the world) the Joseph of Exodus, and that those Sibylline Verses which are most plainly the work of Alexandrian Jews, treat Serapis and Isis with marked tenderness. There is therefore no reason to suppose that the Jewish ethnarch—if it be he who is meant—would be more squeamish in such a matter than others of his co-religionists.

But whatever was the real faith of Hadrian's eclectics, it was to the zeal of a party among the Christians that the Alexandrian gods owed their final overthrow. The severity with which Diocletian in 296 suppressed the rebellion of Egypt under Achilleus rather than any nobler motive, led to the conversion of the native Egyptians *en masse;* and the persecution which followed six years later proved too short to shake their adhesion to the creed with which the Roman Emperors were at war. A great factor in this steadfastness was the institution of monachism, which was, perhaps, a legacy from Pharaonic times, and which certainly had analogies with certain practices common to the Athenian and Alexandrian Orphics.* Moreover, the Egyptians had always, as has before been said, a hankering after the priestly character, and this, coupled with the exemption from the cares of civil life that it even then conferred, caused such a passion for its assumption that the whole male population of Egypt were said a little later to be in holy orders. But even Christianity (to use

---

* Euripides, in a fragment preserved by Porphyry, speaks of certain Orphics as vowed to chastity and abstinence from food which had had life. Cells were reserved for such devotees in the Greek Serapeia of Alexandria and Memphis. See next note.

Pascal's phrase), cannot at once make an angel out of a beast, and there was more of the beast than of the angel about the majority of the Egyptian monks. Sprung from the dregs of a people who had groaned for centuries under the *Kourbatch* and *corvée,* utterly ignorant and unlearned, and with brains set on fire by fearful austerities, they brought with them into their new faith nothing but a fanatical hatred of Greek culture, and a dog-like obedience to the shrewd and ambitious prelates who ruled at Alexandria. With such recruits, the Egyptian Church soon showed that she had gained strength without learning tolerance, and on the adoption of Christianity by Constantine, boasted that she had received the Imperial orders for the extirpation of heresy. The supposed edict may be a forgery, but there is ground for supposing that the Gnostic sects which had formed a bridge between Paganism and Christianity were stamped out at this period with great cruelty. Yet later, the Arian and Sabellian controversies came to deluge Egypt with blood, and to provoke the remark from a contemporary historian that the wild beasts were not so dangerous to man as most of the Christians to one another. The temporary revival of Paganism under Julian did little to check these dissensions, and in the reign of Valens the struggle between Arian and Athanasian broke out afresh. It was not until the accession and baptism of Thedosius that Arianism was finally abandoned by the Court, and the Church found herself at liberty to take up the task of rooting out the ancient worships.

Yet even in the death-throes of Paganism Serapis maintained his supremacy. Although Theodosius had forbidden the practice of any religion but Christianity, and in 384 had given to Cynegius the Praetorian Prefect a commission to destroy all heathen temples, sacrifices to Serapis continued for seven years longer to be offered in the great temple at Alexandria. For the Alexandrian Serapeion was a monument of which the whole city was proud. Within its spacious courts was included the famous library containing the 200,000 volumes given by Antony to Cleopatra, and second only to the great library of the Museum. There, too, was the school of medicine founded on the observation of nature in which

Galen had studied. Then came the shrines of all the gods
with whom Serapis claimed affinity, the vaults necessary for
the celebration of the mysteries, the houses of the ministers of
the cult, and the cells of the recluses who were devoted to
Serapis and ' interned,' like the Enclosed Orders of the Catholic
Church.* In the midst was the temple of Serapis himself,
shining with gold, and adorned with the master-pieces of Greek
art. Conspicuous among them was the colossal statue by
Bryaxis of the god represented with the features of the
Olympian Zeus, but with the mystic head ornament and
caressing the figure of Cerberus which typified his rule over
the lower as well as the upper world. Gold, silver, and ivory
had been lavished on its construction, and many even among
the Christians believed the prophecy which foretold that the
skies would fall if a sacrilegious hand were raised against it.

But all this splendour was now doomed. Theophilus, ' the
perpetual enemy of peace and virtue, whose hands were alternately polluted with gold and blood,' † had for some time filled
the episcopal throne of Alexandria, and had taken a leading
part in the destruction of the smaller temples. At length (in
391) he decided that the time was come to strike a blow at the
Serapeion itself, and unfortunately for science, a pretext was
easily found. A riot after the pattern of those lately occurring
in Constantinople was provoked (as the ecclesiastical historians
themselves admit) by the means taken by the bishop to insult
and vilify the ancient religion.‡ The maddened Greeks, few in
numbers, but still formidable from their wealth and position,
flew to arms, and a fight ensued in which considerable numbers
were killed on both sides. It is reported by Sozomen that the
Greeks threw themselves into the Serapeion in which they stood

---

* The petitions of Ptolemy, son of Glaucias, to Ptolemy Philopator and
his successors show that the recluses of the Serapeion at Memphis were
shut up in cells which they might not leave even for an interview with the
king himself. The papyri on which these petitions were written are now
scattered through the different museums of Europe. See Brunet de
Presle *Notices & Extraits, etc.,* t. xviii. pt. 2.

† Gibbon III., p. 418.

‡ Sozomen, *Hist. Ecclesiast.,* l. VIII., c. 15 : Socrates, *Hist. Ecclesiast.,*
l. V., c. 16, etc.

a siege in form, but this is not stated by other writers, and was probably invented to excuse the acts of vandalism that followed. It is clear, however, that by some means Theodosius was persuaded to give the bishop a free hand in the matter, and that the latter and his monks entered the place under the protection of the Imperial troops. Once there, they broke in pieces or melted down all the statues of the gods on which they could lay their hands, and razed the temple to the ground. There is some doubt as to whether the destruction extended to the library and other buildings, but as M. Botti, the Curator of the Alexandrian Municipal Museum, claims to have discovered the site of the Serapeion, and his excavations will probably solve this question, it seems unnecessary to dwell further upon it. It is at any rate certain that a Church dedicated characteristically enough to no Christian saint but to the feeble Emperor Arcadius, was built upon the ruins of the Serapeion, and that the worship of the Alexandrian gods after having endured for a period of 700 years was thus finally extinguished. Ecclesiastical writers have it that a great number of the worshippers of Serapis immediately received Christianity,* and it is to this fact that Protestant controversialists have attributed the introduction into the Church of the adoration of the Virgin, the doctrines of the Immaculate Conception and the Real Presence, the use of images and incense, and, in short, all the dogmas and practices of the Catholics which the sects rejected at the Reformation. But this matter also is beyond the scope of this paper.

Some notice of the causes which led to the success of this—the first world-religion which appeared in the West—may not be so much out of place. First, it must be remarked that anything like a priestly caste was unknown to the Greeks. In some cities, the priests were chosen for their personal beauty; in others, for their wealth; in all, their functions were so purely ministerial that they did not interfere with their lay occupations, and carried with them no obligation to extend the worship of the divinities whom they served. But in the Alexandrian cult all this was changed. In Ptolemaic Egypt the worship of Serapis was an

---

* Socrates, *op. cit.*, L. V., c. 17.

established and endowed religion, the ministers of which were officers of state. In other parts of the Hellenist world, as in Rome, its propagation was at first the work of voluntary associations, but so soon as a temple was built, its services were provided for out of the offerings of the faithful. In both cases the same result was achieved. The priests of Serapis became, in their own phrase, 'a sacred soldiery,' * devoting their whole lives to the service of the religion and profoundly interested in its extension. From this came stately processions through the streets, a splendid ritual in which even the uninitiated were allowed to join, and the use of all the means by which priests in all ages have tried to arouse the enthusiasm of the indifferent. The Alexandrian worship probably did more to spread the knowledge of its faith in a single decade than did the Mysteries of Eleusis during the thousand years of their existence.

Another point that must not be lost sight of is the great simplicity of its theology. In the Mysteries the devout must always have been puzzled to reconcile their duty to Zeus 'father of gods and men,' but the ruler of a third only of the Universe, with the reverence which the mystic rites taught them for the gods of the underworld. But the universal supremacy of Serapis, 'the greatest of the highest, and the ruler of the greatest gods,' † was asserted from the first. 'He is an independent (*i.e.*, self-existent) god,' says Aristides . . . . . 'not inferior to a greater power, but is present in all things, and fills the Universe.' 'Wouldst thou know what god I am?' said his oracle in the reign of the first Ptolemy to the Cyprian King, Nicocreon; 'I myself will tell thee. The world of heaven is my head, the sea my belly, my feet are the earth, my ears are in the ether; my far beaming eye is the radiant light of the sun.' ‡ The 'monotheistic pantheism,' as it has been called, of the Orphics could hardly be more precisely stated.

But, after all, the world accepted the Alexandrian worship because it came to it in its hour of need. Alexander's conquests had carried the Greek language and culture to the furthest limits

---

* Apuleius, *Metamorphoses*, 1. XI., c. 15.   † *Ibid.*, c. 30.
‡ Macrobius, *Saturnalia*, 1., I., c 20.

of the then known earth, and had broken down the barriers which a jealous patriotism had set up between people and people, as well as between god and god. The rise of the Roman power had followed to establish the reign of law throughout the world, and to accustom the nations to the idea of a Supreme Ruler before whom, as before a father, all the peoples of the earth should be equal. But side by side with this, a conception of the Deity as an all-ruling Providence, the personification of mercy and love, was forming in the minds of men, and only at Eleusis had it found expression in a formal creed. 'Those masculine goddesses,' to quote the words of Renan, 'for ever brandishing a spear from the height of an Acropolis, no longer awoke any sentiment,' nor was it very natural that they should. The Hera of Homer does not conceal her scorn for the 'creatures of a day'; Athena rages with implacable spite against any mortal who is unlucky enough to offend her; even Aphrodite is forward to thrust herself into scenes of blood and battle. Alone among the Greek divinities, Demeter stands as the ideal of the gentler and more humane emotions, the type of divine sorrow and of purified affection. And it was this type that the Alexandrians gave to the world. Isis was to her worshippers 'the haven of peace and the altar of pity.' 'Thou holy and eternal protectress of the race of men,' prays to her the suppliant in Apuleius, 'thou who ever givest good gifts to comfort-needing mortals, thou bestowest upon the lot of the wretched the sweet affection of a mother.' While her consort Serapis, true descendant of the 'merciful lords,' Merodach and Osiris, extends to the human race the protection which they formerly confined to particular nations, 'The protector and saviour of all men'; 'The most loving of the gods towards mankind'; 'He alone among the gods is ready to help him who invokes him in his need'; 'He is greatly turned towards mercy . . . . . turning ever to the salvation of those who need it alway.' Such are the terms in which Aristides addresses him. And in this way, too, it has been said* his worship did much to 'prepare and facilitate' the advent of Christianity.

F. LEGGE.

---

* Lafaye, *op. cit.*, p. 169 (quoting Bottiger's *Isis Vesper*).

Art. III.—THE UNIVERSITIES OF EUROPE IN THE MIDDLE AGES.

The Universities of Europe in the Middle Ages. Hastings Rashdall. 2 vols. Oxford: at the Clarendon Press. 1875.

IT is not so long ago that it was the fashion to say that the days of Universities were over; Carlyle laid it down that the University of the future would be the library of books, where the scholar would roam and read at his will. But so far is this from proving to be the case, that it may well be doubted whether Universities have ever, since their early days, played a more vigorous part in the life of their respective countries than at the present time. In France the freedom of the provincial Universities is being emancipated from the centralization of Paris; in Germany the 'Socialists of the Chair' have contributed and are contributing a powerful solvent to the present organization of the relations between Capital and Labour; in Great Britain the Universities, old and new, have never attracted more students to themselves, while their influence makes itself felt in all departments of education; in the United States so popular is the idea of University culture that it draws from the pockets of the munificent millionaire endowments which bid fair soon to eclipse the ancient wealth of Oxford and Cambridge, and the State subventions of Germany.

It was natural that this revival of present interest should stimulate study as to the past history of the Universities, and it was high time that something should be done in this direction. Not that patriotic sons had failed in the past to write the stories of their Almæ Matres; each old University had its historian, or its many historians; in the case of some of them, *e.g.*, Oxford or Bologna, the mere list of books professing to tell their story, in whole or in part, swells to a treatise. But it was patriotism and not criticism which inspired these studies; few chapters in the history of literature contain more reckless assertions or even more unblushing forgeries, than the works of the University annalists. This was due to several causes, which it may be well to illustrate. In the first place, the Mediæval University attached such importance to authority and prescription that absolute forgery was employed to supply documents, which had all the authority of the 'littera scripta,' and the authenticity of which no one thought of examining. So, probably as early as the beginning of the thirteenth century, a charter was produced at Bologna, which purported to derive the foundation of that University from Theodosius II. in 433. Unfortunately 'the zeal of the forgers somewhat over-shot the mark, and discredited itself by producing two distinct charters, each professing to be issued by the same Emperor in the same year.' At Oxford the forgeries were as unblushing, but they concerned rather individual foundations like University College than the University as a whole; Cambridge, however, was not outdone in audacity even by Bologna. As soon as it began to rise into prominence as an European, and not merely a provincial school, it proceeded to furnish itself with an antiquity commensurate with its new importance, by producing a bull of privileges, purporting to be granted by Pope Honorius I. in 624, in which the Pontiff says that he himself had been a student of Cambridge. This reckless forgery, with other documents equally valuable, was made the base of the legatine judgment, given at Barnwell in 1432, in favour of the ecclesiastical independence of the University. Such stories as these are only interesting in the combination of reverence for authority and of lack of criticism, which is characteristic of the Mediæval mind, and which had such an important influence on the faith of Europe in the ready acceptance it secured for the Forged Decretals of Isidore.

But it was not only by actual forgeries that the University annalists swelled their histories. Mere assertion went for much, without any trouble being taken to substantiate it. Thus Charlemagne had a prescriptive right to be called the founder of the great University of Paris, and its historian Du Boulay ('perhaps the stupidest man that ever wrote a valuable book' as Mr. Rashdall quaintly calls him), fills 2 folios of his colossal work with the history of the University during 400 years of non-existence. Alfred the Great has been so often asserted to be the founder of Oxford that the 'tale still has a kind of underground existence in University calendars, in second-rate guide-books, and in popular histories of England.' And this brings us naturally to the third cause for the vast amount of fiction which has grown up round University history; the popular imagination, especially the imagination of an uncritical period, demands a personal agent; it cannot conceive of a great institution, whether constitutional or educational, without a definite founder. Hence what was really the result of the slow process of time, is attributed to a definite year and a definite person; thus the English Parliament is still put down in historical handbooks as the creation of Earl Simon de Montfort, though scholars have shown clearly that it was the gradual outcome of the union between a centralized government and the local institutions of the English people. This tendency to ascribe the origin of Universities to the definite action of an individual was stimulated by the fact that this really was the origin of later Universities; the generations that saw these institutions being founded by Popes and Kings and Emperors, could not understand that the model had been given by the united work of generations of forgotten scholars.

The critical history of Universities is the work of our own century. Savigny led the way, and his ideas have been developed and illustrated by the labours of generations of scholars, prominent among whom is Denifle, the under-Archivist of the Holy See, whose great work on *The Universities of the Middle Ages to* 1400, is still incomplete. Mr. Rashdall's attention was turned to the history of Universities as long ago as 1883, by its being chosen as the subject for the Chancellor's Prize at Oxford; his essay, which was then successful, has appeared after twelve years of steady work in the two splendid volumes which are before us. He modestly disclaims much originality except in regard to the English Universities, where Father Denifle is for once incomplete (it is curious that, in University history as elsewhere, the giants of Continental scholarship are so incomplete as to things English); but it is a real service to the history of education and of the intellectual movement of the Middle Ages, to have the whole evidence as to them critically considered, and the results set forth with a clearness which leaves little to be desired, and a vigour and humour which enliven the dullest constitutional points.

It is to be hoped that this book of Mr. Rashdall's has, once for all, settled for Englishmen the question of the real meaning of the word 'University;' the old superstition that it had something to do with the universal range of the studies pursued, dies hard; even Mr. Gladstone, in his Romanes lecture at Oxford in 1892, seemed still to favour it, although he also gave the real origin of the word. The mistake is natural, for the idea that all knowledge is the province of a University is a noble one, but it is a mistake all the same; in the mediæval Universities there was no pretence at aiming at universality of study, and 'universitas' simply denotes a corporation or organized body; originally 'scholarium' or 'magistrorum' was always added as a defining term, and the word is used as much for the guilds of traders as it is for those of students. Among the instances which Mr. Rashdall quotes of the use of the word 'universitas,' there is a most curious one which illustrates admirably its wide application. In the year 1284, the Pisans were defeated by the Genoese, and a large number of captives were taken, who were kept in prison for eighteen years: they assumed the right of using a common seal with the legend 'Sigillum *universitatis* carceratorum Januæ detentorum.' 'Universitas' then is originally a word of wide use, which has become specialized just as 'college,' 'convent,' 'corps,' and many others have done.

The causes which led to the formation of these unions were various, and, as will be seen later, the form which they took was various also, but they were one part of the revival of civilization and learning, which begins with the eleventh century. As Mr. Rashdall points out, there is no evidence for the widely spread theory which connects the new birth of Europe with the passing of the millennial year and the relief from the terror of an immediate Apocalypse. The causes were much more mundane, more widespread and slow working; they were the growth of civic life, the cessation or the checking of the raids of Northmen and Saracens, the general restoration of order in Europe, and the increased intercourse with the East: above all the two great institutions of mediæval Europe, the Empire and the Church, had been reformed, and were once more realities; the emperors of the Saxon house had restored the power of the Holy Roman Empire, and had revived the sanctity of the Holy See.

It was Italy which led the way in this Renaissance of the twelfth century, and among the Universities of Italy, Bologna was certainly the first. The medical school of Salerno, it is true, was, from the end of the eleventh to the middle of the thirteenth century, as indisputably the head of European medicine as Bologna was of the study of Law, or Paris of the Scholastic Philosophy; to it patients came to be cured from all parts of Europe, and some of the current medical maxims of our own day may still be traced to its 'Flos Medicinæ,' which was dedicated to Robert Duke of Normandy, as 'King of the English,' when he stayed there to be cured of his wound after the First Crusade. This venerable source is responsible for the dictum 'post coenam stabis aut passus mille meabis,' and for the limitation of a man's proper amount of sleep to six hours (the popular version, however, differs in its further details from that quoted by Mr. Rashdall.)

But Salerno remained exclusively medical, and it seems to have exercised no influence on the formation of other schools. Bologna on the other hand was the great model of the student-universities everywhere; from it (though probably indirectly through Orleans) the Scotch Universities derive the popular election of the Rector, which remains in them alone, among modern seats of learning, as an interesting survival of the freedom of the mediæval student. Bologna has, in our own day, chosen the year 1088 for commemoration of its octocentenary, and the magnificent pageants on that occasion, in which scholars from all parts of Europe and from the New World took part, were a striking evidence of the revived interest in universities and their history; but it is impossible to consider that the University as an organised body dates from that date, even though its great scholar, Irnerius, was lecturing there then or shortly after. For it is not only the presence of one or of many scholars which makes a University; we must be able to trace in it an organised corporate life and definite privileges of self-government. Of these we have the first evidence in the famous decree of the Emperor Frederic I., the 'Authentic Habita,' given at the Diet of Roncaglia in 1158. By this scholars are taken under the special protection of the Emperor, and the privilege is given to a scholar, in case of legal proceedings against him, of being cited 'before his own master or before the bishop of the city.' It is true these privileges are granted not to Bologna alone, but to the students of all Lombardy. The Doctors of Bologna, however, had played a prominent part in the Diet, and we may fairly assume that already there was some sort of organisation, by which a recognised course of study was demanded of those who would be teachers or doctors, and that they were required, before attaining this rank, to obtain the approval of those who were already teaching. Of such a body we have no evidence in Bologna before 1215, but probably it is mere accident that there is no earlier evidence, and the corporation of teachers had some existence very soon after the middle of the preceding century, if not before. It was one of the fundamental ideas of the Roman law that those engaged in any lawful occupation might form themselves into a 'college' or body for the advancement of their common interests, and that admission to this body should be determined by the consent of those who were already members, and should be conditional on proved fitness for the discharge of the duties.

Here then we have the root idea out of which university degrees grew up. The most important element in them always was, whatever other conditions were imposed, that the candidate should have approved himself to those who were masters before him, or to their representatives, and should after this be admitted to be his own master. The degrees of the most modern Universities are still conferred in a solemn convocation, in the presence of those who have already graduated; even

Oxford, where unfortunately the frequency of degree ceremonies has robbed them as a rule of dignity, and sometimes
almost of decency, the form is kept up that no degree can be
given unless there are at least nine M.A.s present to sanction
its conferment.

It was not this organization of teachers, however, which
was the real University of Bologna. As has been said, that
was of the student type. Its origin must be sought in the
crowd of students whom the lectures of Irnerius and his successors had drawn to Bologna. These were often men of
mature age, clerics who wished to improve their knowledge
of church law, or laymen in important positions; and many of
them too came from foreign countries, especially from Germany.
They found themselves in an Italian town without the rights
of citizenship, for in the free republics of mediæval Italy as in
Greece, these depended on birth, and were not lightly given
to the alien ; hence it was natural for the students to organize
themselves into a union of their own, or into a universitas.

The ' universities' of the students then, like any other
mediæval guild, grew up from voluntary association. Its head
received the afterwards honourable title of ' Rector,' because
that was the usual Latin title of the time for the chief magistrate of a town (the Podesta) or for the head of a guild. When
this association of students came into existence we cannot say
definitely, but the first reference to it is just at the close of the
twelfth century when one of the law professors at Bologna
(Bassianus) disputes the right of the scholars to elect a Rector.
Once formed, however, it rapidly grew into a great power ; for
on the presence of the students depended alike the prosperity
of the town and of the professors. Any obnoxious tradesman or
teacher could be ' boycotted,' and so brought to reason. And
here we must notice how the origin of the guilds among the
foreign students led to a very curious result, *i.e.*, that the professors had no share in them. These (as a rule) were from
the first, citizens of Bologna, and in the end all the
' ordinary' chairs were reserved for natives; hence they already
enjoyed that protection by law which the students sought by
association. But this separation between professor and

student, which began thus accidentally, resulted in a position of dependence for the professors, which to modern eyes seems anomalous in the extreme.

We can trace something of the organization of these early student universities from the statutes of the German nation, which have come down to us, and from the accounts of the year 1292, which have been also preserved. The statutes define the object of the guild as 'fraternal charity, mutual association and amity, the consolation of the sick and the support of the needy, the conduct of funerals, the attendance and escort of those taking degrees, and the spiritual advantage of students.' From the accounts we get a livelier picture; the payments are chiefly devoted to convivial purposes, and sometimes the items are very suggestive in their juxtaposition, *e.g.*, when an expenditure of £3 for 'malmsey wine' is immediately followed by an entry 'for broken windows.'

The associations with their common rector and his counsellors came in time to rule the professors with a rod of iron. We may quote some illustrations of this from Mr. Rashdall (I., p. 197, *seq.*)

A professor who wished for a holiday, had to get leave from his own students, and from the rector and consiliarii. By the city regulations he was counted as absent (and therefore fined), unless he had an audience of at least five for an ordinary, and three for an extraordinary lecture. He was bound to begin punctually when the bell of St. Peter's began to ring for mass, under pain of a fine of twenty solidi, and he must not continue one minute after the bell has begun to ring for tierce. To prevent him spending a disproportionate amount of time over the early parts of his book, the law texts were divided into 'puncta;' he was required to have reached each of these at a specified date, and he had to deposit ten Bolognese pounds with a banker, and forfeit a certain part of this for every day that he was late.

It seems at first sight as if the position of the professors must have been almost intolerable: we must remember, however, that a student always depended on these oppressed teachers for his degree, and that the statutes represent only the student's view of the duties of professors. If we reconstructed the behaviour of the modern student from the statutory limitations imposed on him by his superiors, we should arrive at a conclusion which hardly corresponds with the reality; perhaps the mediæval professors were equally able to evade the statutes against them.

The injunctions for the students' own discipline are much less elaborate. They are to wear their gowns of 'statutable or black stuff' under a penalty of three pounds, and there are strict regulations against gaming. Among these the most curious is that which forbids men to play at all, even in their own houses, for three months before going down. Was this to secure those still up and to prevent bad debts? Or was it from regard to the departing student?

The struggles of the University of Bologna against the city, and the gradual growth of its privileges, cannot be entered on here, but it is important to notice how materially it differed from the northern universities, of which Paris was the model, not only in organization but also in the character of its studies and its students. The Bolognese professor or scholar was by no means necessarily a ' clerk,' although the Rector was bound to be at least in minor orders, as otherwise he could not have exercised jurisdiction over clerical students, and the prevailing studies of Bologna were always legal or medical. Before the 14th century, theology was left to the regular clergy, especially the Mendicant Friars, and it was only in 1352 that a theological faculty was founded. This distinction between Bologna and Paris was due to the contrast between Italy and the North of Europe. In the former the life of the old Roman civilisation had never died out; the Roman law had always played an important part in the actual administration of the cities, and the culture of the Old World still survived both for good and for evil. Mr. Rashdall quotes the striking saying of Ozanam that 'the night which intervened between the intellectual daylight of antiquity and the dawn of the Renaissance was but " une de ces nuits lumineuses où les dernières clartés du soir se prolongent jusqu'aux premières blancheurs du matin." '

Before proceeding to speak of the development of the other great archetypal university, that of Paris, it may be well to consider how the conception of a 'university' was developed in imitation of the schools of Paris and Bologna. Originally, as has been seen, the term 'universitas' had nothing to do with teaching; so far as there was any title in the Middle Ages corresponding to the modern use of the word 'university,' it was 'Studium Generale.' This does not become common till the beginning of the 13th century, and at first was purely vague in its signification, just as in England at the present day the title of 'public school' is used in the most various senses; but 'Studium Generale' may be taken to imply three things: 1. That the school attracted, or tried to attract, scholars from all parts, and not from one country only; 2. That it provided teaching not simply in Arts, but also in one at least of the higher faculties, *i.e.*, Theology, Law, and Medicine; 3. That the subjects were taught by a considerable number of masters. Two causes tended to make this vague use more precise. Of these, the first was the growth in the honorary value of degrees; originally the teaching had been sought for its own sake, or at any rate to enable the learner to become a teacher in his turn, but as the number of those obtaining the qualification increased, there grew up a large class who had no intention of devoting themselves to study in any sense, but who were proud to display the much valued title of Doctor or Master. The feeling soon grew up that the degrees of some places were of more value than those of others, and hence by taking to itself the title of a 'Studium Generale,' a new place of learning did its best to convey to the world its claim that its teaching and its examinations were on a level with those of Paris or Bologna. There was a second and a more material reason; by the bull of Pope Honorius III. in 1219, clerks might receive in absence the fruits of their benefices so long as they were teaching theology, and students might have the same privilege for a period of five years, but this right soon came to be limited to those who were studying at 'Studia Generalia.' Hence, in order that students might enjoy their revenues, universities became very anxious to have their right to this honourable title recognized.

And now a new element came in.   In 1224 the Emperor Frederic II. founded a Studium Generale at Naples, and in 1229 Gregory IX. did the same at Toulouse.   The idea rapidly grew that Pope and Emperor could confer the coveted title, and before the end of the 13th century (1292) both Paris and Bologna stooped to have what was theirs, by time-honoured custom, confirmed by grant of the Pope Nicholas IV.   Of the older studia, Oxford and Padua never seem to have received this papal recognition, and based their undisputed title to be world-wide seats of learning merely on prescriptive right; but Oxford tried, though without success, to get her position confirmed by the Pope.   This papal recognition in theory carried with it the 'jus ubique docendi'—*i.e.*, the graduates of these recognised universities could claim admission to the same privileges in all other universities—but in practice this right was very sparingly enjoyed.   Paris refused to recognize Oxford degrees without fresh examinations, and Oxford repaid the compliment, in spite of the privileges granted to Paris by the Papal Bull.

It is not necessary here to enter into the question whether this Papal or Imperial brief was necessary for the creation of a legitimate Studium Generale, or whether the sovereign of any country had the power of founding one.   Mr. Rashdall inclines to side with Denifle in choosing the former alternative, but he is impartial enough to reject the authority of the great German scholar, when he denies the right of Cambridge to the coveted title, before she received the bull of Pope John XXII. in 1318.   However, though he makes it fairly clear that Cambridge was a recognised school for nearly a century before this date, he makes it also clear that mediæval Cambridge was quite an unimportant university, and that it only rises into prominence when Oxford fell under well-deserved suspicion for heresy, at the end of the fourteenth century, by her vigorous championship of the doctrines of Wycliffe.

We must now turn to the Universities north of the Alps, which, as has been said, were different from those of Italy in character and in organisation, and among which Paris is indisputably the first, both in date and in importance. The baseless attribution of its schools to Charlemagne has been already mentioned. His sole connection with it lies in the fact that the organisation of education, which was not the least important part of his many-sided work, established and confirmed the already existing connection between the Church and education. It is not until the end of the eleventh century, however, that Paris has, in William of Champeaux, a teacher of first-rate importance, and it was his fame which brought to the schools of Paris the famous Abelard, who in his turn drew by his lectures multitudes of students to hear him, and whose fame definitely confirmed the intellectual supremacy of Paris. Not that there was any organised university in the time of the famous opponent of St. Bernard, but we can trace in his career the ideas which were later to be the basis of the organisation. Abelard offended his contemporaries by his daring attempt to carry reason into the domain of theology; but he also offended them because he ventured to set at nought the educational traditions of his day, and to come forward as a teacher without having been admitted to the work by those who were teachers before him. Abelard had but scant respect for authority, educational or otherwise. His dialectic reduced his first master, William of Champeaux, to silence, and he irreverently compared his teacher in theology, Anselm of Laon, to the 'barren fig-tree' of the Gospel. But his successes were short-lived, and his independence brought him under the ban of the Church. His eloquence, however, and the force of his intellect had ensured the triumph of the Scholastic Theology and Logic, which henceforth reigned supreme in Paris. The teacher died in disgrace at Clugny, while his pupil, Peter Lombard, rose to be Archbishop of Paris, and by the application of his master's method in his famous 'Sentences,' determined the character of the studies of the next three centuries.

To us, with our wider culture and our numerous objects of interest, the old enthusiasm for logical and metaphysical speculation seems strange. We can hardly now imagine an audience, even of scholars, roused to fury by the question of

'Universals and Particulars,' and breaking each others heads, because one side maintained that there was somewhere an ideal table of which all tables seen on earth were only shadows, while the other side upheld as stoutly the position that the only realities were the individual tables which men saw with their eyes. But so it was. The words of Porphyry in his Isagoge have, as Mr. Rashdall says, roused more controversy probably than any other uninspired words. 'Now concerning genera and species, the question indeed whether they have a substantial existence, or whether they consist in bare intellectual concepts only, I shall forbear to determine.' But this question the Middle Age Students were always trying to determine, and a thorny question it proved. What made it worse was that it was found to have a theological bearing. A man who believed only in the reality of universals was in danger of being reproached for unorthodoxy because his doctrine might be pressed into the view that all genera were included in one summum genus, or, in its theological aspect, into Pantheism. A man on the other hand who denied reality to universals, and admitted it only for particulars, was in great danger of turning the doctrine of the Trinity into the belief in three separate Gods. Each then of the great philosophical schools had its theological pitfalls.

Out of the multitude of students attracted to Paris by the charms of the scholastic philosophy grew up the organised university. Its ecclesiastical character, however, brought into prominence an element which was unimportant at Bologna. The teachers in Paris formed themselves into a 'universitas' or guild, as those of Bologna had done; but they had a formidable foe to their independence in the Chancellor of the Cathedral at Notre Dame, who had the supervision of the schools connected with the cathedral church, and whose license was necessary for a man's entering on the career of a teacher. Round the giving of this license raged the battle for the independence of the University. The Chancellor claimed that he could refuse the license to teach or give it to whom he pleased. The guild of masters on the other hand claimed that they alone were the judges of a man's fitness to be admitted to their ranks, and that the Chancellor must license those whom they approved. He was in authority, but they had on their side the formidable weapon of being able to ' boycott ' the lectures of all who were not members of their body, or who submitted to the Chancellor, and in the end the organised guild of teachers triumphed, largely through the assistance of the Holy See, which saw, with its accustomed wisdom, the assistance for its own claims which was to be found in the new educational body.

The ceremonies by which a man was admitted to the fellowship of teachers may very probably go back to classical times, while survivals of them are found more or less in all universities at the present day. The conferring of the cap (' birettatio ') was the sign that the student was henceforth his own master, just as the Roman slave had received his cap as the sign of his freedom. In the Scotch universities, graduates are still ' capped ' on receiving their degrees, and at the American ' commencements,' the graduates receive their caps from the president. In the more ceremonial South, the further ceremonies of the investiture with the ring and the kiss of peace are preserved. And everywhere the presents to already existing masters, and the banquet and other festivities with which the new master had to celebrate his success, (in some of the Spanish universities this characteristically took the form of a bull fight provided for the amusement of the University), are represented by the payment of fees, which forms an invariable part of all university graduations. The feeling that a new member must pay his footing was as common in these societies of teachers as in other less dignified bodies. It is to be regretted that in Oxford a large part of the degree ceremonies have disappeared ; the new M.A. receives a license to ' Incept,' but he is then dispensed (without his knowledge) from performing this, the most important part, of his graduation.

The guild of masters at Paris can be traced as existing as early as 1170, when we read of an abbot of St. Albans being admitted to the ' fellowship of the elect masters,' and in 1208, in the course of the struggle mentioned above, the University (for we may now strictly call it so) obtained its first written statutes. These are of the simplest kind, and require only three things, the wearing of the academical dress, the observance of the proper order in lectures and in disputations, and the due attendance at the funerals of deceased masters. If this last point shows the origin of the guild of masters as a private society, the second was soon to lead to a change of the greatest importance, *i.e.*, the fixing of a definite course of academical study. This was soon developed in the statutes of the Papal Legate, Robert de Courçon, in 1215, which may be said to mark an epoch in the history of universities. In the previous century, a student had worked much as he pleased ; so we find John of Salisbury, the friend of Becket, passing from lectures on Logic to a study of the Classics which almost seems to anticipate the 15th century Renaissance : henceforth a student who wished for a degree had a fixed course before him to pursue, and this limitation of freedom has been a feature of university studies ever since.

It was in this struggle with the Chancellor that the University developed its constitution, with its Rector at its head, and its Faculty of Arts divided into four Nations, while the superior faculties form independent corporations. The organization of Paris was largely copied in Oxford, and Mr. Rashdall has put forth a most ingenious theory that the very existence of the great English University, as an organized body, is to be traced to a migration of Parisian students between 1165 and 1167. We know at any rate that at that period Henry II., in the course of his quarrel with Archbishop Thomas, issued an ordinance that all beneficed English clerks who might be studying abroad, were to return to England within three months as ' they loved their revenues.' That such a threat would bring home most of the English students from Paris would be probable in itself; we have also evidence that at this time there was a compulsory retirement of ' alien scholars ' from France. It is most natural to suppose that this body of homeless students would settle somewhere in England, and if so, Oxford would have been the natural place for them to choose ; at any rate there is no doubt that the evidence for a large number of students in Oxford begins to become clear very soon after 1170, and almost immediately traces of organization are found among them, which it is most natural to assume were copied direct from Paris.

But in several respects the growth of Oxford privileges has a character of its own; the most important of these is the position of the Chancellor. Oxford was not a cathedral city, but its bishop was more than a hundred miles away at Lincoln; hence there was no great ecclesiastical Chancellor, as at Paris, to attempt to crush the privileges of the university. When the Chancellor appears—as he does in a decision of the Papal Legate, Nicholas of Tusculum, in 1214—he is appointed specially for the university; and though at first the Bishop of Lincoln had the right of nominating him, yet very early the masters of arts seem to have secured the privilege of electing the man who was to be presented to the Bishop for nomination, and by the middle of the 14th century the confirmation of the election seems to have become a mere form. Hence the Chancellor at Oxford is not the would-be oppressor of the University; he is its representative and champion, and Oxford grew up far more free from episcopal interference than did its mother-university under the shadow of the great cathedral of Notre Dame.

Another point in which the circumstances of English life led to an important departure from the Parisian model, is in the comparative unimportance of the division into 'nations.' There are traces that the fourfold division may have once existed in Oxford, but England was far too much one nation to require such a division; the four nations became two, the Southerners and the Northerners, and their representatives, the Proctors, exist to the present day as the executive of the university, but the term 'nation' soon ceases to be used, and the Faculty of Arts votes as a single body.

It would be most interesting to gather from Mr. Rashdall's book a sketch of the development of the privileges of Oxford, and still more to describe the part it played, especially in the development of the Scholastic philosophy at the end of the 13th and in the 14th century, and still more in the Wycliffite movement. But it is necessary to turn to some of the more general features affecting all universities. With regard to the numbers of the mediæval students, Mr. Rashdall shows clearly that they have been enormously exaggerated, *e.g.*, the famous Archbishop of Armagh, Fitz Ralph, in a speech before the Papal Court in 1354, estimates the number of students in Oxford 'in *his own day*' at 30,000, though they had fallen to 6000—Mr. Rashdall, by the way, hardly gives the full strength of the Archbishop's words when he writes there 'had *once* been 30,000 students—but all the evidence that we have as to numbers of those 'determining,' and as to the size of the mediæval city at Oxford, makes it impossible for us to put the academic population of 14th century Oxford higher than 3000, which is the estimate Wycliffe gives. At Paris, which had far more of an international character, Mr. Rashdall thinks there may have been at one time as many as 6000 or 7000 students.

As to the life of these students, we shall not be far wrong in concluding that it was a very stormy one; the history of all universities is one long battle against encroachments on the part of the towns where they were situated, or of the bishop in whose diocese they were, and when the scholars were not fighting against a common oppressor, they fought each other. At Oxford each advance in privileges is won at the cost of some outrage on the part of the town, a process which culminated in the great riot of St. Scholastica's day in 1354, when two days' pitched battle culminated in the complete defeat of the students, the slaughter of numerous "clerks," and then, through the usual interference of Church and Crown on behalf of the University, in the complete humiliation of the city—a humiliation which has only come to an end in our own century. It is curious to note that these Town and Gown rows, which form so prominent a feature at Oxford, are almost equally important everywhere; the clerk and the townsman considered each other sworn foes, though they depended for their existence, or at any rate their prosperity, on each other. The immortal Bailie Nicol Jarvie, in the 18th century, complains of the same insolence on the part of the Glasgow students which had vexed the soul of the mayors of mediæval Oxford.   The conduct of both sides is so full of faults that it is hard to decide between them, but as the Universities triumphed, their historians can afford to be generous, especially now when it may be hoped that the old hostility is a thing of the past.   One point, however, must always be borne in mind; the struggle for University privileges, and especially for exemption from the ordinary jurisdictions, was only part of the great mediæval struggle for the rights of the clergy against lay interference.

The usual success of the universities in these struggles brings us to another point, *i.e.*, that the students' strength was largely due to their poverty.   When any trouble arose the University at once suspended its lectures, and if the trouble was serious, the whole body of students was prepared at once to migrate.   This was easy, for they had no buildings of their own to lose, and the work of the University could be carried on successfully wherever houses or rooms could be hired for the dwelling-places or the lectures of the students, and churches borrowed for the more solemn functions, such as admissions to degrees.   It is a curious feature in the history, especially of the Italian Universities, to read the negotiations between discontented students and towns anxious to attract them to reside, while the universities of established reputation, like Bologna, tried to bind their professors by oaths not to desert and carry their students with them.   By the end of the 13th century, the foundation of colleges in Oxford begins to give the students a permanent stake in the city, but Walter de Merton, to whose thought and munificence England owes its college system, definitely contemplated that his foundation might move elsewhere, and he had secured for it, in 'Pythagoras' Hall, a local habitation in Cambridge.

It is not till the fifteenth century that the age of university buildings proper as distinguished from those of colleges, begins; as the mediæval educational system was losing its real life, so it became rich and increased in goods.   Oxford acquires her Schools, her present magnificent Divinity School, and the Library over it at this period, when her freedom and vigour had been crushed out of her.

Colleges have become so characteristic a part of the English Universities, that it will be a revelation to many Englishmen that such foundations were common in all the mediæval universities; at Bologna, for example, there was the Spanish College, which was founded in 1367, and which is still used by the Government of Spain to train graduates for the diplomatic service, but it was Paris which was the origin of the collegiate system, and Mr. Rashdall gives a list of some seventy which were founded there between 1180 and 1480. They were originally only endowed hospicia for the students, and were not in Paris allowed such complete powers of self-government as were given to the English colleges. In Paris these foundations gradually decayed, and perished finally in the crash of the Revolution, while Oxford has not lost one of the foundations for the learning of the secular clergy which the piety of the Middle Ages gave her.

The history of the Colleges in the Scotch Universities is different. Here, after the German model, they were intended rather to be endowments for the teaching faculty of the University than for independent bodies of students; hence as they had a purpose independent of the common life of their members, this could disappear while the college continued to exist. It was about 1820 that the 'common tables' of St. Andrews and Aberdeen was at last given up.

But though the Scotch Universities have in this respect departed from their original arrangements, yet it may safely be said that in several respects they preserve more faithfully the features of the Mediæval University than do the apparently more venerable, but in many respects more altered constitutions of Oxford and Cambridge. In the first place the ordinary student at Glasgow or Aberdeen is very much younger than in most modern universities, and about the same age as the scholars of Mediæval Oxford or Paris. In spite of this he has kept, as has been said, the now unique privilege of electing his Rector, and the old organization of the Nations is, in Glasgow at least, still used in the election. What is more important, though not more interesting, is that the Scotch degree course is still modelled on the old Trivium and Quadrivium of the mediæval student; hence the prominence of Logic and Metaphysics in the studies of the northern students, a prominence to which Europe owes the development of an important school of philosophy. As Mr. Rashdall says, 'between the time of Hutcheson and that of J. S. Mill, a majority of the philosophers, who wrote in the English language, were professors or at least alumni, of the Scotch Universities.

As to the value of the mediæval degree course as an intellectual training, very various estimates have been formed. Roger Bacon's view of it, at its most flourishing period in the tenth century, is most unfavourable. He complains that the clergy neglect their proper studies for that of Law, which is the sure avenue to preferment, that in theology, the Bible is neglected for the Sentences, that boys begin to study it before they could read their Psalter or had mastered their Latin grammar, and that mathematics is neglected, although in this respect, Oxford was not quite so bad as Paris. But his opinion must not be valued too highly ; he was before his time, and even in our own day, the researcher who is the glory of his university, is not the best judge of the value of its ordinary work. The mediæval degree course can at all events claim that in it were trained the acutest intellects and the highest characters of the Middle Ages ; to take Oxford alone, a course could not have been despicable which produced in one century Edmund Rich, Robert Grosseteste, Adam Marsh, and Roger Bacon himself. And we have the best of evidence that it was valued by contemporaries, in the endowments which were given to enable poor students to enjoy it.

A striking feature in it, especially in the early periods, is the attractive influence exercised by great teachers. The lecture room had something of the charm of the tournament, and the teacher held himself prepared, like the knights in the lists, to dispute against all comers ; ambitious scholars even went from place to place, seeking foemen worthy of their dialectic.

It was this feeling which made the degree ceremonies so important; a candidate who chose some daring thesis to maintain, might hope to attract attention and open the way for his subsequent career. So much is this the case that we even have statutes in Oxford and Paris, to prevent a disputant's friends using force to secure him an audience, and dragging in the passers-by to hear him. When books were rare and costly, the influence of the spoken word, always great, must have been ten times greater; and dry and scholastic as the mediæval studies appear to us, yet a great man like St. Thomas Aquinas or Duns Scotus could make them of vivid interest.

The character of the mediæval examinations is a subject of considerable difficulty. On the one hand there are such remarkable facts as that in Oxford at any rate there is no clear proof of examinations in the modern sense of the word at all, that at Greifswald, where we have the lists of candidates and of those who actually passed from 1456 to 1478, no candidate failed to satisfy the examiners, and that at Paris in 1426, a candidate who achieved the unusual distinction of a 'pluck' brought an action against his examiners, that they had rejected him from odium theologicum. On the other hand there seems no doubt that the examinations at Paris were at first a formidable ceremony; we have a remarkable sermon of Robert, the founder of the Sorbonne, which draws an elaborate comparison between the examination before the Chancellor and the Last Judgment; of course its point is the greater severity of the latter, but the comparison would have been impossible had the university examination been a mere farce. So too we have elaborate accounts of the examination ceremony at Bologna, where at this 'rigorous and tremendous' ceremony, as it is called, the examiner was required to treat the examinee as his own son. Even more significant are the repeated statutes against bribing examiners and the fact that comparatively but a small proportion of those matriculating ever proceeded to their M.A., or even 'determined' as B.As. Even when the actual examination had become a farce, or did not exist at all, there still was a standard of minimum attainment for the degree; it always implied residence and the hearing of the proper lectures during a long period; the course for the D.D. at Oxford for example extended over 20 years.

The personal influence of the lecturer, the importance of the spoken word, is connected with another remarkable feature of the mediæval universities. Though they were clerical in character, it is a great mistake to imagine them as homes of theological bigotry or narrowness; on the contrary they are associated, in their best days, with liberty of thought in matters religious. It was the Universities which insisted on studying the newly discovered works of Aristotle in the Renaissance of the thirteenth century; his logical treatises, or parts of them, had always been known, but the Church at first looked with grave, and not undeserved suspicion, on his scientific and ethical works; the free spirit of the Universities, however, triumphed, and the genius of the great schoolmen succeeded in bringing about a reconciliation of faith and reason. This was especially the work of the great Dominicans of Paris, Albert the Great (1193-1280) and his pupil, Thomas Aquinas (1225-1274). On this occasion the regular clergy were on the side of liberty; as a rule, however, it was the secular clergy who ventured to handle theological questions, and whose lectures were the inspiring cause of so many of the reform movements before the Reformation. In the boldness of their theological teaching and in their popular character, the mediæval universities are specially represented by those of Scotland in our own day; they were essentially the universities of the people, as well as of the classes, and success in the university schools was an avenue by which the low born peasant could rise to position and authority in the Church, just as in Scotland the Presbyterian ministry has drawn to itself, through the Universities, so large a share of the best intellect of the people.

One more point may be noticed as illustrated repeatedly by Mr. Rashdall's book, *i.e.* the constant connection between the educational and the religious movements of the Middle Ages. The great revival of Aristotelian study in the 13th century coincides with, and was profoundly influenced by, the teaching of the Friars, while in the fourteenth century the Wycliffite movement of Oxford and its successor, the Hussite movement at Prague, were especially connected with university privileges and studies. So close is this connection that, as Mr. Rashdall points out, scholasticism maintained itself in the schools of Italy after it had been driven out of those north of the Alps, and only gave way when the Catholic reaction of the sixteenth century produced in its turn a body of teachers, uniting religious fervour with new educational methods.

The number of points of interest in these volumes is endless; the philosophic movements of the middle ages and the life of the students generally we have hardly had time even to refer to, but they are abundantly illustrated; the effect of endowments and the character of the original college foundations and their developments too we have had almost entirely to pass over. We can only hope that in these days of University Reform and Extension, the encouragements and the warnings of the experience of their predecessors may become familiar to the students of the present day, and often it will be found that the true path of reform is that indicated by the old motto

'Antiquam exquirite matrem.'

J. WELLS.

ART. IV.—THE ASIATICS IN AMERICA.

THE question of the origin of the native American races, and of the civilisations discovered by the Spaniards in Mexico and Peru, is one of great interest in connection with the general history of the diffusion of the human race. Many theories have been propounded, according to which the aboriginal Americans were autochthonous, or created in America—an immense antiquity being ascribed to the original traces of man's presence—while some have supposed the Peruvians to be an Aryan people, reaching the Pacific coast from Europe. The Spaniards themselves thought that St. Thomas from India must have reached Mexico and Peru, and thus accounted for the appearance of the Cross in America, and for other similarities in religious rites and customs.

When, however, we study the racial types, the languages, and the civilisations of America, we must conclude that an

Asiatic origin, and a connection with Mongolic races, is far more probable, especially as the distance to be traversed by sea is so much shorter. But in treating this subject two distinct questions must be distinguished : the first being the question of the aboriginal population which was everywhere found by Europeans living in a semi-savage state; and the second, the question of the origin of the two distinct civilisations which existed, in the sixteenth century in Mexico and Peru, while the remainder of the two continents was still barbarous.

As regards the origin of man in America, the existence of a very ancient race, whence the American Indians of both North and South America have descended, is generally admitted. Palæolithic arrow heads, belonging to the Quaternary strata, show a widely diffused but savage race, and rude implements are even asserted to occur in Colorado in Miocene and Pliocene strata; but the evidence requires still to be very cautiously accepted. The earliest American type was long-headed, and approaches nearest to the Turanian or Mongolic, but not to the Chinese or Mongol proper, being rather comparable to the Ugro-Altaic and Burmese, and to that of the early Dravidian races of India. Humboldt was struck, even in South America, with the Mongolic type of the natives; and the main characteristics are the same in both the American continents. The hairless faces, high cheek-bones, prognathous jaws, and even the large curved nose (common among the Kirghiz Tartars, and shewn on the old historic *bas reliefs* which represent Hittites and Akkadians) are Mongolic features. On the Pacific shores the original type is modified by an infusion of blood of some short-headed race, probably representing later elements of population. In Peru the lower class of natives had long heads, but the Incas had short heads. The Azteks had the custom of artificially elongating the head, which is common in America and found in other parts of the world. The longest heads are found among Patagonians and Esquimaux. The prognathic jaw is not found commonly among Thibetans or Mongols, but it occurs among the Chinese. The Wakash tribes are thought to belong to the Tunguse family, and other elements of population may have come from the Aleutian

Islands, or by Behring Straits, from the north-east corner of Asia. Short heads are found in the Ohio mounds, and the later infusion of Malay, and possibly of Chinese and of Japanese stocks, appears probable.

The American languages are numerous, and vary in character, but they are in no cases inflected like Aryan or Semitic languages, and their structure is only comparable to that of the Mongolic or Turanian languages of Asia. Comparative study is rendered difficult by the rapid changes, which affect all languages where there is no literature to preserve the vocabulary. Thus in Africa, and in America, the problem is more difficult than that of Asiatic languages. But grammatical structure is always a safer guide than vocabulary, and the American languages resemble rather the agglutinative speech of Central Asia, with its long words, due to the incorporation of pronouns and particles, its absence of gender and of inflection, its vowel harmonies, its reduplications representing plurals, and its distinctive syntax, than they do when compared with the more advanced Aryan and Semitic tongues. Classification is still very imperfect, but comparative study has already shewn that the classes are fewer and less distinct than used to be supposed. In North and Central America Bancroft recognised three classes, the Tinneh family on the North-West, the Aztek in Mexico, and the Maya. The Otomi language is said to differ from others in being more clearly monosyllabic, and comparable in many features of grammar to the Chinese. The Aztek, though perhaps the most perfect of American tongues, does not distinguish the letters *b d f r g s*, and has no gender or inflexions. All these features also mark the Mongolic languages. The Pima in California is said to present fifteen per cent. of Malay words, but none that are Chinese or Japanese. The Quichuan, which is the classic tongue of South America, presents the same agglutinative features, and the case in favour of a Mongolic connection is therefore strong.

The comparative vocabularies published by Mr. R. P. Greg *

---

* *Comparative Philology of the Old and New Worlds*, by R. P. Greg. London, 1893.

are of great interest in this study. A list may here be given
of about an hundred words generally common to North,
Central, and South American languages, with comparisons
with Mongolic words taken from his pages. In dealing with
modern languages there is no doubt a danger that loan words
may have travelled far from one people to another, but the
words which compare are as a rule those denoting the simplest
objects and acts, and they shew us a savage people living in
the condition of hunters or pastoral herdsmen. The comparisons do not indicate a Chinese origin, but are generally
closest to the dialects of Central Asia and of Siberia, though
some words are so widely diffused that they occur also in the
Indo-Chinese languages, in Thibetan, and in the Dravidian
dialects of India.

Among the words here given we find several to denote
house, boat, axe, knife, bow, arrow, stone, and fire; but the
only metal which has a common name is gold (N. American
ccaxi, Central American *chuqui*, South American *ccaxi*), and
this seems to be a later native word. Among animals the bear
is specially to be noted, with various names for the dog. The
original Americans appear to have recognised family relations,
and had several words for God or Spirit. Their languages
had advanced to the use of pronouns, but their general condition was that of hunters, sowing a little corn, and fishing
in boats. They knew of cold and snow, and may have come
in their skiffs from Asia, but used probably only stone weapons
and bows. They were in fact in that condition of progress in
which they were found still living, in North America, by the
first colonists.

COMPARATIVE VOCABULARY.

	North American.	Central American.	South American.	Mongolic.
House,	Ko Uca	Ku Oigu	Ku Uca	Keui
,,	In Ank	Ngu	In Ngu	Ion
,,	Hi Ho	Hu U	Hi I	Hu Ui
,,	Dum Dimi	——	Dum Tan	Tami
,,	Kotai	Goti	Hit	Kat
Stone,	Tak	Tek	Tika	Tash
,,	Kuk	Kak	Kak	Koch

Stone,	Sileh	————	Silla	Zela
Mountain,	Tipi	Tepe	————	Tepe
,,	Ku Kaak	Kauah	Kakka	Kai, Kgi
Great,	Muck	Noh	Makh	Magh
,,	————	Pacha	Pacha	Paka
Tree,	Kagg	Kagg	Khoka	Aghagh
Boat,	Kayak	————	Kao	Kaiyik
Axe,	Tuk	Tek	Taqui	Taka
Knife,	Akyek	Hasha	Chuki	Chucki
,,	Kiai	Quai	Kiai	Kao
Bow,	Nama	————	Mumute	Numu
,,	Siia	Za	Za	Zaa
Arrow,	Sua	Tzuh	Suu	Sawa
Dark,	Kaak	Akakka	Coca	Gigi
Bad,	Kaka	Ukku	Akaka	Haica
Fish,	Kanu	————	Kanu	Kan
Dog,	Achu Shue	Ochu	Huchuté	Ku Schey
,,	Puka	Pek	Puku	Betka
,,	Keikue	Chiki	Kukui	Kaik
Bird,	Kuku	Kukai	Huku	Kush
Pig,	Cuchi Ak	Ak	Kuch	Gachi
Deer,	Tsick	Kweh	Guaca	Kayik
Bear,	Matto Mavar	————	Mari	Medve Mar
Corn,	Sigi	Saxi	Zaxi	Suk
Salt,	Shukosh	————	Sachi	Saksi
Snow, Ice,	Tek Toosha	Istek	————	Tek Tosh
Foot,	Ooch	Uoc	Kayu	Ayak
Hand,	Paco	Maco	Paco	Baeg
Finger,	Ka	Ca	Ka	Ki
Nose,	Uk	Gu	Cana	Ang
Ear,	Gyu	————	Huchu	Kuo
Tongue,	Del	————	Del	Dil
Hair,	Oshu	Si	Zye	Usha
,,	Shuka	Soz	Socco	Shag
,,	Thaesh	Tusu	————	Thash
Head,	Ca	Que	Gue	Go
,,	Psh Biza	Pacu	Pacu	Bash
,,	Iku	Akang	Yakae	Yok
Tooth,	Itza	Tzi	Dza	Tez
,,	Tong	Tollau	Tullu	Tang
Mouth,	Ku	Ku	————	Ko
,,	Sana	————	Sane	Sun
Eye,	Asu	Siki	Zu	Sei
,,	Na	Nik	Na	Na
Man,	Er	————	Urre	Ere

Man,	Cune	Akun	Canai	Kena
,,	Ka	Ka	Che	Aika
,,	Hama	Huema	Huema	Him
Son,	Saka	Chichi	Chechu	Chuken
,,	Cui	Gua	Ciu	Chu
,,	Cin	Akun	Cana	Ken
Father,	It. Ose	Aitze	Aha	Atya Isa
,,	Tata	Tatle	Tayta	Tato
,,	Aya	——	Aya	Aya
,,	Appa	Aba	Pai	Ab
Mother,	Ma Anna	Maa	Meme Anu	Ema Ana
Woman,	Sun Tan	Dome	Zumo	Zin
God,	Ata	Teo	Ati (Chinese)	Ti
,,	Ogha	Ogha	——	Agha
	Hun	——	Ken	Jin
,,	U Yeh	Ku	Huai	Yo Yahu
,,	Niou	——	Ano	In Na
Daylight,	Tina	Tani	——	Tan
,,	Caan	Chaan	Kin	Kun
,,	Sua	Tse	Sua	Si
,,	Ara	——	Ara Uru	Or
,,	Ene	Andi	Ano Inti	In
,,	Tak Teshe	Tes	Tagg	Tawash
Sky,	Kegek	Quik	Kecai	Kueuk
Sun,	Kon	Kin	Kin	Khon
,,	Sohn	——	Suna	Shun
,,	Suus	——	Suus	Susi
,,	Kese	Cha	Cachi	Kaisa
Star,	Tsohol	Sillo	Silla Tysel	Tysil
Moon,	Aguei	Chic	Yace	Ike
,,	Nosi	Masa	Masa	Mah
,,	Ari Bari	Bari	Ari	Ira
Fire,	Koh Iche	Cha	Iakai	Kuy
,,	Tetsch Tah	Tata	Tesha	Tuz Tet
,,	Teik	Tschuko	Taika	Togo
Water,	Dzu Du	Du	Dzu Du	Zu To
,,	Ia Ui	A Aya	Aah Ui	Ai Wa
To cut,	Kut	Kuta	Kut	Ket Kes
To give,	Da	Da	——	Da
,,	Kia Chu	Caa	Ku	Ka
I,	Noka	Nek	Noka	Ngai
,,	Si Di	De	Su	Si
Thou,	Zu Ta	Ti	——	Su Ti
He,	Na	Nunu	Ni	Na
This,	Huen	Quin	Kim	Kan

With respect to this list it should be noted that a large proportion of the words are very ancient, and occur in the oldest known Mongolic language—the Akkadian of Mesopotamia,* yet the American tribes were apparently offshoots, not directly of that civilized race, but of the rude tribes of Siberia, which had either never learned the arts of the Akkadians, or had lost them as they migrated to wilder lands, remote from the original home of the Mongolic races near the Caspian.

When we continue the enquiry, in the case of words which are not common to the whole range of American languages, we still find that comparisons of vocabulary are more common when the Ugro Altaic, or North Mongolic languages, are used as a basis; and the Aryan languages furnish no comparisons; the Chinese in some cases comes however nearest to the American. The following important words widely spread in North America are very closely like those used by Altaic Turanians in Asia.

	North American.	Ugro Altaic.
Land,	mah amet	ma modu
,,	ti tu	da
Tree,	kan	kona, kanu
,,	tsa	sa
,,	pichu	posu
Knife,	pesh	beechak
,,	seepa	sapa
Axe,	skum	suka
Arrow,	skui	sogau
Fish,	gat	kata
Snake,	osheista	eshdissa
Dog,	cannu	kon
,,	meda	meda
Bird,	mon	motun
Sheep,	una	unet
Deer,	addik	teke
Hare,	yo	(Chinese) yu

---

* Compare for instance the Akkadian words for 'house' *un, ki, tami*: 'stone' *tak*: 'great' *makh*: 'dark' *gig* (also 'bad' 'ill'): 'fish' *kha khan*: 'bird' *kus*: 'head' *ca*: 'mouth' *gu*: 'eye' *si*: 'man' *eri, gan, gum*: 'son' *sak*: 'father' *ai, ab*: 'mother' *ene*: 'God' *An*: 'day' *tan*: 'sky' *gug*: 'sun' *shun*: 'moon' *agu*: 'water' *a*: 'give' *de*: 'I' *anga*: 'thou' *zi*: 'he' *na*: 'this' *gan*.

Bear,	matto	medve
,,	moan	maina
,,	sus	saks
Fox,	chula	koll
Seed,	sum	so
Milk,	chychtya	shiut
Egg,	manig	manu
Ice,	ak	yig
Snow,	kais	kaisa
,,	speu	buss
Foot,	kolo	kol
,,	looga	llagyl
Mouth,	an im	an ama
God,	man	man
,,	u yet	ye
Silver,	shuney (Chinese)	shen
Clothes,	togai	tug
War,	gawi	cooha

In numerals the North American languages differ much, but the commonest words for numbers seem also to indicate an Ugro Altaic connection.

Number.	North American.	Ugro Altaic.
1	ak, ik, cau	aku
2	ako	iki
3	{ taugh { katsa	{ touga { kudem
4	tseto	thett
5	tawit, etsha	vit
6	sih	hat
7	siete, tutsheos	sat seitsa

Up to No. 5 the resemblances are striking, but the numerals for 8, 9, 10, do not shew any remarkable resemblance. The Azteks, as will appear later, had words for 1, 2, 3, 4, 5, and formed the rest by compound words denoting additions.

Not only was the common word for boat in America of Mongolic origin, but the words for the sea in North America shew the same connection. The commonest word for sea among the Aryans and West Asiatics is *mār*, which perhaps means ' great water,' (Sanskrit *mira*, Latin *mare*, Slav *moray*, Celtic *mara*, Teutonic *meer*, Finnic *mar*, Altaic *meri* and *mora*, Lapp *mär*, perhaps the same as the Mongol *nor*), but this word does not apparently occur in America. The Malay, Polynesian, and Australian languages are connected together by another word for sea (Malay *atui*, Polynesian *tai*, Australian *tan*), and the languages of Polynesia and Australia generally compare closely with the Malay. In North America there are many words which as a rule only mean 'waters,' or ' great water'; but some are more distinctive, such as *ta* 'sea,' which is the same as the Corean *ta;* and *vaat* 'sea,' which compares with the Ugro Altaic *vat* or *vut* for 'water' 'sea.' In South America on the other hand we find the word *atun* for the sea apparently of Malay origin.

The indications afforded by such words point to the derivation of the North American Indians from the nearest part of North-east Asia. The tribes which crossed over the narrow straits were in the primitive condition of pastoral hunters. They knew the sheep among domestic animals, but were probably unable to bring cattle with them. They were perhaps acquainted with corn, as well as milk, and they knew the bear, and came from a region where ice and snow were found. The word for silver compares with the Chinese, and is probably of later origin. The numerals, also, though they compare only with the Ugro Altaic, do not seem to have been named beyond 'five.' The words compared for numerals do not in any case recall the vocabulary of any Aryan race.

In South and Central America there are indications, already noticed, that the same northern race penetrated to the extreme end of the continent, but there are also indications of later arrivals from the Malay peninsula. Numerals are the most valuable words for comparison, because the most distinctive of various classes of language. The Otomi numerals, in Central America, seem to show a connection with Mongolic systems, both Ugro-Altaic and Indo-Chinese, though in most cases these are not very close. The Otomi No. 1 is, however, nearest to the Dravidian *onru*, ' one.'

	Otomi.	Ugro Altaic.	Indo Chinese.
No. 1	nura	————	———
2	zooko	kok	kichi
3	hui	uitse	———
4	gooho	ngy	hichi

5	gyta	wit	ngat
6	rahti	hat	re
7	yotho	yedi	tsit
8	hyate	dsghat	thata
9	gythe	gessu	acu

Dissimilar as these may appear, they are closer than any other comparisons with existing numeral systems.

The Aztek system in Mexico included only numerals to 'five,' and these compare with other widely-spread Ugro Altaic words for numbers as far as 'four.'

	Aztek.	Ugro Altaic.
No. 1	ce	aku
2	ume	unem
3	ye	uitse
4	nahui	negy
5	chicu	———

In South America the Quichuan being the most important language, it is interesting to find, in some cases, similar Mongolic comparisons, especially pointing to the northern branch.

	Quichuan.	Ugro Altaic.
No. 1	huk	huca aku
2	yskuy	yike
3	kunsa	kudem
4	tahua	thett
5	picka	besh
6	sokta	kaht
7	kancis	seitsi
8	pussak	sekis
9	yskun	wexum
10	cunka	kamen

These must be taken for what they are worth, but it is conceivable that the two systems may have a common origin, and neither bears any resemblance to the Aryan system common to all European languages of that class.

Before considering the later civilisations of America it is necessary to glance at the early civilisation of Eastern Asia, in order to appreciate the conditions which existed when first the historic races can be supposed to have come into communication with the New World. The oldest civilisation of Asia was that of the Akkadians, whose language (including the numerals) is most closely represented by the Turkish

dialects of the region north of the Oxus.   The Akkadians had
a complete system of syllabic writing, originating in picture
emblems, and they possessed the lunar calendar of twelve
months, which was adopted by the Babylonians and the
Greeks.   It is now very generally recognised that the earlier
tribes of India—preceding the Aryans—were akin to these
Mesopotamian Mongols, but no known remains of their civilisation have been recognised.   The Turko-Mongol tribes, however, who were certainly akin to the Akkadians, spread into
Central Asia, where the Khitai were established in the time of
the geographer Ptolemy.   These latter invaded China, and
brought with them a considerable civilisation including a
system of writing.   The distinctive Chinese system, which is
traced back to about 800 B.C., presents many comparisons with
other Asiatic systems, but these are only pictorial, and there
is so much that is distinctive in the Chinese hieroglyhic writing
that a direct derivation from the Akkadian becomes untenable.
Only a very remote original connection can at most be supposed.

On the extreme north the Siberian tribes appear never to
have been civilised, and in China itself the population was,
from an early period, extremely mixed, many barbarous tribes
being gradually conquered by the Khitai and the Mongols,
while other elements of population entered China from the
west through Thibet, and from the south through Burmah
and the Malay peninsula.   The Malays were a great sea-going
race ; and the communication between China and Arabia, in
the Roman ages, may in great measure have been due to the
boldness of the Malay sailors, who also appear to have popu-
lated the Polynesian islands, and to have found their way to
Australia, as is very distinctly shewn by the comparison of
numerals and of vocabulary as a whole.

But the civilisation of India and of the Malay peninsula was
not of Mongol origin.   It commenced with the establishment
of the Greeks in India and in Bactria.   It was fostered by the
early Buddhists, from the third century B.C. onwards.   It was
also partly dependent on the Arabs of Yemen, who, even
earlier than the Greek period, seem to have been in communi-

cation with Ceylon and India. The astronomy, and especially the calendar, of India was of Greek origin, and Indian architecture is in the same manner based originally on Greek art.

About the sixth century A.D. the Nestorians began to push their way from Persia into Central Asia and Mongolia, penetrating at last even into China. They found the Mongols mainly pagan, but a debased form of Buddhism had also begun to spread among them from India. The Mongol alphabet is of Nestorian origin, and in the twelfth and thirteenth centuries Central Asia was full of European traders. The great Mongol period was that of the successors Genghiz Khan, whose wide empire extended from India to Siberia, and from the borders of Persia to China. The accounts left to us by Rubruquis, Marco Polo, and other travellers, attest the statesmanship and energy of the Mongols, and their mixed civilisation of Buddhist and Christian derivation. The whole empire was bound together by a postal system, which brought news from its furthest provinces to the distant capital at Karakorum, north of China; and the wealth and magnificence of the Khan's Court were astonishing. The tolerance of this great ruler, and of his splendid grandson Mangu Khan, was equally remarkable, and it was not till the later age of Timur that the savage cruelties, which marked the Mongol devastation of Western Asia, led to the revolt of subject peoples, and to the decay of the Tartar power.

Meanwhile in Thibet the corrupt Buddhism of the later Indian schools had already penetrated into the mountain plateau about 640 A.D. The Indian origin is clearly traceable, but it is not impossible that some of the strange similarities to Christian ritual—the use of robes including the mitre, of incense, rosaries, bells, crosses, and holy water, may have been due to the Nestorian influence. Missionaries from the Roman empire penetrated to these regions in 635 A.D., and the Edict of Si-ngan-fu, by the Chinese Emperor Tetsung, which has been found near the east border of Thibet dates from about 780 A.D.* Abu Zeid el Hasan, in the ninth century A.D., speaks

---

* See *Buddhism of Tibet*, L. A. Waddell. 1895, p. 422. Yule's *Marco Polo*, II., p. 23.

of thousands of Christians massacred in China—the south-west provinces—and Marco Polo in the thirteen century found Nestorians north of Yunnan. There were then 30,000 Alans in the Mongol Empire who were Christians, and the Buddhist lamas were familiar with Christian rites and emblems from the seventh century onwards. In Thibet while propagating the later Indian Tantric Buddhism, and even preserving much of the original ethics and philosophy of Buddha, they also permitted the survival of the older savage demonolatry of the country, and added to it much that, in India, was derived from the older Non-Aryan systems. They divided the cycle of existence into six states including heaven, the paradise of the inferior gods, the animal creation, hell, the Hades of starving ghosts, and the human life. Through these six states the soul passed successively in an eternal progress, unless attaining to Nirvana. Their religious system included establishments of monks, hermits, and nuns. They drew terrible pictures of demon guardians on the outer walls of their temples, and recognised all the fabulous beings of India, Nagas, Yakshas, Ghandarvas, Asuras, Garudas, etc., with Indra, Yama, Varuna, Kuvera, and Agni. Their astronomy was that derived from Greece by India, but they possessed the Tartar cycles of 12 and 60 years, and intercalated 7 months in 19 lunar years. They practised both cremation and burial, and burned a lay figure of the deceased on the 49th day, at the close of the funeral ceremonies. Among their emblems the 'wheel of the law,' or *Swastika*, was one of great antiquity, and found in all parts of the world. Their festivals were remarkable for the masquerades, in which actors assumed the appearance of demons with enormous heads and grinning mouths. Human sacrifice and cannibalism existed in Thibet in the seventh century, A.D., but as Buddhism spread a figure of dough was substituted for the human victim. The morsels of this figure, torn in pieces by masks representing bull-headed and deer-headed fiends, were distributed among the crowd. All these customs still survive on the borders of India.

The Tantric Buddhism so described existed not only in Thibet but in China and Mongolia, in Burmah, and the Malay peninsula, and islands. The reasons for thus describing the civilisation of India and Mongolia, and the character of the religion which spread over Eastern Asia to the Pacific shores, will appear when the Azteks and Incas are considered immediately. The history of hieroglyphic systems in China is also important in the same connection, for there is no trace of any hieroglyphic character in India, or in the Indo-Chinese peninsula, where alphabets of western origin were adopted. The florid ornamentation of Malay temples, built in Java and on the main land, and the structure of the topes there found, all point to the Indian origin of this civilisation; but as Buddhism advanced to China the character of its rites and art became further degraded, by the extravagances of Chinese heathenism and pictorial style; and while little survived of the philosophy and humane scepticism of the original religion, little also was left to mark the remote classic origin of architecture and sculpture. The only direct communication of America with any Asiatic civilisation must have been with the deformed Buddhism of the Eastern shores.

We may therefore pass on to consider the earliest known discovery of America by Buddhist travellers *: for there appears to be no reason to suspect the truth of the account given by Hwui-Shan, who came back to China in 499 A.D., under the Tey dynasty, having sailed a distance of 32,000 *li* east, to the Fu-sang country. He first describes the Aleutian Islands, north-east of Japan, and then apparently the Alaska tribes. The distances to Fu Sang point approximately to the position of Mexico. The country was named from the Fu Sang trees, like bamboos, noticed with a red fruit like a pear: the fibre was used for cloth. The agave seems to be intended, which has sprouts not unlike the bamboo. The red pear-like fruit may be that of the cactus in Mexico. The agave has a fibre from which cloth is spun. The houses in Fu Sang were of wood and no citadel or walled tower existed. The people had a written character, and used paper made from the *fusang*, which recalls the agave papyrus of Mexico. They were un-

---

* See *An Inglorious Columbus.* E. P. Vining. 1885.

warlike people and had no weapons. In the north was a
prison for minor offenders, in the south one for more important criminals. This also points to the Mexican polity. When
a noble was condemned to punishment he was shut up in a
hollow tomb and surrounded with ashes. In Mexico the
criminal left to die at the stake was, in like manner, surrounded
with ashes. Crimes were visited on descendants to the third
and seventh generation in Fu Sang. In Mexico the children
of traitors were enslaved to the 9th generation. In Fu Sang
nobles were called *Tuilu*, and the second order of nobles ' the
little *Tuilu*.' In Mexico the title of the nobles is variously
given as *Tecleh-tli* and *Teule-tli*, and a lesser order were called
' Little Chiefs.' The Fu Sang king went in procession preceded and followed by horns and drums. In Mexico the
chiefs were accompanied by horns and drums, and large sea
shells were blown. The Fu Sang monarch, in the first and
second years of the cycle of ten years, wore blue or green, in
the third and fourth he wore red, in the fifth and sixth yellow,
in the seventh and eighth white, in the ninth and tenth black.
In Mexico these five colours in like manner distinguished the
years. Large cattle horns are noticed in Fu Sang, and in
Mexico the buffalo horns were used for drinking vessels. The
pilgrim speaks of carts drawn by horses, cattle, and deer. The
Mexicans had no horses or cows, but they had deer ; and, as
Hwui Shan says, that the Fu Sang people raised deer as
cattle were bred in China, he seems to recognise this, and to
refer to the tame deer and large deer forests of the Mexican
nobles. The inhabitants had no iron, but plenty of copper in
Fu Sang, and did not value gold or silver. The Mexicans also
had no iron, but much copper. They had a great quantity of
gold and silver, but did not use either for money. Among the
customs of the Fu Sang people the pilgrim notes that a lover
would erect a hut outside the girl's home, and sweep and
sprinkle the ground for a year. The girl could dismiss him
afterwards if unwilling. The marriage ceremonies resembled
those of China. Among the Apache Indians similar courtship
occurs, and the newly wedded pair live in a cabin before the
father's house for the first year. It is also to be noted that

similar customs existed among the early Chinese tribes. The Fu Sang people mourned during stated times for various relations, as did also the Mexicans. They set up an image of the deceased, and poured libations before it noon and eve. This was also a Mongolic custom in Thibet and China, and in Yucatan wooden statues of parents were placed in oratories, while the statue of a Mexican king was adorned with offerings of clothes, food, and jewels. Hwui Shan concludes his account by stating that these people had been ignorant until visited by five Buddhist Bikshus in 458 A.D., who are said to have come from *Kipin* or Cabul, in Afghanistan. He also speaks of a country, 1000 li east of Fu Sang, called the 'Country of Women,' where a fair, long-haired race lived, who fled from strangers. He may refer to *Clhuatlan,* 'the place of women,' on the Pacific coast ten days journey from Mexico.

This interesting account, as explained by Mr. Vining, would thus appear to give a faithful picture of Mexican life about 500 A.D., and contains indications, not only of the Buddhist origin of Mexican civilisation half a century earlier, but also of the Mongolic customs of the people so civilised. When we compare this account with the existing remains of Yucatan,* and with Spanish accounts of the Azteks in the sixteenth century A.D., we find further reasons for believing the truth of Hwui Shan's account.

As regards existing remains, the temples of Central America, rising in steps to a building above, bear a striking resemblance to the Buddhist topes, especially to those of Java and the Malay peninsula; and the florid art of the statues is equally like that of the same Asiatic region. The hieroglyphic character does not recall any of the syllabaries of Western Asia. It is clearly ideographic, and few symbols are repeated, except certain strokes and dots added to the left of the emblems, which appear to denote terminations of words. The inscriptions of Palenque are in the same character used in Aztek MSS. The writing may have been in horizontal lines, but in some cases it is vertical. There is no system known which,

---

* *Central America.* J. L. Stephens. 1841.

in general character, bears as close a relation to the Aztek as
does the Chinese; and if the inscriptions ever come to be read
(the language being known) it will probably be by aid of the
oldest Chinese hieroglyphics—the seal character. The evidence of Hwui Shan would point to this having been introduced from Mongolia, or Central Asia, into Mexico by Buddhists in the fifth century A.D.

At Copan, on the borders of Honduras, one of the pyramid
temples is adorned with a row of sculptured skulls, and this
symbol of sacrifice and death was derived originally from the
terrible symbolism of India by the Eastern Asiatics. At
Palenque the kings, standing on slaves, are represented with
long pig-tails, like the Mongols, who introduced this custom
into China. Terrible masks, like those noticed in Thibet, are
represented. The winged sun is also a Mexican emblem, and
one widely spread in Asia. The use of stucco for these bas-
reliefs also recalls the Buddhist art of Eastern Asia. The
'lion throne' on which Buddha sat is represented at Palenque
on the east border of Mexico, and a figure carrying a child
recalls perhaps the mother goddess of Eastern Asia. The cross
is represented as an object of worship; but the cross was an
Indian and a Buddhist emblem. The figures are beardless
and of Mongolic type; and Herera speaks of the Azteks as a
beardless people, who wore their hair long and coiled up, with
a pig-tail hanging behind.

Humboldt, who was struck with the Mongolic type of the
American Indians, collected many important indications of
their Asiatic connection. He pointed to the monastic institutions, symbols, etc., but especially to the Mexican zodiac, as
compared with that of Thibet and the Manchu Tartars:—

Tartar Signs.			Mexican Signs.
Rat,			Water.
Ox,			Sea monster.
Tiger,	...		Tiger (ocelot).
Hare,			Hare.
Dragon,	...		Serpent.
Serpent,	...		Reed.
Horse,	...		Flint knife.
Goat,	...	...	Sun's path.

Monkey,	...		Monkey.
Bird,			Bird.
Dog,			Dog.
Hog,	...	...	House.

The variations are equally remarkable with the coincidences. The Mexicans had no oxen or horses, and probably no hogs or goats. The signs were therefore changed in these cases, probably by the teachers who introduced the Tartar calendar.

Mr. Vining has given a useful *resumé* of the customs and other details which connect Mexican civilisation with that of China, Japan and Mongolia. Among their religious ideas were the transmigration of souls, monastic life, penances, ablutions, alms, the use of household gods, the festivals, the knowledge of astronomy or astrology, the cloistered virgins, the dragon standard, and a kind of heraldry as among the Japanese. They also used incense, charms, amulets, and chants, like the Buddhists, and burned the dead, preserving the ashes in vases. The clothes of bride and bridegroom were tied together, but they lived apart for the first four days. Both these customs are found among the Hindus.

Prescott's *History of the Conquest of Mexico** gives other indications of this connection. The four cycles of Mexico, in which the earth is successively destroyed by each of the four elements, answer to the Indian Kalpas, carried to Thibet and East Asia by the Tantric Buddhists. The dead were buried in a sitting posture, which is also an Indian custom. The mitre-like crown of an Aztek monarch recalls the Buddhist mitres—perhaps borrowed from the Nestorians; and the armour of quilted cotton is equally suggestive of that worn by the Mongols in the Middle Ages. The helmets made to resemble the heads of wild animals recall Chinese and Japanese helmets, intended to terrify the enemy. Baptism, confession, and absolution were customs common to Azteks and Buddhists; and, like Mongols, they believed in 'one god by whom we live,'—an expression used also by Mangu Khan in the thirteenth century in speaking to Rubruquis. But, as among Mongols, this belief in a supreme god, who knew all things

---

* *Conquest of Mexico.* W. H. Prescott. New edition, 1878.

and gave all gifts, incorporeal and invisible, perfect in goodness and purity, 'under whose wings is a sure defence,' was accompanied by the worship of inferior deities, chief of whom, among Azteks, ranked the terrible war god, to whom human victims were offered in hecatombs. They also believed in three future states—hell, hades, and heaven, answering to three of the six conditions of existence among Tantric Buddhists. Paper charms were strewn on the corpse, as in China they are burned at a funeral. The soul was conceived to make a long journey to the North, and to pass between mountains which, moving together, crush the suffering shade; this was a feature also of the Lama's hell. Every year the ghost returned to the family, recalling the Buddhist yearly feast of the dead. A green stone was buried with the corpse, as jade is buried with the dead in China. The children sacrificed for rain were eaten by Aztek worshippers, but such sacrifices were unknown to the milder Toltecs who preceded them. They possessed also a custom of 'eating god,' in the form of a dough image, which recalls that already noticed in Thibet. They spoke of this world's wealth as an 'illusory shadow,' in the language of original Buddhism; and mendicant pilgrims came to visit the shrine where first the foreign teacher of Aztek tradition had taught religion and arts, just as Buddhists visited the sacred land of their faith in Northern India.

Mexican traditions spoke of more than one such teacher. Quetzalcoatl entered Mexico from the east. He wore a long sleeved robe with crosses on it, and a mitre like that of the lamas of Thibet. He taught various penances and ascetic customs, and is said to have introduced the calendar. In his time various artizans disembarked in the north at Panuco, including jewellers, smiths, architects, painters, and sculptors, with agriculturists. His assistants could cast metals, and engrave gems. Cukulcan, another teacher, came to Yucatan from the west, with nineteen companions, who were bearded and long-robed. They introduced a written character, and forbade human sacrifice. They taught the duty of confession, and finally disappeared and were deified. After them the rulers who followed made roads, palaces, temples, schools, almshouses, retreats for widows and orphans, inns, baths, and ponds. The Chilan Balam, or Sacred Book of Yucatan, reckoned back to the second century A.D., or according to another calculation to 583 A.D.

The civilisation so introduced among the peaceable Toltecs was, in time, developed by the Azteks, though the religion of the country decayed, and human sacrifice was reestablished. The Azteks are reported by the Spanish writers to have been able to cast metals, and to have understood the art of enamelling and of lacquer, they used jade and glazed terra cotta, as in Japan and China, and had tesselated pavements. Their lake dwellings on piles resembled those of Eastern Asia, and they had regular posting houses on the high roads like the Mongols. The American legends included that of the Deluge whence Coxcox and his wife escaped in a boat to a mountain, sending out a dove, as shewn on ancient paintings. The Flood story is also found in the high plateau of the Andes, where Tezpi is said to have sent forth a vulture and a humming bird from his boat, in which he preserved many animals. The humming bird brought back a twig in its beak. An Aztek picture represented a single tree in a garden, round which was coiled a human-headed snake. At Cholula giants are said to have begun a tower which the gods destroyed by fire. These legends are traceable to Mesopotamia, but they were known also to Indians, Mongols, and the Chinese. The Flood story is preserved in an Indian Purana, and in Chinese tradition, as well as in Persia ; and the Persians, Indians, and Chinese all possessed legends of a paradise garden.

Among other points of comparison may be mentioned the suspension bridges of the Azteks, resembling those of India and Eastern Asia. The king was also called the child of the sun and earth—a Mongol idea. The Aztek calendar consisted of twenty months of 18 days, with four weeks of 5 days, and an extra week of unlucky days. In every cycle of 52 years 13 days were intercalated. This calendar was reformed in 1091 A.D. The astrological year, with months of 13 days, is comparable to the vague year which, in a sothic cycle of 1491 years, returned to its starting point. These ancient systems,

originating in Chaldea, spread eastwards in Asia, and appear
to have been introduced by Buddhist ascetics into America.
The pantomimic dances of the Azteks, with their masks, like
heads of birds and beasts, also recall those of Tantric Buddhism
already noticed. The Toltecs came into Mexico from the
north probably about 650 A.D., and spread abroad during the
four following centuries, till dispersed by famine. The Azteks
followed about 1196 A.D., entering Tula north of the Mexican
valley; and in 1325 A.D. they settled south-west of the Lake
of Mexico. Dialects resembling the Aztek language have
been found in New Spain, a thousand miles north of Mexico,
and a similar architecture is here said to be traceable. The
existing skulls of the more civilised race are said to resemble
those of the eastern Tartars.

The numerals of the Aztek language have been mentioned.
The language was not a Chinese dialect though it possessed
no letter *r*, which occurs in Mongolian and Japanese, but not
in Chinese. The general character of the grammar is more
akin to that of eastern Tartar dialects. Its greatest peculiarity
was the affix *tl* to nouns. The numerals are nearest to the
Ugro Altaic or North Turanian. A few words may be compared with Mongolic words, as examples of possible comparative study.

Aztek,	*Teo* 'god,'	-	-	Chinese *ti.*
,,	*To* 'mother,'	-	-	Dravidian *tay.*
,,	*Calli* 'house,'	-	-	Altaic *kalle.*
,,	*Cu* 'lord,'	-	-	Chinese *chu.*
,,	*Mez* 'moon,'	-	-	Malay *masi.*
,,	*Canoa* 'boat,'	-	-	,, *chuma.*

Words like these seem to point to a later condition of language in Eastern Asia, and to a more southerly origin than
that of the original American race.

The general result of these comparisons tends to show that
the Mexican races were of East Asiatic origin, but that the
civilisation introduced in the 5th century was foreign, and due
to the energy of the Tantric Buddhist missionaries, at a time
when Buddhism had spread very widely in Eastern Asia, and
when trade and navigation were boldly prosecuted. It

remains to consider the civilisation of Peru under the Incas, which, though presenting many similarities to that of the Azteks, was in other respects distinct, and superior to Mexican conditions.

The Incas traced to a mythical pair representing the Sun and Moon—a married brother and sister who drove a gold wedge into the earth in Peru.* The story of the gold wedge occurs in the Persian legend of Yima, and Mongol kings traced their origin to a similar divine pair. Only thirteen Incas ruled before the Spanish Conquest in 1524 A.D., and the period is variously estimated at 200 or 550 years. The word Inca itself suggests the Tartar *un* or *unk*, ' Lord,' and their conquest must have occurred between 1000 and 1300 A.D., the period of Mongol Empire in Eastern Asia. Among their customs and institutions many recall those of Eastern Asia. They had a ceremony, when youths assumed the ' girdle,' which recalls the sacred thread of Parsees and Brahmins. They used litters in travelling, and had regular stations, called *tambos*, on the high roads. The palace was fitted with silver pipes to the baths, and had gold and silver carved objects in the gardens, just as Mangu Khan's palace at Karakorum was fitted by his French goldsmith in the 13th century. The bodies of the Incas were mummified, and seated in gold chairs. The laws were strict, and the land was held by village tenure as in India. Care was taken of the sick and aged, widows and orphans. The Peruvians knew how to spin and weave wool, and wore cotton dresses. Their country is full of the ruins of temples, palaces, forts, aqueducts, and roads. The latter were paved, and bitumen cement was used. Milestones were erected about a league apart, and suspension bridges were carried over the rivers. In the tombs of the Incas are found vessels of fine clay, gold and silver vases, bracelets, collars, utensils of copper, mirrors of silver or of hard, polished stone, and earrings in the form of wheels. Post-runners carried news along the roads between the *tambos*—ten or twelve miles apart—where military stations were established. These runners—mentioned by

---

* *The Conquest of Peru.* W. H. Prescott. New edition, 1888.

Herodotus in the Persian Empire — were also a feature of Mongol organisation in the 13th century A.D.　By their means fish, game, and fruit were brought 150 miles in a day to the Inca's palace.　The arms in use—bows, lances, darts, swords, battle-axes, slings, etc.—were of copper, or tipped with bone, iron not being used.　The quilted cotton armour, noticed among the Azteks, was also used in Peru, and was, as already stated, common among Mongols.

The Peruvians had not only the Deluge story but, according to Father Charlevoix, a legend also of Virgin birth.　It must not however be forgotten that the Mongol monarchs claimed descent from a Virgin mother, and the same birth was attributed to the Buddha, and to Zoroaster in Persia.　The Peruvian religion recognised an immortal soul, a resurrection, and a hell in the centre of the earth, as well as a Heaven beyond the clouds.　The sun was the Inca's father—as in Mexico—and worshipped by sacrifices on altars.　Pilgrimages to sacred shrines, human sacrifices of children—but not, as in Mexico, accompanied by cannibal feasting—the institution of vestals, or nuns, who fed the sacred fire, and became brides of the Incas, feasts with dancing and drinking, and distribution of bread and wine, were among the religious customs.　As among Mongols, there were registers of property, births, marriages, and deaths.　Plays were acted, and poets composed songs.　Diviners and astrologers had small repute, but augury by entrails was practised, as in Asia generally.　The Peruvians had cycles of years, like the Azteks, and used gnomon stones to correct the calendar.　They lamented (like Indians and Chinese) the occurrence of eclipses, and watched the planet Venus.　They had a calendar of twelve months, and divided the month into weeks.　This calendar is remarkable as being almost identical with the old Asiatic zodiac, which, as already stated, reached India from Greece.

	Peru.	Greek.
April,	lamb,	ram.
May,	ram,	bull.
June,	two stars,	twins.
July,	crab,	crab.
August,	tiger,	lion.

September,	mother goddess.	virgin.
October,	crossing,	scales.
November,	pleiades,	scorpion.
December,	*unknown,*	archer.
January,	buck,	capricorn.
February,	rain,	aquarius.
March,	*unknown,*	fishes.

The custom of inaugurating the ploughing season, by use of a gold plough driven by the Inca, was also a Mongol custom. The Peruvians had silver balances, and were in this respect apparently in advance of the Azteks. They had idols, some of which, still extant, resemble those of Eastern Asia. They used the indigenous transport by llamas and vicunas, instead of camels, and the wool of the alpaca, cattle being unknown.

It is thought that the Incas had no literary character, using only the *Quipu*, which consisted of coloured threads with knots—a system chiefly applicable to registers and short messages, white signifying 'silver' or 'peace,' red 'war,' and yellow 'gold;' but in the museum at Cusco * a sixteenth century MS. appears to indicate the native system of writing used before the Conquest. The Aztek character, as already noticed, was ideographic and not syllabic, and in its general appearance—especially the square and equal forms of the emblems—approaches most closely to the Chinese; but the Peruvian character seems to have been a syllabary of about 100 signs, often repeated and quite different to the Aztek. Among these emblems is found the cross—as in Central America; and on Peruvian pottery, as well as among the Lengua tribes of North America, and in the mounds of Yucatan, the *Swastika* or 'croix cramponée' occurs. This ancient emblem was much used by Buddhists, to represent the 'wheel of the Law,' and wherever the Bikshus travelled they carried with them this remarkable symbol, which however does not occur on the MS. in question in Peru. The grinning mask of the Tantric Buddhists, mentioned in Mexico, is also found in Peru. Among the Peruvian hieroglyphics one of the most

---

* *Wiener. Peru et Bolivie*, p. 775.

distinctive is a kind of tree; and the legend of the sacred tree, by which heaven was reached, is found in Paraguay as well as in India and China, in Persia, and even among the Maoris.

These indications point to a separate civilisation in South America, which may have been introduced as late as the thirteenth century A.D. The skulls of the Incas are said to resemble those of Burmans rather than of Mongols; and Malay enterprise may have carried the conquerors over the Pacific. In New Grenada, close to the equator, a legend referred to the arrival from the East of a stranger called Bochica, (probably Pachcheko or 'Saint') who taught chastity and abstinence. He, too, may have been a Buddhist missionary, reaching the plateau of the Andes perhaps from the Toltec settlement, but by an eastern route, and bringing no doubt with him the *Swastika* found in Peru. The fact that the lion is replaced by the tiger in the Peruvian Calendar seems to point to Indian origin, unless it be due to the absence of lions in America. The ram takes the place of the bull because cattle were unknown. The Pleiades, which replace the Scorpion, were generally observed by Eastern Asiatics, and the legend of the lost Pleiad was carried by the Malays to Polynesia.

It was not surprising that the Spaniards should suppose that certain features of religion, in Mexico and in Peru, were only explicable on the theory that Christian missionaries had visited America. The Cross, the flood story, the images with rayed glories, the traditions of virgin-birth and of paradise, the use of incense, the existence of monks with shaven crowns, and of nuns, the practice of confession and penance, all recalled Christian ideas. But the Spaniards knew nothing of the history of Buddhist systems, or of the early contact of Buddhism with the Christianity of Central Asia. The civilisation of Mexico was distinct from that of Peru, but both shew more points of contact with that of Eastern Asia, and with the strange degraded Buddhism of Mongol peoples, than with any western ideas; just as the languages of America, by grammar even more distinctly than by vocabulary, are related to Mongolic speech, and have no connection with Aryan languages; or as the racial types are Tartar and Malay, and not European. America was so much nearer to Eastern Asia than to Europe that it is natural to suppose that it was discovered by Mongols, and by the hardy Malay sailors, long before the Atlantic was crossed with such difficulty by Columbus, and even before the Norsemen found Vineland in the far North-East.

The evidence here collected seems to shew that, at some early period, the Siberian tribes crossed over the straits, and spread gradually south even to Patagonia. That by the fifth century A.D., Buddhists from the Corea, or from China, reached Mexico, and perhaps travelled on to Peru; and that in the eleventh or twelfth century a Malay or Burmese Conquest civilised the Empire of the Incas. The study of Aztek and Peruvian hieroglyphics can thus best be prosecuted by aid of the old graphic systems of Eastern Asia, which were at most very remotely connected with the yet older hieroglyphs of Egypt, Chaldea, and Syria.

C. R. CONDER.

ART. V.—SCOTLAND UNDER THE ROUNDHEADS.

IN the last issue of the Scottish History Society's publications is included a volume of much and varied interest—*Scotland under the Commonwealth*, 1651-3. If a statue to the Lord-General should again become a question of the hour, even to the imminent peril of an English ministry, this volume ought to recommend the tardy honour, for it goes far to justify the favourable judgment on his usurpation of Scotland as 'tolerant, wise, and just.' It entirely wants the commanding personality of Cromwell himself, who finally turned his back on the Kirk and her cantankerous leaders in the early autumn of 1651, to close with Leslie and the Royalists at Worcester. But it deals with questions of considerable moment at the time, and of constitutional interest now, such as the incorporating Union of the two kingdoms, the reduction of the Highlands, and the settlement of difficult ecclesiastical, judicial, and economic pro-

blems. The sources of the narrative are the Oxford MSS. of
William Clarke in Scotland, acting as secretary to Cromwell, and
thereafter to his right-hand man, Monk. That office he continued
to hold, till the Restoration, under the officers that succeeded
Monk. The *lacunae* in Clarke's Journal have been supplied
from the Tanner MSS. in the Bodleian, consisting of letters to
the Speaker, supplemented by news-letters of the day and inter-
cepted Royalist correspondence.

The narrative opens with Monk's march through Fife to the
reduction of Stirling Castle. He crossed the Forth, not by the
bridge but at the Ford of Frew, a few miles farther up, where
in the '45 Prince Charlie's men passed southward. William
Cunningham, *anciente of the Castle,* gave in after a week's feeble
pounding at the ramparts from the kirk steeple. The mortars
proved too much for the nerves of his Highlandmen, among
whom they produced a panic and mutiny. These would appear
to have been the most advanced type of ordnance, worked only
by Mr. Joachim Hane, the Dutch Engineer, of whom, on a later
occasion, Lilburne says, writing to Cromwell, ' we have an ex-
ceeding great want. Should we have any occasion to use a
morter peece without him, there is nobody to undertake that
business that is fitt for itt." Among the spoils we find,
' 4 *leather* guns, 2 coaches and a sedan, the Earl of Murris
coronet and Parliament roabes.' Monk lived in the interesting
old Stirling mansion, Mar's Wark, from which the Countess of
Argyll had to retire during the siege, *being sik,* and there terms
of capitulation were signed. The siege of Dundee, which Monk
reached from Stirling by Perth, has made a profounder mark in
history, for it proved a Scottish sack of Drogheda, for which the
General gets off much more lightly in history than his master over
the Irish affair. Hither most of the portable wealth of the country had been transported. With two wide firths between it and
the Sectaries it was deemed safe. The townspeople were very
confident, remembering their success in beating off Montrose, but
Engineer Hane *plaid* again *with his morter peece,* the troopers
poured through the breaches on the east and west, ' divers of the
enemy retreated to the church and steeple, and among the rest
the Governour, whoe was kild with between foure and five

hundred souldyers and townsmen. The souldyers had the plunder of the town for all that day and night, and had very large prize, many inhabitantes of Edinburgh and other places having sent their ware and geere thither. Captain Eely led on the Pioneers, whoe made way for the horse, and the Lt.-Generall went in person. Our word was, God with us, and the signe a white cloath or shirt hanging out behind.' The minister of the town was among the slain. Such is the brief contemporary narrative of a massacre which great historians, like Burton and Gardiner, have disbelieved. Two days before had been enacted the Crowning Mercy of Worcester, of which Monk heard 'the happy news' here, September 9. Shortly before this (August 27) Colonel Alured accomplished his smart feat, the Raid of Alyth, and curtly tells in due course, 'From my Tent at the Leaguer before Dundee,' how 'It hath pleased the Lord to give a great mercy to us,' no less indeed than the capture of the whole committee of the Scots Estates, barring two. He rode with his dragoons 'on a darke rainey night in rough and tedious way to a Towne called Ellit,' where lay the Scots Parliament, at the foot of the Sid-laws, in full security of its Highland supports. The Earls of Leven (General Leslie) and Marischal were among the batch of captives that Monk shipped off to a long captivity in the Tower, from which the old Captain of the Covenant was ultimately liberated to die in peace at his beautiful Fifeshire retreat of Balgonie. Another of the caged Scots was the notorious Lauderdale, and him we can fancy having a crack over the adventure, after the Restoration, with his companion renegade, the now glorified Duke of Albemarle. Thus was the curtain rung down on that Covenanted Republic, Carlyle's 'theocracy without the inspiration,' which Jenny Geddes and Duns Law had brought into being.

Scotland was now left to the tender mercies of that 'very precious instrument,' General Monk, unfortunately seized with a very desperate sickness after the fall of Dundee. Clarke gives him a high character in writing to Speaker Lenthal—'the most properly fitted for the management of affairs here. His temper every way fits him and none could order the Scots so handsomely as himself, he carries things with such a grace and *rigid gentle-*

nesse.' The Secretary writes a pretty style it must be admitted. Monk certainly lost no time in getting his men well in hand again after the sack, proclamations following, on the next day, to 'forbeare further plundering or rifling of the houses in Dundee.' Court martials severely punished offenders who had been scouring the district for plunder. For robbing two country-men a brace of dragoons are led with ropes about their necks to the gallows, tied up, flogged with thirty stripes a piece; then on their knees they have to beg forgiveness of their victims, and restore the plunder four-fold. Others have to ride the *tree mare* for similar offences—' so severe,' says Clarke, ' is the Lt.-General and officers against injuring the countrey, to whom we endeavour to show as much favour as may be (especially to the poorer sort) to convince them of the slavery they have been under and freedom they may now enjoy under the English.'

Monk followed up his success with the reduction of the coast towns and the establishment of small garrisons. A good footing was gained as far north as Aberdeen, 'one of the richest and chiefest cities,' where the officers were handsomely entertained. No doubt both parties were anxious as to the attitude of that great scourge of the north, the Marquis of Huntly, but he proved powerless both in health and purse to interfere in the struggle. Before the renewal of active operations in the spring of 1652 Monk's weak health compelled him to retire to Bath for the waters, and Deane assumed command for a few months, but the really active officer was Lilburne. To him fell the hardest task of all, to reduce the Highlands and keep the active royalists at bay. The situation reached its acute stage in the summer of 1653, when the Roundhead government was put to the severest strain. The Dutch War absorbed its whole energies and Lil-burne was in despair for men and means. One cannot but sym-pathise with his efforts to be honest and faithful. In a letter to Cromwell he speaks his mind—' Our want of money seemes to be an incouragement to our enimies, who conceives we are not able to subsist long at the vast charge the Commonwealth is at; the foote eate biskett and cheese on Pentland hills, and hath not money to buy them other refreshments, being now 2 months and above in arreare and our fortifications readie to stand still, nor do I know where to gett 100l. in the treasury ; this hath bene often represented above and hinted to your Excellencie.' In the early days of the occupation the troopers had lived at free quarters on a rough system of local billeting, but latterly about £8000 a month had been uniformly levied, which sum, however, had to be largely supplemented from England. The assessments for the different shires and burghs are detailed in this volume and give a valuable indication of the economic situation. Fife and Perth head the list of the shires by a long way, then follow Aberdeen, Ayr, Midlothian and Lanark. Of the burghs, Edinburgh pays more than five times Dundee, the second on the list, closely followed by Aberdeen, Glasgow, and Perth. Rutherglen has to contribute £3 less than Rothesay, and only half the cess from the ancient burgh of Culross. From Argyle-shire Lilburne had to accept the cess in kind, cows at 26s.—28s. if fat, and trees at 4s. each if from 20—24 feet long and a foot square. Here he had an eye to the substantial forts he was constructing as at Ayr—*sconces* (Ger. *schanze*), these were called after the Dutch masters in gunnery. The term is still used in South African warfare, and is heard, in modified form, in *ensconced*. This volume corroborates the tradition that the Cromwellian rule pressed hard on the few native woods as well as the historic churches. Thus Lilburne tells Cromwell that the broken men under Glencairn and Kenmure had come down from the hills as far as Falkland and secured four or five men in charge of the timber in the park at Falkland, designed for the citadel at Perth. The meat supply was an even greater difficulty, the country was so poor. The ships had to go often to Newcastle and Hull for beef and pork ; hay and meal the country provided, but in the hills the men had to subsist on the biscuits and cheese they carried with them. In the Lowlands trade flowed on in the usual channels. Thus we find Lilburne telling Cromwell that it ' was strange that the Treasurer should hinder the return of money and put the State and the soldiers to the trouble of bringing it out from London and York in waggons when it might be almost every groat received here upon bills.'

The untiring energy displayed gives one a high idea of the

splendid stuff developed by the army of the New Model. In all directions there is the greatest activity. The mosstroopers of the Border were dragooned into decent dalesmen. The coast towns were made ready to meet the Dutchmen. Arbroath Abbey, for example, was turned into what was deemed a very tenable fort; while the Scots navy, taken in Dundee—sixty sail of 10, 6, and 4 guns—along with one that had escaped to Aberdeen, having ' 6 peeces, and stoare of wines and other good comodityes,' were pressed into the service. To checkmate the Dutch, who set the greatest store upon the Orkneys and Shetland for the Great Fishing, Overton fortified Kirkwall, making tenable the Cathedral Kirk of St. Maans (Magnus) and the Earl of Morton's house, *where a regiment can lodge.* Lilburne, writing to Cromwell, tells how the Dutch have especially an eye upon Shetland. 'There have bin sometimes 1800 saile in and about Birssie (Bressay) Sound,' the narrowest part of which he proposes to secure with a strong fort. For a time the Lewes had been thought well worth securing, and here Cobbett worked hard at making a strength at Stornoway. It was found, however, that the course of trade did not at all lie in that direction. Montrose's destructive raid had taught the lesson that there was a real danger from Ireland through the West Highlands, where another Colkitto might any day appear; and so Ayr and Brodick, Dunstaffnage and Dunolly were strongly held. Inverness was relied upon as the chief defence for the central Highlands, and in an interesting letter we read the story of the building of a citadel and particularly of the great feat of dragging a forty ton pinnace across six miles of dry land for service on Loch Ness, ' to the admiration of the spectators. The men broke three cables, seven inches about, with hawling of her . . . The west end of the Lough is near unto the Irish Sea, it wanting not above six mile of ground to be cut to make the shires north of it an entire island of itself.' Inverlochy, at the western side of the Great Glen, was held strongly to keep down what was the main-stay of the Royalists, the cattle-lifting caterans of Lochaber, the Macdonalds and the Camerons. The attitude of Argyll, the great leader of the Covenant and the rival of Montrose, was a constant source of anxiety. With a caution characteristic of these old times, when the head of the clan remained in one camp while a son or brother stuck by its rival, the Marquis had frequent friendly correspondences with the Roundheads, doing them valuable service, while his son, Lorn, was a leading spirit among the Royalists. In consequence Argyllshire required constant watchfulness, and was often the scene of really plucky marchings and counter-marchings. It would be something even in these days to take, as Colonel Read did, 700 horse, dragoons and foot, from Tarbert to Dunstaffnage 'after four hard dayes march,' find no provisions there nor in Dunolly, and after a stay of two nights, 'be forced to act the King of France's part,' to face about 'and by a nearer cut return to his base.' A still more toilsome undertaking was the marching and the dragging of guns from Athole over the stiffest part of the Highlands to Inverlochy in Lochaber. Nor again was that a small feat of which we read in a Letter from Paisley, August, 1652. Here we can follow the handful of surly Roundheads as they marched from Inveraray across 'an impregnable Passe, called Glen Crow (Croe), where onely one could but file over,' for not till a century later did Lascelles' regiment make the present road. The jagged cliffs that frown upon the gloomy tarn at Rest and be Thankful, were dotted over with crowds of excited clansmen, 'to know if the E. of Argyle were our prisoner; yet God, who restrains the fury of the most savage beasts, doth also muzzle the mouthes of bloody-minded men. Wee drew up our men under their noses until our rear-guard was got over. I doubt whether these things are in order, to war with these base and beggerly wild beasts, a thing to be avoided for many reasons, especially their poverty and un-accessiblenesse of every passe and place, where each hill is no less than an invincible garrison.'

Worcester had proved a heavy blow to the Royalists. For some time the exiles suffered the greatest straits. But the Dutch War revived their hopes, absorbing as it did all Cromwell's energies and resources. The difficulty, however, was to find money for an expedition. Late in 1652 we have the King, *young Charles,* or *the lad* of the Roundhead letters, writing from Paris to Middleton, 'I have scarce received 200 pistoles since you went.' By the spring of 1653 everything seemed favourable for action, all the more urgent that the fall of Dunnottar, the last of the Covenanting strengths to succumb, was imminent. Heie were stored the royal plenishing and the regalia, the preservation of which forms a well-known romantic incident of the time. Agents scoured the Baltic provinces to raise money from the Scotch merchants there. One letter from a General Douglas at Stockholm breathes the most touching loyalty. In answer to His Sacred Majesty's own letter he says that all he can do 'must be in a private way; however, your goodness will not reject the harte affections of your subjects abroad, quhairoff a few with my selfe have maide boulde to send your Majeste a somme of 5200 rixdollars' through William Davidson, merchant in Amsterdam. The King himself writes, asking a loan of £300 from the Earls of Southesk and Panmure. Hyde entreats Middleton, appointed General in Scotland, 'not to be angry at the sum' he sends, 'being but £100, God knowes the King had rather give you £1000.' Middleton, originally a Fifeshire trooper in Hepburn's regiment, rose to be the King's Viceroy in Scotland with an evil reputation for rough measures and manners and drunken habits. The cruel agents of the Secret Council during the Killing Times all occur in this correspondence as working for the King—Strachan, Turner, Ballantyne, and that truculent trooper, Dalzel. Great efforts were made to secure the co-operation of the Dutch, the Royalists offering them fishing stations in the isles 'to be possessed by them forever.' All this activity resulted in the Glencairn Rising of 1653, which we can now study here in most interesting detail. There were high hopes of the Highland chiefs, with Glengarry at their head. Charles took great pains to reduce the friction of jealousy by giving the chief command to Middleton, but with little success. Lorn and Glengarry one day drew their claymores on each another. Glencairn, one of the most active leaders, was a Cunningham, an Ayrshire laird, and his henchman, that energetic raider, Kenmore, was the head of the Galloway Gordons, who took to the hills with but a hundred followers. Scott's *Lochinvar* and that stirring Jacobite March of The Fifteen, *Kenmure's on and awa!* will forever preserve the memory of the lords of the grim fortalice at the head of Loch Ken. There was no Montrose now among these leaders, and, if there had been, the Roundhead troopers would have made his tactics impracticable. The King cheered on his followers with the sham hope of joining them, but he secretly had no wish to be up a tree again. Nothing more serious than horse-stealing was done. A slight skirmish at Aberfoyle, a Roundhead raid into Athole in which the Laird of Macnab got killed, Kenmore's futile landing in Cantire and attack on Campbeltown, then known only as Lochhead—these summed up the exploits of the Royalists; and, when Cromwell assumed the Protectorate and dismissed the Long Parliament, his officers in the north could assure him of the support of Scotland.

Lilburne's reports prove him an admirable administrator. The backbone of the rising he rightly conceives to be the bankrupt position of the gentry, impoverished by civil war and a vicious land system. To Cromwell he more than once strongly represents the situation. The creditors of the lairds were using the increased strictness and despatch of the reformed Court of Session to harass their debtors, and again and again we find Lilburne pressing them to leniency, their action driving many to the hills. To this the scarcity of money contributed. All this bears out the gloomy picture of the economic situation drawn by Baillie in his *Letters,* ' Our nobility weel near all are wracked,' and accounts for the exaggerated strain of Glencairn's appeal to the United Provinces, how ' the cry of our blood hath reached to Heaven, soe we doe not at all doubt but the extremities of the Earth are acquainted with the horrid actings of those men of blood,' the Roundheads. Lilburne tells Cromwell that there are (December, 1653) ' 35,000 *captions* (arrest-warrants for debt) out against men. Huntly being one of that number, sent this day to me for protection.' About the same date Lord Cardross was writing to the Stirling bailies to allow the Earl of Mar to come south without fear of arrest, the revenue of the town's hospital depending upon monies that had been lent to him. Lilburne also strongly urged the policy which President Forbes and Argyll pressed upon the Hanoverian Government after the Fifteen. This was, ' That libertie may bee given to any Scotchman to transport regiments to Forraine princes in amity with us.' Forbes's plan contemplated service under the British flag, and this was left to Chatham to carry out.   Had it been adopted earlier, we should probably never have heard of the Forty-five.

Cromwell, finding the country at his feet, lost no time in promoting an Incorporating Union.   A commission of eight, on which sat such famous Roundhead officers as Vane, Lambert, Monk, and St. John, arrived in Scotland early in 1652 to confer with the local leaders with a view to union.   Argyll held out in the hope of resuscitating the old Scots Estates, and even summoned them to a futile meeting at Finlarig, on Loch Tay, but after a conference with Monk at Dumbarton he gave in, and rendered valuable assistance in reducing the Highlands.   Cromwell evidently looked upon Scotland as won by his sword, and was disposed towards annexation pure and simple.   Convinced that the advantages of union were all on the side of the poor Scots, he and his officers were astonished that they were so little grateful for the boon.   It offered a mild form of Home Rule in place of a military occupation, Parliamentary representation by thirty members, most of them drawn from the officers of the English, and three peers, among them Argyll and Johnston of Warristoun.   This was the outcome of the instrument of Government, or declaration for Union, ' proclaymed with much solemnity att the Markett Crosse in Edinburgh by beate of drum and sound of trumpett, and the Crosse adorned with hangings,' all which can be read in this volume in a letter from Leith, April, 1652.   There was a great concourse of people, and after the reading the soldiers shouted their approbation with the ' free conferring of liberty upon a conquered people, but soe sencelesse are this generation of theire owne goods, that scarce a man of them shew'd any signe of rejoycing.'   The citizens evidently thought this a poor substitute for the riding of the Parliament, the glories of which made Miss Damahoy wax so eloquent to her neighbour, Peter Plumdammas.

Of greater moment than this abortive Union, on which the volume throws but little light, was the creation of a new bench of judges in place of the corrupt Court of Session.   They were seven in number, four English and three Scots—James Dalrymple, better known as Viscount Stair, Johnston of Warristoun, and Lockhart of Lee.   They were no longer paper *lords,* but designated Judge Smith and the like, in colonial fashion. Henceforth, too, all legal documents were to be in English. This Southron justice proved popular, for it was pure and expeditious. A *laudator temporis acti* of a later date, who admired the old style of ' tholing an assize with a formidable *tail* of supporters,' disposed of them sneeringly with a ' Deil thank them ! a wheen kinless loons.' They appear to have valued their salaries, regularly paid them, better than the gifts and favour of kinsmen. Nicoll, the diarist, an Edinburgh writer who acted as agent for the city of Glasgow at this time, laments that the old legal officials dare not show themselves for fear of the English. To his disgust people had to seek justice from the English governors and officers. There was no magistrate or Council for Edinburgh, and petitioners had to go to the Castle and Leith, ' whose officers (to speak truly) proceeded more equitably and conscientiously nor our own magistrates.' The Commissioners sat at Dalkeith, in what had been the castle of the Regent Morton in Queen Mary's time, and thither had many a deputation from the burghs to trudge and make a poor face over the paying of the cess and the quartering of soldiers, or take their commands as to the ordering of burghal affairs. They contrived, however, to *thole* their troubles. In the burgh accounts of Stirling at this date appear the items—' Spent with Tammas Bruce the nicht befor going to Dalkeith, on wine, succar, tabacco, and *other necessaris ;* on return with Tammas, in John Cahouns, 9 muchkins (quarts) canary, tobacco, and pypes; *mair,* when Tammas gaed to his awn hoose, 1 muchkin canary.' Nor did these hard-driven bailies deny themselves the compensations of the *deid chack,* as witness the item (1651)—' Spent wi' the auld provist and bailyeis in Jas. Swordis efter the execution of the man quba murderit his chyld, on wyn, aill, and tibac., £3 11s. 6d.'

The wars for Covenant and Crown had proved the ruin of Scottish feudalism and prepared the way for that degradation of public spirit and character among the governing classes which made the Restoration period the most scandalous in our annals. Robert Baillie pithily sketches the condition of the peers— ' Hamilton execute and the estates forfault, one part gifted to

English sojours, rest not fit to pay the debt, Argyll amost drowned in debt, Douglas and his son Angus quyet men of no respect, Loudoun ane outlaw about Athole, Balmerino suddenly deid and his son for *captions* (warrants) keips not the causey, Eglinton and Glencairn on the brink of bankruptcy.' Lilburne's letters amply corroborate Baillie. He shows how this state of matters was feeding the flames of disaffection, 'many broken men of desperate fortunes running to the Hills daily, and from thence fall downe in parties in the night time into the Lowlands, and steal horses,' thus putting the garrisons to much trouble and expense. Of course one cannot expect sympathy with broken barons from such militant republicans, whose leanings were all towards ·the *poore commonis.* The news-letters seem to delight in showing these royalist barons at a disadvantage. Thus the *Mercurius Politicus*, of October 1653, tells, with a chuckle, how Kenmore ' marches with a rundlet (keg) of strong waters before him which they call Kenmore's Drum.' On the other hand the peasantry are cordially supported as the victims of their feudal masters, whose ruin proved in fact to them a genuine relief from rent and harassing exactions. The raising of the royal standard at Killin, July 1653, was virtually a No Rent manifesto. The burghers were more to be pitied, for they had to contribute heavily to support the military occupation in spite of disorganised trade and great scarcity of money. There are frequent petitions for abatements. Lilburne, ever considerate, presses the Committee for the Army to be lenient and not charge any more than £8,500 a month, with abatements to *depopulate* places. Perth, Dundee, Glasgow, and other great burghs, he adds, pay little or nothing, Argyle and most of the Highlands nothing at all. Especially sad was the case of Glasgow, ' fair and beautiful, the flower of Scotland,' of which the fourth part was burnt down in 1652. It took forty-eight hours to quench the fire in spite of the help of the garrison. ' Yesterday, when we went to view it, it drew tears from my eyes, and not mine alone, but many,' says a contemporary letter. The burghers wofully petition that ' the poore widowis and orphaunts wha hes no scheildis to creipe in may be timeously supportet.' The times had wrought sad reverses among even the well to do burgess class. Sir William Dick, who had been a great merchant in the Lawnmarket of Edinburgh and architect of his own fortune, died a pauper in Westminster, December, 1655, and without a decent funeral, yet his advances in hard cash, the sacks of dollars that Davie Deans describes, really gained the victory of Duns Law and turned the tide of history. Lilburne, in November 1653, pleads with the judges to grant a suspension to his sons from personal execution, 'being very sensible of the sufferings of the old gentleman, their father, at London agitating for some public satisfaction for his great sacrifices.'

The poverty of the country, unable as it was to bear the military burdens, and the disaffection of the chiefs, formed not the only rocks on which Cromwellian rule split. The real rock was the clergy. The divisions among them were more political, and more bitter than those among the Sectaries whom they detested. There were a few Malignants, professed Royalists with no great love for Presbytery. They pretended to be most ready to submit to Cromwell, but, in reality, merely from hostility to the Kirk. A letter from Hyde to Middleton in this volume is a curious commentary on Church politics and royalist tactics. For some years after 1660 he ruled Scotland, and, himself a cavalier toper, presided over that Drunken Parliament at Glasgow, 1662, which sent so many of the westland clergy to the moors and the moss-hags. Hyde tells him, 'I fear you are *not Presbiterian enough*, for I do not find any of that trybe who are ther (in Scotland) have any confidence in you.' At the other extreme were the Remonstrants, the true-blues of the west, who protested against certain resolutions of recent assemblies in favour of the King, passed by a party that they dubbed in consequence Resolutioners. These Resolutioners were the Moderates of the time, who clung to their *simulacrum of a Covenant* and hoped to *purge* and *plant the church* and bring in their covenanted king. Chief of these were Robert Baillie, and 'that very worthy, pious, wise, and diligent young man, James Sharp.' Cromwell upon the whole preferred the Remonstrants as more thorough-going Puritans. In truth the Moderates had an intense hatred of that Brownism or Independency which had neutralised the victory of Presbyterianism in the Westminster Assembly. The Roundhead officers were diligent apostles and exemplars of Brownism, trying their best among the common people with a fervour worthy of rivals such as that John Menzies who used to change his shirt always after preaching, and to wet two or three napkins with his tears every sermon. Under their example the devotional aspect of the old service of Knox and Melville deteriorated. The Brownists made great ado about their hats during sermon, sitting covered during the preaching. A Cross-michael minister objected to this among his own people. ' I see a man,' he said from the pulpit one day, ' aneath that laft wi' a hat on. I'm sure ye're clear o' the sooch o' the door. Keep aff your bannet, Tammas, and if your bare pow be cauld ye maun just get a grey worsit wig like mysel.' Lilburne believed that ' there is an increase of good people who daily some way or other are sweetened towards us, only there wants some meanes to lead many into a clearer light that are waiting for it.' He expects some favourable movement among 'the people in the west, who have bin always accounted most precise.' There were a few *gathered churches* or meetings of converts to Brownism here and there. Lilburne soon comes to see, however, that even the Remonstrants detested the Cromwellian subordination of the Church to the State and its lax toleration of Anabaptists, Quakers, Papists, and even Atheists. That dour Precisian, Andrew Cant, who was watching so sedulously over Aberdeen for the Covenant, rejected the advances of Colonel Overton when apologising for some incivilities offered by his men to one ' who he heard was a friend · to us ; to which Mr. Cant replied in plain Scottish that he was a lying knave who told him so, for he neither respected him nor his party.' At Cupar there was a conference between the Puritan and the Presbyterian preachers, where were discussed, with much cry and little wool, such *kittle pints* as Adam's sin, infant baptism, and universalism. Among the benighted Highlanders progress was made, it was believed, ' some having heard our preaching with great attention and groanings. They are very simple, and ignorant in the things of God, and some live even as brutish as the heathen.' In 1651 Lambert had received overtures from Warristoun, Rutherford, and others of the

rigid sect 'in name of those who would be called the godly
party,' but he sees their drift, which is to 'exalt their government in the Kirk.' By the summer of 1653 Lilburne has become
convinced that the disaffected clergy are secretly encouraging
the rebel Malignants in the Highlands, and on his own responsibility orders Colonel Cotterell to treat that popular and godly
Parliament, the General Assembly, to his master's stern *Get thee
gone!* He 'besett the church (St. Giles) with some rattes of
musketers and a troop of horse,' marched the members ignomin-
iously out at the West Port and so on to the quarry holes on
Bruntsfield Links, and there at the foot of the thieves' gallows
set them about their business. The two prelatic Stuart kings
had never dared to do so much.

The divided state of public opinion on church matters showed
what a loss the country sustained in the death of a real statesman like Alexander Henderson. King-made Prelacy and drum-
head Independency had both been tried and Scotland would
have none of them. The position of parties made compromise
impossible, and so a great opportunity was lost. And while the
Kirk learned little or nothing of 'sweet reasonableness' from
the piety of the Independents, their example destroyed much of
that 'beauty of holiness' in ritual which Knox and Melville had
left untouched.

By vehement harangues in sermon and prayer the clergy
sought to show forth the power of grace, resulting only in an
incongruous blend of secular and sacred. Thus, in Edinburgh,
there was a daily service in the kirks every afternoon at four, in
which the officers were wont to play the part of the church militant. Nicoll sarcastically extracts good out of the practice,
'which benefited soul and body, the soul being edified and fed
by the Word, the body withhalden from unnecessar *bibing*, whilk
at that hour of the door was in use and custom'—an early
authority for that time-honoured institution, the *meridian*. The
diarist tells us that in its social aspects the Usurpation was still
more aggressive. The Independents 'proclamit the day called
Christmas to cease, demolished the King's seat in the High
Church, pulled down the King's arms and dang down the unicorn, hanging up the crown on the gallows,' which stood at

the cross on the High Street. They struck too at the Kirk's
police control over public morals, for the dragoons took out and
burned the repentance stool wherever they went, making fun of
it as a Popish relic of penance. No doubt the Church had
shown the absurdity of giving legislative importance to trifles.
They had found the most scandalous offenders among self-
accused demented creatures. In this volume we are told how the
English judges sat for three days (October 1652) on a long list
of arrears, cases under the seventh commandment, all more or
less shocking. Above sixty offenders were libelled, most for
deeds done years before, the chief proof being found to be their
own confession. With all this the Sectaries had little sympathy,
though in a practical way they studied public decency. The
garrison at Leith was made the nucleus of a sort of model community, and here the governor tried (January 1652) to put down
immorality with a strong hand, forbidding the employment of
women and maid-servants as tapsters and the marriage of any
soldier with a Scots woman without official sanction. Military
discipline was admirably maintained, and there are here many
proclamations against the breaking into 'orchards, gardens,
yards, to plunder fruits, cabbage, roots, also green pease or
beanes in fields, or killing rabbits belonging to warrens, and
house-pigeons,' the object being to conciliate the people. 'Free
the poor commoners, and make as little use as can be either of
the great men or clergy,' sums up well the policy of the Usurpation.

Cromwell's officers followed on the lines of the old Privy
Council in interfering, for a social good, with the liberty of the
subject. They fixed the price of hay and stabling charges, restrained the extortions of the boatmen and ferrymen of Burnt-
island and Leith, inspected and regulated the quality and price
of bread. Bakers must expose their bread for sale only on
Fridays and Tuesdays at the Brig-end of Leith, and not run
from house to house with it. Moderns will have more sympathy
with the efforts to improve the comforts of the capital. The
order that householders must hang out lanterns and candles at
their doors and windows—6 p.m. to 9 p.m.—almost turned,
according to a contemporary, night into day. The provost, too,

was to give present order to clean wynds and closes, and that none throw water from their windows, or be fined 4s. Scots, half to the informer, half to the poor. Not till 1731 did the Edinburgh Corporation make any real headway in repressing the *throwin owre* practices. In Cromwell's time the thrifty magistrates complained of the enormous expense of the enforced scavenging (£50 Scots a week), landing the city, as it did, in debt.

Scotland suffered badly from the witch mania that disgraced so many countries and centuries. These poor creatures had reason to bless the Roundhead officers, under whom they enjoyed something of a respite. Thus Clarke, in reporting to Lenthall the doings of the judges on that notable three days' assize in 1652, mentions a witch case of several years' standing. On their own confession, the unhappy wretches had been turned over to the civil magistrate, and this is how they had been proved witches—' By tying their thumbs behind them and then hanging them up by them when they were whipped, after which lighted candles were set to the soles of their feet and between their toes, then they burnt them by putting candles into their mouths.' Of the six so treated, four died of the torture. The judges appointed the sheriffs, ministers, and tormentors to be found out, and to give an account of the ground of the cruelty. Another suspect was 'kept on bread and water twenty days, stript naked and laid upon a cold stone, with only a hair-cloth over her. Others had hair-shirts dipt in vinegar put on them to fetch off their skin. Here is enough for reasonable men to comment upon.' The humanity of Puritanism was never more conspicuous than at this time.

The editorial introduction to this curious volume is excellent, but the annotation of the text, and especially the indexing, leave much to be desired. As the material of the volume has been deciphered and pieced together with great difficulty, often from rough notes and jottings in shorthand, we ought to be thankful that it has been made so intelligible. The numerous topographical references on every page, a matter of very great and lasting interest, have been but perfunctorily handled. This may be one of the disadvantages accruing to

Scottish history made or edited in England.   Many of the
place-names are almost hopelessly disguised.   As the index offers
no help here ingenuity might be directed to such as Bohanty,
'the best of the three ways out of the Highlands,' Bonnywher,
'neere Ruthven Castle' in Badenoch, Canygeles, 'Huntly's
house,' Carversa Castle, '20 miles from Inveraray' (?) Tarbert,
Gillogaer somewhere on the northern bounds of Athole.   These
are only a few of the unexplained.   They include such very
obvious ones as Dagettee in Fife, Finlarge at the west-end of
Loch Tay, Logyerate, Envernes, Rowborough, and Bigtoune,
indexed as Biscoptoune (Bishopton).   The editor queries 'Knap-
drale betweene Swin Castle and Rosse,' suggesting Knapdale,
and leaving the other tempting bits of topography unexplained.
And yet the ordnance maps are not difficult of access.   Baginoth
is Badenoch in the index, but Badinoth in Ruthven and Baggon
are never mentioned though obviously the same place.   When Kenmore went from Busse to the head of Loch Long to meet Colonel
Macnaughten, we are left to conjecture that Luss on Loch Lomond
is meant.   Another passage surely calling for explanation is, 'The
Marquess of Huntley died last week at his house at Bogy-geith.'
This place is not even indexed, so it may be well to say it is on
p. 289.   It is the famous Bog o' Gight, that gives its name to
Strathbogie.   Slezer in his *Theatrum Scotiæ* blunders strangely
over this name.   He gives a view of Heriot's Hospital, which he
labels *Boghen-gieght*.   Now and again the Roundhead officers
preserve the local pronunciation very correctly as in 'our new
garrisons att *Buhannon* and Cardrus,' and again in '*Kirkmichill*'
(near Blair Athol).   The index affords no help, though we have
obviously here Buchanan Castle, Cardross, and Kirkmichael.
One would never guess, again, from text or index, where Loch-
heid is.   In this connection falls to be noted the strangest bit of
editorial obscurity.   'For the Major General who went by sea
from Inverary to Ayre, came to us by boat (to Peasly *i.e.* Paisley), and wee heard by him of the surprizall of our garrisons of
Lough, Kincairn, and Turbet.'   The comma after *Lough* is in
the text.   Kincairn stands in the index with a reference only.
Now we have here Kenmore's famous dash at Kintyre and a very
pretty bit of topographical lore.   The fort on the beautiful loch

at Campbeltown had the honour of first appearing in history as Dalruadhain, the capital of Fergus King of Scotia. When Kiaran, the black-visaged, settled here in his cell as an Irish saint, the spot became the holy Kil-cerran and in Gaelic to this day *Ceann locha chille Chiaran,* head of the loch of Kiaran, or, in this Roundhead officer's letter, Lough Kincairn. During the early Protectorate Argyll induced many westland Whigs to settle here from Ayrshire, and they Saxonised the spot as Loch-head. On the site of the old castle that Kenmore stormed, at the head of Main Street of Campbeltown, a church was built in 1780. In the *Expedition of Argyll,* 1661, the town is called Cean Loch or Loch-heid, and in a church register of 1671 it appears for the first time as Campbeltown in honour of the Argyll family. After these faults of omission it is venial to find the editor telling in his preface that Monk's soldiers learned at Dundee, *Aug. 9th,* of the victory at Worcester at the beginning of September.

The personal names in the text offer most tempting bits of family history. Not to speak of the crowd of Macs, disguised by outrageous spelling, we have such members of noted historical families as Hope of Craighall, Sir John Chiesly, Sir James Stewart, Lord Dundas of Arniston. Most of the King's agents in the Persecution (1662-87) are here—Middleton, Turner, Ballantyne, Dalzel—all active in stirring up opposition among the Tories, as Lilburne calls his Highland enemies, 'people who speak Irish, and go only with plaids about their middle, both men and women.' It may be observed here that all through our literature Scottish Gaelic generally appears as *Erse* or *Irish,* and this even so late as the poetry of Burns, a fact not always recognised by his editors. Of the clergy Lilburne was much pleased with Mr. Galeaspe, honest Robert Baillie's *bête noir,* Patrick Gillespie, whom Cromwell made Principal of Glasgow University, paying also Charles I.'s subscription to the building fund, to which the King had signed his name. Lilburne's name for him is that which Milton thought as inharmonious as his own Tetrachordon. Here, too, is Master Robert Leighton, as yet minister of Newbattle, and going to London to help the poor clergy whom Captain Alured had captured in the Raid of Alyth. But the most curious personal name occurs in a letter of Hyde to Middleton, who had wished 'the King should write to Mr. Junius of Amsterdam in Latine,' probably that he might be another Salmasius and catch the ear of academic Europe for the woes of royalty in exile. Junius was among the first to draw attention to Old English, publishing Caedmon's *Paraphrase*, and the Moeso-Gothic *Gospels* of Wulfila, two of the most notable finds in the whole range of English philology.

JAMES COLVILLE.

———————

ART. VI.—CHRISTINA, QUEEN OF SWEDEN.

1. *Christina, Queen of Sweden.* By T. W. BAIN (Fellow of All Souls College, Oxford). London: W. H. Allen & Co. 1890.
2. *Mémoirs concernant Christine, reine de Suede.* Par JEAN ARCKENHOLTZ (cons et bibl du Landgrave de Hesse Cassel). Amsterdam. 1751-60.
3. *Memoirs of Christina, Queen of Sweden.* By HENRY WOOD-HEAD. London, 1863.

Many other works and pamphlets.

I.

AN enigma on the page of history! A queen descending from her throne—the heiress daughter of a famous Protestant warrior voluntarily placing herself under obedience to the Holy See—the virgin representative of a Scandinavian crown choosing of her own free will to reside in the sunny palaces of intriguing Rome!

Such acts and deeds are suited to the pages of romance, or to the heroic age of the world's history, but seem to be out of place in the dull monotony and exhausted energy of the seventeenth century. The battle of the Reformation had been fought out. The awful brightness of the fires that had been kindled in the previous century had died away. Only here and there a bright spark remained of that fiery flame, which had driven nations into fiercest conflict, and well nigh consumed the noblest souls of earth. An ordinary mortal in the latter half of the seventeenth century lived in the great reaction from intensity of belief to the indifference of satire, in matters civil and ecclesiastical. All too strange, therefore, for the comprehension of her age and her surroundings, were the life and doings of Christina, Queen of Sweden.

In truth, the Queen possessed many heroic qualities, and yet withal was deeply embued with that same spirit of the age. Whether the fulsome flattery of Roman authors, or the fierce scorn of Protestant detractors be most objectionable and most absolutely removed from the truth, it were hard to determine. Certain it is that Christina's contemporaries all agreed to estimate the value of her life by that one act which they deemed the best and only test of human merit—her translation from the Church of her fathers to the Church of Rome. Such a test is hardly conclusive. Motives, though often difficult enough to trace, and often appearing contradictory, are yet for moral purposes the true test whereby the value of actions must be estimated ; and further, in judging of the very life itself, not one event, however great or however important, must be seized on to the total exclusion of the remainder, but all the events in due order of merit must be allowed their appropriate share of weight in preparing the final verdict.

The life of Christina falls into several very strongly marked periods. There is, in the first place, the period of her youth, during which her great powers were being rapidly matured, while her days were for the most part spent in isolation. Then the ten years follow during which she was a real Queen, surrounded with nobles and men of letters and courtiers ready to do her bidding, but from nearly all of whom she was separated by that great gulf which lies between a sovereign and her subjects. It was during this period that she had to cope seriously, and with but little external aid, with the more solemn matters that distract the human mind, politics, religion, and marriage.

Finally comes the period during which she lived in Rome and frequented the Papal Court. It was in reality more than

half her life. The earlier portion of this residence in the States
of the Church was frequently broken by expeditions into
various parts of Europe, but the latter portion was seldom interrupted by any ventures of this kind. A certain concealed
regret seems to hang over these closing years, subdued alike
by literary interests and the dignity of true self-respect, and
softened by the consolatory exercises of religion.

II.

The earlier days of Christina's life were passed in circumstances of great peculiarity. If it were needful to characterise
her position by one emphatic word, that word must needs be
Isolation. The only child of a mighty warrior, cut off in the
prime of life, Christina was early left with but two near relations in the world—her mother Maria Leonora, and her aunt
Catharine.

Gustavus Adolphus, her father, loved her passionately while
he lived, but her mother, the records say, shewed less affection. She had hoped that her child might have been a boy,
who might have become a worthy heir of the great champion
of the Protestant cause, in the Council and the battle-field.
Once, it is said, just as the northern hero was starting for his
last descent on the German Empire, so utterly paralysed by
internal feebleness and want of organisation, his little daughter,
no more than four years old, ran towards him and wished him
prosperity in his arduous undertaking. The King was at the
moment giving some important orders, and did not notice her
approach: but, she, refusing to be ignored, pulled with all her
tiny might at his sword belt, and so drew him towards her.
In a moment, by means of this military appeal, Gustavus'
whole thought became suddenly fixed upon his darling child.
The simple anecdote is characteristic of both the persons concerned in it. Both were impetuous, eager, passionate. And
the general interest of the story is heightened by another fact.
For neither at the time knew that they would never meet
again on earth.

Gustavus, on the eve of his journey southwards, appointed
John Matthiæ to be Christina's tutor. The appointment was

well made. Matthiæ was one of those gentle and devotional spirits, who long above all things for the religious union of Christendom. And it is undoubtedly true that this noble desire, however chimerical, must always possess a peculiar charm to the most liberal and enthusiastic minds. Still, at a later time, this pure and simple ecclesiastic was destined to be deprived of his Bishopric on a somewhat vindictive charge of heresy. Nevertheless, he fared better at the hands of the State than of the Church, and in after years his children were ennobled. One lesson at the least Christina learnt from this excellent man, which never faded from her memory throughout all the vicissitudes of her later life; and that lesson was Love of Toleration.

Before his final departure, Gustavus made such arrangements as would be necessary in case of his own death. He appointed his beloved Chancellor Oxenstiern the guardian of his youthful daughter during her minority, and the appointment took effect much sooner than might have been expected, owing to Gustavus' sudden overthrow at the important battle of Lutzen. When the kingdom of Sweden had recovered its consternation at the sad news, Christina was proclaimed Queen, and of the five regents then appointed Oxenstiern was the chief. Hence this skilful and adroit statesman became possessed of the larger share of authority in the entire government of Sweden. His political position was further strengthened by the fact that two of his near relatives held the offices of Constable and Treasurer. The complete control which he exercised on the young Queen's education was calculated to extinguish all feminine qualities, although he was careful to provide the best instruction in art, science, and literature. The Grand Council of the nation consisted in Sweden of five colleges or ministerial departments, comprising altogether twenty-five persons. The heads of these departments formed the executive Government. When Oxenstiern and his colleagues assumed office, they found the affairs of the nation in great confusion. The expenses of the war in Germany were ruinous to the royal exchequer, yet all attempts to equalise taxation by withdrawing the privileges of the nobles or clergy were distinct failures. Within the Empire, the baffled hopes of Ferdinand's troops revived after the memorable fight at Lutzen. In fact, the position of the Swedes seemed becoming untenable. The upright Chancellor, however, disdainfully scorned to notice the bribes which the Austrians with foolish cunning offered. He only wrote home to the Council at Stockholm, 'a dog who growls and shows his teeth, can make better terms than one who puts his tail between his legs and runs away.'

Yet when Bernard of Weimar was overthrown in the battle of Nördlingen, in the month of August 1634, it was necessary to commence negotiations for peace : and the truce which Axel Oxenstiern was obliged to sign with Poland cost him many sighs. Any admission, even indirectly, of Uladislaus' false claim to the crown of Sweden seemed to his patriotic soul utterly intolerable. He returned to his own land in the month of July 1636.

Meantime, while weighty affairs were being discussed abroad, internal strife divided the royal family at home. Christina, it has been already hinted, never loved her mother, Maria Leonora. In fact they disagreed about the merest trifles as well as matters of greater moment. Moreover, Maria Leonora was unpopular with the Council and the people. Her jealousy was aroused by the large incomes appropriated by the regents, and the small allowances paid over to her own privy purse, and in an evil moment for her own best interests, she entered into communications with Christian of Denmark. Subsequently she fled to that country, and remained above eight years on the continent.

Maria Leonora's deserved unpopularity induced the Council to place their future ruler under the official care of her aunt, the Princess Catharine, who was the only surviving child of Charles IX. Her influence, while it lasted, was most beneficial, but unfortunately she died towards the close of the year 1638. This event was a turning point in Christina's life.

Bereft at the early age of thirteen of the only relative, in whom she placed any confidence, the young Queen was forced to rely entirely on her own resources. She pursued with increased vigour her studies in all branches of literature, giving especial prominence to history and theology, but she became hard and unsympathetic, and, ignoring her own sex,* sought only the companionship of the learned. The records concerning Elizabeth of England afforded her peculiar delight, and most likely presented models for imitation. Her interest in politics was early awakened, and on hearing of the likelihood of Baner's death after an exhausting and difficult campaign she wrote to the Prince Palatine, 'I cannot conceal the bad news that has just arrived. Baner is dangerously ill, and not likely to recover . . . such men are not met with every day, and if he dies, our affairs will not go on well.'

The first debate which the young Queen of Sweden heard at her Council Board concerned the much disputed question of the Sound Dues. A certain coldness had arisen between Sweden and Denmark, due partly to Maria Leonora's strange conduct, and partly to King Christian's subservience to the Emperor. Hence the majority of the Council were in favour of war, and even the Chancellor maintained that the expenses of fighting would be less burdensome than the excessive tolls. The dispute arose in this way. Sweden, by her treaties with Denmark, was exempt from this tax, and she made use of the privilege to cover with her flag the goods of foreign merchants. The Danes retaliated by seizing three Swedish vessels. The Swedes determined on invasion, and Torstenson was intrusted with the guidance of their operations. The attack was conducted with skill and secrecy, but in no very honourable fashion, and, although Denmark was overrun, was not decisive.

It was one of Christina's first cares on her complete assumption of government to negotiate a peace with Christian of Denmark. It was arranged that the Sound should be free, and that certain concessions in the shape of territory should

---

* 'It is almost impossible that a woman should perform the duty required on the throne. The ignorance of women, their feebleness of mind, body, and understanding makes them incapable of reigning.'—*Vie par elle-même*, ch. ix.

be made in favour of Sweden.   Oxenstiern's services on this occasion were rewarded with the title of Count.

While the war with Denmark continued to disturb the peace of Sweden, Christina reached her eighteenth year.   Sovereigns usually come of age earlier than the rest of mankind, and, as in the case of our own Queen, eighteen was fixed by lawful authority as the appropriate time for Christina's majority. Henceforth she must enter on a wider and more brilliant field of action, and, escaping from the trammels of the regency, must become mistress of a regal Court.

III.

As soon as Christina had attained her majority, she was proclaimed, in deference to her own wish and the desires of the people, *King* of Sweden in the month of December, 1644. The masculine gender was adopted in preference to the feminine to avoid running counter to an old tradition.

Her first measure after her complete establishment on the throne was to grant an Indemnity to the Regents, who for above ten years had directed the executive Government. This she was bound to do, not only to conciliate the nobles but as an act of simple justice.   She was bound to start fair if she was ever to rule her country with success.   Nevertheless, the Act of Indemnity gratified the aristocracy alone.   The fact was that Sweden, for the last decade of years, had been entirely in the hands of an aristocratic oligarchy, who, amongst other things, had freely alienated Crown lands for the benefit of their own Order.   The other Estates of the realm, therefore, had looked for some partial resumption of these alienations previous to the grant of the Indemnity.   But it would have been impossible for Christina, even if she had been inclined, to commence her reign by serious disagreement with the friendly and all-powerful Chancellor.   She felt that at first she must learn from Oxenstiern what he had learnt from her father, and not strive to direct him with the ignorance of pride. The Chancellor was alone intimately acquainted with all the minute intricacies of home and foreign affairs, and was the only man capable of conducting the Government of Sweden.   Moreover, from long experience, every one trusted his judgment and admired his integrity.

Who should be the favoured possessor of this northern heiress' hand was a question mooted alike amongst the noble houses of Sweden and the royal courts of Europe. The following princes have been enumerated among her suitors— Ulrick and then Frederick of Denmark, Philip IV. of Spain, the Archduke Leopold of Austria, Charles Louis Elector Palatine; Ferdinand, King of Hungary, and the three sons of Sigismund of Poland. Besides these more distinguished persons, there were numerous inferior aspirants, but there were never more than two who had any chance of success—Magnus de la Gardie, a Swedish nobleman, and Charles Gustavus. The former of these was really in love with Maria Euphrosyne, Christina's cousin, whom he finally married. The latter became Christina's successor on the throne, but not her husband. Once or twice it seemed as if they might have married, but the Queen could never quite make up her mind. Like our own Elizabeth, she became so enamoured of the sweets of absolute power that she was unwilling to share her authority with another, and she was not sure of the purity of Charles' motives. Did he seek her or her power? The Queen herself declared that heiresses proverbially remained single, and that the Court was a hot-bed of intrigue. Neither the beauty, elegance, and courtly manners of Magnus de la Gardie, nor the high rank and near relationship of Charles Gustavus, could win Christina's heart.

The retirement of Torstenson from the command of the troops belonging to the Swedish Crown within the Empire was regretted by the whole country. He was one of the ablest of Gustavus' generals, and was much beloved by the soldiery, whom he had generally led to victory. Meantime the successes of the French, who were allies of Sweden, were very brilliant in the north of Germany, and Christina took opportunity to congratulate Condé by letter. She soon saw, however, that the war had become chronic, and determined, against the wishes of her own nobility, to support with the utmost of her ability the proposed negotiations for a lasting peace. 'What I desire most,' she wrote privately to her representative Salvius, 'and esteem above everything else, is the power of restoring peace to Christendom.' The colleague of the clever plebeian Salvius was the proud patrician John Oxenstiern, and it was indeed needful that the Queen should give clear and distinct orders to prevent these ill-matched envoys from openly quarrelling.

Intricate and brimful of diplomatic subtlety were the debates that preceded the final settlement of peace. Some of the Great Powers sent ambassadors to the Congresses, more out of deference to public opinion, than from any desire of seriously arranging preliminaries. Their representatives talked of the interests of religion, but, while they squabbled about precedence, they thought only of the best means of obtaining power and influence. Once it is said the Papal Nuncio enquired of Cardinal Richelieu whether he was not greatly embarrassed by the war. The great minister of France only observed that he had obtained, when he became Secretary of State, a dispensation from his Holiness which he deemed wide enough even to include giving aid to heretics.

The terms which Sweden finally obtained at the Peace of Westphalia, though satisfactory for the purposes of a general pacification, were unworthy of the amount of blood that had been shed. Western Pomerania, certain cities and islands, and two secularised Bishoprics were ceded to her as hereditary fiefs.

All northern Europe breathed freely again at the happy Restoration of Peace after thirty years of miserable warfare. Each nation found time to investigate the condition of its internal politics. The peasantry of Sweden declared that they had many grievances. The nobility strenuously opposed all efforts for reform. The people demanded the resumption, the aristocracy sought the further alienation, of the royal domain. Christina found herself unable to satisfy these contradictory demands, and the Lutheran Church, which was at first neutral in regard to this dispute, soon sided with the people owing to the overbearing arrogance of the nobility. Matthiæ's attempts to quell the rising outbursts of party spirit were fruitless.

About the year 1650, the antagonism between the two parties had reached the highest pitch. Christina, with the truest moderation, held the balance between them. She could not reconcile the opposing parties, but she gave way to neither the one nor the other. At the same time, by occasional concessions, she succeeded in averting the outbreak of civil war. She found herself placed in a position of the greatest difficulty,* with but few trusted advisers, and it seems likely that the extreme anxiety of this troublesome period of her reign first suggested the idea of abdication. At any rate she made up her mind to propose Charles Gustavus as her successor to the Estates of Sweden : and after some opposition, headed by the Chancellor, the proposal was adopted. By this step she facilitated her own abdication : she also crushed the aspirations of that section of the nobility that longed for an aristocratic republic, and escaped for the future the irritating importunity with which proposals for marriage had been thrust upon her in the past. Her general health too was indifferent, and at times the doctors became thoroughly alarmed.

In many ways the youthful Queen of Sweden's reputation stood high among the princes of Europe. It was admitted on all sides that she had shewn considerable skill in the conduct of public affairs in times of unparalleled difficulty ; but above all she was renowned throughout the world on account of her extensive patronage of the savants distinguished in various branches of learning. Grotius, the well known writer on International law—a study then in its infancy—was for a short time her representative at the Court of Versailles. His death occurred before any intimacy could arise. The famous philosopher, Descartes, visited Stockholm in the spring of 1649, and was royally received. He had corresponded with Christina on various subjects of interest previous to his journey northwards. Descartes always maintained that he was a good Catholic, holding that the study of philosophy and theology should always be kept separate. Our own Lord Bacon held

* About this time a lunatic attempted to take the Queen's life without success.

the same opinion.* The philosopher's health suffered much from the coldness of the northern climate, and his constitution, already impaired by excessive study, entirely gave way at the early age of fifty-three. He died in the month of February, 1650. The Queen received the sad news with floods of tears. The rude but clever Salmasius, who delighted in abuse under the title of criticism, and the learned Vossius, who died a Canon of Windsor by a curious freak of fortune, were received with great favour at the Court of Sweden. Other persons of less general distinction, who likewise obtained royal favour, were Burœus, Manasseh Ben Israel, Stiernhielm, John Paulinus, Rudbeck, Bishop of Westeras and his son Olaus, Francenius, Stiernberg, and Sigfried Forsius.

Milton and Gassendi wrote eulogistic letters, and Ménage, Benserade, Scarron, and Claude Sarrau addressed adulatory epistles, and Scuderie dedicated a poem to the distinguished Queen of the North. Bochart of Caen, and his friend Huet, afterwards Bishop of Arvanches, visited Christina in her own country. It was a favourite plan with Huet to overthrow the principles of philosophy by suggesting doubts as to their reality; and it seems likely that he, all unconsciously, commenced paving the way which afterwards led Christina to the Roman Church.

It is no wonder, under the circumstances above recorded, that the Queen of Sweden's reputation for learning continued to steadily increase throughout Europe. The Court of Sweden was free from that cold formality and endless amount of etiquette, which formed an essential part of the popular estimation of royalty in the seventeenth century. Individual genius had fair play. Each courtier could prove his title to excel. Hardly any bound was set to the license of repartee, or any limit prescribed to brilliant sarcasm. Unlike the formal and tedious ceremonial, so popular in autocratic Spain, at Stockholm entire freedom of action was the rule. The gay

---

* "Both religion and philosophy have received and may receive extreme prejudice by being commixed together, thereby making a heretical religion, and an imaginary and fabulous philosophy." *Advancement of Learning.* Ch. II.

scene consisted of a perpetual round of mental and bodily enjoyment. Day followed day in quick succession, and the happy players had no thought beyond the present season of pleasure. Sometimes a single courtier obtained undue influence. This was especially the case with Bourdelot, the royal physician. Christina considered that he had saved her life, and was therefore naturally well disposed towards him. Bourdelot's character has been variously represented, but never in a very favourable light. It is certain that his knowledge of medicine far excelled his notions of morality, and his general influence on the Queen and her Court was, we think, injurious. After a time, he lost favour, and was forced to retire to France, where some preferment was procured for him. Magnus de la Gardie was also disgraced about the same time. The insolence of his conduct had become unbearable, when he ventured to accuse the Queen's friends before her face, and he was advised to retire into the country. No complete reconciliation ever took place : and in after years when Christina visited the country in the capacity of a private person, Magnus spoke against any prolonged stay, lest there should be a disturbance amongst the peasantry.

The sovereigns of Sweden from time immemorial had been crowned at the old capital Upsala, just as the kings of Scotland were for centuries crowned at Scone. A tradition of such ancient authority ought to be upheld. But when it was found that Upsala was incapable of providing sufficient accommodation, and was altogether too small for the requirements of the public, it was resolved to set aside the authority of tradition, and allow the coronation to take place in the new capital, Stockholm,—a town furnished with all the most modern improvements. The usual round of festivities preceded and followed the solemn event. Fountains of red and white wine played for the entertainment of spectators. Fireworks, masks, balls, royal salutes, and masquerades representing the muses, and other goddesses of heathen mythology, were given. Gifts and pensions were freely distributed. While the restless Christina was thus enjoying herself to the full, she tired of pleasure. Even in the midst of these gaieties, the thought of abdication was sometimes present.   She longed for honourable ease and learned leisure.   She desired to travel in foreign lands, and to see the treasures preserved in the Vatican.   She felt unable to reconcile the differences between class and class, between peasant and noble that distracted her own land.   She could not resuscitate the well-nigh bankrupt treasury.   She could not, as she was, join the Roman faith.

It was impossible to devise any matured plan for abdication without much forethought.   Chanut, the French ambassador, was the first person to whom the Queen definitely confided her intentions.   He at once did all in his power to dissuade her from so strange a course.   When Charles Gustavus first heard of this idea he doubted the Queen's sincerity.   He thought the whole theory of the abdication was only a clever plot to ascertain the state of his own private feelings.   He dared not show how keenly he longed to succeed to the throne, and he wrote a cautious letter, recommending Christina to retain her crown.   When the whole affair became known to the public, the nobility and people were equally opposed to the Queen's abdication.   The Chancellor, Oxenstiern, was particularly annoyed, and declared that the constitutional obstacles to such a course of conduct would prove insurmountable.

Just at this time the pulse of Europe was quivering under the pressure of democratic influences.   Signs of conspiracy against the throne made their appearance in Sweden, which ended in the execution of the two Messenii.   The revolutionary changes in England caused Whitelocke to be appointed ambassador to the Court of Sweden on behalf of the English commonwealth.   His lengthy journal conveys a favourable impression of the northern capital.   So stern a Puritan was content to describe Christina's * entertainments as 'genteel.' The ring which she gave Pimentelli, the Spanish ambassador, he calls 'a memorial of her favour.'   Her enemies call it a love-token.   His conversations on the Sound dues led to no results.   When he heard of the proposed abdication, he

---

* In these days Christina fancifully instituted the knightly Order of Amaranta.

repeated a quaint parable, which by interpretation meant that repentance after the event would be too late for amendment.

Both the Puritan, Whitelocke, and the Catholic, Pimentelli, left Sweden in high favour. The jealousy of the French ambassador was aroused at the favour shown to the Spaniard, and Christina's efforts to terminate the war, then raging between France and Spain, were rendered unavailing. The arrival of the Portuguese ambassador, Pareira, with two Jesuits in his suite, exercised a marked influence on the religious sentiments of the Queen of Sweden. For a long time she had silently weighed in her mind the contradictory arguments of the Protestant and Roman Churches. She had never loved the cold severity of the Lutheran formularies. Her philosophical studies had taught her to doubt their absolute truth. She was just in the right frame of mind to readily accept dogmas claiming infallible truth. Macedo, the Jesuit interpreter of the Portuguese ambassador, was determined not to lose his opportunities. With the connivance of the Queen, his interpretations of the political remarks of his master were really dissertations on Papal theology. The innocent ambassador was frequently surprised and delighted at the evidently favourable reception of his observations. After a while, Macedo, at the royal request, secretly escaped from Sweden with a message to the General of the Jesuit Order, who at once despatched to the north Francesco Malines, Professor of Theology at Turin, and Paolo Casati, Professor of Mathematics at Rome. These distinguished personages reached Stockholm in disguise in the month of March, 1652. Christina was the first to detect their real character. When she privately questioned them on the origin of evil, and the nature of the contrast between faith and reason, they not only asserted the sufficiency of the Papal authority to decide such points, but also used the argument from analogy—those parts of religion which were beyond the reach of reason were no wise opposed to reason.

How deeply the Queen was at the time impressed is shown by her inquiry whether the Papal authority (if so vast as they declared) was not able to grant a dispensation for the reception of the Sacrament once a year according to the Lutheran rites.   On the receipt of a negative reply, the resolution to abdicate became firmly fixed.   Yet the distraction of her mind is well illustrated by the fact that on the eve of her own change of creed, she addressed an epistle to Prince Frederick of Hesse urgently pressing him to remain on the Protestant side.

Christina was not so singular, as at first appears, in her strange desire to join the Church of Rome.   Many learned men, whom perhaps the Queen treated with excessive respect, took a similar step in the seventeenth century.   All the courtiers tried to retain her, as a good Lutheran, on the throne of her fathers without success.   Her answer to Chanut's letter of expostulation was vehement and haughty.   ' You know this whim has lasted a long time . . .   I allow every one to judge me according to their capacity, and although it is true I cannot hinder them, yet I would not do so if I had the power. . . .   I have possessed power without pride, and I relinquish it without regret.   Do not fear for me, my wealth is beyond the power of fortune.   I am happy whatever may chance.'   Surely the concluding sentence is the climax of proud humility.   Though the people of Sweden knew it not, the abdication and the change of creed went hand in hand. One could not have happened without the other.   Other motives, besides the theological, had their share in prompting the abdication.   That accomplished, the adoption of the Papal creed was the natural sequence.

In the month of February, 1654, the intended abdication was formally announced to the assembled Estates of the realm. The Senate demurred, but the Queen remained resolute : and so the discussion of details was commenced.   It was settled that Charles Gustavus should be King in her room.   The payment of a fixed pension, slightly below the original demand, was charged upon the Swedish Pomerania, and certain islands in the Baltic.   The retention of the sovereignty of these districts, and a future right to interfere in the regulation of the succession, was denied.   The members of the Third Estate manifested their grief openly, and a deputy of the peasantry shouted out of genuine sympathy 'Continue in your gears, good madam, and be the fore-horse as long as you live, and we will help you the best we can to bear your burden.'

At the close of the month of May Christina made her final address, and on the sixth of June the Act of Abdication was duly performed in the presence of the assembled Diet. The Queen was clad in white, Charles Gustavus in black. She spoke of the blessings of peace which then prevailed, and her father's glorious victories, and then surrendered the sword, the sceptre, and the other emblems of royalty, which were delivered in due form to Charles Gustavus. The same afternoon he was crowned in Upsala Cathedral.

A reign of ten years was thus brought to a sudden termination. They were the happiest years of Christina's life. Peace had been restored to Europe. Internal dissension had been for the time allayed. A fresh impetus had been given to the study of literature and the fine arts. Though darkened by some disappointments, clouded by some failures, and distracted by agitating thoughts on politics and religion, these days that had slipped rapidly by, were bright and happy and gay. The sunshine of life felt warm.

Unlike the Emperor Charles V., who deserted the Imperial throne, weary and worn by anxiety and trouble, Christina retired from public life at the early age of eight and twenty. There was something of knight-errantry in the manner in which she started from her northern home to seek her fortune in the sunny south. A medal was struck, representing Olympus with Pegasus on the summit adorned with the motto, 'Sedes hæc solio potior.' There was something of sadness in the vehemence with which she afterwards asserted her increased happiness. Not quite what she expected was the treatment she received from the flattering but deceptive world, when stripped of the realities of power. She stilled her disappointment by the intensity of her study. For she soon discovered by stern experience that a Queen surrounded by a brilliant court and all the externals of royalty was in a very different position to a Queen without a throne.

IV.

Immediately after the Act of Abdication Christina started for the mainland of Germany. The news of her resignation of the Crown had created so great a stir that the details of her journey from Sweden to Rome were industriously circulated throughout Europe, and soon assumed an absurd prominence in the pamphleteering literature of the day.* The attempt to preserve secrecy only increased the popular curiosity. After the circulation of a report that she would visit Spa, she travelled in male disguise through Denmark under the name of Count Dohna. She scandalized the orthodox citizens of Hamburg by openly lodging for three weeks with a Jewish banker, and leaving the town suddenly in the middle of the night. At Antwerp she formally received the Archduke Leopold, and the other dignitaries who happened to be in that city. She travelled thence in state to Brussels, where she privately abjured the Lutheran doctrines. Advices from Sweden brought a gentle rebuke from Matthiæ, and a keen reminder of the need of union throughout Christendom, as well as the solemn tidings of the death of Oxenstiern and Maria Leonora. It seéms needless to pursue further the numerous but unimportant details of her journey.

In the ancient city of Innsbruck, nestling beside the Tyrolese Alps, consecrated as the last resting-place of those proud champions of the Roman creed, the princes of the House of Hapsburg,† Christina appropriately made the public confession of her new faith in the presence of Holsteinius, papal legate on behalf of Alexander VII. Clothed in black silk, kneeling before the high altar, she distinctly read the required declaration, ‡ asserting her thorough belief in every doctrine of the

---

* Of above sixty books and tracts relating to Christina preserved in the British Museum, there are four copies of the *Vera Relazione del viaggio fattosi,* and two copies of a pamphlet concerning her entrance into Florence.

† The tomb of Maximilian I. occupies a considerable part of the nave of the cathedral, and is ornamented with statues of his ancestors and other princes.

‡ The confession is found thus stated. ‘Ego Christina firma fide credo et profiteor omnia et singula quæ continentur Symbolo fidei, quo Sancta Romana Ecclesia utitur.’ *Vera Relazione,* n., p. 37.

Roman Church, and listened to a clever Jesuit's sermon on the suggestive text, 'Hearken, O daughter, and consider, incline thine ear; Forget also thine own people, and thy father's house.'

From Innsbruck she wrote to inform Charles Gustavus of her change of religious belief. The devout conduct of his new convert greatly pleased the Pope, and Christina's entrance into Rome became one long triumph. Fireworks and illuminations, processions and triumphal arches honoured her approach. After a regal reception in the Vatican, Alexander VII. conferred the rite of confirmation with his own hands at the High Altar of S. Peter's, and bestowed upon Christina the additional name of Alessandra.

The name of Rome has always possessed a strange fascination. First as the capital of the heathen world, and then as the seat of the chief Bishopric in Christendom, the wealth of the nations flowed into it. Christina, fired by no ordinary enthusiasm, visited in turn the museums, and the picture-galleries, and shared in the fêtes and solemn feasts of the eternal city. In turn, each form of amusement palled upon the taste. Soon tired by the monotony of the Italian festivals, she determined to test the world-wide reputation of the elegant and brilliant entertainments provided by the Court of France.

The States of the Church were the home of throneless princes and princesses. In other countries *de jure* without *de facto* title is little worth. Though treated with every mark of external respect, Christina soon discovered that she could exercise no real influence among the fickle Parisian courtiers of Louis XIV. Her ordinary disregard of detailed etiquette became the subject of ridicule. Her extensive knowledge of the picture-galleries of Paris was considered remarkable but peculiar. Her intimate acquaintance with the intrigues of the Court was deemed offensive. On one occasion she quietly advised the young King to marry Mademoiselle Mancini, Cardinal Mazarin's niece, if he were so inclined. Henceforward ceaseless efforts were made to facilitate her return to Italy.

Yet Christina soon recrossed the Alps with the object of

again visiting the gay capital of France. To postpone her arrival the Palace of Fontainebleau was assigned as her official residence by the Court of Versailles. Within the walls of this Palace the fatal tragedy was enacted, which was doubtless the most serious blot on the otherwise honourable character of the Queen of Sweden. Irritated by the delay, enraged at the discovery of treachery amongst her own servants, over whom she conceived that she still held the power of life and death, she insisted with the wild haste of excitement on the immediate execution of the Marquis Monaldeschi. The pleadings of Father le Bel, the appeals of Sentinelli, the Marquis's own earnest entreaties, were of no avail. Nothing could revoke the unalterable decision. In the Gallery of the Stags, among the hunting trophies of the Kings of France, Monaldeschi was stabbed to death.

The deed in itself cannot be justified. It was the work of passion. The forms of justice were neglected. Nevertheless, it appears Monaldeschi deserved his fate. It seems likely[*] he had revealed in a traitorous manner a political intrigue with the Pope which was intended to bring the Crown of Naples to his royal mistress. Here, as elsewhere, Mr. Bain endeavours to represent the conduct of the Queen in a more favourable light than critics have been accustomed to do in the past, and certainly seems to sum up the intricate facts connected with this painful incident in a more impartial vein than the majority of previous writers.

Louis of France was furious when the news of the execution reached him. He altogether resented Christina's conduct in this affair. He maintained that the execution of any person, especially within the precincts of a royal Palace, without the sanction of the reigning sovereign was a direct insult to the Majesty of the Crown. It was no judicial punishment for proved treachery. It was little else than murder.

Modern authorities on International Law have confirmed Louis' view. Reason and common sense do the same.

---

[*] *Evelyn-Diary*, II., 149. The vulgar story as to a love affair is repeated in the *Diary of the Shah*, p. 200.

Nevertheless it is certain that, when she resigned the crown of Sweden, Christina honestly believed that she retained absolute power over her own suite. So great an authority as Leibnitz has been found ready to support her opinion.

There is some analogy to this painful and curious case in the treacherous conduct of Manning, whom Lord Clarendon calls 'a proper young gentleman, bred a Roman Catholic in the family of the Marquis of Worcester.' Charles II., while an exile, had passed in disguise from Cologne to Zealand in the year of grace 1655, and it was discovered that this fact, as well as some other actions of the Royalists, had been communicated by Manning, under the pseudonym of And. Butler, to Oliver Cromwell. On discovery a confession of guilt was at once made, and an excuse offered to the effect that the treacherous letters were, in fact, untrue, except the relation of the journey to Zealand, and their object was the extortion of money from the Government now carried on in England in the name of the Commonwealth.

Lord Clarendon omits to mention the manner of Manning's death, but he was quietly shot after his detection in a wood near Cologne, in the month of December, 1655, by Sir James Hamilton and Major Armourer. For the space of three years he had been in the receipt of £1200 per annum from the Lord Protector.

While Christina was thus passing her time, partly in the enjoyment of Italian society, and partly in wandering over the face of Europe, Charles Gustavus was King in Sweden. His reign of five years duration was one perpetual campaign. He commenced his military operations by overrunning Poland, and then attacked Brandenburg. He next crushed an insurrection of the Poles at the battle of Warsaw, after which John Casimir resigned his crown. Then turning northwards, he made a successful inroad against the Danes, whose country was only saved from annexation by the opportune mediation of England, France, and Holland. Angry at thus losing the fruits of his last campaign, he perfidiously attacked Copenhagen after the peace was signed. The Danes with the assistance of the Dutch made a desperate resistance, and totally defeating Charles were able to enforce their own terms. The King of Sweden's pride was cruelly wounded, and his constitution undermined by the hardship of the war. He died suddenly in the month of February 1660 with the words on his lips:—'The loss of Fyen kills me.' The war in Pomerania impoverished Christina. Many of the towns allotted to provide her pension were sacked by the violence of the soldiery. Her own attempts to introduce an higher culture among the Swedes were nullified. She was herself forced to become a pensionary of the Pope, and Cardinal Azzolini was appointed to manage her household. His administrative ability introduced tolerable efficiency and economy into the Queen's domestic affairs. Enough money was still forthcoming to supply the requirements of literary and scientific tastes, and considerable sums were annually spent on chemistry and alchemy without much practical result. Christina was thus forced to become more subservient to the Papal Court, and undertook to persuade some of her retinue to adopt the Roman Catholic faith, but she declined altogether to resign her freedom of action, and disputes not unfrequently arose with his Holiness in regard to the discipline of the Swedish servants, and the political condition of Southern Europe.

After the sudden death of Charles Gustavus, the payments from Pomerania became more irregular, and Christina determined to visit Sweden, not now as Queen, but for the purpose of effectually securing her income, and asserting her own claims in case of the death of Gustavus' infant heir, Charles XI. She was hardly received with respect, much less affection.

As the wandering ghost of the quaint old laird, who has long rested beneath the grassy sod, is sometimes said at dead of night to revisit the favourite haunts of long forgotten days, and scarce to recognise the stiff Elizabethan garden or the cool secluded bower owing to the silent ravages of time ; so the Queen, bereft of her throne, revisited her former capital, and scarce recognised its altered aspect, and transformed features. A few brief years had changed all things. New courtiers were stationed round the throne. New faces filled the Diet. New interests swayed the minds of the deputies. A few nobles who remembered Christina in her wealth, avoided her in her poverty.

While yet in Hamburg, she ascertained that Magnus de la Gardie, Brahe, and the rest of the dignitaries of Stockholm, were anxious to delay her approach. Brahe even suggested she should be 'sent to Aland, in charge of an honourable and determined man.' On her arrival in Sweden, powerful resistance was offered to the just demand for the confirmation of her revenue. The celebration of mass in the royal chapel was forbidden. The claim on the succession under certain contingencies was rudely rejected. A second act of renunciation was arranged, and signed.

Christina now thought it best to retire to Norköping. After obtaining some promises as to the payment of her revenue, she left for the continent. During a year's stay in Hamburg, she became acquainted with Borri, a well known student of alchemy, and Lambecius, afterwards distinguished as librarian to the Emperor.

In the autumn of the year 1666, Christina planned a second visit to Sweden ; but she met with such an unfavourable reception at Norköping, that she immediately returned to Hamburg, where she heard from Algernon Sydney that her imprisonment had been positively proposed in the Council at Stockholm. The foolish illumination of her hotel in honour of .the election of Clement IX. to the Papal throne caused a tumult in the streets of this Protestant city in which several lives were lost. Soon after this unfortunate display of enthusiasm, she left Hamburg for the south.

During the intervals between these various journeys, Christina resided chiefly in Rome. She took the keenest interest in the different questions that were agitated in the University and among the members of the Sacred College, and became absorbed in literary pursuits. The Archbishop Angelo della Noce, Pallavicini, Menzini, Guidi, Filicaja, Cassini, and other men renowned for their acquaintance with the arts and sciences, frequented her palace. She founded a learned Academy, and thus exercised a decidedly beneficial influence on the development of Italian literature, by checking the tendency to prefer style to substance in composition. She never allowed her Italian courtiers to indulge in personal flattery. In fact, there was nothing she more thoroughly despised. 'I think,' she wrote on one occasion, ' that flattery, which is the poison of princes, might be their best medicine if they knew how to use it properly.' And again, ' If all comparisons are odious, what must a comparison be between me and Alexander the Great?' Christina was too clever and many-sided to care for flattery, and she always saw through it. A remarkable proof of the general respect with which she was regarded by distinguished men is afforded by Bernini on his death-bed bequeathing to her his famous statue of Christ.*

Christina's time passed happily in the capital of Christendom, yet her lively restlessness, though diminishing with advancing years, urged her to seek variety in distant travel, and the study of the political intrigues carried on in the principal European courts. Once she failed in her efforts to mediate between Louis XIV. and the Pope, who was justly indignant at the insolent behaviour of the French Ambassador. His Holiness was most unfairly forced to give way, when the French king, without attempting to argue the matter, took the decided step of occupying Avignon, which had been handed down amongst the possessions of the Papal See ever since the days of the Great Schism.

Christina must have greatly delighted in the superiority of southern manners and customs over the rougher habits of the Swedes, though she was herself no lover of false delicacy. Swearing and other vulgarities were common among the uneducated nobles at Stockholm, whereas external decorum and politeness were always the rule in Rome. Nevertheless, intellectual refinement and extreme attention to the formalities of etiquette, frequently concealed (as at the Court of France) the shameless character of many a vicious life. In fact, nothing could be more complete than the entire contrast between the external aspect and general habits of the northern and southern Courts—the one genuine, rough, rude; the other intriguing, polished, refined. The happy charm of Italian society cast its subtle spell around Christina's life, and fastened her soul with silken chains to the Papal Court, in conjunction with the earnest

---

* She bequeathed it to the Pope.

desire for the golden coin which opened the door to the celestial regions, spoken of by a contemporary poet, named Bassus :—

> ' Romuleam Christina gradus contendit ad urbem,
>   Olli ut luce fluat candidiore Polus ;
> Regia Virgo lares patrios Regnumque relinquit,
>   Coelestem Drachmam sedula ut inveniat.
> Pectore magnanimo juvat Hanc expendere Regnum,
>   Quo redimat gemmam, quæ pretiosa beat.'

It has been already mentioned that the Cardinal, John Casimir, in disgust and grief, resigned his crown. After trial by experience, he discovered that the dignity of prince of the Roman Church was far preferable to the regal cares annexed to the troublesome Crown of Poland. He obtained a French abbacy from Louis XIV., determined that no barren dignity, but quiet peace, should embrace his declining years. The world beheld the curious spectacle of the two last representatives of separate branches of the house of Vasa wandering over the face of Europe voluntarily stripped of their crowns.

Christina, tired of that privacy which the Cardinal sought, sent her chaplain, Father Hacki, on a political mission to Warsaw. Her candidature, however, was not acceptable to the Poles, who elected one of their own nobles to the vacant throne. It was well that Christina, after resigning the Crown of Sweden, was thus prevented from being involved in the hopeless difficulties and endless feuds connected with the administration of unhappy Poland. It was too late to begin life afresh with a new kingdom. It was better to be content to remain among the palaces of Rome, in the midst of ecclesiastical pomp and intellectual refinement, rather than to risk the chance of easy failure in regions yet untried.

v.

In the autumn of the year 1668, Christina was welcomed, on her return to Rome, with a magnificent reception from the recently elected Pope Clement IX., which bore some comparison to her happier entry within the walls of the Eternal City in all the ardour and enthusiasm of a new convert. From this date to the time of her death in 1689, she seldom journeyed beyond the

limits of the states of the Church.   These last twenty years
were, in comparison with the earlier days, years of quiet and rest.
Christina now dropped that active interference in European
politics with which she had previously loved to occupy her mind,
and gave her whole time to study and meditations on the strange
vicissitudes of human life, though in public she always maintained her usual vivacity.

After being an actor in the gay pageant, she came to regard
the scene from the point of view of a spectator.   With the
majority of persons who take part in the public business of the
world, the reverse is the case.   In youth they watch the progress
of the world's history ; in manhood and old age they are permitted to direct the course of events.   Christina, in later life,
probably felt that the transition from sovereignty to privacy was
really unnatural, and in many respects placed her in an impossible position.   There is no doubt that the resignation of the
crown of Sweden was the great mistake of her life, but it was
an honourable mistake, a royal error.   The hope of freedom
from the control of mechanical ceremonial and the cares of
royalty, and the honest striving after religious truth, prompted,
while still young, the complete abandonment of the highest
honours that the world can bestow—honours which some men
have sacrificed integrity and honesty of purpose to obtain.   Her
genius, tempered and properly directed, would have conferred
lasting benefits on mankind, instead of simply dazzling and
astonishing her own generation.

The Queen of Sweden was thoroughly kind-hearted.   Whenever she had the power, she loved to help others.   Her conduct
towards Count Wasenau was a signal instance of her general
kindliness.   This Prince was a natural son of Uladislaus, King
of Poland, and on the resignation of John Casimir, he wisely
retired to Rome.   Christina strongly advised him to seek refuge
for the remainder of his days in some retired monastery.   When
she found that this advice was not followed, she induced Cardinal
Albani to procure him an office in the Papal Court.   Her letter
of advice is expressed in terms of great freedom, and in an earnest
spirit :—

'It seems to me that your best course would be to retire either to Monte-Casino, or to Vall' Ombrosa. . . . There is nothing for you nor for me to hope for, and one is happiest when one does not expect or hope for anything in this world. Man is made for something greater, and the world has nothing which can satisfy him. If you could become a monarch, and be surrounded with glory and pleasure, you would not be more satisfied than you are at present. . . . Give bravely the little that you have to God, and do not fear to lose by it. . . . What glory and pleasure to serve so good a master, and how happy am I to have given up so much for Him! This satisfaction is worth more than the empire of the world.'

At one time a report without any foundation was circulated in Sweden to the effect that Christina was dead. She at once wrote to Olivecranz, the governor of her domains, a characteristic epistle —

'Regarding the report of my death I am not surprised at it : there are many people who desire it. It is natural they should indulge in flattering illusions. . . . Above all let me assure you that neither fear nor interest will kill me. If there were no other cause of death than these, I should be immortal.'

The Council at Stockholm, to whom the executive functions of government were entrusted during the minority of Charles XI., was composed of the leaders of the nobility. This aristocratic rule bore no good fruit. A series of long and intricate intrigues and a declaration of war against Brandenburg was really the outcome of French bribes adroitly distributed amongst the more venal councillors. Dishonest policy proved vacillating. Frederick William, active and determined in council and the field, drove the Swedes out of Brandenburg, and pursued them into Pomerania. The payment of Christina's revenue was thus temporarily suspended. Just when the fortunes of Sweden appeared desperate, Charles XI. won the battle of Lund, and saved the Swedish possessions on the mainland. At the Diet of 1680 he threw off the aristocratic yoke that had hitherto enthralled him, and became in reality King. The nobles were forced to refund public money, and even to permit the resumption of crown lands. Thus Christina curiously enough lived to see the Swedish noblesse obtain almost unlimited power, and then submit to a complete overthrow. One of her own greatest troubles in the administration of government had been the con-

tinual effort she was forced to make to hold the balance between
the contending interests of the Three Estates of the realm.
During her own reign, she had successfully achieved this difficult
object.

Though no longer taking part in the world's politics, Christina
watched the course of events with keen interest. She had frequently declared her apprehensions in political circles as to the
total insecurity of the Hungarian frontier on the side of Turkey.
When she heard of Sobieski's magnificent defeat of the immense
invading host with very inferior forces, she could not refrain
from writing to congratulate the King of Poland on these heroic
victories. 'Your Majesty has displayed to the world a great and
noble spectacle by the deliverance of Vienna, and the memory of
it should be immortalized in the annals of Christianity.'

Moreover Christina did not lose her love of toleration even in
the atmosphere of suppression so prevalent at the Papal Court.
Although a convert, she heartily hated religious persecution in
all its forms. She rescued at least two fortunate persons from
the terrible tortures of the Spanish Inquisition, and she was not
afraid to express her absolute disapproval of the Dragonades,
somewhat to the annoyance of the French Court. She was
entirely free from that fanatic spirit which the adherents of a
fresh creed are so often given to exhibit.

Though truly religious after her own fashion, her mind was
not cast in a theological mould. There was nothing ascetic in
her view of life. She considered that the good things of this
world were given for man's enjoyment, and she had no scruple
as to her full right to as much innocent pleasure as came in her
way, nor was she careful to contradict the calumniations and
depreciatory reports spread abroad by her enemies. As might
be expected, the wildest stories were current in various parts of
Europe. She once came across a book purporting to be a history
of her own change of religious belief, and wrote on the fly leaf,
'he who knows nothing has written, he who knew has not
written.' She was a faithful daughter, but no slave to the Pope.
She even ventured to maintain her exclusive jurisdiction over
her own household (a sore point with her) in spite of the resolute
opposition of Innocent XI., and consequently lost her papal

pension of 12,000 dollars. For this deprivation she haughtily thanked his Holiness:—'The pension which the Pope gave me was the one blot of my life, and I received it from God as the greatest humiliation to which He could put my pride. . . . I beg you to convey my thanks to the Cardinal Cibo, and the Pope, for relieving me from this obligation.'

On principle, it seems clear the Pope was in the right. It was a most obnoxious and injurious privilege to allow the houses of foreign ambassadors to be sanctuaries, and so to free their retinue from the ordinary civil jurisdiction of the Papal Courts. As a matter of fact, the embassy became an asylum for all sorts of criminals; the retinue became embroiled in every tumult. Only recently has international Law laid much practical restriction on such privileged abuses, and therefore the Papal action in this respect deserves the more credit. As soon as this conflict with the Pope became known over Europe, the Elector of Brandenburg invited Christina to visit his dominions. His invitation was wisely refused. Sometime she had rested in Rome, and the day was past for seeking another home. Soon she would require but a few feet of earth for her resting place.

In the evening of her days Christina retained her accustomed liveliness and vivacity, combined with the full use of her mental faculties. She announced that in her opinion Sweden ought to remain neutral in the European crisis of 1688, and foretold the wonderful success of the Prince of Orange together with its political effect on the nations—'England and Holland united will make all Europe tremble, and will impose laws both by sea and land.' When the time of fulfilment came, she entreated William III. to be kindly to his Roman Catholic subjects.

It seems probable that grief at the sudden death of a favourite servant, the Marquis del Monte, whose real character is very variously depicted, hastened on her own end. 'I am inconsolable,' she writes to the Marquis' son, 'at the loss we have sustained in your father, who as I trust surely is now in eternal glory.' Early in the year 1689, she had a sharp attack of erysipelas from which she recovered contrary to her own expectations. A second attack in the month of April of the same year proved fatal. She died in full communion with the Roman

Church, and after the reception of the Papal absolution passed away so peacefully that it was hard to mark the moment of departure. She framed her own simple epitaph: ' Vixit Christina annos sexaginta tres.'

Pope Innocent gave her a public funeral of great magnificence, and his successor Clement erected a monument to her in the Church of S. Peter. Her own desire had been to find a quiet resting place in the Rotunda. After making suitable provision for the payment of her debts, and for the majority of the servants in her suite, Christina bequeathed the mass of her property to Cardinal Azzolini. No mention was made of Charles XI. in her will. At the hour of death the separation from Sweden was complete. Ultimately, the larger portion of her excellent library found its way into the Vatican Palace, that vast treasure house of literary spoil. Among the host of sepulchral monuments in the great Basilica of S. Peter—amongst the stately memorials erected to the honour of fallen royalty and the memory of impossible causes, a fit place was found for Christina's tomb.

VI.

An attempt has been made in the foregoing rapid sketch of the chief points in Christina's life to illustrate the real character of this remarkable woman, freed alike from the extravagant praise of Roman Catholic writers, and the unfair insinuations of Protestant criticism. Modern historians have been too much in the habit of dismissing this most interesting Queen of the North in a satirical strain, which has dealt out but scanty justice.*

Christina had doubtless many faults, but she possessed also brilliant virtues. The very acuteness and versatility, the very strangeness and manysidedness of her life and character, the wide experience of the world, combined with the different capacities in which she mixed with that world, all tend to enhance the general interest, and add to her special peculiarities. It would not be possible to state her striking characteristics in one terse sentence, yet if it be admissible from a certain point of view to

---

* *e.g*, Russel's *Modern Europe*, III., 384-8, ed. 1822.

speak of the first Napoleon as an epitome of the French idea of glory, then Christina might be described as an epitome of the literary tendencies of her age.

Just as Christina's sense of satire was so keen, and her appreciation of irony so vivid, so her humility was combined with much pride. The forced humility with which she endeavoured to crush her insulted pride after she had deserted her throne occasionally burst forth in its true colours. The fulness of her submission to the Roman Church is now and then limited by strange assertions of individual freedom and individual authority in the region of theology or the domain of politics. Her absolute devotion to the pursuit of truth in the wide, and then unexplored, field of natural science, is sometimes marred by superstitious yearnings after the forbidden secrets of alchemy and astrology. Nevertheless, it must be admitted that Christina Alessandra was in a peculiar manner open to all the better impressions that came across her path, and was possessed of many earnest cravings and true aspirations far in advance of her own age and country. Amid all her restless playfulness and curious elasticity, and at times what we should now call indelicacy, she sought knowledge for its own sake, and she was content to believe in her better moments that the Christian religion was the highest good.

Perhaps it was not so much that her own genius was very extraordinary, but that she knew how to collect around her all the greatest wits and most distinguished philosophers of her own day, and quick as lightning to catch their more brilliant and salient points. Her *Reflections on Alexander and Cæsar* never obtained wide circulation. In fact, her own compositions show intense subtlety of intellect, and a keen knowledge of human nature, but are often wanting in moral grandeur. In the excellent portrait which has been preserved, the features are strongly marked, and appear capable of great variety of expression. The nose is large, the mouth powerful, and the eye bright. Some light has been thrown on Christina's character by what has gone before. Yet the real character of so subtle and refined a woman must ever be difficult to unravel. One thing at least is certain. She was a perfect lover of paradox—at one moment loving power, at another despising all its pomp and ceremony; at one moment conceiving of religion as the only good, at another half doubting whether there were any religion at all. At one time she would be totally immersed in political affairs, at another she would regard the arts of diplomacy as little better than a childish game of chance. One day she was the keen votary of satire, on the next she became the stern devotee of philosophical abstraction. 'The sea,' she once said, 'resembles great souls: however agitated the surface may be, the depth is always calm.' And again; 'the good and evil of this world is like those perspectives which only amuse or deceive at a distance.'

R. S. MYLNE.

SUMMARIES OF FOREIGN REVIEWS.

THEOLOGISCHE STUDIEN UND KRITIKEN (No. 3, 1896).—
Dr. Link, Professor of New Testament Exegesis at Königsberg
discusses here at considerable length, under the title, 'Die Dol-
metscher des Petrus,' the question as to whether the Apostle
Peter had or had not a sufficient knowledge of, and a sufficient
facility in the use of, the Greek tongue to enable him to
address in the course of his missionary journeys, Greek speaking audiences, and to write in that language. The discussion
as to this has arisen from what Eusebius reports as taken from
Papias, viz., that the presbyter John spoke of Mark as the
hermeneutes of Peter. The same office is assigned, by Clement
of Alexandria, to one Glaucias. But what function does the
term indicate? Dr. Link briefly refers to the controversy on
this point, and discusses the usage of the word in Greek
writings, chiefly at the times of the Cæsars. He shows that
its best equivalent is simply our dragoman, one who translates
the utterances of a person addressing an audience, or a person,
whose language he cannot himself speak, into their or his
native tongue. It did not mean a secretary, an amanuensis, a
help to a busy man, but one who rendered the speech or
writing of one man into the language of those for whom it
was intended. The necessary inference is that Peter was
unable to address his hearers in certain districts in their own
tongue. But then what tongue was that? Bleek maintained
that it was and could only be Latin, which Mark had mastered
when in Rome with Paul. This idea has found little favour,
the consensus of opinion being that it was into Greek that
Mark rendered the Aramaean of Peter. Dr. Link regards this
as certain, and refers for one of the proofs of it to the fact that
Peter was pre-eminently the apostle to the Circumcision, even
in Rome, and that Greek was the language familiar to the
Jews there, and the language in which their intercourse with
their brethren in all provinces to the East was carried on.
Further, he shows that the language of Papias indicates that
Mark was Peter's *hermeneutes,* not in Rome only, but constantly
in his missionary journeys. Dr. Link defends the same sense,
against Zahn and Neander, of the term *hermeneutes* as applied
to Glaucias by Clement of Alexandria in relation to Peter.
His conclusion is, therefore, that Peter was not skilled in the
use of the Greek tongue, and that the epistles and addresses

that have come down to us as his were not penned or spoken
by him in the form in which they have come down to us.—
The second article is by Professor Fredrick Blass, Professor of
Classical Philology, at the University of Halle. It is titled,
'Neue Texteszeugen für die Apostelgeschichte.'   The new
witnesses are chiefly three; a Latin text from the early part
of the thirteenth century and now in the Bibliotheque Nationale of Paris, No. 321; another, which is in the Royal Library
at Wernigerode; and next a Provencal translation, dating from
the thirteenth century. All vary in some important particulars
from the Vulgate, and Professor Blass gives us, so far as the
Acts of the Apostles is concerned, a list of these variants, as
likely to aid in getting at a correct text of the original work.
—Dr. Carl Clemen, Privat-Docent at Halle, follows with an
elaborate and extremely interesting paper on 'Der Begriff
" Religion " und seine verschiedenen Auffassungen.' He gives
a series of the definitions of religion given by the most distinguished German writers, who have adventured such, group-
ing them according as they have regarded religion from the
intellectual, aesthetic, or practical point of view. He then
discusses the most important of them, and points out their
merits and defects respectively.—Dr. Otto Kirn, Professor of
Theology at Basel, treats of the significance of Law, and the
Mosaic Law as a special form of it, for, or in, Christian ethics.
His article bears the title 'Das Gesetz in der christlichen
Ethik.'—The only other article here is by Herr Pfarrer Paul
Durselen of Berlin, 'Uber eine Darstellung des christlichen
Glaubens vom Gnadenstande aus.'—Professor Beer of Halle
reviews Dillmann's 'Handbuch der alttestamentlichen Theo-
logie,' a posthumous work of the celebrated Oriental scholar.

RUSSIA.

Voprosi Philosophii i Psychologii (January, 1896).—
The first number of the present year opens with extracts or
brief selections from the far-famed Indian writings, the Upanishads. The selections appear to have been made by a lady,
who signs herself Vera Johnston. They are fitly opened by a
brief motto from Schopenhauer, who says that ' Deep, independent, high thoughts meet one on every page of the Upanishads.
This very rich and very high subject is a teaching for the
world. It was a comfort in life and will be a comfort in death.'
The translator has undertaken no easy task. As a medium of
expression Russian is not at all to be compared with Sanscrit.
As compared with Sanscrit it is as a language but of yesterday. Moreover it is so poor in expressions for *abstract* concep-

tions, that even when translating from a tongue so near to itself, in comparison with the Sanscrit, as the German, the translator has to occupy himself more and more with the selection and composition of such expressions as *things in themselves* or with *world-conception* in order to translate such terms as *Das Ding an sich* and *Weltanschauung.* Difficulties of this kind are the more hard to overcome when we have to do with translations from the Sanscrit tongue, which for fulness, of colouring and richness of expression is superior to any old or new European language.— The second article is on the autonomy of man and its various stadia or halting places, by L. E. Obolenskie.—The third article is by Prince Serge N. Trubetskoi, who takes for his subject the 'Foundation of Idealism.'—The last article but one in the general part of the journal is by the Russian thinker, Vladimir Solovieff, 'On the Reality of the Moral Order.' This article is immediately connected with a former, which appeared in No. 30 of the 'Voprosi,' November, 1895. The author sets out from the logical development of the religious sensation, the unconditional moral element, which is the source of the ful- ness of good, containing in itself the obligatory relation of all to all. This again realises itself as a complete moral order, otherwise a kingdom of God. But how pure moral good ought to be experienced, though admitted by every preacher of the Categorical Imperative, is according to the author a position which is not so easy to make out. He then enters upon a discussion of the validity of the *Ought—Das Sollen*, as formulated by Kant, conditioned by the unconditional obliga- tory.—The concluding article is on the 'Development of the Idea of Imperial Necessity and Social Right in Italy,' as shown especially by the writings of Botero and Campanella.—On this follows an article on 'Temperament,' and the usual critical notices and bibliography.

ITALY.

NUOVA ANTOLOGIA (April 1).—P. Molmento describes the encyclopedic art of the Middle Ages.—G. Boglietti faithfully notes the progress which socialism has made in England, but asks what grounds William Morris and Belfort Bax have for their opinion that 'the advent of socialism is as inexorable and inevitable as the daily rising of the sun?'—P. Lioy writes on 'The Suggestions of the Unknown.'—G. Ricca Salerno dis- cusses the progressive tax in England and France, giving a brief account of taxes in general.—The serial story 'The Sin of an Honest Woman,' by E. Castelnuovo, is continued; and also the 'Origins of Poetry in Rome,' by E. Cocchia.—The

bibliographical bulletin praises General Booth's *Life and
Labour of the People in London.*—(April, 15th).—A portion of
this number is devoted to a chapter from a book by Senator
Finali, just published, entitled *Le Marche nel* 1860,' in which
Finali points out that hitherto an error has been committed by
historians in attributing the victory of the battle of Castelfi-
dardo to General Cialdini. That General was not in the battle,
and knew nothing of it, only arriving when all was finished.
But he had so far contributed to success, in that he had, by
an able manœuvre, prevented General Lamoriciere from rein-
forcing the troops under General De Courten at Ancona, which
fact greatly retarded the advance of the royal army into the
kingdom of Naples. The greatest brunt of the battle, however, was borne by the Regina brigade, which had been led
to victory by General Cialdini the year previous at Sesia.—
C. F. Ferraris contributes a translation of part of Marx's *Kritik
der Politischen Oekonomie.*—G. Goiran writes on military reform.—E. Montecorboli has a long and appreciative article on
Paul Verlaine.—The remaining numbers are continuations.—
(May, 1st).—R. de Cesare points out the beginning of a new
phase in the ecclesiastical policy of the Italian government,
and that its new direction has already pacified the Vatican.
Only a united action responding to the moral and political
necessities of the State can exercise a beneficial influence and
be productive of good.—F. Torraca writes about Sicilian
schools, and 'Historical Materialism' by Signor Ferrari, and
Castelnuovo's romance are continued.—G. Cimbali explains
the political wisdom of Giovanni Botero.—E. Mancini describes the progress made by and the future of electric lighting.
—(May 16th).—E. Pinchia gives an interesting account of the
family Debormida, the last hero of which lost his life at the
battle of Adowah.—A. Salandra writes a statistical paper
entitled 'Two Years of Finance,' and D. Carraroli a long
article on the Hungarian Milennium.—'Africa in the Green
Books,' by E. Arbib, clears up a great deal that was obscure
in the Italian campaign.—(June, 1st)—C. Ricci contributes a
careful study on the paintings of Tiepolo, who was neglected
during the period following his own, but has now received
the acknowledgment of which he was worthy.—E. Catellani,
at the close of a paper describing events in the Soudan, advises
Italy not to forget, should she be called to co-operate in the
Soudan, that a *universal* equilibrium has succeeded or is rapidly
succeeding to *European* equilibrium, and just as, in commerce,
science has brought the most distant countries near, so in
general politics, the world exists now as a whole, the parts of

which are the organs, and that in less than half a century to come, that European State which has no colonies and interests in all quarters of the world, will be simply wiped out from the list of great powers.—A. Luzio and R. Renier commence a series of papers on the luxury of Isabella of Este, describing her wardrobe, the customs of the Renasence, the influence on Italy of foreign countries, the inefficacy of sumptuary laws, and the setting of the 'fashion' by Isabella.—P. Lioy writes an interesting article on rustic literature.—O. Grande begins a novel 'The Cloud.'—D. Cortese writes on the 'New Spirit,' which he says is as old as the world.—E. G. Boner discusses the Finnish 'Kalewala.'—(June, 19th).—Besides continuations of previous papers, F. d'Ovidio writes on the sonnet addressed to Dante by Cavalcanti; and I. Guidi on ' Ancient Abyssinia.' —C. Segrè criticises Thomas Hardy's *Jude the Obscure* in an unfavourable manner. He calls the book 'the strongest example of the modern spirit ever seen.' 'If Thackeray or Dickens could rise from the grave and hear the applause bestowed on this book, they would think modern men had been seized with a fit of madness.' 'The author,' the critic goes on to say, 'tries to prove that man is the mere victim and tool of his social surroundings. Love is the theme of the book, but the reader who looks for the old tenderness and calm in that passion will be cruelly disappointed. It is a saddening thing that a book like *Jude the Obscure* should have been conceived and found admirers in a country like England, where usually there prevails a simple and strict sense of justice. The evil has penetrated deep, and it is time to rise and oppose the poisonous current, which will otherwise gain ground. With Carducci, the whole field of art should cry out "We must return to the traditions of our grand masters !"'— G. Fraisan writes on money circulation in Italy.—O. Z. Bianco reports the latest researches in 'Uranos' and 'Neptune.'

LA RASSEGNA NAZIONALE (April 1).—G. Zaccagni contributes an article on the late Signor Bonghi.—G. Villa concludes his paper on 'The Naturalist Romance,' in which he criticises the modern French, Russian, and German psychological writers, and comes to the conclusion that art should not be monopolized by any one school, for a really good work of art is neither classic, romantic, realistic nor socialistic; neither idealistic nor psychological in its tone. Who would think of classifying as belonging to a special school the ' Don Quixote ' or the 'Promessi Sposi ?' When a work of art arouses discussion, it is a proof that it may have all qualities but the supreme one of being a masterpiece of art. No one dreams of discussing the artistic value of Shakspeare's dramas, while those of Victor Hugo stir up tempests of argument; and, to come lower down in the scale, no one thinks of discussing Daudet's romances, while every one fights about Zola's. Ibsen is violently discussed, but not Sundermann. Art is derived from intuition of life, and no æsthetic or philosophical theory can give that intuition when it is wanting.—J. Isola writes a 'Memoir of Cesere Cantu,' in commemoration of the first anniversary of the historian's death.—' Regulus ' briefly relates the story of the rule of the Dervishes from the rise of the Mahdi till now. He alludes to the struggle of the English, Abyssinians, and Italians with the dervishes, and insists on the necessity of exterminating their barbarous race. If the Italians and Abyssinians had allied themselves against the common enemy, and the English had not waited for the battle of Adowah before moving on Dongola, the power of the Dervishes would have been already broken. The present expedition of the English will perhaps have greater consequences than is now foreseen. It is to be hoped that a blow will be struck against the dervishes from Kassala and Dongola from which they will never recover, and that the fanaticism which has devastated, some fifteen years, the region which Europe believed she had reclaimed for civilization, will cease.—P. Stoppani writes on Lourdes, a paper which gives the Catholic point of view.—(April 16).—G. Grabinski, writing on the new *Vie de Saint Francois d'Assise,* by Paul Sabatier, says that while rendering due homage to the literary and paleographic value of this work, he is constrained to conclude that Sabatier has not given the world a page of objective history, but a treatise too much imbued with Protestant prejudice and the rationalistic spirit of negation. Sabatier is no doubt sincere, but his book is, in times like the present, a danger. Grabinski then subjects the book to strict criticism, and concludes by hoping that some literary man of value will take upon himself the easy task of writing a history of the Saint worthy to rival that of Sabatier, while combating the errors in the latter.—P. Rossi furnishes a statistical article on the industries of the province of Verona.—(May 1st).—In an article called 'Abandoned Infancy' C. Bassi cites the example set in England by the 'National Society for the prevention of cruelty to Children,' describing what it has done. He says that Italy has 30 millions of inhabitants, and if only a fourth of that number would subscribe the trifling sum of one *soldo* a day for such an institution much could be done. At least 55,000 abandoned children could be cared for and educated.—

E. Artoum describes the financial syndicates of England. —The dialogues on the Temporal Power are continued, and T. Regulus writes on Sicily.—(May 16th)—A. von Scwarz describes the ancient divination by fire, traces of which superstition may still be traced in some parts of Italy.—N. Bardelli reviews M. Sigogue's ' L'Art de parler.'—R. Mazzei contributes a paper on ' God in Art.'—Then follows the pastoral letter addressed to his people by the Bishop of Cremona on emigration, full of good advice to struggling Italians.—G. Grabinski contributes a memoir of the late Cardinal Galimberti.—(June 1st)—I. Petroni discusses the philosophy of law in the light of critical idealism.—There is a review by A. Ghigusni of a recent volume of remarkable poems by G. Bertache.—The proceedings of the trial of General Baratieri are fully published.—(June 16th)—G. Marcotti writes a long interesting article on 'Unknown France' describing caverns, valleys, the various churches and abbeys, ancient ruins, etc.—T. Luxow has much to say on the bestowal of prizes on art productions.—P. S. writes on social legislation. —Regulus on the recent deplorable events in Crete, and V. Recci on decentralization.

LA VITA ITALIANA (May)—' To the Marquis of Rudini.'— ' Africa in legend and history,' by Prof. De Gubernatis.— ' Tarquinia Corneto.'—' Baroness Corti.'—' Enrique Serra.'— ' The Cock's Tower at Florence.'—' A glance at the sky.'— ' Venetian charity.'—' Paolina Leopardi.'—' The Valley of Pompei.'—' Constantinople.'—' Veronese dialectic poets.'

IL PENSIERO ITALIANO (May).—' A morphologic problem regarding the superior vertebrates.'—' Vittorio Alfieri.'—' The genesis of moral sense in relation to the organic sexual differences of the human race.'—' A musical drama,' by Metaotasis.—' The perils of Vaticanism in the Italian State.'— ' Positivism and the problem of liberty.'

NAPOLI NOBILISSIMA (May).—Contains : ' The Bass-relief at Porto and the legend of Nicolo Pesce,' by Benedetto Croce, in which are noticed recent studies on the curious legend above mentioned, and a very rare Spanish romance of the beginning of the 17th century is described.—' The Church of S. Teresa agli Studi,' by G. Ceci.—Documents, notes, etc.

EMPORIUM (May).—' Adolf Menzel.'—' Astronomers and Observers,' by F. Porro.—' Elizabeth Barrett Browning.'—' The House of the Vettii at Pompei.'—' A Precursor of Lombroso in the 17th century.'—' The Scientific Hygienic Institutions in Italy,' etc.

GIORNALE DEGLI ECONOMISTA (May) contains: 'The *Spread* of the Americans.'—'The Agronomic Base of the theory of Rents.'—'The Reform of Local Taxes.'—'The Banks in the Province of Reggio Emilia.'—'Providence,' etc.

NATURA ED ARTE (April 1)—contains: 'The Resurrection of Italian Art.' — 'The Poets of the Country — Giovanni Guidiccioni.' — (April 15). — 'Women and Jewels.' — 'The Descendants of the Queen of Sheba.'—'The Evangelists of Francesco Podesti.'—'Giannino Baglioni,' pretender to France, which is a curious and little known story of a pretender to the throne of France. A certain Guccio Baglioni, who lived in Siena at the end of the 13th century, went to establish himself in Paris, and there secretly married a noble lady, Marie di Carcy, by whom he had a son, who was named Giannino. The marriage being discovered, the father was obliged to fly, but, nine years later, was able to return to France, where he went to fetch Giannino, with whom he returned to Siena. But, so the story runs, it was not his son whom he had fetched but the Dauphin of France! During the ceremony of baptism this son of King Louis had been exchanged with the son of Baglioni, in order to save the former from the intrigues of Prince Philip, who aspired to the throne. The real son of Baglioni died in infancy. The exchange of children was revealed by Marie di Carcy to her confessor on her deathbed, twenty years later. The confessor went to Rome, and told all to Cola di Rienzi, then a tribune, who sent for the supposed Giannino Baglioni, who was still living at Siena, and revealed to him his real personality, proving it by documents and the testimony of Marie di Carcy's confessor. Cola di Rienzi urged the young man to claim his rights, promising to give him his support. Soon after Rienzi died. The pretender returned to Siena and compiled a memorandum begging the sovereigns of Europe for their protection, and forwarded six copies in Italy and six abroad. He received no reply whatever, and went to Venice to induce that Republic to take his part, but without effect. He then made another attempt with the King of Hungary, but failed, and thereupon returned to Siena, where a rich Jew furnished him with money on the promise that if he attained to the throne he would not allow the Jews to be persecuted. In 1360 Giannino went to Avignon, where the Pope refused to receive him. He then gathered together a troop of adventurers and marched on Lyons, but he was betrayed, arrested by order of the Pope, and imprisoned in the castle of Marseilles. Thence he was sent to Naples, and kept in the Castle dell' Voo, where he died in 1363. There exists a document in the parish of Saint Domenic in Siena, a book containing the lists of death, wherein is registered the death of Giannino Baglioni, with the note that on his corpse was found the cross which it was the custom to impress on the shoulder of a dauphin of France 'and all dependents of the Royal House of France.' The author of the article, Signor Arrighi, suggests that the foreign archives should be examined in order to ascertain whether any of them contain a document relating to the subject of this story. —'On the Julian Alps.'—'Submarine Telegraphs.'—'Pictures in *tempora* and *al fresco.*'—'Marat as a Journalist.'—An inedited letter written in Italian by Alexander Dumas *fils*.— (April 15)—In this number is published, contributed by a lady residing in Reggio, a letter in *broken Italian*, by Alexander Dumas *fils*, which, translated, runs thus:—'Sir, only to-day have I returned from a little journey into the interior of France; I found your book, for which I thank you a thousand times. My first moment shall be employed in reading it, and I shall be honoured and fortunate in finding myself at once your admirer and political friend. Pardon my bad Italian; I shall be more learned when I have read your book. Believe me, your devoted, A. Dumas. Rue St. Lazare, 40.'—The May numbers contain: 'Prizes at the Rome Exhibition of Fine Arts.'—'Melan's Hermitage at Little S. Bernard and Aosta.'— 'Scraps of Medical Science.'—'Marco Mingheltd as a Soldier.' —'Ostende and Scheveningro.'—'The Springtime of Italian Painting.'—'G. Rouvetta and his First Historic Drama.'—'The 15th May, 1848, at Naples.'—'A French Doctor, Friend of Italy, Peter de Nolhac.'—'The Commensalism of Animals.'— 'The Olympic Games,' etc.

FRANCE.

REVUE DE L'HISTOIRE DES RELIGIONS (No. 2, 1896).—M. J. Philippe continues and concludes his series of studies on 'Lucretius in Christian Theology from the first to the thirteenth century, and specially in the Carlovingian Schools.' In this, the third of the series, he shows from the writings of the distinguished theologians of the eighth century, and after, that Lucretius continued to be read and studied by them, and that his influence was very widely felt in the whole Western Church, and affected the exegesis, the physics, and the metaphysics of the schools. Though branded as a heretic and an atheist of the deepest dye, and volumes were devoted to the refutation of his opinions, yet copies of his works were carefully treasured in abbeys and monasteries, and the reflex of his teaching is seen in the writings of many who scrupulously avoid mentioning his name. M. Philippe establishes all his points by numerous quotations, and often places the lines of Lucretius in footnotes so that the value of his assertions may be tested by his readers for themselves.—There follows the second part of M. Frederic Macler's article on ' The Apocryphal Apocalypses of Daniel.' In accordance with the promise given in the last section, he gives us here a translation of the Coptic version. It is only the first part of the translation which is given in this number ; the rest will follow in order. It is here preceded by a brief introduction, describing the persecutions which the Copts suffered at the hands of the various powers that ruled over Egypt. It was these persecutions which furnished the cause of the rise and development of this kind of literature in the Christian communities there, as elsewhere. The persecution under Diocletian, and those instituted by the Byzantine emperors, were followed by even more terrible measures taken against the Copts by the Arabs, whom the former had invited to come to their help. Driven to despair by their severe and prolonged sufferings, the Christians in Egypt sought refuge in the hope of the future,—in the foretold coming of the Messiah a second time to gather together his redeemed and deliver them from all their enemies, introducing then a glorious era of peace and felicity. Mr. Macler, in his introduction, gives us also a short summary of the contents of this apocalypse, while in a series of footnotes, which accompany the translation, he shows how closely the writer, or writers, of it adhered to the historical setting and form of the canonical Daniel. After the introduction to the apocalypse, which, like that of Daniel itself, is in appearance historical, the prophet depicts a vision concerning the kingdom of the children of Ishmael. During the reign of the nineteenth and last king of that race over Egypt, his enemy, Pitourgos, will come against him, and put him to flight and to death. Next will come the king of the Romans. Gog and Magog will after that convulse the earth; then will appear the antichrist; and finally the Ancient of Days, who will destroy the antichrist, and then reign for ever. At the close of the apocalypse Daniel receives from God the command to seal up all these things unto the time of their accomplishment.—M. L. Marillier next continues, and here concludes, his exhaustive review of Dr. Edward Caird's Gifford Lectures on the ' Evolution of Religion.' It is nearly a year and a half since the first part of this review appeared, and we had begun to fear that surely the sequel of it had miscarried. The first part gave a summary of the contents of the work, and paid a warm tribute to the lucidity and charm of the author's style, and to the philosophical value of the work; the reviewer then promising to subject the volumes to a careful scrutiny later on. That promise is fully fulfilled here. M. Marillier's criticisms, however, are given with a kindly hand. Of course the title of the work, read in the light of its contents, is found fault with, as by almost all its critics on this side of the channel. The limits within which Dr. Caird confined himself in treating his subject, M. M. thinks, as many others have done, have necessarily prevented him from giving anything like an adequate account of the evolution of religion. It is the evolution of Christianity only that he has traced, and sought to trace, in his lectures. His conclusions, therefore, as to the evolution of religion may be correct, but it is impossible for him, excluding, as he has done, so many religions from account, to demonstrate their accuracy. Another fault found with Dr. Caird's treatment of his subject is, that he constantly looks at religion from the intellectual side, regards it, that is, as a system of opinions, as the product of human reason, or reasoning, and so fails to take, or to take sufficient, note of the complex parentage of it,—the emotions, sentiments, fears, and fancies, that all play their part in the genesis and development of religion. Dr. Caird is here throughout the metaphysician, and has forgotten that to carry out his self-imposed task it was necessary for him to lay aside for the time being that character, and to become the historian pure and simple. M. Marillier's article here is not only a masterly review of Dr. Caird's lectures, but forms in itself a valuable contribution to religious science.

REVUE DES RELIGIONS (No. 2, 1896.)—M. the Abbé de Moor continues here his essay on 'The origin of the Egyptian people and its civilization, according to Egyptian legend and the Bible.' It will be remembered from previous summaries that the learned Abbé thinks he has discovered the secret of, or the key to the right interpretation of, the Osirian legend, which has hitherto puzzled Egyptologists, folklorists, and others. He has found the key, he thinks, in the Genesis narratives, which bear on the origin and early history of the race, and in the references, elsewhere made, chiefly in the apocalyptic literature, Jewish and Christian, to the revolt of the angels and their consequent expulsion from heaven. All these things, the learned Abbé takes, of course, to be historical facts, and, taking them as such, he here endeavours to show in detail how the Osirian legend, when read in the light of these facts, becomes intelligible, and is seen to be in harmony with the Biblical

record.   The Osirian legend, he regards, as a much corrupted
and disfigured version of the story of the revolt of the angels
under Satan, of the history of the Cainites, the Abelites, and
the Sethites, and of the corruption of the race through sin, and
its subsequent destruction by the flood.   In these facts we
have, M. de Moor tells us, the real foundations of the Egyptian
legend; and with these facts before us, we are now able to
spell out its true significance.   They enable us to strip off
the accretions due to generations of fanciful *conteurs*, who endeavoured to make up for their pardonable ignorance, or
faulty memories, by the liveliness of their poetic imagination.
M. de Moor carries forward here his self-imposed task of un-
ravelling this tangled skein of fact and fancy.   The details,
of course, are very numerous, and the success of his effort can
only be judged by those who carefully read the learned Abbé's
paper throughout.   The revolt of the children of Ra against
him, in the Egyptian legend is, it seems, a distorted reminiscence of the Satanic revolt.   The Isis of the legend is the
Satan of the Biblical tradition.   The punishment ordered to
be inflicted by Ra, is also but a distorted version of the destruction of the race as given in the Biblical story of the flood.
In fact we have but to read the Egyptian legend in the light
of the early chapters of Genesis, making liberal allowance for
forgetfulness of details inevitable in the course of time, and
the process of identification becomes comparatively easy.—
M. Castonnet des Fosses continues next his paper on 'Japan
from the religious point of view.'   He gives us here an historical outline of the planting and growth of Buddhism in
Japan.   The ancient Shinto faith, he tells us, is professed to-
day by about a third only of the people of Japan.   The various
sects that continue to exist up to now are described, so far as
their leading tenets are concerned; the number of their temples·
respectively and of their priests is roughly given; and the
attitude in which their adherents stand to the sects differing
from them, or the members thereof, is indicated.   It is an
attitude of contemptuous, rather than of benevolent, neutrality.
—Dr. P. Bourdais follows with a study in Egyptian hierology.
It bears the title 'La production des êtres par la Divinité.'
The writer seeks in his article to show from several Egyptian
hymns that the idea that everything was created, (all beings
included), not by God, the Supreme Being, but by one who
bore the name of the Word, and the Truth, la Parole, la Verite,
was familiar to the Egyptians from the most remote times.
He concludes, therefore, that we have here a reminiscence of
the primeval fact, preserved to us in the Bible in its purity,

that all things were created by the Logos, the second person
of the Trinity.—M. the Abbé Loisy furnishes a short study on
the last fragment of the book of Jashar, ' Le dernier fragment
du Jasar.' The last quotation from that lost work is not, as
M. Renan, and others with him, have thought, David's lament
over Saul's and Jonathan's death. There is a still later quotation from it, one which belongs to the time of Solomon. It
appears in the prayer of Solomon at the dedication of the
temple. It occurs in 1 Kings, viii. 13. It is awanting in that
place in the lxx. version, but appears later on in the prayer,
viz., at the end of it, and is there accompanied by a valuable
note, ' Behold, is not this written in the Book of the Song?'
The translator from the Hebrew has, however, M. Loisy thinks,
slightly misread his text here, in fact confounded the final *resh*
of the word before him with *daleth*, and so read 'Song' instead
of ' Jasar.' The study is of considerable interest, and merits
the attention of Biblical students.—The ' Chronique ' here, as
usual, is of a somewhat cosmopolitan character; and the
appreciations of the literature of the two months cannot but
be helpful to all the readers of the *Revue.*

REVUE DES ETUDES JUIVES (No. 4, 1895).—M. Theodore
Reinach has the first place here with an article headed
' L'Empereur Claude et les antisemites alexandrines d'apres un
nouveau papyrus.' The new papyrus has a somewhat curious
history. Part of it, but in a very mutilated condition, was
discovered lately in the Berlin Museum, and was published,
translated, and commented on, in *Hermes*, xxx. 485ff., by Herr
Wilcken. But another fragment of it has since been discovered in the Museum at Gizeh by M. Pierre Jouguet, and
was reported by him in his annual Memoire to the Academie
des Inscriptions of Paris. M. Reinach saw at once that it
formed part of the document lately published by Herr
Wilcken, and, acquainting M. Jouguet with the fact, was
promptly furnished by him with a copy of the Gizeh papyrus.
M. Reinach, taking advantage of this kindness, and with M.
Jouguet's permission, publishes here both fragments, and
details the legal process of which it gives an account. It tells
of a trial which took place before the Emperor Claudius at
Rome in presence of an august assemblage of notables, one of
whom was the Empress. The accused was King Agrippa
(Wilcken identifies him with Agrippa II., but M. Reinach disposes of that idea very summarily, and shows that it must have
been Herod Agrippa I.). The accusation was evidently
brought against Agrippa by certain bitter opponents of the
Jews in Alexandria in Egypt, who had been enraged at the

pomp displayed by Agrippa when passing through that city on his way from Rome in 38 A.D. to take possession of his Tetrarchy, as also, doubtless, by the many favours he had then and afterwards shown to the Jewish colony there whenever occasion offered. It was he, too, who secured for the Jews in Egypt an edict from Claudius, when he came to the throne, securing to them the enjoyment of all their former privileges. To those in Alexandria who hated the Jews, and they were seemingly not few, this was an unpardonable offence. Fragmentary as the papyrus still is, it enables M. Reinach to follow so far the course of the trial, and to show that Claudius was favourable to the accused. If M. Reinach is correct in this, then the trial took place in the year 41.—The second article is by M. Ludwig Blau. It is on the 'Origine et Histoire, de la lecture du Schema et des formules de benediction qui l'accompagnent.' M. Blau acknowledges that it is now impossible to say with any certainty when the use of it was first introduced into Jewish services. He thinks, however, that what forms the first part of it, viz., Deut. vi. 4-9, came very probably to be repeated early in the Persian period by the officiating priests in the temple, just before the offering of the morning sacrifice, and this as a testimony that the sacrifice was offered to Jahveh, the true and only God, and not to the Persian deity, the god of light. The history of the additions that were made to the first formula in the course of time is also involved in considerable obscurity, although it may be traced with more certain results in regard to many points. The references to the reading or repetition of Shema are very numerous in the Talmudic writers, and M. Blau here adduces a large number of them to establish the time and place he assigns to the additions made to it up to its receiving its present form. He discusses the whole question with great learning and quite scholarly patience.—M. Israel Levi next devotes a few pages to refuting the claims so long and so often made by Jewish writers in regard to Hillel that he was of Davidic origin. He examines the documents on whose testimony the claim has been based, and shows very clearly how little value can be placed on them. He brings forward also a formidable array of very strong objections against the validity of the claim.—There are several noteworthy articles in addition to these in this number, though they do not extend to such dimensions. M. Martin Schreiner furnishes interesting 'Contributions á l'histoire des Juifs en Egypte.'—M. D. Kaufmann two short studies, viz., (1) 'Les 24 martyrs d'Ancone,' and (2) 'Deux lettres nouvelles des Marranes aux Levantins

touchant l'interruptions des affaires avec Ancone.'—M. Kohut
discourses on 'Le Had Gadya et les chansons similaires.'—M.
Bloch concludes his paper, 'Une expulsion de Juifs en Alsace
au XVI. siecle.'—M. Weill writes on 'Les Juifs et le Saint
Simonism.'—The 'Notes et Melanges' are also very numerous,
and embrace a rich variety of exegetic, grammatical, and
historical matters.—The 'Bibliographie' is contributed by M.
Mayer Lambert and M. W. Bacher. It contains critical appreciations of recent works by Landau, H. L. Strack, and Samuel
Poznanski.

REVUE PHILOSOPHIQUE (May, 1896).—A. Fouillée's 'Necessity
for a Psychological and Sociological Interpretation of the
World' discusses the various theories of the universe, and
concludes that the psychological can explain the physical but
not *vice versa*—'how can we explain this reality [which lies
behind sensible appearances] except after the type of the sole
reality known to us immediately and in itself, I mean our
conscious existence?' In the same way the author lays stress
on the idea of organism in the universe as well as in human
society.—The first portion of a paper by F. Le Dantec on
'The Chemical Evolution of Species' considers the effect of
surrounding fluids in destroying or altering low forms of life.—
George Fonsegrieve concludes his 'Generalisation and Induction.' He denies that there is aught in induction which constitutes a special form of reasoning, an original discursus of
the mind.—A note on experiments on perception of coloured
objects by L. Duprat.—(June, 1896).—'Experimental Researches on Joy and Sorrow,' by G. Dumas. The present
instalment deals with joy in its physical aspects. 'The
primitive and essential condition of joy is cerebral vaso-dilation,
accompanied by acceleration of the pulse and respiration, and
by excessive mental activity.' Several observations of cases
of insanity from the Sainte-Anne Hospital are given, from
which M. Dumas shows that those madmen who imagine
themselves kings, millionaires, etc., owe their delusions to their
physical condition. 'In the case of general paralysis, vaso-
dilation is anterior to any intellectual condition.' In short the
mental and physical phenomena of joy act and react on one
another.—In 'The Involution and Relative order of Ideas as
revealed by Language' M. de la Grasserie draws attention to
the importance of language as an index of mental habits.—
M. Ch. Féré in 'The Hand, Prehension, and Touch' has a
variety of interesting information to offer. He concludes that
'like all other organs of sense and motion the hand offers considerable individual varieties. A considerable number of de-

fects are incapable of being corrected by exercise. Just as deaf and colour-blind persons should be debarred from certain studies, so should those furnished with imperfect hands. Just as in some individuals the eye or the ear can convey only incomplete or false notions to the mind, so the hand in others. The hand is at once the agent and the interpreter of mental development, and deserves more attention on the part of physiologists and psychologists, who have somewhat neglected it.'—A note on the idea of the Social Organism.—Reviews of Books.—Summaries of Russian (May) and German (June) philosophical journals.—(July, 1896).—M. L. Dauriac continues his 'Study in the Psychology of the Musician,' and seeks to investigate the nature of the pleasure produced by music.— Dr. Dumas' 'Experimental Researches on Joy and Grief' (second part) deals with the physical phenomena of grief.— An interesting paper on 'The Logic of the Infant' by Dr. Bernard Munz, translated by A. Keller.—The 'General Review of Psychophysics' analyses the articles on the subject which have appeared in German periodicals from April 1895 to April of this year.—Reviews of Books.—Summaries of American and English psychological magazines.

REVUE SEMITIQUE D'EPIGRAPHIE ET D'HISTOIRE ANCIENNE (No. 2, 1896).—M. J. Halévy's 'Recherches Bibliques' in this No., continue his critical examination of the text of Genesis, and his notes for the interpretation of the Psalms. The Genesis section embraces chap. xxviii. 10, on to the end of chap. xxxi., that is, the history of Jacob from his flight from Beersheba to his return from Haran as far as Mount Gilead, where he finally parted from Laban. The order followed by M. Halévy is the same as in the former sections. A brief summary is given of the contents of the section; the Hebrew text is then minutely examined, emendations, where thought necessary, are suggested, and explanatory notes are given of words or phrases, which the fuller and more accurate knowledge of Hebrew as a language, and of Semitic customs, in these days, enables a scholar like M. Halévy to give; and finally, there is a section devoted to showing the unity of the text throughout, in opposition to the dismemberment and partitioning of the text to this and that writer, as is done by the so-called modern critical school. M. Halévy's explanatory notes are often very ingenious, if not always convincing, while his emendations of the text are invariably such as are, at least, justifiable, and render the meaning clearer and more consistent with the context. As in the margin of the Revised Version, so here, M. Halévy in Gen. xxviii. 13, renders the proposition as 'beside,' not as 'above,' as in our Authorised Version. Jahve stood *beside* Jacob, when he spoke to him, and not at the top of the ladder. As instances of M. Halévy's explanatory and illustrative notes, both of their strength and of their weakness, we might select the following. Jacob's astonishment was not, we are told, caused by the theophany itself; it arose from his own ignorance of the sanctity of the place, seeing that it had been a consecrated place since at least the days of Abraham. Again we are told, Leah received but one servant on the occasion of her marriage, because Jacob brought no dowry ; while Rebecca was sent away with a numerous retinue of servants because her parents received, through the negotiating messenger, numerous and costly gifts. Again, the reason why Rachel stole her father's teraphim, M. Halévy tells us, was merely to prevent her father from divining by means of them the route the fugitives had taken, a somewhat foolish precaution, surely, when we think of the number of retainers that accompanied Jacob, and the numerous flocks and herds he owned. The chief interest of these Genesis studies, however, lies in their vindication of the substantial unity of the text. In regard to the section before him here, he has chiefly Dillmann in his mind ; and it is in opposition to his arguments that he here defends the consecutiveness of the narrative, and its perfect harmony with all that precedes it. The section devoted to the Psalms embraces Psalms xlvi. to lvii. inclusive. Here again the text is subjected to a minute and scholarly analysis, its errors, arising probably from the mistakes of copyists, are noted, and corrections suggested; explanatory notes are given where thought to be needed, and reasons are offered for assigning, where possible, the date of composition and originating occasion for each. A lengthy inscription from a cuneiform text follows, here transcribed and translated by M. Halévy also.—M. Alfred Boissier furnishes, in the same way, two fragmentary texts relating to Shamash-shum-ukin. They are accompanied with explanatory notes.—An interesting article follows, again by M. J. Halévy, on the influence of the Pentateuch on the Avesta. The similarity between these works in their account of the creation of the world and of the human race through a single pair ; in their account of the introduction of sin into the world, and of the destruction of the race that followed ; their descriptions of the intimate relations existing between the Deity and the pre-eminently just man ; these points of similarity have been long observed, and have frequently provoked the question, which of the two works is the older and has been utilised by the other. At first the Avesta was favoured, and Genesis was regarded as having borrowed from it. M. Halévy has always been inclined to award the priority to the Pentateuch. He succeeded in bringing the late M. James Darmesteter to the same opinion. M. Halevy here re-states his conclusions on this subject, and adds some weighty reasons for still holding to his early conviction.—M. Blochet furnishes a short note on the form of the future tense in Pehlevi; M. J. Perruchon continues his 'Notes pour l'histoire d'Éthiope;' M. Halévy gives a revised and corrected version of the first inscription of Bar-Rekoub, and some short notes on other matters: and finally reviews several recent books on subjects kindred to those to which this *Revue* is consecrated.

REVUE DU MONDE LATIN (March, 1896).—'The Monk in the XIth and XIIth Centuries, a Study in Social Psychology,' by A. Baure.—'Letter from Roumania.'—'Phosphates of Lime,' by E. Plauchud.—'Letter from Portugal,' by E. Castilho—'Promenades Fructuenses,' a slight sketch by Madame Fertiault.—'Voiles en Vue,' and translations of Horace's odes to Virgil and Lydia, by M. Durand-Gonzague.—Chronique Théatrale by the Editor.

SPAIN.

LA ESPANA MODERNA (April, 1896.)—Juan Valera criticises a work on the Jesuits, recently issued anonymously, and dealing with their claims to superior humility and actual pride. The writer claims to review the position of the Jesuits with knowledge, as he does with acumen, and seeks to show that the anonymous author does them injustice. He acknowledges at the same time, that the Jesuits of the present day display a limitation and narrowness of aim opposed to their original aspirations. 'They forget that the letter kills and the spirit vivifies, and forget what the spirit of truth will do to glorify all truth before the eyes of those who follow it.' A criticism of the 'Sample Tales of Cervantes,' Las Novelas Ejemplares, notes that the author claims them to be the first to appear in Spanish; to which the Marquis of Casa-Torre adds 'even in any language.'—Echegaray continues his Reminiscences, and these are followed by 'The Adventures and Misadventures of an old Soldier,' which continue to give a curious insight into the ordinary life of the country during the century. The anecdotes are not always such as could be printed in an English periodical! The tradition that literature is for male creatures has not yet been dissipated in Spain.—'The Salons of the Countess of Montijo' continue to afford interest and amusement to the historian and society reader.—A. de Valbuenna tells a curious tale of the condition of Spanish official maps, which may help to explain the state of ignorance of Cuban geography amongst the military.—'The Literary Chronicle' deals with Scandinavian literature, and the orthographic reform in Chili. The writer appeals against the *democratisation* of the spelling, by the elimination of what is historic and erudite. 'The International Chronicle' explains clearly and well the situation in Egypt, and shows how the French blundered in retiring from the dual control there.' 'The International Press' handles Tolstoi's Parables ; Wolf's Spanish and Portuguese Literature is continued, and Book Notices are full.—(May, 1896)—'The Salons of the Countess of Montijo' ends in this number, with the notice of the private theatricals that inaugurated the proclamation of Alfonso XII. as King of Spain.—'The Adventures of an old Soldier' show how utterly ignorant the common soldiers were of the cause they died for, or why or for whom they fought. 'The people who rob and kill are not the people but the *mob*,' or the *roughs* as we might say, is given in a popular distich. The old soldier sums up with the assurance that 'everything political is evil,' and in better managed lands than in Spain this is becoming an accepted axiom. It is clear also from his account that Spain does not treat her veterans any better say—than England ! 'Reminiscences,' the chatty recollections of Echegaray, continue. 'Recollections of Bequer,' by Miguel S. Oliver, is written with appreciative sympathy. Emilio Pardo Bazan completes her smart novel of 'Adam and Eve,' the memoirs of a Highlander.—'The International Press' translates a clever article from the French *Review of Reviews*, on the Russian Nobles, showing how they have nothing in common with Western aristocracy at any period of the growth of the latter. In commenting on an article in 'Social Science' of Barcelona, on 'The Intellectual Youth of Spain,' by Sr. Unamuno, a frank admission is made—'One may say that intellectual progress follows the wealth and power of nations. Our culture corresponds, in this respect, to our present historic situation '; and he acknowledges that after a century of struggle, internal and otherwise, Spain is exhausted and asleep. A valuable paper on an interesting subject, Bibliography and 'Castilian and Portuguese Literature,' close a good number.—(June, 1896)—'The Sociological novel,' of which *Looking Backward* is a type, is the theme of a good paper by A. Builla y Alegre.—'The Adventures of an old Soldier' continues full of short anecdotes, mainly of the civil wars in Spain. In this connection he justly remarks, that especially in civil wars should it be the case that the combatants fight to conquer and not to slay. —The 'New Biography of the Abbe Manchena,' by Menendez y Pelayo, is a small edition for scholars.   For the reviewer explains, that this notable propagandist of the irreligious philosophy of the 18th century, and foremost revolutionist of that age in Spain, finds no intellectual sympathy, but the reverse, in him, his biographer.   His life was full of interest and activity, and it is well for it to be within the reach of students of history and human progress.—'The Evolution of Political Parties in Spain,' is a critical study of the growth of the present political divisions in that country, by Rafael Salillas.—'The International Chronicle' treats of the dangers in Europe and Asia, and sees great cause for anxiety in the conduct and position of Prince Ferdinand of Bulgaria.—'The Spanish Criminal' is a study, philological, psychological, and sociological, by Sr. Salillas.—A clever work from Richter commences in the 'International Press,' entitled 'After the Victory of Socialism—The Feast of Victory.' It commences: 'The red flag, symbol of international democracy, flutters in the royal palace and in all the public buildings of Berlin,' etc., etc.   'Castillian and Portuguese Literature,' Bibliography, and new works published, make up a full and useful number.

HOLLAND.

DE GIDS (May.)—This number begins with a story by Cyriel Buysse, 'Mr. Ongena's Vexation,' a story which is a clever delineation of lower middle class life but the *denouement*—the finding of a tape worm inside one of the characters is inexpressibly disgusting.—'A theory of Smell,' by Dr. H. Zwaardemaker, is a scientific article of much interest, and seems to open the way to a more succinct and simpler explication of the difficult and delicate problems which this sense proposes to investigators.—Professor Kalff concludes his article begun in April on 'Vondel's Life,' an extremely interesting paper, as Vondel shared fully in the rich and varied life of his time, religious, political and scientific, always keeping a high ideal before him.—'Adventures of a Dutch ship on the return voyage from the East in 1665,' gives a vivid picture of sea-life of old days and of encounters with English ships of war.—'The Origin of the name of the Island Celebes,' is a curious account of how a name arose from a concatenation of errors unequalled in the history of geography.—Dr. van Bemmelen contributes 'A Visit to the Natural History Museum, London.' Comparing the arrangements there with those in similar museums in Holland, he remarks that anyone wishing to see a different state of matters and things as they should be ought to visit the London Museum.—A. L. W. Seyffardt reviews at great length (June, July,) the views of De Roo van Alder-werldt on the actual war strength of Holland, and how to make the best of it. Though that great authority is now somewhat antiquated there is still much to be learned from him, especially in regard to the training of militia and on the subject of compulsory service.—Van Deventer (June, July,) gives an exhaustive study of Balzac and his works.—Mr. W. H. de Beaufort continues his 'Thirty Years of our History, 1863–1893,' a valuable but not very interesting chronicle of party strifes and the effects on Holland of more widely-felt events of that period.—'Ape or Man,' is a discussion of Dubois' find in Java of the bones of Pithecanthropus erectus, supposed to be the missing link. This is extremely doubtful seeing that bones of so many other animals were found in the same spot, but it is possible the skeleton in question may be correctly arranged and may even be that of a progenitor of man, but it settles nothing.—An obituary article by Professor van Hamel is devoted to Allard Pierson, the well known theologian and a frequent contributor to the *Gids*, who died in May of this year. He was specially devoted to the subject of ethics and in the end gave up the orthodox theology for a sort of agnosticism, but he preserved still as his ideal the love of all that is noble and pure and believed in love as the solution of all ethical problems.—'The Father,' by George Sylvius, is a story of Scotch West Highland life, only entertaining as a Dutch view of what is possible in Scotland.—'Clericalism in the Italian State,' by C. E. de Vries Robbé, who writes from Rome, is a brightly written paper in which the growing influence of clericalism in school and social life, and generally everywhere in Italy, is noted, and the causes of the successes of the clerical party are pointed out.

DENMARK.

YEAR-BOOK FOR NORTHERN ARCHÆOLOGY AND HISTORY (Vol. X., Part 4, 1895). A valuable contribution to the study of the oldest Scandinavian poetry is made by Dr. Finnur Jónsson in an article on 'The Oldest Skalds and their Poems.' This is an answer to Prof. Bugge's recent attempt to discredit the antiquity of the poems ascribed to Bragi and Thiódólf, the date commonly assigned to these being too early to suit his theories on Scandinavian mythology. It is a case of 'so much the worse for the theories,' Dr. Finnur evidently thinks. He brings out in the clearest fashion the striking want of actual proof in Prof. Bugge's arguments, which is, to a great extent, disguised by the professor's eloquence and wealth of illustration. By a searching analysis of the poems themselves he shows that whether historically, philologically, or metrically, there is nothing whatever in them to cast any doubt on the traditional accounts of their authors and dates. Bugge and Zimmer, from different points, have tried to establish an early literary connection between the Celts of Ireland and the Scandinavian peoples; Dr. Finnur is convinced that so far as there is foreign matter in Old Norse literature it has come from the south rather than from the west. Bugge's theories have been taken so seriously by many scholars that this criticism of them is of the greatest value for students of northern literature.—Chr. Blinkenberg contributes a notice of an Etruscan bronze vase with a wheeled stand, found in a mound near Skallerup in the south of Sjælland : it had been used as a funeral urn. The whole find belongs to the early bronze period, c. 800 B.C. The vase is the first of the kind found in Denmark, though two others have been got in South Sweden and North Germany. In the south of Europe specimens are not uncommon, and they probably reached the north in the way of trade, even at that early day.—(Vol. XI., Part 1.) The same writer gives an account of Pre-Mycenean antiquities, illustrated by the specimens in the possession of the National Museum at Copenhagen. He enters at some length into the general bearings of the question, and dissents in various points from the views of other archæologists as to the age and significance of the finds. The most interesting section is perhaps that which deals with toilet articles, and the practices of tattooing and shaving. He is not inclined to accept the theory that the finds belong to a Carian population, and points out that it rests on a very slender foundation. A topographical list of the finds shows their distribution throughout the Greek islands.—Prof. Petersen details the results of excavations begun on the site of Vitsköl church in Jutland. This was founded as a Cistercian erection in 1158 by Valdemar I., in gratitude for his escape from, and victory over, his enemies. It was once famous as 'the finest church in the North;' now it is covered with earth and vegetation. From the excavations it may be inferred that its reputation was due to its brick-work and the width of its nave and transepts, but the building is of much later date than the twelfth century.

GREECE.

ATHENA (Vol. VIII., pt. 2, 1896).—G. N. Hatzidaki deals with a variety of subjects in his 'Koskylmatia,' the formation of Greek proper names, the Athenian pronunciation of ypsilon, modern verbs in-ôno, hybrid words, two Cretan inscriptions,

and his paper on the Macedonians in the previous number.—
The fourth part of his paper on 'The Language Question' is
occupied with a translation of the section on 'Common Dia-
lect' in Hermann Paul's 'General Principles of Linguistic.'—
M. I. Pantazês, 'The Spuriousness of Plato's Laws'—J. N.
Hatzidaki on 'Divergent Integrals.'

SWITZERLAND.

THEOLOGISCHE ZEITSCHRIFT AUS DER SCHWEIZ (First quarterly part, 1896).—Pfarrer Nabholz discusses the means of
promoting the Church's welfare, especially in Zürich associations.—'Johann Peter Romang as a Religious Philosopher,' by
Professor Bloesch of Bern.—'The Influence of Syrian Literature on the West,' by V. Ryssell, gives a short but very full
account of the advance made in our knowledge of Syrian
writings. The latter part of the paper deals with the Seven
Sleepers, the Finding of the Cross, and the Sylvester Legend,
which, according to recent investigations, are Syrian in their
origin. Examination of the various versions current in mediæval European literature proves that these Syrian versions must
have been widely known. A curious piece of evidence occurs
so far west as Ireland. In the Leabhar Breac's account of the
finding of the cross, Satan, in anger at the discovery, is made to
say, 'I will find a plan against you,' which is meaningless, but
on turning to the Syrian text we find that what he really said
was, 'I will raise up a king against you,' viz., Julian the
Apostate, and the inference is that the Irish writer mistook
'malka' king, for 'melka' plan. He must have been
acquainted with the original, as this error is found in no other
extant version.

AMÉRICA.

THE AMERICAN HISTORICAL REVIEW (April, 1896).—The
contents of this number are varied and attractive. The first
place is given to an article by Mr. C. F. Adams on the Battle
of Bunker Hill, who maintains that the battle was won by
the Americans not in consequence of any great skill or capacity on the part of their leaders but in consequence of the
superior capacity for blundering on the part of the British
commanders.—In 'The Bohun Wills' Mr. M. M. Bigelow
examines several of the wills of the Bohuns, Earls of Here-
ford, for the purpose of ascertaining how people lived and
fared in their day. The study may be commended for its
minute details and for the vivid way in which it sets the life
of periods dealt with before us.—Another extremely interesting paper, which bears the signature of Wilbur H. Siebert,

has for its title 'Light on the Underground Railroad.' It is accompanied by a map showing a multitude of roads by which the slaves fled and the houses in which they were sheltered.— Mr. Justin Winsor contributes 'Virginia and the Quebec Bill,' and Mr. W. P. Trent 'The Case of Josiah Philips.'—Mr. J. F. Rhodes writes on 'The First Six Weeks of M'Clellan's Peninsula Campaign,' treating the campaign as 'a chapter of blunders,' and as showing how 'decisive events fail of accomplishment for the lack of a great general.'—Mr. H. Morse Stephens contributes an article on 'Recent Memoirs of the French Directory.'—Hitherto unpublished documents are represented by 'A Memorial of Lord Burghley on Peace with Spain, 1588,' and a continuation of Richard Smith's 'Diary.'—Among the Books reviewed are Mr. Rashdall's *Universities of the Middle Ages*, Lord Aston's *Lecture on the Study of History*, and Grosvenor's *Constantinople*.

CONTEMPORARY LITERATURE.

History of Christian Doctrine. By GEORGE PARK FISHER, D.D., LL.D. Professor of Ecclesiastical History in Yale University (International Theological Library). Edinburgh, T. & T. Clark. 1896.

In this closely printed volume Dr. Fisher has managed to give a very fair account of the history of Christian Theological opinions. The history of Christian dogmatics is, of course, treated, but the comparatively narrow limits of Christian dogma are overpassed, and the theological opinions of a great number of writers, more especially of recent times, are discussed. The work, though not without its merits, is not altogether such an one as might be desired, either as to arrangement or style. The style, while usually clear, is here and there a little tautological, and not always sufficiently explicit, as in the introductory chapter. In a work like this the free use of the paragraph with head lines in a type different from that of the text cannot be too strongly commended. Dr. Fisher divides his history into three parts, viz., Ancient Theology, Mediæval Theology, and Modern Theology, the first bringing the history down to A.D. 600 ; the second to the time of Luther ; and the third ending with the Agnosticism of Mr. Huxley. These, so far as they go, are good ; but the subject is susceptible of sub-divisions. Dr. Fisher attempts something of that kind by the arrangement of his chapters ; but the contents of these are determined in a number of instances not so much by the development of any specific doctrine as by the history or locality of the writer or writers. What one desires to see in a work of this kind is a clear statement of the stages through which a doctrine or dogma has passed, and the attempts which have been made to modify or counteract its development during a definite period in its history. The later chapters in the volume assume the shape of sketches of recent religious opinion in different countries. Dr. Fisher's citations are numerous, as are also his references, but it is a question whether his volume would not have been more useful to the student if the exact words of the authors had been given, even at the expense of cutting down the text. Of course they may, for the most part, be found in German Handbooks and Histories of Dogmatics, but to those for whom this International Theological Library has been projected these are not always accessible. One misses the elaborate introduction which a German author would have written for such a volume, defining his subject, terms, sources, etc., etc. Dr. Fisher's introductory chapter, which runs to over twenty pages, and stands for it, seems to us less satisfactory than other parts of his volume. However, in dealing with the question : Is theology possible ? he says some very useful and true things against the Agnostic position. On the other hand, he is not so successful in dealing with Clement's doctrine of the relation between faith and knowledge. It is doubtful, too, whether he has caught the meaning of the Apostle when he says : ' But faith, we are taught by the Apostle, merges at last, not in science, but in sight.' Science, we should say, is knowledge, and ' sight ' can scarcely imply more. Nor does the sentence refute, as it is intended, Clement's position that knowledge is more than faith. The remark ' Faith " abides " until beyond the veil it is resolved into vision,' is scarcely a sufficient exegesis of the words, 'Now abideth faith;' nor does it tell against Clement any more than Dr. Fisher's arguments tell against the position of St. Thomas Aquinas 'that as fast as science advances faith is displaced.' With a somewhat strange inconsistency Dr. Fisher says, 'Faith, to be sure, includes a perception of truth;' and, again, he defines faith as 'a practical experience.' There is a sense, of course, in which these statements are true, but in writings of this kind more precision is expected. When we come to the body of the work, and to the statement of the opinions he has to cite and discuss, Dr. Fisher, in the chapters we have taken to test his work, is always fair and impartial. When dealing with the opinions of St. Augustine, as for instance, as to faith, he is a little perplexed, as writing from his strictly orthodox Presbyterian point of view he might almost be expected to be. The chronology of the concluding chapters is somewhat mixed, and the presentation of opinions, as, for instance, those of F. D. Maurice, is somewhat sketchy. There is no attempt to show, or rather to sum up, the gains of theological thought during the long course of its history; nor is there to show the influence which science has had upon it, or the way in which its contents have been enriched by scientific discoveries. Assuming with Dr. Fisher that 'phenomena are revelations of reality,' and with Spencer that there is an 'Ultimate Reality which all things are continually making manifest,' a doctrine, we suspect, which Dr. Fisher does not deny, one would have thought that in a book on the History of Christian Doctrine, and abounding so much in *obiter dicta* as Dr. Fisher's does, a chapter on this subject would have found a place. Still, though scarcely reaching up to the high standard set by Dr. Driver's work for the series, Dr. Fisher's volume fills a place hitherto vacant in English theological literature, and will doubtless prove acceptable to that large class of readers for whom it has been specially prepared.

The Apostolic Gospel with a Critical Reconstruction of the Text. By J. FULTON BLAIR, B.D. London: Smith, Elder & Co. 1896.

This volume divides itself into three parts, viz., an Introduction, a translation of what the author conceives to have been the text of the Apostolic Gospel, and lastly, an elaborate commentary, consisting for the most part of proofs and arguments in support of the reconstructed text. It will thus be seen that the volume is one of considerable importance, and that it is devoted to the solution of one of the most controverted theological problems of the day. Mr. Blair is not in entire agreement with the foremost critics in Germany. He is in agreement with Weiss and Wendt as to the existence of an Apostolic Gospel, but at variance with them as to its contents and the way in which it has been used in the compilation or construction of the first and third Gospels and as to its relations to the fourth Gospel, as also on other points. Like them he accepts the second Gospel as forming the framework of the first and third, and admits that if we had no more than the second and third Gospels any reconstruction of the text of the Apostolic source would be impossible, and the question he seeks to answer is, 'Can we with the help of the parallel incidents and logia in Matthew and in the fourth Gospel, or from a comparison of the data given in the whole of the Gospels, construct the text of the Apostolic source?' His argument is not without considerable ingenuity. First of all he calls in the aid of the scientific imagination and asks: If Luke had in his hands besides Mark's Gospel, a Gospel of high authority which he wished to combine with Mark's; if this Gospel consisted not merely of logia with a few selected events, but of all the facts which were known to the writer from the beginning of the ministry to the Cross ; if these facts were narrated in their chronological order, and in many cases were parallel to Mark's facts ; and finally, if for reasons which are capable of definition, this Gospel had been largely superseded by Mark, which was richer in incidents but contained much less of the teaching, so that Mark had become the standard of history before the third Gospel was written, what would be the probable characteristics of the combination thus proposed and effected ?   Mr. Blair's answer is—' It is quite conceivable, on the one hand, that the editor, with such documents before him, would supplement Mark's narratives *seriatim* by material derived from the other authority, and would gather into long discourses the teaching which permitted such treatment. Or, on the other hand, he might. while not altogether neglecting this method, insert in Mark's framework, at appropriate places, accumulations of loose material derived from the other source ; and in such a case the following phenomena might be confidently predicted. First, the incidents taken from Mark, and already recorded in the history, would not be repeated by the editor, although contained in the other source, if such incidents were recognised as identical. Secondly, a few incidents in their different versions would not be recognised as clearly identical, and therefore duplication would arise. Thirdly, Mark being accepted and followed as the standard, the original arrangement of the other source would be entirely upset by combination ; the bones would be removed from the body, and thus a new editorial arrangement, especially of the teaching, would be permitted, and indeed would be inevitable.' Assuming the existence of the ' Apostolic Source ' all this is of course quite conceivable. It is quite as conceivable also that an editor may have adopted another course. So too is it that the editors of the first and third Gospels may have used what were practically independent sources in order to fill out the framework supplied by the second Gospel. At the same time it cannot be denied that on the assumption of the existence of the Apostolic source, what Mr. Blair here says furnishes what may at least be called a working hypothesis, and is borne out by the contents and differences of the Gospels Matthew and Luke. For, as he points out, the characteristics of the combination, in the case of the first Gospel, agree precisely with the first of the imagined alternatives, while the method adopted in the third Gospel, on the other hand, is in agreement with the second, even to the extent of exhibiting the phenomena which might be expected in the case supposed. This fact, which has hitherto been overlooked by critics, is of supreme importance for Mr. Blair's theory. Accordingly in the passages occurring in the third Gospel and not occurring in the second, and in those occurring in the first Gospel and not in the second and third he finds traces of the Apostolic source ; but not all the Gospels contain. ' We possess additional data,' he says, ' which enable us to advance to much larger results.' Some of these additional data are in the passages where the first and third evangelists differ both from St. Mark and from each other ; others are supplied by textual evidence and a comparison of Luke's digressions with Mark, a process which brings to light the fact that Luke's omissions are much more numerous than they are usually supposed to be. So far Mr. Blair has dealt with the evangelical narrative from the Sermon on the Mount to the discourse on the Coming of the Kingdom, and he now proceeds to argue backwards and forwards, maintaining that the narrative preceding the Sermon on the Mount presupposes an earlier history, and that the discourse on the Coming of the Kingdom in like manner presupposes a subsequent history bringing the narrative down to the Passion. He is prepared to go further and to maintain that the critic who proceeds to the work of reconstruction and is faithful to the data observed cannot stop short until ' he stands beside the empty tomb with a clear conception of the ministry, a new comprehension of the teaching, and a firm appreciation of that great personality which has gained the homage of men.' Want of space prevents us from dwelling upon any of the many points which Mr. Blair's argument raises, as well as from entering more minutely into it. What we have said, however, is sufficient to show the line of argument he follows, and to exhibit his theory. The further and larger question which his hypothesis raises Mr. Blair does not argue. As might be expected he is prepared to join issue with those who uphold the generally received opinion as to the origin of the synoptic Gospels, and the relation in which their sources stand to each other, and to the fourth Gospel. 'He does not believe,' he says, 'that the two sources are really independent. On the contrary, he is prepared to prove—by arguing, of course, from probabilities—that the second Gospel is not a recollection of the preaching of St. Peter. He believes that the Apostolic source, which existed at first as an oral tradition, was committed to writing, at different places by different men, to meet the requirements of the Christian society, and that Mark is a combination of the versions. He is also prepared to prove that the fourth Gospel is a primitive commentary, or in other words an elaborated version of the Apostolic source, with the incidents adapted to the evangelist's purpose, and the logia partly reproduced and partly displaced by reflections which the original suggested. He does not accept the common assumption that the synoptic problem is altogether distinct from the Johannine. He maintains that the two coalesce, and that in solving the one the critic will solve also the other. He believes, in short, that the four Gospels are simultaneous equations, that the unknown quantity is the Apostolic source, and that the value of x can be discovered.' This belief has certainly the merit of simplicity. It has that also of reasonableness. Whether it can be vindicated is a question on which we cannot enter. We can only commend Mr. Blair's scholarly volume to the careful attention of students, and leave them to form their own opinion as to the theory it so ably maintains.

A Synopsis of the Gospels in Greek after the Westcott and Hort Text. By the Rev. ARTHUR WRIGHT, M.A. London and New York: Macmillan & Co. 1896.

This scholarly piece of work on the part of one of the members of the new School of Cambridge theologians will attract attention both on account of its comparative novelty, and because of the skill and thoroughness with which it has been done. It is an attempt to analysis the Gospels, and to exhibit their primitive sources. Mr. Wright has brought much painstaking labour to his task, and whether his results be wholly accepted or not, what he has done will considerably facilitate the work of the student in arriving at something like definite conceptions as to the sources whence the Gospels were derived, and the way in which they have been brought into their present shape. The truth of the oral hypothesis is assumed, and in a carefully written preface Mr. Wright exhibits the principles by which he has been governed in the construction of his synopsis. Accepting the theory, the truth of which is now generally but not everywhere admitted, that there were at least two main sources from which the materials for the synoptic Gospels were obtained, and that these sources correspond to what Papias calls ' St. Peter's Memoirs of Our Lord,' and the ' Logia,' or ' Utterances of St. Matthew,' and that the former consisted chiefly of narrative, and the latter of discourses or isolated apophthegms, Mr. Wright inclines to the opinion of those who hold that on the whole the second Gospel corresponds to St. Peter's Memoirs, and that the author of the said Gospel was unacquainted with the Logia. That this and not the Logia is the oldest source is shown, he argues, by its wide diffusion, its contents, and its frequent mixture with the other sources. Hence in his first Division he places the Gospel of St. Mark, and side by side with it the identical or equivalent passages from SS. Matthew and Luke, together with the parallels from St. John and other sacred writers. In his second Division he places thirty-six discourses from St. Matthew's Gospel with the identical or equivalent passages from St. Luke, and parallels from St. Mark and other sacred writers. The third Division contains nineteen discourses, parables, and stories from St. Luke, chiefly in the central third, ix. 51—xviii. 14, five of which find parallels in the first and second Gospels, two in the first only, and one in the fourth. In the fourth Division, we have no fewer than a hundred and thirty-four fragments, some of which are common to SS. Matthew and Luke, others of which are peculiar to the first Gospel, and others to the third ; but none of which are to be found in the second Gospel. The fifth Division contains a group of sixteen historical narratives peculiar to St. Luke. In the sixth Division we have a number of Editorial notes contributed by the writers themselves, and not by their authorities. The analysis is made still more exhaustive by the use in many places of brackets and different kinds of type. To appraise a work of this kind, or to enter into anything like an examination of it in the space here assigned to us, is of course impossible. We must content ourselves with but one or two remarks. That an oral Gospel or Gospels preceded the written Gospels must be assumed. But whether there were originally but two written Gospels from which the present Synoptic Gospels were derived is an open question. If Mr. Wright's Analysis be correct, there were more ; at any rate the solution of the problem is made much more difficult. By Mr. Wright the *Logia* is reduced to a minimum. It is quite possible that many of the fragments included in his fourth Division are derived from this source. Any how, it will be exceedingly difficult to prove that they were not. That no principle of selection was adopted by the authors of the primitive written sources, and that any one who undertook to write a life of Christ would endeavour to put into it all that he knew, or all that was accepted in the Church to which he belonged, or all that he could collect from trustworthy witnesses, are positions which seem to us to be too confidently assumed. It is reasonable to suppose that a modern author would do something of this sort, but whether the authors of the primitive Gospels or of the Synoptics did this is another and different question. Altogether, while we cannot but admire the skill and scholarship, and patient industry which Mr. Wright has brought to bear upon the problem he has sought to solve, it seems to us that its final solution is not yet in sight. Perhaps it never will be so long as our knowledge of the written sources remains what it is. All the same, such work as Mr. Wright has here done can not fail to incite to a more detailed study of the evangelical narratives, and to prove of great assistance to the student.

The Bible for Home Reading. Edited with Comments and Reflections for the use of Jewish Parents and Children by C. G. MONTEFIORE. First Part. London and New York: Macmillan & Co. 1896.

This volume of Bible readings, the first of two, has been compiled, as the title-page bears, for the use of Jewish parents and children. The period covered by the readings is from Abraham to the second visit of

Nehemiah to Jerusalem. The first eleven chapters of the book of Genesis are represented by a series of extracts given at the end of the volume, in which are the stories of Creation, Paradise, etc. The chapters from which these extracts are taken, are, in the opinion of the author, 'too full of grave moral and religious difficulties to form a suitable beginning.' The text used in the extracts is virtually that of the Authorised Version, though here and there Mr. Montefiore has adopted readings which seem to him to be better. Besides selecting the passages and editing them, Mr. Montefiore has contributed to each of them an introduction with comments, sometimes explanatory, sometimes historical, and sometimes of a homiletic nature, which are all remarkable for the frankness and freeness of their criticism, as well as for the spirit of devout appreciation of the Scriptures by which they are pervaded. More remarkable than the notes, however, is the general introduction to the volume. Here Mr. Montefiore treats of the origin and character of the Bible, and touches upon many points of the greatest interest. His critical standpoint is that almost of the most advanced school of Biblical criticism ; but though one may not be always able to agree with him in his critical opinions, when he comes to speak of the moral teaching of the Old Testament one's sympathies go entirely wth him. He emphasises the fact that it exhibits different stages of morality among men ; but his main point is its intrinsic value and wherein this value consists. ' The Bible,' he says, ' tells us about God and Goodness ; this is what gives it its unity. This is what gives it its unique value. No other book has told men so well and so truly of goodness and God as the Bible. All that it says about God, and all that it says about goodness, is not indeed of equal value, of equal truth ; there are degrees of excellence and of worth. But, taken as a whole, no book has spoken and still speaks of God and goodness as this book, the Bible. And this is what has made the Bible precious and beloved through so many ages, and to so many different peoples. For God and goodness never grow old. Men and women always want to know about them, and in this respect one age is the same as another.' In this passage we have the key to most of his comments, and an indication of the spirit in which the volume has been compiled. Mr. Montefiore's aim is edification, and his volume may be read with profit by the old as well as the young, whether Jews or Christians. A second volume is promised to complete the work.

Documents Illustrative of English Church History. Compiled from Original Sources by HENRY GEE, B.D., F.S.A., and WILLIAM JOHN HARDY, F.S.A. London and New York : Macmillan & Co. 1896.

This volume will serve a very useful purpose, and help to lighten the labours of the student of English Church History. All the documents illustrative of English Church History it does not contain, nor does it profess to contain them ; but in its pages will be found many of the more important, and especially those to which reference is most frequently made. Sixteenth and seventeenth century documents are fairly well represented, but for a number, as for instance some of those belonging to the reigns of Elizabeth and James I., the student will require to consult other collections, such as the volume prepared for the Clarendon Press by Professor Prothero. The selection from pre-Norman documents is admittedly meagre. Originally it was not intended that the collection should contain any, but, acting on the suggestion of Dr. Bright, twelve of the more important, beginning with the British signatories at the Council of Arles, 314, and ending with selections from the Constitutions of Odd, 943, are given. Still, taken as a whole, and remembering the limitations of space with which the Editors have had to contend, the selection has been made with tact, and is thoroughly representative. The Editors' notes are always to the point. If any fault can be found with them it is that they are too brief. The Latin and Norman-French documents have been translated, and the spelling of the rest, the latest of which is dated 1700, has been modernised. The Editors, in short, have done their work so well as to encourage the hope that a new edition will be called for, and that they will then avail themselves of the opportunity of making their collection more complete by including the more important of those they have been obliged to omit, making use if necessary, as in all probability it will be, of an additional volume.

The Union of England and Scotland: A Study of International History. By JAMES MACKINNON, Ph.D. London, New York, and Bombay: Longmans, Green, & Co. 1896.

An impartial narrative of the events which led up to the union between England and Scotland, of the various stages through which the negotiations passed, and of the terms on which the union was finally agreed to, has for some time been wanting. Recent publications of official and hitherto inaccessible documents have made the task comparatively easy, and it is perhaps fortunate that at a time when the subject has been pushed forward into public controversy that it has been taken in hand by one who has proved himself so competent to deal with it as Dr. Mackinnon. At any rate he has not only made himself thoroughly conversant with all the published sources of information connected with his subject; here and there his pages bear evidence of independent research and of the use of papers and documents which have not seen the light in print. And what is of more importance he has threaded his way with a firm hand through the tangled web of negotiations he has had to contend with, and written his narrative in a spirit of judicial impartiality which is to say the least commendable. At the time both public and private feeling ran high. Each party was jealous of the other, many were opposed to the union, obstacles were thrown in the way of the negotiations, and many things were done to provoke ill-feeling, but all through Dr. Mackinnon is eminently fair and never allows himself to be led astray by the storm of feeling in which he has to work. Over the earliest attempts at union between the two countries he passes lightly, pointing out that they were of two kinds, attempts by force and attempts through marriage. Henry VIII.'s scheme of a matrimonial and political alliance, which he had arranged with Arran, was wrecked, he shows, by the opposition of Cardinal Beaton and his conservative following. The scheme devised by Somerset after the battle of Pinkie, he speaks of as ' his memorable offer of a liberal treaty of union.' Scotland, however, he adds, was not prepared for amalgamation of interests and policy, but preferred the old French alliance, a preference which in the end may be said to have hastened on the union which subsequently took place. Among attempts at union of a forceful kind those of James VI. and Cromwell are rightly placed. Cromwell's scheme simply meant the complete absorption of Scotland by England and the suppression of every national institution. The only generous thing about it was the offer of free trade ; but this, on the other hand, while, as Dr. Mackinnon observes, it ' served to open the eyes of the Scots to the material advantages connected with a closer union with a more powerful and wealthy neighbour,' awakened the spirit of opposition to the union in England,

and at the same time contributed to increase the dissatisfaction already felt there against his arbitrary rule. In dealing with the events which led up to the treaty of union Dr. Mackinnon dwells at considerable length on Paterson and the Darien Scheme, and the influence which the failure of that ill-fated scheme had in embittering the two nations against each other. Simon Fraser and his intrigues also come in for a large share of attention. The chapter devoted to him is probably the most interesting piece of reading in the volume. Those which deal with the negotiations between the Commissioners are of course of more importance, but they are unintelligible without it. Fletcher and the Patriotic party are spoken of with approval, and Dr. Mackinnon has done wisely to quote liberally from Saltoun's speeches and essays. The state of feeling in Scotland immediately after the inauguration of the union is dwelt on at length, and attention is called to the fact, which has hitherto been seldom noticed, that all through the long war of the Spanish Succession the affairs of Scotland formed an important factor in the calculations of French statesmen. That the state of public feeling in Scotland had much to do with the continuance of that great struggle seems to be certain. 'The hope of dealing a blow at the power of the allies by means of a rebellion in Scotland was,' as Dr. Mackinnon says, 'never absent from the mind of Louis and his ministers.' In his concluding chapters Dr. Mackinnon speaks of the attitude of Parliament towards Scotland after the union, of the unconstitutional character of the legislation of the period, and of the risings in 1715 and 1745, and of the industrial and social progress of the country during the eighteenth century. Dr. Mackinnon is not of opinion that the union has been an unalloyed blessing. There have been and still are he thinks serious drawbacks to it, to some of which he refers in his concluding chapter, a chapter, however, which is more political than historical.

The History of Civilisation in Scotland. By JOHN MACKINTOSH, LL.D. New edition. Vol. IV. Paisley and London, Alex. Gardner. 1896.

With this volume Dr. Mackintosh finishes the new and revised edition of his principal work. As we have before remarked, when noticing the earlier volumes, this edition is in every way a great improvement on the first. The emendations are such as almost to make it a new work. The present volume opens with an account of the state of philosophy in Scotland at the end of the last century, and continues it down to the death of the late Professor Croome Robertson. The five chapters which follow are devoted to the history of literature in Scotland from Allan Ramsay down almost to the present day. These are followed by chapters on the history of science, medicine, and education. Then we have chapters on agriculture, manufactures, shipbuilding, as well as on architecture, music, and painting, and, lastly, a couple of chapters dealing with the social, political, and religious movements from the year 1832 almost to the present. It is hardly necessary to say that, like the previous volumes of this work, the one now before us is a mine of information on a great variety of topics, and traces the development of the civilisation of the country with a sure hand during the period with which it deals. An elaborate index to the four volumes fittingly concludes the work.

A History of Fife and Kinross. By Æ. J. G. MACKAY, Sheriff of these Counties (The County Histories of Scotland). Edinburgh and London: William Blackwood & Sons. 1896.

The learned Sheriff of Fife and Kinross has made no attempt, as he tells us, to write an exhaustive and complete history of these counties ; his endeavour has been 'to catch the spirit rather than to follow the letter of the history.' His work, therefore, is cast on lines quite different from those on which Mr. A. H. Millar wrote the two volumes of his *History of Fife* which was noticed in these pages some time ago. But though not exactly a history in the usual meaning of that term, Mr. Mackay's volume contains a delightful account of the most important matters connected with what was formerly known, and indeed is still known, as the kingdom of Fife. In the preparation of it he has made large use of the 'Sketch' of the history of the two counties which he published in 1890. The present volume may be said in fact to be a second and enlarged edition of the 'Sketch.' No one, however, will be disposed to quarrel with it on that score. The additions are all in the right direction and enhance the interest and value of the work. As a popular history of a county it is probably without a rival and is a model which may be followed in the rest of the series with advantage. That it contains everything one would like a history of Fife to contain cannot of course be said, but it contains sufficient to furnish a clear idea of the course which history has run in the ancient kingdom and of the relation in which it stood to the general history of the country. One omission we notice. There is no reference to the Session of Parliament held at St. Andrews, November 20th, 1645, an incident sufficiently important and singular, we should say, to be recorded in any history of Fife. Two excellent maps are given—one is a *facsimile* of Blaeu's two quaint maps on the county, and the other is a reproduction of the Ordnance Survey Map. It was a mistake, however, to print the first of these on brittle paper. Both of them would have been better on cloth and in a pocket. A very commendable feature of the work is the long list of books and publications on the county. The volume presents a handsome appearance and altogether promises exceedingly well for the series which it inaugurates.

The Life and Works of Robert Burns. Edited by ROBERT CHAMBERS, revised by WILLIAM WALLACE. 4 vols. Edinburgh and London : W. & R. Chambers. 1896.

Various attempts have been made to commemorate the centenary of the death of Robert Burns by publishing special editions of his works and biographical sketches of the poet. Editors and biographers, with diverse degrees of fitness for the task, have arisen in unsuspected quarters ; and 1896 is likely to be memorable in the publishing trade for the variety of editions of Burns that have been issued or are in progress of preparation. One might have thought that a poet who had been biographised voluminously for ninety-six years would long ere this have been exhausted as a subject ; but every year has been adding fresh material to Burnsiana, until the topic has assumed gigantic dimensions. The very embarrassment of the riches at his command might terrify the conscientious biographer from the task of writing a new life of Burns, or giving a complete edition of his poems. For Burns shares with Shakespeare and Mary, Queen of Scots, the doubtful honour of having been a favourite subject of debate amongst literary critics. Amongst the heterogeneous volumes written about Burns only two works stand out with prominence,—those, namely, which owe their origin to Dr. Currie and to Robert Chambers. Dr. Currie, who was a native of Dumfriesshire, had encountered the poet accidentally during the clouded years of his later life, and had become deeply interested by his personality. After the poet's death, Dr. Currie, with com-

mendable devotion, strove to excite compassion for the bereaved widow
and children of Burns amongst the literary circles of Liverpool, and at
length he undertook to edit an edition of the poems, with a biographical
introduction, to provide a fund for the hapless family of the poet. Though
one of the most benevolent of men, Dr. Currie was not a model biographer,
and he allowed discreditable stories to appear in this sketch, possibly with
the notion that these would increase commiseration for Mrs. Burns and
her children. He was a fluent writer, and his graceful periods were so
easily copied that for many years his biography was prefixed to numerous
editions, without alteration or question. Attempts were at length made
by J. Gibson Lockhart and Allan Cunningham to give true versions of the
life of Burns ; but these were only partially successful. It was not until
Robert Chambers took up the subject, and devoted himself to collecting
materials for his notable edition of Burns that a reasonable effort was
made to give an accurate account of the poet's life, and a critical edition
of his works from which spurious pieces were excluded. Chambers was a
book-worm with a wide knowledge of literature, a sleuth-hound in tracking
items of evidence, and an intelligent and impartial antiquary, and was
thus admirably fitted to carry the task he had undertaken to a successful
issue. There have been countless biographies since his edition was published in 1851 ; but those which did not imitate Chambers, or crib from
his pages, have been deservedly forgotten. During his investigations Dr.
Chambers unearthed much material which, for various reasons, could not
be published at the time when his edition was issued. It is likely that he
contemplated a second edition ; at all events he was too acute an antiquary
to destroy the evidence he had collected at vast personal trouble and expense. Other projects occupied the later years of his life, and his second
edition did not appear. It was a happy thought which led the members
of the publishing firm which he had founded to bring out, in this present
memorable year, an edition which should not only include what had
formerly been excluded, but also contain the results of inquiries made
by other investigators since Chambers's time. And it was also a fortunate circumstance that the firm was able to secure so competent an
editor as William Wallace to carry out this new edition. Since 1851 a
new literature of Burns, of the most scrappy and incoherent character, has
accumulated ; and the new editor who seeks to be abreast of the times
must be able to select from this miscellaneous heap, whatsoever is of good
report. Judging from the two volumes which have already been issued,
Mr. Wallace has succeeded in his onerous task beyond expectation. Recent
discoveries have made it necessary for him to re-write great portions of
the original work, and though he has carefully followed the lines laid
down by Dr. Chambers, Mr. Wallace has practically produced a new
edition of the life and works of Burns which will certainly hold its own
against all rivals for many a day to come. In bringing out a new edition
of such a work the editor may either give fresh matter in footnotes (always
a disturbing method for the reader), or he may incorporate additional
material with the text, thus making the book continuous. The latter
course has been wisely adopted by Mr. Wallace, though the result is that
only those acquainted familiarly with the original will be able duly to appreciate the labour of the new editor. By doing so, however, Mr. Wallace
has thoroughly effaced himself, his aim being apparently to produce a
satisfactory edition, whether he receives full credit for his own work or
not. Possibly there are few editors who would be willing in these days to
pass a 'self-denying ordinance' of this kind, and still fewer who would
carry it out so thoroughly as Mr. Wallace has done. For his additions are
not only numerous but also important. For instance, he prints the whole

of the famous autobiographical letter written by Burns to Dr. Moore, which has formed the well-spring from which all biographers have drawn their accounts of the poet's early career. Again, Mr. Wallace has examined the various contradictory versions of Burns's genealogy which are afloat, with much discrimination, and has drawn up from this puzzling maze what seems to be a credible account of the Burnes family. Another point on which Mr. Wallace has thrown much light is that of the theological attitude of Burns. It is too readily assumed that Burns was either an active scoffer at religion or an indifferent Gallio who ' cared for none of these things.' When Dr. Chambers wrote it would not have been prudent for him to have cast himself wilfully into a theological controversy, and he left the question of Burns's religious convictions rather indefinitely explained. Professor Wilson (Christopher North), when preparing the letter-press for *The Land of Burns,* was greatly exercised on this point, and wrote a letter to Mr. Aird asking if it would be possible to discover whether Burns regularly had family worship in his house ; but Aird could not find the desired information. However, Wilson was decidedly inclined to the notion that Burns was a religious man, despite his severe satires on some of the ministers of his time. Mr. Wallace very lucidly explains Burns's attitude to the formalism of his time, and points out that while he resented dogmatism, Burns was thoroughly imbued with a belief in an all-pervading Creator to whom every creature owed the deepest devotion and reverence. He was not a sceptic as Voltaire was sceptical ; his quarrel was rather with humanly-devised creeds than with religion. Much foolish nonsense has lately been ventilated regarding Highland Mary, and she has been traduced by recent writers as the equal of some of the frailer women with whom Burns's name was associated. Into this matter Mr. Wallace has made elaborate and intelligent research, and has succeeded in triumphantly vindicating Mary Campbell from the slanders of ill-advised traducers. The peculiar episode of Burns's dispute with the Armour family is placed in a clearer light than ever it has been by Mr. Wallace's lucid recital of the circumstances connected with the quarrel. While he does not excuse Burns for contemplating the desertion of Jean Armour, he shows that the attitude taken up by Jean's father was calculated to irritate a sensitive nature like that of the poet's, and to drive him to extremities which he would afterwards bitterly regret. Mr. Wallace has also brought out new matter regarding Burns's relations with Elizabeth Paton, and the evidence tends to obviate the charge of heartlessness sometimes brought against Burns with reference to this incident. The second volume carries on the story of Burns's life from November, 1786, till December, 1788, and deals with the first visit to Edinburgh, the tour through the Highlands, the Clarinda episode, and the marriage of Burns and Jean Armour. This was the most stirring period of the poet's life, and the relation of the varied incidents demands care on the part of the narrator and accurate knowledge of the characters introduced and their relations to each other. On comparing this volume with the corresponding volume of the first edition it will be seen that Mr. Wallace has almost entirely re-written the text, so numerous are his additions. He has printed the whole of the correspondence of Clarinda and Sylvander, thus making it easy to follow the development of this romantic episode. When dealing with the brilliant period of Burns's visit to Edinburgh and the production of the first Edinburgh edition of the poems, Mr. Wallace vindicates the poet from the charge of having been spoiled by his literary success. He shows that amid all the temptations to overestimate the patronage accorded to him, Burns kept a cool head, and valued the applause bestowed at its true worth. The later passages in the poet's life will occupy the third volume, and Mr. Wallace purposes giving an estimate of the poet's work in the concluding volume. The illustrations to this edition are worthy of high praise.

Life and Letters of Fenton John Anthony Hort, D.D., D.C.L., LL.D., etc. By his son, ARTHUR FENTON HORT. 2 vols. London and New York, Macmillan & Co. 1896.

As the author of this memoir remarks, the subject of it was little known outside the world of scholars. In that world, however, he was both well and widely known and highly appreciated. Outside of it his influence is likely to be much greater than his fame, though that also, we should say, is destined to grow. The New Testament is not likely to lose its hold upon men, and wherever it is read as a subject of serious study few men will be regarded with greater respect than that remarkable triumvirate of whom the present Bishop of Durham is the only survivor. Each, in his own way, has done much for its elucidation, and Dr. Hort not less than the others in theirs. A scholar's life is, as a rule, barren of incident, and Dr. Hort's was no exception. He was born in Dublin, April 23, 1828, and though of English extraction, could count among his ancestors an Irish Archbishop, who married into the Butler family, and an Irish baronet. The third son of the baronet was the father of F. J. A. Hort. On his mother's side Hort could claim to be descended from the celebrated Dean Colet. His father settled at Cheltenham when he was nine years old. He was at Rugby under Arnold, and subsequently under Tait, where he was distinguished for his scholarship rather than for athletics. From Rugby he went to Cambridge in 1846, and entered at Trinity, his father's College. Here he became a member of the mysterious company of the 'Apostles,' graduated, obtained the Hulsean Prize in 1850 for an essay on 'The Beneficial Influence of the Christian Clergy on European Progress in the first Ten Centuries,' and was one of the founders of the *Journal of Classical and Sacred Philology.* In 1854 he was ordained by Dr. Wilberforce, then Bishop of Oxford. Two years after he married, and was appointed the same year, and shortly before his marriage, to the College living of St. Ippolyts-cum-Great Wymondley, near Hitchin. Here he remained till 1872, when he returned to Cambridge as Theological Lecturer at Emmanuel's, having been defeated four years before in his candidature for the Knights-bridge Professorship of Moral Philosophy by F. D. Maurice. Six years later he was appointed Hulsean Professor of Divinity, and in October, 1887, was unanimously elected to the Lady Margaret Readership in Divinity, which had become vacant through the death of Dr. Swainson, the Master of Christ's College. This was his last piece of preferment. He died November 30, 1892. A man of more ambition with Dr. Hort's abilities might have attained to a yet more distinguished position ; but of ambition he had little. His interests were numerous and his activities many-sided, but he always preferred to remain in the back-ground. His great work, the preparation of the Greek Text of the New Testament in collaboration with Dr. Westcott, which for thirty years was always before his mind, originated in a suggestion made in 1854 by the late Mr. Daniel Macmillan that he should take a part in a New Testament scheme which was then afoot. According to this 'Hort,' we are told, 'was to edit the text in conjunction with Mr. Westcott ; the latter was to be responsible for a commentary, and Lightfoot was to contribute a New Testament Grammar and Lexicon.' Subsequently the idea was modified. The preparation of the Text was to go on as before arranged ; Lightfoot was to write the Commentary on St. Paul's Epistles, and Westcott that on the writings of

St John, while Hort was to undertake that on the Synoptic Gospels and Catholic Epistles. But for these and many other literary projects which were before Hort's mind, as well as for the reasons why so many of them fell through, we must refer the reader to the letters contained in the two volumes before us. These are wonderfully varied in their contents, and, unless we are mistaken, will pleasantly surprise those who have known Dr. Hort only through his published writings, or were not his intimate friends. Here he throws aside the hesitancy and caution which always served to hedge him in, and unbosoms his mind with a freedom quite unexpected. Mr. Arthur Fenton Hort has done his work well, and has succeeded in producing what, to say the least, is one of the most charming biographies we have met with for some time.

Memoir of John Nichol, Professor of English Literature in the University of Glasgow. By PROFESSOR KNIGHT, St. Andrews. Glasgow, James MacLehose & Sons. 1896.

The father of the late Professor of English Literature in the University of Glasgow was himself a Professor in the University of Glasgow, where he filled the chair of Astronomy with great acceptance, and was the friend and correspondent of such men as the two Mills, Herschel and Airy, Longfellow, Wordsworth, and De Quincey. No memoir of him has ever been written, much, apparently, to the regret of Professor Knight, whose first intention was to write a biography of the father as well as of the son, but who, in deference to the advice of the family, 'that it would be inexpedient to combine a sketch of both men in a volume especially devoted to the son,' has, fortunately or unfortunately, given up his original plan, and, with the exception of a couple of pages in which a brief sketch is given of the Professor of Astronomy, confined his labours to the life of the Professor of English Literature. The result is a volume of moderate size which, thanks to the publisher, is admirably printed and light in the hand. It divides itself into two parts, unequal alike in their length and quality. The first is from the pen of the late Professor of English Literature himself ; the second has been written and compiled by Professor Knight. Professor Nichol's part takes the shape of a series of autobiographical letters written to his wife shortly after their marriage, and bringing the story of his life down to the death of his mother in 1851, when he was about eighteen years of age, still resident at the Observatory in Glasgow, and a student at the University there. They were written in 1861, and though printed at the time, under the title *Leaves from My Life*, they were not written for publication. It is fortunate, however, that they have been preserved. They form by far the most attractive feature of the volume, and are remarkable for their simplicity and eloquence. The glamour of poetry is everywhere upon them, and here and there are passages of singular beauty. Here is one in which Mr. Nichol speaks of his father and mother, to the latter of whom he appears to have been devotedly attached. 'More wise than clever,' he says, 'she gave me more sage advice than I have ever seen in books, and all I have seen of life has only served to confirm its excellence. One of the best and greatest of those who have ever, in storm and sunshine, toiled through the earth, she ever seemed less than she was. My father spoke at times scornfully of the world ; but in his happier days it "came out a perfect round," and hope made it seem rich in glorious promises. She saw it just as it was, rather a cloudy land ; but her anchorage was firm beyond it. It seemed to me as if my father had power to see all the stars, but my mother alone could hear the music they made. Her speech was melodious, like silver, but her silence was like gold, and when she spoke, her noble words were clenched with noble deeds. She said to me, "Be faithful," and lived like an emblem of faith ; "Be loving," and her love was deep as the sea ; "Be true," and she was true as the eternal stars.' Referring to her death he says, 'I have had many trials since but never one which made me desolate like that, when I moved about calm and cold and shed no tears.' Very little of Professor Nichol's correspondence has been preserved. This is to be regretted, and probably accounts, in a large measure, for the somewhat scrappy character of the rest of the volume, which may be said to consist of letters from Professor Nichol's friends, estimates of his character by pupils and others, and Professor Knight's notes and comments. Much the best and most important of the letters written to Nichol are those from the late Master of Balliol. Dr. Jowett seems to have understood Nichol's failings quite as well as his merits, and touches them with a kindly, sympathetic hand. His wide knowledge of men and affairs comes out in every letter, as well as his anxiety lest Nichol should give way to disappointment, or overtax his powers. Dr. Donald Macleod contributes some reminiscences of his classmate, which are as discriminating as they are generous. Professor Knight is not exactly an ideal biographer. Here, however, he seems to have worked under difficulties. His materials were scant, and now and again one has the feeling that he is in too great a hurry. One thing he seems to have to learn yet, notwithstanding his practice in biographical writing, and that is that what nine out of every ten readers of biography desire to see is not the opinions of the biographer but the deeds and words of the individual whose life he is narrating. It is to be regretted that more of Professor Nichol's unpublished verses have not been printed. The present volume contains several of great beauty. From a remark in the introduction it would appear that a chapter of the biography has been by some chance left out. Reference is made to Chapter XI., but no Chapter XI. can be found.

Henry Callaway, M.D., D.D. First Bishop of Kaffraria: His Life-History and Work. A Memoir by MARIAN S. BENHAM. Edited by the Rev. CANON BENHAM. London and New York: Macmillan & Co. 1896.

Bishop Callaway has left behind him a very considerable name both on account of his devoted labours as a missionary in South Africa and because of the many and valuable contributions he made to the literature of anthropology. Miss Benham in the memoir which she has written of him dwells to some extent upon the scientific side of his labours, but makes no attempt to appreciate it. A more complete account of his studies in connection with the Zulus, their language, customs and folk-lore she has apparently left for other and probably more capable hands. To the religious side of his life she does ample justice. Her narrative is brief, but graphic. Few memoirs are so replete with interest, and whatever partiality the editor may have for the work, as having been written by his daughter, it is well deserved. The son of an exciseman, Bishop Callaway was born in January, 1817. He became a teacher, and coming under the influence of Mr. Dymond, in whose school he acted as an assistant at Heavitree, he was drawn towards the Society of Friends, a body which he afterwards joined, and in which for some time he acted as a minister. Abandoning teaching, he studied medicine, and began practice in London, but his health failing, and having joined the Church of England, to which his parents belonged, he, in 1853, offered his services as a missionary to Bishop

Colenso, who had just been appointed to the See of Natal. The letter in which he made the offer missed the Bishop, who had set out for Natal, but he was accepted by the Board of the Society for the Propagation of the Gospel, when it was arranged that he should be ordained at home and in the following summer accompany Bishop Colenso on his return to Natal. Accordingly, in the August of the following year, along with Mrs. Callaway, he left England, and landed at Durban on the 5th of December, when he at once began work. While the earlier pages of Miss Benham's narrative show the religious doubts and difficulties with which Dr. Callaway was troubled in his own mind, the remainder are a record of calm, earnest, and strenuous work. Though always delicate in health Dr. Callaway's capacity for work was extraordinary. Few men have been more devoted or unselfish. From the fierce controversy which broke out in the South African Church in consequence of the publications of his Bishop's criticisms on the Pentateuch, he endeavoured as far as possible, though holding views entirely at variance with those of Dr. Colenso, to keep himself aloof. What he desired was above all things peace, with freedom to carry on his work. But for the slight part he took in it, as also for the difficulties he had to contend with, and his remarkable success as a missionary, and for much else that is interesting we must refer the reader to Miss Benham's attractively written and instructive volume.

Richelieu. By RICHARD LODGE, M.A., Professor of History in the University of Glasgow. *Philip Augustus.* By WILLIAM HOLDEN HUTTON, B.D. ('Foreign Statesmen' Series). London and New York: Macmillan & Co. 1896.

The series to which these two volumes belong promises to be a very fitting sequel to the series whose publication is almost completed under the general title of 'Twelve English Statesmen.' The excellence of the monographs forming that series is generally admitted, and taking the two volumes before us as samples of those which are to follow them, there is every apparent probability that this new series will at least equal, if not excel, in interest its predecessor. The general editor is Mr. J. B. Bury, than whom no more scholarly and capable editor could have been found. With considerable propriety, the initial volume of the series is devoted to Richelieu, whose character has been so variously represented, but who is fairly entitled to be called 'the greatest political genius' France 'has ever produced.' In sketching his life and character, Mr. Lodge has necessarily to travel over a wide space. His private and domestic character he for the most part leaves aside, and is occupied with him chiefly as a politician, and as 'the chief founder, not only of France before the Revolution, but of much that is most characteristic of France at the present day.' The sketch is admirably done. There is not an uninteresting page in the volume. Both sides of Richelieu's character as a statesman are brought out. While laying stress on his industry, skill, sagacity, decision and breadth of view, Mr. Lodge does not seek to exonerate him from the charge of cruelty and vindictiveness. All the same, he is of opinion that he was neither capricious nor unjust, and that 'his methods, though often arbitrary and contrary to legal custom and tradition, were always fearless and above-board.' If Mr. Hutton's volume is scarcely so attractive as Mr. Lodge's, it is not by any means due to any defect in his treatment of his subject, but rather to the fact that Philip Augustus is less known than the brilliant minister of Louis, and lived at a more remote period. In his time, however, he played a scarcely less conspicuous part. The conquerer of Bouvines and the successful opponent of Henry II. of England, he laid the foundations of the French Monarchy sure and strong, and restored it from the ruins into which it had fallen under the Capets. English history does not forget his intrigues against Richard I., as little does it forget John's subserviency, and the way in which he allowed Philip to strip him of his French possessions. The worst stain of Philip's character was his treatment of his wife Ingeborgis, whom he renounced on the very day of her coronation. The conflict which arose in consequence between him and Innocent III. is graphically described by Mr. Hutton, as well as the measures he took for the defence of the Church against the rapacity of the feudal lords. Altogether, he has produced a very readable volume, interesting in many ways, and bearing evident marks of careful study and preparation.

Studies in Judaism. By S. SCHECHTER, M.A. London: Adam & Charles Black. 1896.

Mr. Schechter, the accomplished Reader in Talmudic in the University of Cambridge, has here put together a number of essays on topics connected with Judaism both ancient and modern, which, though they have already appeared in the pages of the *Jewish Quarterly* and the *Jewish Times*, are of sufficient value to justify their publication in a permanent form. Dealing with the topics they do, and written with a vivacious, if not brilliant pen, they will commend themselves to the reader both as bringing to his notice various phases of life and thought, about which to the general public very little is known, and as presenting him with a large amount of information, which, while singularly interesting in itself, is set before him in a most charming way. Some of the papers are biographical, others of them theological, one or two of them are bibliographical, and the rest of them are of a somewhat lighter texture and might almost be called gossipy ; only the gossip is always that of a scholar with a memory overrunning with all manner of information about Jewish history and literature and the ways of the Jews. The essays are in all fourteen. The first of them is on the Chassidim, or the Pious, a dissenting sect among the Jews in Eastern Europe, originated by Israel Baalshem, a native of Ukop, in Bukovina, who was born about the year 1700. Mr. Schechter has both loved and hated the Chassidim, and 'even now,' he says, 'I am not able to suppress these feelings.' But he adds, 'I have rather tried to guide my feelings in such a way as to love in Chassidim what was ideal and noble, and to hate in it what turned out bad and pernicious for Judaism.' The life of Baalshem was not without its elements of romance, and his followers have added to it many things which are purely legendary. In its origin Chassidim was a revolt against the excessive causistry of the contemporary Rabbis. 'It was in fact,' says Mr. Schechter, 'one more manifestation of the yearning of the human heart towards the Divine idea, and of its ceaseless craving for direct communion with God. It was the protest of an emotional but uneducated people against a one-sided expression of Judaism, presented in cold and over-subtle disquisitions which not only did they not understand, but which shut out the play of the feelings and the affections, so that religion was made impossible to them.' Baalshem had no Rabbi for his master ; his teaching, the key-note of which was the Immanence of God, he worked out for himself and communicated to his disciples for the most part orally. On the study of the Law or the observance of its precepts in themselves, he laid little stress ; he regarded them as means to an end, and the end, he taught, is union with God. Out of this mysticism was developed the doctrine of the Intermediary which gave rise to the Zaddikim, a class of men who were supposed to form a connecting bond between God and His creatures, and soon became the distinguishing feature of Chassidism. In other words, Chassidism soon gave way to Zaddikism, and before long dwindled away to little short of man worship. The sect was early rent by divisions; it was persecuted by the orthodox and by the Government; but it still remains. 'Amid much that is bad,' Mr. Schechter remarks, 'the Chassidim have preserved through the whole movement a warm heart, and an ardent, sincere faith.' The three essays which follow, while biographical, are largely expository, and have for their subjects R. Nachman Krochmal (1785-1840), R. Elijah Wilna, Gaon (1720-1797), and R. Moses ben Nachman, or Nachmanides, as he is now commonly called, of Gerona (1195-1270), all of whom were great teachers, and have had a marked influence on the course of Jewish thought. The fifth essay contains a brief sketch of a Jewish Boswell, R. Solomon of St. Goar, who took down the sayings of R. Jacob, who filled the office of Chief Rabbi in Mayence and Worms, some three hundred years before the Laird of Auchinleck did the same for Johnson. The next four essays are theological. Two of them deal with doctrine, and amply refute the saying of Maimonides, that Judaism has no dogmas. Mr. Schechter shows that while Judaism has no definitely elaborated creed or symbol similar to the symbols of the Christian Church, it has nevertheless a fairly numerous set of well defined doctrines, which he illustrates with a variety of quotations from the Talmud and other writings. An essay having for its title 'The History of Jewish Tradition,' may be said to be a short treatise on the history of the interpretation of Scripture among the Jews. Two delightful essays bear the titles respectively of 'The Child in Jewish Literature' and 'Woman in Temple and Synagogue.' 'The Earliest Jewish Community in Europe' approves of the removal of the Ghetto in Rome, and contains much interesting reading about the Jews in the Eternal City. 'Titles of Jewish Books' notes the curious titles Jewish authors were in the habit of giving to their books. Among others mentioned are 'Principal Spices,' 'Meat Offerings Mingled or Dry,' 'Two Young Pigeons,' Forests of Honey,' 'The Offering of the Poor,' 'One Kid No Israel,' 'Meat or Coals.' 'Choice Pearls,' however, is more attractive than the prosaic 'Collection of Proverbs and Sayings,' which is what the book contains. 'The Lips of those who Sleep' recommends itself, Mr. Schechter remarks, 'as a very suggestive title for a catalogue, especially when one thinks of the Agadic explanation given to Cant. vii. 10, according to which the study of the book of a departed author makes the lips of the dead man speak. R. Jacob Emden named one of his pamphlets 'Rod for the Fool's Back,' while for a mathematical book R. Joseph Tsarphathi devised the title *City of Sihon,* alluding to Numbers, xxi. 27, for Hesbon (reckoning) is the City of Sihon. In his essay on the Collection of Hebrew books in the British Museum Mr. Schechter laments the little interest which is taken in that magnificent collection, and enumerates a number of the most valuable of its MSS. and volumes. The fame of the collection has penetrated, it would appear, into some of the most obscure places in Poland, where legends circulate about the 'millions' of books which belong to the Queen of England, and a certain autograph copy of the Book of Proverbs. presented to the Queen of Sheba on the occasion of her visit to Jerusalem, and brought by the English troops as a trophy from Abyssinia. We have said sufficient, however, to show the character and contents of Mr. Schechter's *Studies.* Since the publication of Dr. Deutsch's volume nothing equal to it has appeared.

The Poetical Works of William Wordsworth. Edited by
WILLIAM KNIGHT. Vols. I.—V. London & New York:
Macmillan & Co. 1896.

The students to whom this edition of Wordsworth is dedicated are
already under a heavy debt of gratitude to Professor Knight, and this
debt promises to be largely increased rather than diminished by the work
he has now begun. Whatever may be thought of his work as an editor,
there can be no doubt that Professor Knight possesses information, and is
in a position to give to the world an edition of Wordsworth such as no one
else at present can, and such an one as might well be counted ' final.' His
edition of 1882-6, notwithstanding its numerous mistakes, and the Life of
1889, notwithstanding its errors, marked a distinct advance, and placed
him easily amongst the foremost, if not at the head, of editors of Wordsworth. The present edition, we are glad to say, is not a reprint, nor even
an amended edition of that of 1882-6. It retains some of its features, but
has others which entitle it to be regarded as new and more complete.
The editing in fact has been recast, and as it seems to us, with advantage,
the alterations made being, as we venture to think, without exception,
improvements. Whether other improvements might not have been added
with advantage is perhaps an open question. As for the features of the
1882-6 edition which have been retained the following may be mentioned :
(1), The poems are printed in the chronological order of their composition,
not in the order of their publication, nor as they were arranged by Wordsworth. (2), The changes made in the text by Wordsworth in successive
editions are given at the foot of the pages and duly dated. (3), Other
changes suggested by Wordsworth but not printed are also given in the
footnotes. (4), The Fenwick notes are printed in full. In addition to
these there are the topographical notes, the poems and verses not included
by Wordsworth in any of the editions he brought out of his works, the
bibliography and the Life. Among the changes, it may be noted that the
heavy and clumsy volume of the 1882-6 edition has been discarded for the
more convenient size of the ' Eversley Series.' The poems are to occupy
eight volumes, and along with Wordsworth's poems are to be printed those
of his sister Dorothy, and others which the poet published among his own.
The notes to the poems are re-arranged, distinguished and dated. All
Wordsworth's prose works are to be given in full and are to occupy
volumes nine and ten. Dorothy Wordsworth's journals are to be printed,
though, for reasons to be explained, not all of them in full. We are also
promised the letters of the poet and his sister Dorothy, with many that
have not hitherto seen the light, besides a new bibliography and several
other items of great interest. The Life is to be re-written and shortened
so as to occupy only a single volume. Whether this new edition of the
Poet will be final it is much too soon to say. For our own part we are not
particularly enamoured of the chronological arrangement of the poems.
Professor Knight defends it on the ground that it exhibits best the development of the poet's genius. We are not so sure that it does. A poet's
mind does not work like a machine, nor can it be said to work evenly.
There are tides in the inspiration of genius as there are in intellectual
vigour. It is subject to ebb and flow. More perhaps than any one else
the poet is a creature of circumstance, and during what may be called his
best periods, he may produce, as he often does, work which is much below
the level of what he is capable of doing. Besides, in the case of Wordsworth, we have the fact that in regard to some of his poems it is difficult
to fix their date either of inception or completion as well as the other, that
the poet himself refused to adopt the chronological order and was at great

pains to classify his poems on a different principle. Professor Knight, however, admits that 'the chronological method of arrangement has its limits,' and in several instances, as he explains, departs from it. Still one feels disposed to say, even with this admission : If a principle is worth anything it is worth sticking to. The errata in the 1882-6 edition were striking ; here they hold out the promise of being numerous ; but leaving these for others who have more space at their command, to point out, we may observe that the word 'gill' is not as Wordsworth believed (Vol. I., p. 10, Note), and as his editor seems to assume, 'confined to this country,' *i.e.*. the Lake District. It often occurs in Scotland, as, for instance, in the name of Normangill, etc., and may be found pretty liberally annotated in Jamieson. On page 253 of the same volume the singular misprint occurs, 'of went years,' for 'twenty years.' Four pages further on Professor Knight's correspondent is not quite accurate as to his translation, nor has the Professor himself laid hold on the right passage from St. Bernard of Clairvaux. It occurs in Ep. ·106, and runs as follows : Experto crede : aliquid amplius invenies in silvis quam in libris. Ligna et lapides docebunt te, quod a magistris audire non possis. The table of contents to the first volume exhibits the singular omission of all mention of the Preface which runs out to over sixty pages and deserves better treatment. Each volume, we should add, is provided with a beautifully executed portrait and vignette.

Catvlli Veronensis Liber. Edited by ARTHUR PALMER, Litt.D., LL.D., D.C.L. London and New York : Macmillan & Co. 1896.

Professor Palmer has here edited for Messrs. Macmillan's 'Parnassus Library,' the poems of Catullus, for whom he claims the high honour of being 'the most passionate and brilliant, if not the greatest of the Roman poets.' That he was 'the most passionate and brilliant,' will probably be admitted by most ; that he was the greatest is probably more than many will admit. In some respects, however, Catullus stands out before any other of the Roman poets either of the Republic or the Empire. In his sincerity, his love of beauty, his rich pictorial power, the startling vividness of his language and imagery, and his mastery over the art of expression, he is often unrivalled. There is no knowing what he might have done had his life been spared, but judged by the works which have survived, though entitled to a high place among the Roman poets, he can scarcely claim to be placed first. Even as a lyrical poet he cannot, as Sellar observed, be placed on the same level with Horace. It is with the text, however, that Professor Palmer has mostly to do. Here he has for the most part followed Professor Robinson Ellis, though not always. The ·plan of the series does not admit of notes, but to justify his text, Professor Palmer has supplied a list of various readings and added a couple of excursus. An all too brief introduction sketches the life of Catullus and deals with the metres, MSS., and other matters. Like the other volumes in this series the work is handsomely printed and bound, and of a handy size. The elaborate index with which Professor Palmer's volume concludes is an excellent indication of the admirable manner in which he has discharged his duties as editor throughout.

The English Dialect Dictionary. Edited by JOSEPH WRIGHT, M.A., Ph.D. Part I. A to Ballot. London and Oxford : Henry Frowde. New York : Putnam's Sons.

This is the first instalment of a great and important work which has not been begun too soon. It has been long in preparation. Dr. Wright, its accomplished Editor, has had, and still has, many helpers whose joint efforts, it is to be hoped, will meet with the handsome recognition they deserve. The aim of the dictionary is to include as far as possible the vocabulary of all English dialect words which are still in use, or have been in use, during the last two hundred years in England, Scotland, Ireland, and Wales, and any American and Colonial dialect words which are still in use in Great Britain and Ireland, or have been found in early printed dialect books and glossaries. The difficulty of compiling such a work is obvious. To ensure success, readers and contributors must be found in every district, and they must work promptly, we should say, as the tendency of things in the present seems to be to assimilate the language all over the country, except in the most remote parts, or where the modern means of locomotion have not yet penetrated. After a careful examination of the Part before us, we have no hesitation in saying that it is scarcely possible to speak too highly of the exhaustive and scholarly way in which the work has been done. Over two thousand simple and compound words, and five hundred phrases, have been treated, and these have been illustrated by 8536 quotations, without counting those which have been cited at the end of each article from early writers. A careful search for omissions has not resulted in the discovery of more than a dozen, and some of these may be at least excused. Under *adder* the Scotch form *nadder* has not been given. *Agate*, a word used in the north for *ajar*, a little open, is omitted. *Agog* sometimes has the sense of ' amazement.' *Alane* is given under *alone*, but it should have been registered separately ; so also should *ance*, ' once.' *Awne* is not given, though *awny* is. *Backwater* as a verb, though common enough, is omitted. *Baffing*, making rough sport, though other senses of the word are given, is also omitted. *Baffing-spoon*, the name given to a club used in golf, is wanting, though *to baff* is rightly defined. The cross entries are numerous, yet a few more might have been given ; *aicht*, to own, for instance. Perfection in a work of this kind is, we should say, impossible, and Dr. Wright may be congratulated upon reaching the very high standard he has.

A New English Dictionary on Historical Principles. Field— Fish. By HENRY BRADLEY, M.A. *Diffluent—Disburden.* By Dr. JAMES A. H. MURRAY. Oxford: at the Clarendon Press. 1896.

The first of these quarterly issues of Dr. Murray's great Dictionary has been prepared under the editorship of his able coadjutor, Mr. Bradley. The number of pages in it is the same as in the other quarterly sections, but the number of main words which are dealt with in it is smaller than in any previous section. The reason is that to a greater extent than in any other portion, the words which are here treated of are among the oldest and most frequently used in the language, and that on this account many of them, in consequence of the multiplicity of their senses and applications, have required to be illustrated at much more than the average length. The total number of words recorded is, on the other hand, much larger owing to the extraordinary abundance of combinations of certain important substantives. The combinations of ' field,' for instance, occupy a couple of pages, and those of ' fire,' six. While between ' Field and Fish,' Johnson records 168 words, the number here recorded is 1985. Johnson's illustrative quotations number only 556, Mr. Bradley gives no fewer than 8526. These numbers speak for themselves and show with what extraordinary care and elaboration the work of this monumental Dictionary is being carried on. Novelties in the way of derivation are in this section rare, but the development of meaning is, in a number of words, such for instance as 'file,' 'fine,' 'field,' 'fight,' and 'fire,' interesting. The section edited by Dr. Murray, though appearing later than the section just noticed, deals with an earlier part of the alphabet. A great number of the words explained are furnished with the prefix *dis-* or its variants. Here, as in the rest of the Dictionary, the words registered are much more numerous than those given in any of the larger dictionaries, while in the matter of illustrative quotations no comparison can be made. In short, the more carefully each part is examined, the more is one struck with its extraordinary value of the work to which they belong, and its marked superiority over all other works of its kind.

Introduction to Political Science: Two Series of Lectures. By Sir J. R. Seeley, K.C.M.G., Litt.D. London and New York: Macmillan & Co. 1896.

The two series of lectures contained in this volume of the 'Eversley Series,' were delivered by the late Sir J. R. Seeley as Professor of Modern History at Cambridge, mainly during the Michaelmas and Lent terms of the academic year 1885-86. They have been prepared for the press by Professor Sidgwick, than whom no more skilful or sympathetic editor could have been found. Written for oral delivery, they do not form a manual of political science ; still less do they aim at the communication of a complete system. Their aim is rather to communicate a method and to excite the reader to an independent exercise of thought in applying it. During his occupancy of the Modern History Chair it was the author's custom to give instruction in history and in political science, the former by means of formal public lectures and the latter by means of a conversation class. Of this latter many of Professor Seeley's old students have grateful recollections, and some time ago Mr. J. R. Tanner described the way in which the class was conducted. 'The subject,' he says, ' was political science studied by way of discussion, and discussion under the reverential conditions that prevailed, resolved itself into question and answer— Socrates exposing the folly of the Athenians. It was mainly an exercise in the definition and scientific use of terms. What is liberty ? Various definitions of the term would be elicited from the class and subjected to analysis. The authors of them would be lured by subtle cross-examination into themselves exposing their inconsistencies. Then the Professor would take up his parable. He would first discuss the different senses in which the term had already been used in literature. . . . From an examination of inconsistent accounts the Professor would proceed to the business of building up by a gradual process, and with the help of the class itself, a definition of his own.' At times the Professor would vary his method and treat political philosophy in formal lectures as well as in his conversation class. To the objections that his proper function was to teach history and not political science, he was ready to reply that to lecture on political science was in his opinion to lecture on history. The two, he used to maintain, are not distinct but inseparable. To call political science ' a part of history,' he says in his first lecture, might do some violence to the usage of language, but I may venture to say that history without political science is a study incomplete, truncated, as on the other hand, political science without history is hollow and baseless, or in one word :

' History without political science has no fruit,
Political science without history has no root.'

Hence the chief aim of the lectures before us is to enforce and illustrate the two-sided doctrine that the right method of studying political science is an essentially historical method, and that the right method of studying political history is to study it as material for political science. The fruitfulness of this doctrine is obvious. Its treatment has afforded Professor Seeley the opportunity of dealing with many current opinions and of exposing numerous modern political fallacies. The second of the two series of lectures will, in all probability, prove itself the more attractive to the majority of readers as it is here that different forms of government, a number of points in English constitutional history and the practice of Parliament, and such terms as ' aristocracy ' are trenchantly discussed.

A Handbook of Greek Sculpture. By ERNEST ARTHUR GARDNER, M.A. London and New York : Macmillan & Co. 1896.

Both as to subject and author, Messrs. Macmillan & Co. have been exceedingly fortunate for the initial volume of their new series of ' Handbooks of Archæology and Antiquities.' In any such series, Greek Sculpture, on account of its intrinsic importance, deserves the first place, and the task of treating it could scarcely have fallen into more capable hands than those of Professor Gardner, who for some years discharged the duties of Director of the British School of Archæology at Athens. The present volume is only an instalment and does not bring the history of the subject down to a later date than the year 400 B.C. In a subsequent volume it is proposed to continue the narrative down to the date of the foundation of Constantinople in 324 A.D., Byzantine Art being entirely beyond the scope of the work, but reserved, we may hope, for separate treatment. The plan adopted by Mr. Gardner is simple, and such as will commend itself to those who are acquainted with what is required in a handbook by those for whom handbooks are written. In an introductory chapter of considerable length, Mr Gardner deals with the sources, literary and other, for the history of Greek Sculpture ; then with the materials used by the sculptor, the uses to which he put them, and the technical processes he employed in working them. There is also a useful section on the application of colour to sculpture, and another on the use of pointing from a finished model, and one on decorative sculpture. In the first of the two and a half chapters which follow, Mr. Gardner endeavours to appreciate the influence which Egyptian, Assyrian, and Phœnician Art had upon the Greeks and indicates the way in which the rise of Greek Art was conditioned and fostered by the great national games and festivals. From 600 to 480 B.C. is taken by Mr. Gardner as the period during which the Greek sculptor ceased to be an apt imitator of foreign masters and Greek art began to show signs of that development ' which was to lead to the works of Phidias and Praxiteles, and when their chief interest' is 'in their promise for the future.' Here the Schools of Samos, Chios, and Crete, as also of Athens, Argos, and Sicyon are treated, and the monuments of the different schools of the period are classified according to their various localities and described. The first half of the third chapter which is here given is devoted to the fifth century B.C. After pointing out the immense influence which the Persian Wars had upon the development of Greek Art, Mr. Gardner proceeds to deal with the Olympian Sculptures and the works of Calamis, Myron, Pythagoras, and Phidias. Everywhere Mr. Gardner avails himself, as far as possible, of the assistance afforded by Greek writers. In many cases the evidence he has to work upon is slight, but he is always careful in the case of controverted points to put the various opinions which have been held, and to write as undogmatically as possible, believing it better that the student should be left in doubt than that he should take up with views which he may afterwards require to unlearn.

Darwin, and After Darwin: An Exposition of the Darwinian Theory and a Discussion of Post-Darwinian Questions. By GEORGE JOHN ROMANES, M.A., LL.D., F.R.S. Vol. II. London; Longmans, Green, & Co. 1895.

In this, the second and posthumous volume of his discussions, the late Mr. Romanes carries on his exposition of the doctrine of Darwin and his defence of Darwin against some of his followers. Of the ten chapters it contains, the first is introductory and treats of the general theory of descent as held by Darwin and as it is now held by the several divergent schools of thought which have arisen since Darwin's death. The next five chapters are devoted to a discussion of the theory of heredity, and the remainder to the theory of adaptations. The point explained in the first chapter is the fact that Darwin always held, and with increasing firmness, the doctrine that selection has been the main and not the only means of modification, but has been supplemented and assisted by other causes. With this the theory of Wallace and Weissmann, that selection has been the only cause of modification, is strongly contrasted, and the points of difference between the two theories are set out at great length. Mr. Romanes also discriminates between the true Darwinian theory and the ideas propounded by Sachs and Pfeffer, Geddes, Cope, and Hyatt. In the chapters on Heredity Mr. Romanes expresses his conviction that, notwithstanding the arguments of Weissmann, the doctrine stands exactly where it was left by Galton twenty years ago. On the doctrine of utility Mr. Romanes differs from both Wallace and Huxley. In his opinon, regarded as a universal principle, the doctrine of utility is purely *a priori* and being founded exclusively on grounds of deduction, it is impossible to combat it by an appeal to facts. 'The question,' he says, 'is not one of fact ; it is a question of reasoning. The treatment of our subject matter is logical, not biological.' As usual, Mr. Romanes here sets forth his ideas and arguments with great force and clearness. The latter are trenchant and exhaustive, and one can only regret that the hand which penned them is no longer with us, and that a career so conspicuously brilliant has come to what to all appearance was, in the interests of science, a premature end.

SHORT NOTICES.

The Book of Job and *Ecclesiastes, The Wisdom of Solomon* (Macmillan) are two volumes of Professor Moulton's series entitled 'The Modern Reader's Bible.' To the general features of this series we called attention last quarter when noticing the first two numbers of it The two before us amply bear out the promise of their predecessors. As was remarked then critical questions are avoided and the introduction with which each book is prefaced is for the most part taken up with an explanation or analysis of the text. Mr. Moulton's introduction to the Book of Job is particularly interesting. The analysis is lucid and will help the reader very materially to the understanding of a book whose meaning is not very generally understood, and as to which there is, and probably will continue to be, notwithstanding Professor Moulton's arguments, considerable difference of opinion. The passage in the introduction devoted to the exposition of the idea of Satan and the part he was supposed to play at the time the book of Job was written, though not new to Theologians, will strike many as peculiar. The introductions to Ecclesiastes and the Book of Wisdom are equally good, but here, again, it is more than probable that Theologians and Biblical critics will have something to say against the views they contain as to the ruling idea of each book. As in the other volumes the text of the Revised Version is used. The notes are frequent and apposite. Those to the Book of Job contain a brief account of Hebrew prosody.

An Ethical Movement (Macmillan) by W. L. Sheldon, is chiefly remarkable as illustrating a movement, which has sprung up in the United States of America and has a few representative societies on this side of the Atlantic, having for its object the study and practice of Ethics of a more or less altruistic kind as a sort of substitute for the Christian religion. The lectures may be called Lay Sermons. There is nothing new in them, but they will serve to show the kind of teaching which is supposed to satisfy a number to whom Christianity, so far as they have heard or understood it, seems to be defective.

Hugh Miller, by W. Keith Leask, *John Knox*, by A. Taylor Innes, and *Robert Burns*, by Gabriel Setoun, are three volumes of Messrs. Oliphant, Anderson & Ferrier's 'Famous Scots' series. The volumes are being issued with commendable rapidity. The sketches they contain are necessarily, owing to the limitations of space, slight, but so far as they go, they have evidently been written with the intention of making them as attractive and popular as possible.

John Chinaman (Hitt, Edinburgh), by the Rev. J. Cockburn, M.A., is an excellent little volume. The author was formerly stationed at Ichang, and has had many opportunities of studying the Chinese on their native soil. The account which he has given of their ways and ideas is remarkably instructive. More accurate information about them may be gathered from these pages than from some volumes, the perusal of which requires the expenditure of more time and patience.

The summer number of *The Evergreen* (P. Geddes & Colleagues) is full of varied and interesting reading. There is a careful and attractive paper in it by Mr. J. A. Thomson, with the title, 'The Biology of Summer," and another equally good by the Editor, with the somewhat curious title, 'The Flower of the Grass.' Over the signature of Dr. Bellyse Baildon we have a sonnet on Robert Burns of more than average quality. Among the poetry of the volume may also be mentioned a charming song by Sir George Douglas, and one or two effective renderings from the Celtic. If the number is not a specially strong one, it is at anyrate of more than average quality.

Under the title, *Milk, its Nature and Composition* (A. & C. Black), Dr. Aikman has published a small handbook for the use of farmers and the information of the general reader, in which he treats briefly, but lucidly, of the chemistry and bacteriology of milk, butter, and cheese. No attempt has been made to deal with the practice of butter and cheese-making, but the scientific principles underlying these processes have been stated in as popular a way as possible. Incidentally, Dr. Aikman mentions that between the years 1890 and 1892, no fewer than 1013 papers were published in connection with the study of bacteriology. A list of the principal works on dairying is given in an appendix.

In *The Authorship of the Kingis Quair* (MacLehose), Mr. J. T. T. Brown subjects to a very close and searching examination the claims of King James I. to the authorship of the poem mentioned on his title-page.

Writers and Editors, including **Dr.** Skeat who edited the poem for the Scottish Text Society, have all along assumed that its author was undoubtedly the first of the Jameses, and have gone so far as to fix the year and month in which it was written. Mr. Brown criticises adversely the grounds on which these opinions have been based, and by a variety of evidence, external and internal, attempts to show that the author of the poem cannot have been the King to whom it is usually attributed, but an unknown author, who took for his model the *Court of Love*, a poem written not earlier than 1440, or thirty-five years later than the date to which the authorship of the *Kingis Quair* has hitherto been assigned. Mr. Brown's arguments are strong if not decisive ; but perhaps Dr. Skeat may have something to say on the subject.

Scottish Poetry of the Eighteenth Century (Hodge & Co.,) is another volume of the 'Abbotsford Series of the Scottish Poets,' which has been issued under the editorship of Mr. George Eyre-Todd. The selections begin with Lord Yester's 'Tweedside,' and conclude with a couple of pieces by William Julius Meikle. Among them are examples from Alexander Ross, Allan Ramsay, Hamilton of Bangour, and John Skinner. The pieces are carefully edited and a short account is given of the authors from whose works they are taken. To many, one of the surprises of the collection will be to find that 'Rule Britannia' owes its origin to a descendant of the proscribed MacGregors. A second volume is to follow.

The Story of Burns and Highland Mary (Alex. Gardner), by Archibald Munro, M.A., is a book which will find many readers. Mr. Munro has been extremely diligent in his quest for information about Burns and Mary Campbell, and has succeeded almost beyond expectation. There is much that is new in his volume, while his manner of telling the story of the two lovers is skillful and attractive.

The Duties and Liabilities of Trustees (Macmillan), is a series of six lectures delivered by Mr. Birrell, M.P., in the Inner Temple during the Hilary Sittings, 1896, at the request of the Council of Legal Education. They were delivered to law students, but are as free from legal technicalities as possible and can scarcely fail to be intelligible to all whom they concern. Mr. Birrel, in fact, has put what he has to say so clearly and forcibly that no Trustee need have the slightest difficulty in understanding what his duties and responsibilities are. The reading of his lectures is almost as pleasant as that of his *Obiter Dicta*. The same hand is apparent on almost every page as well as the same genial spirit. Law has seldom been expounded in the same luminous and felicitous way. With Mr. Birrell's lectures accessible to him no Trustee will henceforth be able to excuse himself for not being acquainted with the duties and responsibilities of his position.

The publication of the sixth and seventh volumes of the late J. R. Green's *History of the English People* in Messrs. Macmillan's 'Eversley Series,' leaves but one more volume to be issued in order to complete the work in this Series. Its publication in this form is an undoubted gain. Like all the rest of the works in this Series, it is admirably printed, while its low price should place it within the reach of a vast number of readers whose means will not allow them to indulge in the luxury of the more expensive edition.

THE

SCOTTISH REVIEW.

OCTOBER, 1896.

ART. I.—THE ANNANDALE FAMILY BOOK.

The Annandale Family Book of the Johnstones, Earls and Marquises of Annandale. By Sir William Fraser, K.C.B., LL.D. 2 vols., 4to. Edinburgh : 1894.

WHEN the twentieth century has reached maturity, and the Scottish historian of that period is engaged making researches as to the early history of Scotland, there is one writer of the present time whose memory he will hold in special veneration. He may esteem highly three successive Historiographers-Royal—Dr. John Hill Burton, for his masterly studies of eighteenth century life ; Dr. Skene, for his patient investigations of early Celtic history, and Professor Masson for his laborious work in transcribing and annotating the Register of the Privy Council. But for really valuable historical matter, for documentary evidence of an irreproachable character, and for the publication of the correspondence of prominent characters in general history giving curiously intimate glimpses of social life in bygone days, the future historian will feel particularly indebted to Sir William Fraser. Before reviewing *The Annandale Family Book,* one of the latest products of Sir William's prolific pen, the reader of the present day may be interested in the story of the author's long and industrious career. It is a record of unexampled success in a field of labour that is often barren and unfruitful even to the most 'eident' worker.

The modern method of historical research in Scotland, by which traditional evidence is carefully separated from that which is founded upon documents, may be dated from the beginning of the nineteenth century. Thomas Thomson, who held the office of Deputy-Clerk-Register from 1806 to 1841, did much to clear away the myths and baseless traditions that were accepted as veritable history even by serious historians of Scotland. Trained as a lawyer, and accustomed to estimate the value of documentary evidence in the Courts of Law, Mr. Thomson brought the same logical processes to bear upon historical questions. With him, as with every sane historian, the written document, when its authenticity was proved, entirely superseded the oral evidence of tradition; and though he did not produce any elaborate history of Scotland, he accomplished a far greater work by placing all future histories upon a secure and steadfast basis. His labours in the Register House were of incalculable service, for he reduced the chaos of documents committed to his charge into something approaching order, and made valuable discoveries of neglected papers that have since been utilised profitably by every historian of Scotland. It is sufficient to mention his edition of *The Acts of the Parliaments of Scotland, The Register of the Great Seal* (an interrupted work now approaching completion), and *The Chamberlain Rolls*, to show what he accomplished as a pioneer. In his position as President of the Bannatyne Club, Mr. Thomson was also able to render efficient service to historical literature. His immediate successor in office was William Pitt Dundas, grandson of Lord President Dundas, but it was not until Sir William Fraser became Deputy Keeper of the Records that Thomas Thomson's place was adequately supplied.

Sir William Fraser, who is now an octogenarian, began his career as a Solicitor in Edinburgh, and was admitted as an S.S.C. in 1851. He had turned his attention at an early period in his life to the study of those family documents in which the real history of a nation is more accurately displayed than in any formal work that deals exclusively with State Papers; and Peerage Law became one of his specialties. Long before his name was made prominent as an author he had gained a high reputation in professional circles as an authority on family history; and he was frequently entrusted with researches in private charter-rooms for the purpose of discovering and preparing documentary evidence in important cases. So highly was he esteemed as a competent 'black-letter lawyer' that, in 1852, Mr. Alexander Pringle of Whytbank, then Keeper of the Register of Sasines, offered Mr. Fraser the responsible position of Deputy-Keeper, and induced him to give up his legal practice for this post. At Mr. Pringle's death in 1857, it was expected that Mr. Fraser would have succeeded him as head of the Sasine Office; but that place was bestowed upon the late Mr. John Clerk Brodie of Idvies, who retained it till his death in 1888. Mr. Fraser remained in his post as Deputy-Keeper of the Register of Sasines until 1880, when a new arrangement of the staff in the Register House, Edinburgh, left the office of Deputy-Keeper of the Records vacant, and Mr. Fraser was promoted to this position. For the next twelve years he filled this post with conspicuous success; but in 1892, when he had reached the official limit of 40 years' public service, his retirement became necessary. As he was still vigorously prosecuting his life-work it was thought that a special arrangement might be made to prolong his term of service. The fear, however, of establishing a precedent that might not always work well, prevented this reasonable proposal, and he retired, but not to inactive seclusion. His ability had been recognised by the conferring upon him of the degree of LL.D., by Edinburgh University in 1882, and by his enrolment as a Companion of the Bath in 1885 by Mr. Gladstone. He was advanced to the dignity of K.C.B. in 1887 by Lord Salisbury—an honour rarely bestowed for purely literary services.

While Sir William Fraser's work in organising the various departments in the Register House that have been under his charge has greatly expedited both professional and historical researches, he will be most highly appreciated by posterity for the wonderful books on Scottish family history—24 in number

—that have issued from his pen. These have placed the writing of Scottish history upon an entirely new basis. The imaginative historian who accepts local tradition as if it were unchallengeable verity has been effectually put to flight, and fact is properly preferred to fancy. In this respect Sir William Fraser's books are models of accuracy, for though he may sometimes theorise upon the contents of a charter, or suggest a tentative explanation of a letter, he is always careful to give a copy of the document in dispute—often in fac-simile—so that the student may draw his own inferences from the veritable parchment or epistle. How many violent historical feuds between rival partizans would have been avoided had it been possible to refer to originals and verify quotations! The literary career of Sir William Fraser has extended over nearly half-a-century. During that time he has not only produced an unique library of books on Scottish history, but has also been actively engaged in making reports of private Scottish collections for the Royal Commission on Historical Manuscripts. In this department of labour, first as joint reporter, and then on the resignation of the late Dr. John Stuart, as sole reporter for Scotland, he has worked assiduously since 1869, and has examined the principal charter-rooms of the Scottish nobility, and prepared elaborate statements as to their contents. The results of his work are made available in the valuable series of Reports published by the Royal Commission. The great expense involved in the preparation of Sir William Fraser's books necessarily prevented them from being taken up as a publisher's speculation, and their existence is due to the liberality and public spirit of the noblemen and gentlemen for whom they were 'privately printed,' and by whom they have been distributed. Occasionally stray copies come into the market and bring very large prices, but it may be doubted if there is any private library in Scotland which contains the whole of these splendid volumes. To book-lovers and collectors the following full list of these books will be of especial interest. *The Stirlings of Keir* (1858) was undertaken for the late Sir William Stirling-Maxwell of Pollok and Keir, and was the earliest volume brought out by Sir William Fraser. It

was followed by *The Montgomeries, Earls of Eglinton,* (1859);
The Maxwells of Pollok, (1863), both in two volumes; *The
Maxwell, Herries and Nithsdale Muniments,* (1865); *The Pollok
Maxwell Baronetcy,* (1866), each one volume; *The Carnegies,
Earls of Southesk,* (1867), in two volumes, for the present Earl;
The Red Book of Grandtully, (1868), two volumes, for the late
Sir William Stewart; *The Chiefs of Colquhoun,* (1869), two
volumes; *Registrum Monasterii de S. Marie de Cambuskenneth,*
(1872), for the Grampian Club; *The Book of Caerlaverock,*
(1873), two volumes; *The Cartulary of Colquhoun,* (1873), one
volume; *The Lennox,* (1874), two volumes; *The Cartulary of
Pollok Maxwell,* (1875), one volume; *The Earls of Cromartie,*
(1876), two volumes; *The Scotts of Buccleuch,* (1878), in two
large volumes, for the late Duke of Buccleuch; *The Frasers
of Philorth,* (1879), three volumes, written in conjunction with
Lord Saltoun; *The Red Book of Menteith,* (1880), two volumes;
The Chiefs of Grant, (1883), in three large volumes: *The Douglas Book,* (1885), in four large volumes, for the Earls of Home;
The Family of Wemyss of Wemyss, (1888), in three volumes, for
Mr. Randolph Erskine Wemyss; *The Earls of Haddington,*
(1889), in two volumes; *The Melvilles, Earls of Melville, and
the Leslies, Earls of Leven,* (1890), three remarkable volumes
projected by Thomas Thomson in 1820 and finished by Sir
William Fraser seventy years later; *The Sutherland Book,*
(1892), three volumes, for the late and present Dukes of Sutherland; and *The Annandale Book,* (1894), in two large volumes,
for Mr. J. J. Hope-Johnstone of Annandale. The two last named
works have been completed and published since Sir William
Fraser retired from his public duties; and it is by no means
unlikely, despite his advanced years, that he will be able to
finish some of the similar volumes which he has long had in
view.

From this list of his works it will be seen that Sir William
Fraser's researches have covered the whole of Scotland, from
Annandale to the remotest parts of Sutherland; from the
'kingdom of Fife' to Ayrshire, the Colquhoun country, and
the land of the Lennox. There is not a shire in Scotland
which has not figured in some form either in his Reports or in

his volumes. His experience, therefore, transcends that of any other living Scottish writer upon family history or genealogy, and his position is unique in this respect. His later works are full of that ripe knowledge of affairs which is only gained by wide experience and research; and *The Annandale Family Book* to which attention is now to be directed, is a typical example of Sir William Fraser's style.

Amongst the families that ruled the Scottish Borders the Scotts, the Johnstones, the Maxwells, and the Jardines long held prominence, and for centuries they contested among themselves for precedence, though they united against the common foe, 'oure ould innemyes of England.' The chief power in Dumfriesshire was divided between the Johnstones and the Maxwells, and many a fierce contest took place to decide the supremacy of the one or the other. An old colloquial phrase (utilised by Burns in one of his poems) asserts that whatever plea might arise on the Borders 'the Johnstones had the guidin' o't.' They seem to have held much the same position in their own district as the Kennedies in Ayrshire, or the Douglases in Clydesdale; and they exercised baronial rights of 'furk and fosse, of pit and gallows,' and waged war upon their neighbours as well as against the English invader with the irresponsibility of independent sovereigns. It is difficult to settle precisely the date when the Johnstones were established in the Annandale country, nor is it easy to tell from what place they came when their location was taken up there. Recent investigations have traced the family back to a certain 'John' who received lands in Dumfriesshire, either by inheritance or gift, from Robert Bruce, Lord of Annandale, in 1170, and who called the place 'Jonestun,' afterwards corrupted into Johnstone. His son Gilbert de Jonestun was in possession in 1194, and was knighted some time before his death in 1230. Two of the grandsons of this Sir Gilbert swore fealty to Edward I. on 28th August, 1296, and most of the genealogists begin the Johnstone pedigree with Sir John Johnstone, the elder of these two brothers, though there is documentary evidence to carry back the line of the family to 1170. Of the personal history of these early Johnstones little is known, and even their names are only discovered in ancient charters. As the names of Gilbert and John prevailed in the family for three centuries, it is sometimes difficult to identify individuals; but Sir William Fraser has made out a consecutive pedigree which shows the successive heads of the family from 1170 till the present day. The Johnstones were vassals of the Bruces, Lords of Annandale, from the time of their first appearance in 1170 until King Robert I. resigned the lordship to his nephew, the famous Thomas Randolph, Earl of Moray; and it would have been interesting could we have found proof that John of Johnstone atoned for the unpatriotic deed of his father in acknowledging Edward of England as his overlord. It seems probable that the father, Gilbert, adhered to the fortunes of Robert Bruce, since he received a gift of land in Annandale from that King in 1309, and it is likely that John of Johnstone distinguished himself at Bannockburn, as he still remained in possession of the ancestral property till 1332; but this is merely conjecture.

The first warrior-hero of the family whose deeds are celebrated in verse was Sir John Johnstone of that Ilk (1370-1413) who was one of the Wardens of the West Marches at a time when incursions from England were frequent and sanguinary. In describing an encounter on the Water of Solway in 1378, Wyntoun refers specially to Sir John's prowess, coupling his name with that of Sir John Gordon, who had defeated the English at Carham,

> When at the wattyr of Sulway
> Schyr Jhon of Jhonstown on a day
> Of Inglis men wencust a gret dele.
> He bare him at that tyme sa welle
> That he and the lord of Gordowne
> Had a sowerane gud renowne
> Of ony that was of thar degre,
> For full thai war of gret bounte.

Adam Johnstone (1413-1454), son and successor of Sir John, has received an adventitious prominence in the annals of the family to which his own deeds may not have entitled him. The various claims for the dormant Annandale peerage which have been repeatedly made within the last hundred years have turned to a large extent upon the question whether this Adam Johnstone was the common progenitor of the Johnstones of Annandale and the Johnstones of Westerhall. When Sir Frederick Johnstone of Westerhall preferred a claim to the Marquisate of Annandale in 1876 he brought forward evidence to prove his descent from Adam Johnstone, and as it is impossible to enter here into the details of that famous case, it must be sufficient to state that the Committee of Privileges of the House of Lords decided that he had not made good his claim. Adam Johnstone was both a soldier and a statesman. He took part in the battle of Lochmabenstone in 1448, and several times he visited England on pacific missions to the Court. There is a romantic story of his courtship told by quaint old Sir Richard Maitland of Lethington. According to Maitland, this Adam Johnstone was in love with Janet, widow of Sir John Seton, but could not prevail upon her to wed him. Her only son, George Seton, a mere boy, had been seized by Lord Crichton, then high in power, and had been straitly warded in Edinburgh Castle. The sorrowing widow promised to Adam Johnstone that if he released her son from captivity she would lend a gracious ear to his suit. With the courage of a Quixote and the diplomacy of a Machiavelli, the Border baron succeeded in liberating the youth, and brought him safely to his own castle of Lochwood. The end of the romantic tale is thus narrated by Maitland :—

'The said lady heiring tell that the said laird had convoyit hir sone out of the lord Crichton his handis, sho was contentit to marie him, and bair to him monie sones quhilk war all brether to lord George on the mother syde, of the quhilk the eldest was callit Gilbert, quha was efter ane valiant man, and maid knight.'

One would like to believe that a romance of this kind was veritable reality ; but Sir William Fraser is inexorable. He points out that the Janet Seton whom Adam Johnstone married was not the widow of Sir John Seton, but of his son William ; though he admits that George, first Lord Seton, was uterine brother of Johnstone's family. And as Sir Richard Maitland's own mother was a Seton, and he was born in 1496, it is possible he may have heard the story from the lips of those who knew of the episode at first hand.

The Annandale country had been under the superiority of the Douglases, but the Johnstones, though formerly vassals of that powerful race, took the side of the King against the Earls, and actively contributed toward the downfall of Douglas supremacy. John Johnstone (1454-1493), son of Adam Johnstone, took part in no less than four battles, with the purpose of breaking down the Douglas tyranny, and was the recipient of royal favour as a recognition of his valour. He was succeeded by several Johnstones, regarding whom little is known, although they must have contributed largely to the increase of the power of the family on the Scottish Borders. With John Johnstone of that Ilk (1524-1567) the historical importance of the Johnstones really begins. He was born in 1507, and before he had attained his majority he was a member of the King's Council. The rise of the Johnstones had provoked the jealousy of the Maxwells, and during this laird's long tenure a feud was begun which continued with varying intensity for many years. James V. was disposed to favour Johnstone, and he intensified the ill-blood between the families by practically superseding Maxwell and making Johnstone responsible for the keeping of the West Marches. Fortune did not always smile upon him, for the English overran Annandale in 1547, and attacked Johnstone in his own Castle of Lochwood and bore him away to captivity in England. He was carried from place to place as a prisoner, and according to his own account, published by Sir William Fraser, his enemies several times attempted to poison him while in prison. At length through the interposition of the Queen Dowager he was liberated early in 1550, and permitted to return home. It was during his time that the lands of the Johnstones in Annandale were united into the free barony of Johnstone and entailed upon his heirs male. Though he sympathised with the Reformers (as far as a free-booting baron could distinguish between nice theological points) he did not interfere much with the progress of the Lords of the Congregation, preferring to 'keep his ain hand' on the Western Borders, and to rule from the saddle.

Johnstone was succeeded by his grandson, Sir John Johnstone (1567-1587), whose lot fell upon more troublous times. He was at first a partizan of Queen Mary, but after the hopes of her supporters were blighted at Langside, Johnstone submitted to the party in power, and gave his allegiance to successive Regents with volatile impartiality. During his time the feud with the Maxwells reached an intense degree. Outrages and reprisals were frequent. No Sicilian vendetta was ever pursued so relentlessly as this hereditary dispute between two Border barons and their followers. At length matters reached a climax when, on 6th April, 1585, Lord Maxwell, at the head of one hundred and twenty English and Scottish rebels, attacked Johnstone's Castle of Lochwood in the night-time and plundered it, afterwards setting fire to the place, and burning not only Lady Johnstone's jewels but also the charter-chest containing the family papers. But for the loss of that chest with its invaluable contents, the question of the Annandale peerage might have been settled long ago. Retaliation followed upon this outrage, and for nearly twenty years the Borders were kept aflame by the quarrels between these two families—the Montagues and Capulets of Scottish history. From 1587, when Sir John Johnstone died, till 1613, when the eighth Lord Maxwell signed a reconciliation on his way to the scaffold, constant warfare was maintained between the two clans, and the utmost exertions of King and Parliament were powerless to arrest this feud 'bequeathed from bleeding sire to son.' Referring to the rival families, Sir Walter Scott says, that during this period each of them lost two chieftains; one dying of a broken heart, one on the field of battle, one by assassination, and one by the sword of the executioner.

Some time before his death, in 1567, John Johnstone, grandfather of Sir John, showed signs of relenting towards his hereditary enemies the Maxwells, and appointed John Maxwell of Terregles to bring about a marriage with some of the Johnstone family, which was then the favourite method of terminating a feud. His grandson, Sir John Johnstone, was married to one of the Scotts of Buccleuch, but his great-grandson, Sir James Johnstone, at length fulfilled the request. Sir

James had taken part with his father in several of the raids against the Maxwells, and during the life of his father the feud had raged more fiercely than ever. Yet almost his first action when he came of age, one year after his father's death, was to enter into wedlock with Sara Maxwell, daughter of Lord Herries and full cousin of Lord Maxwell. This portentous experiment was sure to result either in complete reconciliation or in bitterer animosity. The latter was the consequence, and this fatal marriage was the indirect cause of his own assassination. In the very year of the marriage (1588) Sir James Johnstone had to take up arms against the Maxwells by the King's command, as it was known that Lord Maxwell was preparing to assist the Spaniards when the Armada had reached the shores of Scotland. Disputes followed upon Maxwell's submission, but at length in 1590 a formal reconciliation took place, and was confirmed by a Bond of Amity in April, 1592. The peace did not last long; it was only a truce before the renewal of hostilities.

As head of the Johnstone clan Sir James was summoned to meet the King and Council at Edinburgh in March 1592-3. For some unexplained reason he failed to appear, and was promptly ordered into ward in Edinburgh Castle. He managed to escape from his prison, and this was reckoned so serious a crime that he was at once denounced as a rebel. Meanwhile a raid had been made by the Johnstones of Wamphray (celebrated in the well-known ballad " The Lads of Wamphray "), upon the Crichtons of Sanquhar, and the latter appealed to Lord Maxwell as Warden of the West Marches for redress of their grievance. That nobleman was nothing loth to find an excuse for attacking his foes, and he obtained a commission of fire and sword against the Johnstones. Maxwell summoned out his forces, numbering 1500 horse and foot, and Johnstone could only muster about 800 men; yet when the combatants met at Dryfesands on 6th December, 1593, Johnstone managed his little army so skilfully that the Maxwells were defeated, and their leader fell, slain, it was said, by the hand of Sir James Johnstone. This lamentable incident still further embittered the opposing clansmen, and for several years afterwards the strife between the Maxwells and Johnstones raged more fiercely. Sir James made repeated attempts at reconciliation, both for his own sake and that of the rival clans, but these were unsuccessful. At length, years after the conflict at Dryfesands, a meeting was arranged between Sir James and the new Lord Maxwell, but at the very moment when the feud seemed likely to be terminated, a dispute arose between two of the retainers, a pistol was fired, and Lord Maxwell, fearing some treachery, drew his own pistol and shot Sir James Johnstone, wounding him mortally. This felonious deed took place on 6th April, 1608. Lord Maxwell escaped to France, and though he was closely pursued, he eluded capture. Wearied out with the constant dread of pursuit, he returned to Scotland, a broken man, in March, 1612, and by the treachery of his kinsman, the Earl of Caithness, he was delivered into the hands of the avengers. His cousin, Sara Maxwell, the widow of Sir James Johnstone, relentlessly urged his execution, and the King wrote a letter to the Privy Council expressing his surprise at their delay in putting the murderer to death. The final act in this tragedy is thus described :—

'On 18th May [1613] the Council issued a warrant for the execution of Lord Maxwell to the Provost and Bailies of Edinburgh. By that warrant he was to be taken from the tolbooth to the market cross on the 21st, and to be beheaded. Lord Maxwell was at once apprised of the decision of the King and Council. On the day fixed upon he was brought to the scaffold, where he acknowledged the justice of his sentence, asked mercy from God on account of his sins, and expressed the desire that the King would accept his punishment as an atonement for his offences, and restore his brother and house to the rank and place of his predecessors. He also craved forgiveness first from James Johnstone of Johnstone, his mother, grandmother, and friends, whom he acknowledged he had wronged, although without dishonour or infamy "for the worldlie pairt of it," and from Pollok, Calderwood, and his other friends present, to whom he had contributed harm and discredit instead of safety and honour. After giving himself to devotion, and taking leave of his friends and the Bailies of the town, Lord Maxwell placed his head upon the block, and was executed. His lordship was buried in the cemetery of Newbattle Abbey.'

With the execution of Lord Maxwell the long-standing feud between the Johnstones and Maxwells was brought to a close, although it was not until 1623 that the murderer's brother and

successor, Robert Maxwell, first Earl of Nithsdale, met Sir
James Johnstone's son, James (afterwards first Earl of Hartfell), and in the presence of the Privy Council entered into a
bond of friendship. It was not likely that a dastardly deed
like the murder of Sir James Johnstone—so inexcusable as to
provoke the indignation of King and Parliament even in an
age when many heartless actions were tolerated—would be
soon forgotten. But lest the Johnstones might forget the circumstances of the assassination, the bereaved widow caused a
tombstone to be erected to the memory of her husband bearing
an inscription calculated to perpetuate the desire for revenge.
That ' stone of remembrance ' still exists, and must have acted
as a stirring call for vengeance while the murderer was at
large. The quaint inscription reads thus :—

Heir lyis the Ry^t. Honorabil Sr Iames Iohnstone of that Ilk, Kny^t.,
Depairtit [this lyf] of 39 zeirs : Qvha vas maist tresonabillie mvrtherit
vnder traist be the schot of ane pestolat behind his bak be Lord Maxvel
on the 6 day of Apryl, the zeir of God 1608 zeirs. For the crevel mvrther
He vas maist ivstlie forfatit of his haile landis, his armeis rivene in
Parliament, and himself banischit the Kingis dominiovns for the trason
don be him.

The murder of Sir James Johnstone marked an epoch in
the history of the family, for from the time of that event may
be dated the rapid rise of the Johnstones in the political life
of Scotland. James Johnstone, son of the murdered knight,
was only six years of age when that event occurred, and his
nearest kinsman on the father's side was distantly related, and
had neither position nor influence to take upon himself the
onerous duty of guardian or ' Tutor ' of the young head of the
Johnstone clan. But the sad circumstances attending the
death of his father had awakened the interest and sympathy
of James VI. for the fatherless youth, and the King wrote
several letters (printed by Sir William Fraser) commending
him to the care of the Privy Council. When Johnstone was
fourteen years of age he applied to the Council to have tutors
appointed for him, and his kinsman, Robert Johnstone of Rae-
cleuch, was not one of them. In 1622, Johnstone made an
important alliance with a powerful family through his marriage

with Margaret Douglas, eldest daughter of William Douglas of Drumlanrig, afterwards Earl of Queensberry. When Charles I. visited Scotland in 1633, Johnstone was elevated to the peerage with the title of Lord Johnstone of Lochwood. He cast in his lot with the Covenanters, and was a member of the famous Glasgow Assembly of 1638 which abolished Episcopacy. He afterwards raised a regiment in his own district to oppose the advance of the King at the head of the English army, and was actively engaged with the Covenanting army under Montrose. He signed the Cumbernauld Bond along with Montrose, which certainly contemplated the protection of the King against the Covenanters; but as that document was afterwards declared treasonable and publicly burned by order of the Parliament, he joined with the other signatories in the declaration made in January, 1641, asserting that the Bond had been signed under a misapprehension. After this time, however, his ardour for the Covenant grew rather cool, and he was not with the Scottish army at Newburn.

While appreciating the honour which Charles I. had conferred upon him, Johnstone's ambition was not satisfied with the mere title of a Scottish Baron. There are several letters quoted in Sir William Fraser's work which show that he expected a much higher dignity, but he had to wait patiently for ten years ere his preferment came. In 1643 he was created Earl of Hartfell for his 'many conspicuous services' to the King. His loyalty was soon put to the test, for when Montrose—then acting as Lieutenant-General for the King—made his ill-advised raid on Dumfries in April, 1644, the Earl of Hartfell refused to join him, and was reported to the King as having 'stumbled his service.' Nevertheless the Parliament looked upon him as a dangerous person, and he was ordered into ward and confined without trial for seven months in Edinburgh Castle. Ultimately he was liberated on payment of a fine of £1000 sterling and heavy cautionry. This did not prevent him from joining Montrose at Bothwell after the battle of Kilsyth, and raising men in the Annandale district to support the Royal standard. The Earl of Hartfell was present at the battle of Philiphaugh, and though he escaped from the scene of conflict, he was captured by some of the country people and handed over to the Parliamentary forces. He was brought to trial at St. Andrews in December, 1645, and condemned to death. He and Lord Ogilvie were ordered to be the first executed, on 6th January following. The night before the execution Lord Ogilvie escaped, and the Marquis of Argyll, deeming this evasion had been managed with the connivance of the Earl of Haddington, used his influence, on the other hand, to procure a mitigation of Hartfell's sentence, and was successful. After a year's imprisonment Lord Hartfell was liberated, but was compelled to pay the bond of caution of £100,000 Scots, which had procured his former release from confinement. The Earl of Hartfell did not again meddle with warlike politics, and even during the troubled days of Cromwell's occupancy of Scotland, he seems to have remained at home extending and supervising his estates. His death took place in April, 1653, and he was succeeded by his eldest son.

James Johnstone (1653-1672), second Earl of Hartfell, was born in 1625, and took his share of military work with his father, being also partaker in his father's imprisonments. By his marriage with Lady Henrietta Douglas, eldest daughter of the first Marquess of Douglas, he still further increased the power of his family. He had suffered both fines and captivity for the Royal Cause, and when Charles II. came to his own again he did not forget the claims of the Earl of Hartfell. On 13th February, 1661, the King bestowed upon him three new peerages, creating him Earl of Annandale, Viscount Annand, and Lord Lochmaben. The earldom of Annandale had formerly been the title held by a cadet of the Murrays of Cockpool, but had become extinct on the death of the second Earl in 1658, and had reverted to the Crown. The patent conferring this title upon Lord Hartfell expressly states that ' no one is so worthy to enjoy the said title, as well because of his merits as of the proximity of the estates of Annandale to those of Hartfell.' The title was conferred upon him ' and his heirs male, whom failing the eldest heir female of his body, without division, and the heirs male of the body of the said eldest heir female, whom all failing, the next heirs whomsoever of the said Earl.' This very comprehensive destination of title might have been thought sufficient to secure permanency; and yet the title became extinct or dormant in less than a century and a half. The first Earl of Annandale and Hartfell died in 1672, aged 47 years, and was succeeded by his eldest surviving son, William, in whom the honours of the family culminated. Referring to the second Earl of Annandale Sir William Fraser says :—

'This great chief of the Johnstones, the greatest of all the long line of his family, lived in the reigns of six Sovereigns. Born a few years after the Restoration of King Charles the Second, and surviving till the accession of King George the First, he was thus a subject successively of King Charles the Second, King James the Seventh, King William and Queen Mary, Queen Anne, and King George the First. Annandale was too young to serve in any official capacity under King Charles the Second, but under all the other Sovereigns named he was more or less actively engaged in prominent official positions. Under King James the Seventh he first came into official life in the not very enviable position, in company with Sir Robert Grierson of Lag, of putting down the risings of the Covenanters in the western counties of Scotland, a work apparently very uncongenial to the young nobleman. King James also made him a Privy Councillor. When William of Orange made his descent upon England, the youthful Earl of Annandale warmly espoused the cause of the Revolution. But immediately after, on account of his youth and inexperience, he was easily misled and induced by his brother-in-law, Sir James Montgomerie of Skelmorlie, to join in the plot which had for its object the restoration of King James the Seventh. Annandale, speedily repenting of this political indiscretion, cordially confessed his fault, and was the means of ending that intrigue. His frank confession led to his ready pardon by Queen Mary as acting for King William. His revelations showed the extent to which King James the Seventh was ready to make concessions to recover his lost kingdoms. Annandale himself was to be Commissioner to Parliament, and a Marquis, and commissions and patents of peerages were lavishly bestowed upon Montgomerie and Ross, the other two members of the Club engaged in the plot, as well as upon their partizans.

'Escaping from this youthful error, Annandale was afterwards received into Royal favour both by King William and Queen Mary, and the Royal commissions both by these and subsequent Sovereigns granting important offices of State to Annandale, which are still preserved in the Annandale charter chest, are probably more numerous than were received by any subject at that time. The mere enumeration of these royal commissions will show the extent to which Annandale was employed and trusted by his

Sovereigns. By King William he was sworn a Privy Councillor, and appointed an Extraordinary Lord of Session in 1693, while still comparatively young, being in his twenty-ninth year. Two years later he was constituted one of the Lords of the Treasury and President of the Parliament of Scotland which met in Edinburgh in 1695. In 1701 King William appointed him Lord High Commissioner to the General Assembly of the Church of Scotland. Queen Anne appointed him in 1702 Lord Privy Seal of Scotland, and in the same year President of the Privy Council of Scotland; and in 1705 and again in 1711 she appointed him Lord High Commissioner to the General Assembly of the Church of Scotland. In 1705 the Queen also made him one of her principal Secretaries of State for Scotland. In 1714 King George the First appointed him Keeper of the Privy Seal and a Privy Councillor, and next year, when the Rebellion broke out, he made him Lord-Lieutenant of the counties of Dumfries, Kirkcudbright, and Peebles. In that office he displayed great zeal and energy in support of the Government, and contributed largely to the suppression of the Rebellion in these counties. Such in general outline is the official life of this distinguished statesman.'

This quotation affords a very comprehensive panoramic view of the busy life of the second Earl of Annandale. His high rank and important offices brought him into many critical positions, and he has hastily been condemned as a waverer who gave up the Stuart Cause when the Orange party seemed likely to prosper. But the perusal of the detailed biography, written impartially by Sir William Fraser, and largely founded upon authentic documents not hitherto published, should convince every candid reader that the charge of treachery is an unjust one. A nobleman in so exalted a position had many enemies. His early connection with Grierson of Lag in suppressing the conventicles raised the feelings of the religious party against him, and Wodrow's few references to Annandale are evidently tinged with personal animus. The strong attitude which he took up against the Jacobites after he had seen how futile was their plot made them virulent in denouncing him; and even yet there are historians who accuse him of infamous treachery. Alluding to the Montgomerie Plot, Sir Walter Scott says that Annandale was secreted by Robert Ferguson the Plotter for several weeks, 'a kindness which the Marquis repaid by betraying him to the Government.' In the same strain the author of a recent book called 'Ferguson the

Plotter,' repeatedly refers to Annandale as a faithless conspira-
tor who won favour through his treachery.

Sir William Fraser's calm and judicial examination of the
chief incidents in the career of Annandale seems more worthy
of acceptance than the opinions of inflammatory partizans. The
papers connected with this Earl of Annandale, published by
Sir William Fraser, throw much light upon the Massacre of
Glencoe, and the Darien Expedition—two of the important
events of that period. Lord Annandale's attitude towards the
Union of Scotland and England is made very clear both by
the biographical sketch of him and by the letters and papers
included in the second volume. He was opposed to the
Union, contending that the first step should be the regulation
of the commercial relations of the two countries; and even up
to the very last day of discussion upon the Treaty of Union
he was ready with protests against it. But when he found he
could make no way with the pro-Union Members, and was
powerless to prevent or delay the Union, he resolved to do his
best to make it beneficial to Scotland. This was not the
wavering of a 'trimmer,' but true patriotism.

That Annandale was ambitious cannot be questioned, yet it
has not been proved, though often asserted, that he was ready
to take devious ways to accomplish his own preferment.
Honours were liberally bestowed upon him by the Sovereigns
whom he served; and it is no slight testimony to his worth
and integrity that successive monarchs esteemed his moral
character and highly valued his counsel.

'The personal distinctions which he received from his Sovereigns were
as marked as his official appointments. He inherited all the peerages
which had been conferred on his father and grandfather by King Charles
the First and King Charles the Second. By King William the Third in
1701, when he represented His Majesty in the General Assembly, he was
advanced to the dignity of Marquis of Annandale, Earl of Hartfell,
Viscount of Annan, Lord Johnstone of Lochwood, Lochmaben, Moffatdale
and Evandale. And after his appointment as President of the Privy
Council in 1702, he was, in 1704, invested by Queen Anne with the ancient
order of the Thistle, re-established only in December of the previous year
by Her Majesty. Although Annandale enjoyed so many principal offices
of State and personal dignities, there was still another office and a still
higher dignity to which he aspired. The office was that of Lord Chan-

cellor of Scotland, and the dignity that of Duke of Annan. But he did not survive to receive either of these appointments.'

The Marquess of Annandale died at Bath on 14th January, 1721. By his first wife, Sophia, daughter of John Fairholme of Craigiehall, he had three sons and two daughters. His second wife, Charlotta Van Lore, daughter of John Vanden Bempde of Hackness, had two sons. James Johnstone, the eldest son, succeeded as second Marquess of Annandale, and died unmarried in 1730. As both his brothers had predeceased him, unmarried, the succession fell to his half-brother, George Vanden Bempde Johnstone, who became third Marquess of Annandale. The latter was born in 1720, and became Marquess when only ten years of age. The death of his brother. Lord John Johnstone, in 1742, deranged the mind of the Marquess, and in 1747 he was declared incapable of managing his affairs. He was never married, but he survived till 1792, when he was succeeded in the estates by his grand-nephew, James, third Earl of Hopetoun, directly descended from Lady Henrietta Johnstone, the eldest daughter of the first Marquess of Annandale. As the patent of the Earldom of Annandale provided the titles to the descendants of the eldest heir female, failing the direct male line, James, third Earl of Hopetoun, as the heir female, claimed the title by petition in 1792, but did not assume the title of Earl of Annandale. As he had only female issue the Earldom of Hopetoun passed to his half-brother, Sir John Hope of Rankeillour, great-grandfather of the present Earl of Hopetoun. Lady Anne Johnstone Hope, eldest daughter of the third Earl of Hopetoun, succeeded to the Annandale estates and claimed the titles, but she died while her case was in preparation. Her son, John James Hope Johnstone of Annandale (1796-1876), took formal proceedings to have his right to the titles of Earl of Annandale and Hartfell declared; but in 1844 the House of Lords resolved that he had not made out his claim. An important document was accidentally discovered by Sir William Fraser in 1876, which seemed to make the claim of Hope-Johnstone unimpeachable. The case was re-heard in 1876, and after a long investigation the decision of 1844 was adhered to. Mr. Hope-Johnstone was succeeded by his grandson, the present Mr. John James Hope-Johnstone of Annandale, who has not made a formal claim for the titles. Sir William Fraser, who has been engaged in the Annandale Peerage case since 1841, and is thoroughly acquainted with all its mazes, has written a most interesting appendix to his second volume, entitled ' A Century of Romance of the Annandale Peerages,' in which he details all the proceedings, and very clearly sets out the basis of the Hope-Johnstone claim.

The second volume of *The Annandale Family Book* is entirely occupied with letters and documents connected with the history of the Johnstones. Some of these are important historically as throwing light upon obscure incidents; while others are of value as affording glimpses of social life in the seventeenth and eighteenth centuries. One of the latter may here be quoted as showing the literary taste as well as the defective orthography of ladies of the highest rank in the Scottish nobility two centuries ago. It was written by Christian Leslie, daughter of the famous Duke of Rothes, and wife of the third Marquess of Montrose, and was addressed to Sophia, Countess of Annandale. The Marchioness had married Sir John Bruce of Kinross, Bart., and she wrote her letter from Kinross House, the now deserted mansion near the town of Kinross.

'Kinröse, July 4, 1693.

' Madam,—I render yow a thowsant thankes for your play, which is vere good, and I heve rettornead itt with the bearear, and if your ladyshipe heve eather enay mor good playes or novells which yow heve read, and will be plesead to lean them to me, I shall be vere fathefouell in restorenge, and teke it a great faver, for they ar vere deverting in the cuntery. Your lord did me the honouer to dayn hear yesterday, and was vere well. I hertely wished your ladyshipe had come alonge, for itt wold heve bin bott a devertisment in this good wather, and yow wold heve bin vere wellcome to, dear madam, your ladyshipes most humble servantt,

' C. MONTROSE.

'For the right honorable the Counttes of Anandeall, att hir logeng in Netherayes Waynd, Edinburgh.'

It used to be a favourite joke with both Sir Walter Scott and Lord Macaulay to ridicule the spelling of John Graham of Claverhouse, Viscount Dundee; but not the wildest cacography of that much-abused hero could surpass the epistolary style of this daughter of a Duke and wife of a Marquess.

So rarely has the reviewer an opportunity of finding an error in Sir William Fraser's works that the pointing out of the solitary mistake in these two bulky volumes may be pardoned. In his sketch of Sir James Johnstone (1587-1608) he writes:—'For the purpose of marrying the Princess Anna of Denmark, King James set sail for Denmark on 22nd October, 1589. The marriage took place at Upsal on the 23rd November, etc.' Sir William has followed Tytler and other historians in giving to the place of marriage the name of 'Upsal.' David Lindsay, minister of Leith, who accompanied the King and performed the ceremony, wrote a letter home (quoted in full by Calderwood, Vol. V., p. 69) dating it from 'Upslaw.' In the Register of the Privy Council under date 1589 the name of the place is given as 'Opsloe.' The name 'Upsal' which Tytler gives is not unlike Upsala, but that town is in Sweden, and the King of Denmark of the time had no control over that country. The whole question was examined in the *Scottish Review* for 1893 (Vol. XXI., p. 142) in an article entitled 'The Wedding Tour of James VI. in Norway,' and the town was identified as Oslö, the old Norwegian burgh now one of the suburbs of the comparatively modern capital, Christiania. Even the very house in which the ceremony of the marriage took place is still in existence.

A. H. MILLAR.

ART. II.—VICTOR HUGO, THE POET.

WHEN a great controversy has for ten years circled round a dead poet's name, we may assert without fear of contradiction that the world, with its many chisels of individual opinion, is already hewing his niche in the solid rock of fame. But it is Time alone which, in some mysterious manner, settles whether the shrine which the poet is to occupy shall be small or great. In the meanwhile a prophet may resign himself to the fact that many will cast doubts upon his prophecies. And indeed he has no easy task, for to arrive at any satisfactory conclusion he must compare with the poet under discussion not only the singers of classic days but also those who for many years have influenced his literary life.

Was Victor Hugo a great poet? That is, not only a poet of his day and a poet of his country, but a world-wide recognized poet? Each country has its own answer as to what constitutes true poetry. Though England and France have but a narrow bracelet of opal sea between them they are widely severed by many differences of opinion, and one of these refers to the question, 'What is poetry?'" No Englishman will challenge the inspiration of Shakespeare, the stately march of Milton, the greatness of Dante, and the sweet singing of Tennyson, but many, and Matthew Arnold was one of them, will deny that Victor Hugo deserves a place among the immortals, in spite of the fact that Mr. Swinburne has placed the Frenchman in Shakespeare's company.

It is but fair to say that the majority of Englishmen, even those who possess 'a liberal education,' chiefly know Victor Hugo as the writer of *Les Misérables,* but of his claim to be a great poet, a Titan of inspired song, they know nothing at all, and they will excuse this ignorance by the *quid pro quo,* 'What do our neighbours know of Shakespeare?'

Certainly for many generations the French have lived in deplorable darkness on the subject of him who was 'self-schooled, self-scann'd, self-honour'd, self-secure,' yet there are evident signs that a change is coming, and that soon Shakespeare's best commentator may be a Frenchman. Before this happens let us at least give some passing study, if not to Victor Hugo's entire poetic productions—an impossible task— at least to the best poetry of his best period. Leaving his prose works entirely on one side, we are still confronted by an immense volume of verse, and the task of sifting it is not made easier by Mr. Swinburne's pages of panegyric. We naturally feel shy of contradicting the unhesitating and almost unqualified praise found in his 'Study of Victor Hugo.' For a time, indeed, it leaves us silent and bewildered. A humble critic, who knows that he is mortal and therefore that he may be in error, is swept away by such oft repeated words as—'immeasurable '—' incomparable '—' vast and profound sense '— ' immensity of imaginative range '—innumerable beauties '— ' magnificent and rapturous hymn.' Worse, he is in danger of losing all his bearings when he reads in print such verdicts as these upon the French poet. ' There is nothing in Homer, or Dante, or in Shakespeare, the three only poets who can pro- perly be cited for comparison, of a pathos more poignant in its bitter perfection of sweetness.'—' The man by whose name our century will be known for ever to all ages and nations that keep any record or memory of what was highest and most memorable in the spiritual history of the past.—" *Onorate l'altissimo poeta.*" '

But turning next to a French critic of repute, strangely enough we find this last prophecy unhesitatingly contradicted.

' Others,' says Lemaitre, ' are persuaded that Victor Hugo has incar- nated the philosophy of the century and that posterity will say '' the age of Victor Hugo,'' as we talk of the '' age of Voltaire.'' This is a most extraordinary illusion. I assure you that in 1900 no one will use this expression. The poet of the '' Légende '' has often delighted our imagina- tion, but he has hardly stirred our thoughts, having but few of his own. The men of my generation owe him but little, those who follow will owe him nothing at all.'

These are indeed opposite poles of opinion ; no wonder that lesser wits remain silent, uncertain how to refute the poet and not quite willing to give in their adhesion to the critic ; and so they go on in search of some other landmark of critical thought, or else—which is perhaps a wiser course—they refer to Victor Hugo's own works without offering a fee to any guide. Be- fore following this last course let us first listen to the opinions of other writers, remembering that all of them are helping time to formulate its unerring verdict, that is when each shall have been weighed in its perfect balance.

M. Bourget who, on many subjects, possesses deep insight, was honest enough to own, when writing soon after Victor Hugo's death, that the poet's literary work was so immense, and so complex, that the ordinary methods of criticism failed before it, and that this man who for more than sixty years had startled the world with his varied productions, paralysed analysis so that no single formula could comprise all that he had produced.

'In the form of his work,' says M. Bourget, 'he at once rises above his peers. Lamartine was more melodious, Alfred de Musset more pathetic, De Vigny more thoughtful, but no one before him manipulated rhymes and rhythm with so much ease, and no one has so strongly bitten in the right idea with the acid of the inevitable word. Compared with him, other poets sound a little dull, and other prose writers a little insipid. He was a great visualizer and like Rembrandt he worked in strong colours. He was the great master of light and shade, revelling in the lightning that immediately precedes the thunder, and in the hailstorm that is chased away by sudden sunshine. His liking was for sharp effects and violent contrasts, so that classic restraint must have appeared somewhat monotonous to him. Very early in his career he burst the bonds of French poetry, displacing the cæsura, and making the Alexandrine bend before the breath of his special genius. Like the vision of the sheet let down from heaven he declared, once for all, that no work was unclean, exclaiming, "Plus de mots sénateur, plus de mots roturier." Having done this he then threw all the force of his genius into the enrichment of rhyme.'

In that admirable French series of 'Les grands Ecrivains Français,' M. Léopold Mabilleau, whose book on Victor Hugo should be read by English readers, gives us what appears at first sight a very fair study of the poet as a thinker and a singer. Here the question is plainly asked, 'What trace will Victor Hugo leave on human thought? Can his philosophy be compared to that of an Aristotle, a Leibnitz, a Hegel, or a Darwin? Will he rank with Plato, Spinoza, or Kant, or can his poetry, as Louis Veuillot has insinuated, be summed up by the words "Vain imaginations circling round nothing," a mere windmill of words that has never let fall one of measurable weight?'

M. Mabilleau declares at once that this accusation can be easily refuted, that Victor Hugo has more than most poets enriched the world with ideas, and that he has allied abstract thought with popular phraseology. He realized the mystic union of the thought with the word, of nature with art, and brought about this unity with superabundant imagery. But the poet in fact outlived his own poetry. He had been a great romantist and romanticism was struck down. He had been called the master of lyric poetry, and he was superseded, so that presently young scornfuls, calling themselves naturalists, symbolists, or decadents, threw mud at their former idol, at the forger who had wrought with his own hands the spears which now they hurled at him.

Many modern poets who have failed to be original, have blamed Victor Hugo for not having been able to show them the path of fame, but we must not forget that *Les Orientales* was like a mighty revolution as well as a startling revelation to the votaries of rhyme. (We in this country must remember also that there is no such thing as blank verse in French, it simply does not exist). Henceforth all French poetry was of necessity and in spite of all detractors 'Hugonized.' Moreover the poet was full of that vital strength which is an inherited birthright, indeed he was all life, and what he really felt he felt strongly. We may compare him to a modern instrument, played on by all the winds of thought, the breath of science only excepted. He was a reflection of everything and was influenced by everything, feeling as Keats felt, and as we believe all true poets feel, that he was but as strings vibrating to every passing touch, but as the echo of all voices, —that is, the least original of all men, because so highly sensitive as to respond to all.

Representing thus all human sounds he yet added a personal note, though at times, indeed, he lost all sense of proportion, allowing the *ego* to become far too pronounced. This often caused blasphemers to point the finger of scorn at him, but on the other hand he delighted those—and they are many—who can but feel the impersonal through the personal, and who love to look through a microscope, so that for them the real may be ten times magnified. Shall we for this reason say that such people do not see the truth because all they look at is enlarged? What they see is at the same moment truth and untruth, but if they cannot mentally correct the proportion, at least they can take in what otherwise they would never have seen at all.

Théophile Gautier, that perfect workman in prose, had, as we know, a very near view of the poet. He did not in consequence lose for him his feeling of enchantment, for he was always unsparing in his praise, but writing in 1867, he finds no difficulty in classing him amongst other French poets, and he shelters himself from a conclusion as to their relative worth by referring to the verdict of time. Lamartine, Victor Hugo, Alfred de Musset, are the names he joins together, and then he owns that he himself is fairly puzzled as to which poet shall be accounted the greatest. By this we see that in his estimation Victor Hugo was not, though the 'Légende des Siècles' was already written, the unapproachable Titan whom some would have us think him.

This uncertainty of opinion whether a man is a world-wide genius or merely one among other equals is a very interesting subject of thought to the ordinary reader. He asks himself, 'Has chance some weight in the balance? How is it that if the standard of an author is immeasurably high, every judge, however small, does not immediately recognise it, or is it that the ordinary mortal cannot lift his head high enough to see what rests upon the mountain? Is it ignorance or humility? Is the reader blind or dazzled, or is poetry, like love, a mystery, which only the initiated can really understand? In fact, what is the aim of poetry, and what do we expect it to give us?' If we could answer this question we could more easily judge whether the poetic metal sends forth a true ring, or whether, on the contrary, it is debased or hollow.

In whatever dress poetry may clothe itself it must not be an exact reproduction of reality. In this arena poetry would easily be conquered by truth. Poetry must not reproduce, but it must create; nevertheless, its means are merely human, it cannot 'speak the word' and work a miracle, it can but create the ideal from the real. If poetry chooses history for her theme, she must give us the essence of abstract character by making use of new combinations. If she decides that the soul shall be her province, she must clothe this most ancient of subjects with new imagery and paint the ideal with a brush dipped in new and wondrous colours. If inanimate nature is her province, she must add new grace to the graceful, new beauty and new sublimity to the sublime. By these tests, then, shall we recognise true poetry, for they at once sweep away, amongst other evils, all that savours of the common-place.

Further, poetry must never be the slave of reality, but, strange paradox, she must make the ideal appear to be the real. Her ever present aim must be to ennoble all that she touches, and thus to react on all who touch her, so that the progress of poetic thought shall be possible only upon a higher plane. ' Il faut avoir de l'áme pour avoir du gôut ' has been said and we might adopt for poetry this truth about taste. But let us remember that poetry is on the lowest plane when she merely circles round the poet; so that the greater the poetic impulse, the farther will poetry soar away from its own source.

Did Victor Hugo ever err on the side of the common-place, or in other words, did he ever strive to rival nature on her own supreme ground? To this accusation we must plead guilty for him, especially when considering the poetry of his earlier period. Hence the feeling which we occasionally experience of being in company with the common-place. Then it is that we realize that nature requires no dictionary and needs no inventory, so that the poet fails where the ready reckoner begins. Very often also he fails to rise above himself, for the personal is so strongly impressed upon his poem that this low flight of necessity never carries him up to the highest plane of poetry, that plane where the poet is as if he were not, and where only the heavens are to be seen. How little do we know of Shakespeare, how much of Victor Hugo! On the other hand his imagination, though at times failing in true humour, was boundless. He would touch an object and immediately that object lived its own new life, whilst round it would surge new and endless images, like a fully grown tree whose branches spread out on all sides of the tapering stem, but all of them having sufficient room to expand and each being perfect in itself. In this, when he forgets to be his own echo but becomes the mouthpiece of earth's endless voices, we recognize the true poet.

Another very noticeable feature in Victor Hugo's poetry is his constant use of, and his perfect manipulation of the crescendo in thought and in construction. As he ascends, the metaphors and the varied visions unroll themselves fuller and stronger, till without warning comes the contrast, then hovering on the summit for a longer or shorter time the gradual descent follows and he gently takes us back to earth, unless indeed, which is often the case, the poem breaks off suddenly like a horse pulled up on its haunches by the firm hands of an experienced rider. In these cases we are carried away by the pure force of his genius and we forget the man and the manner : as in ' La Comète ' and ' La Vérité,' and that most perfect of all descriptions of battles, ' Le Cimetière d'Eylau.'

But then suddenly we pause and we try to analyse what it is which has just moved us. Was the thought adequate to the accumulated feeling, and were all the images true reflections of the central idea ? Some there are who have coldly analysed the poet's subject matter and scornfully asked, ' Do these themes adequately represent the philosopher of the nineteenth century and the deep thinker among poetic prophets ? ' In many cases he is a true philosopher, but we must not look for deep philosophy from the man who was but little influenced by science, though he lived in the very midst of a scientific age. He was not one who could gaze for long together down into the heart of things; but on the other hand may we not ask, is this absolutely necessary for a poet ? We think not, especially if the tests which we have suggested are not found wanting. He was accused of giving us merely everybody's ideas in his own words—words forming a style which was eminently his own and to which he had given birth. We all know that everybody's ideas may too easily be expressed in platitudes, and before his best period we find platitude in Victor Hugo. But everybody's ideas clothed in new and costly attire and adorned with new imageries, till the commonest word appears to palpitate with life, this is certainly a poet's crown of glory, and we may unhesitatingly accord it to Victor Hugo.

When the volumes entitled *Châtiments* and *Contemplations* appeared, Victor Hugo had perfected this new style, this original and living imagery which is so extremely difficult to discover, because the ordinary mind is strongly wedded to old grooves and the race is essentially conservative of its old forms. We still use worn out imagery, though for us it has long lost its true meaning. We say, 'The rosy dawn,' 'The gentle zephyr,' etc., but Victor Hugo, by the instinct of his genius, cut the chains that bound us to these old thoughts and in their stead substituted new imageries ; always well chosen, and when in company never jostling each other. Neither was he satisfied to give us merely one new image to serve an old idea. Like a ball kept bounding by repeated blows, the old idea is kept renewed with many and various similitudes and new interpretations, till the reader is left amazed and delighted, hardly finding his way in the enchanted labyrinth full of living and personified thoughts and of personified nature.

There was yet another effect which Victor Hugo trusted in and which, in the end, he sadly exaggerated, though perhaps no master has used it so ably. This was his extraordinary power of enumeration. We are swept away by the torrent, though our sympathy and our admiration are most often left high and dry. It savours too much of the reference dictionary and of prepared lists. At times, indeed, when we take the trouble to examine these lists, we are left still more confirmed in our feeling of disappointment, for however much they may tickle the ear they remind one too closely of a conjuror and of his wonderful bag full of incongruities. In like manner the names and places which Victor Hugo strings together, with no break or stop, are often hopelessly indefensible if the reader pauses to think. The leading idea is drowned in the whirlpool of words, being unable to find a reasonable support either from the historical or from the other allusions presented for our edification. Further, perhaps Victor Hugo's own character inclined him to love paradox, the paradox which startles the reader and arrests his attention. This habit, if we can call it so, may easily be carried too far, though often, as in Victor Hugo's case, it adds just that touch of personal character which is much to be admired. For instance, what can be more lovely than this idea,

'Aux champs, d'où l'on voyait un si vaste horizon
  Qu'un petit enfant seul pouvait l'emplir.'

Or again when he says that God sometimes replaces a
mother by a grandfather,

'Et fait, jugeant l'hiver seul capable de flamme,
  Dans l'âme d'un vieillard éclore un coeur de femme.'

But after a time this strophe and antistrophe becomes a
little irritating, because we soon learn to expect its arrival,
and even when it is most perfect—(as to imagery and suit-
ability it is nearly always so in Hugo's best period) we are
not so much moved as we should be, for it savours too
much of a trick, or of a confirmed habit, and loses the beauty
of the unexpected. Because of this, however, Victor Hugo's
poetry becomes a mine of good things, though not always the
familiar friend with whom one loves to saunter in all weathers
and in all moods. On the other hand, how few poets have the
wit to create a perfect contrast, and how often it is a failure
when they attempt it; Hugo's source was never dry, but language is a very delicate instrument which should never be
hurled about like a football. Every thought, however refined,
has, could the author find it, its perfect vocabulary. Every
image, however subtle, has its right colour, could the artist of
words paint it; but to connect ideas together—that is ideas
which in reality should never touch each other—this will certainly produce an effect, but it will not be the right effect, and
it will only help to deteriorate that perfect taste to attain
which, as we have said, the possession of a soul is needed.
Victor Hugo's taste is often at fault, and at times even leads
him into ridiculous places, especially when he makes himself
the mouthpiece of God. For instance in 'Quelqu'un met le
Holá' in the first 'Légende,' after enumerating what God can
do—a list which decidedly lacks dignity—he thus ends with
this violent antithesis.

'Et qui, lorsqu'il lui plait, donne des millions
  D'astres aux firmaments et des poux aux lions.'

But when kept within its just limits, this power of contrast
adds brilliancy to what is brilliant. In 'Le cimetière d'Eylau'

which is perfect throughout, the subject and the words are exactly fitted to each other, and the juxtaposition of ideas is not too startling for the occasion. We doubt if a battle has ever been, or can be, better rendered. Out of it we might select a dozen perfect lines, but the whole should be read.

> ' Mais rien ne sait mourir comme les bons vivants.
> Moi je donne mon coeur, mais ma peau je la vends.'
>
> .   .   .   .
>
> ' Les rois ont les soldats comme vous vos jouets.'
>
> .   .   .   .

Notice also the delicate irony which inspires this simple touch,

> ' Tacher de n'être morts qu' a six heures du soir,
> En attendant tuer, c'était notre devoir.'

When Hugo deals with children his metaphors are never exaggerated. Here he can use the right word and we have not to reproach him, as so many of the modern writers have reproached 'le père Hugo.' for his bombastic language.

Of the child a year old he says in ' L'idylle du vieillard,'

> ' Il a le tremblement des herbes et des feuilles,
>
> .   .   .   .
>
> La jaserie avant le langage est la fleur
> Qui précède le fruit, moins beau qu'elle, et meilleur
> Si c'est être meilleur qu'être plus nécessaire.'
>
> .   .   .   .
>
> ' Ses premiers mots ont peur comme ses premiers pas·'

Another example of the perfect strophe and antistrophe we find in the poem entitled 'A quoi songeaient les deux cavaliers dans la fôret' in *Contemplations* which again avoids any exaggerated antithesis.

> ' En ce moment, des yeux pleurent, d'autres yeux veillent,
> Et je lui dis " Hélas" d'autres sont endormis.'

But on many other occasions the poet seems to lose sight of the relative worth of words and of facts, making the historian shudder and the mystic frown. M. Lemaitre, having steeped himself in Victor Hugo whilst writing about him, expresses this opinion somewhat in Hugo's style, when he says of him, 'A man for whom Robespierre, S. Just, and even Hébert and Marat are giants, and for whom Bossuet and De Maistre are odious monsters, for whom Nisard and Mérimée are fools, that man may have genius but be certain that he has nothing else.'

We must remember, however, that this genius—who was 'nothing else '—wrote for sixty-nine years and published fifty or sixty thousand verses. Posterity has to weed out his many faulty lines and to enshrine the perfections of his special genius. When it has done so, we do not doubt but that the residue will live and will become classic, and that Victor Hugo, in spite of his many faults, will take his place amongst ' Ces grands esprits parlant avec ces grands fantômes,' even if he has to accept the lowest seat. For, as a modern writer has said, 'He in whom blind hatred for particular classes of men and great political institutions, has become a passion, can never be a poet of the history of humanity, for the muse of that history is love and not hatred. A man must be a partaker of Shakespeare's all entrancing toleration before he can ascend to Shakespeare's altitude. True tolerance, wisdom and judgment are the requisites of every great work, and therefore of every good poem. The failure of men of the first order is thus a lesson in the highest morality as well as in the highest criticism.'

To help those who have no leisure to hunt for pearls we will briefly notice a few poems of the poet's best period. Anyone who takes up the Victor Hugo theme feels quite at a loss to select examples, for even these must often only resolve themselves into the writer's favourite selection from a limited number of his poems.

Though *Les Orientales* gave great promise of his genius, *Les Châtiments* and *Contemplations*, published in 1856, have been generally accepted as the best volumes from which to date this period of perfection of workmanship and of highest poetic flight. In this period we include *La Légende des Siècles*, *Les Chansons des rues et des bois*, *L'année terrible*, *Seconde Légende*, and *L'art d'être Grandpère;* this last was published in 1887. Ten out of his eleven plays had appeared before *Les Châtiments*, and form a period apart. His last play, *Torquemada*, was published in 1882, and has not received much general favour, yet if we examine *Ruy Blas*, the last but one of his plays, we shall see

all the best and all the worst of his dramatic wit in it, and not
for one moment can a critic—endowed with less genius than
Mr. Swinburne—bring his lips to breathe a comparison between
the author of *Hamlet* and the writer of *Ruy Blas, Cromwell,* or
any other of the eleven plays. Hugo is infinitely superior—
according to our present ideas of superiority—in the art of
construction. The *mise-en-scène* is excellent, the characters
live and move, come in and go out, as stage folk should do.
They follow laws of expectancy and laws of contrast, laws of
surprise and laws of satisfied justice. Shakespeare, actor as
he was, does not satisfy modern dramatic art in this way,
therefore let us, if we like, place Hugo far above the singer of
the Avon for stage knowledge; but does all this trick of
machinery constitute a great dramatic poem? Does perfect
rhyme and rhythm only give us what is necessary to make the
poet, or does the portraiture of the inner depth of character,
the magic mirror, held up to human motives and to the strange
irregularity of human thought, count for little? Take this
speech of *Ruy Blas* and compare it with the lines spoken by
Hamlet.

> ' Ecoutez, quelle que soit sa sphère,
> Monseigneur, lorsqu 'un traître, un fourbe tortueux,
> Commet de certains faits rares et monstrueux,
> Noble ou manant, tout homme a droit, sur son passage,
> De venir lui cracher sa sentence au visage,
> Et de prendre une épée, une hache, un couteau !
> Pardieu ! j'étais laquais ! quand je serais bourreau ?'

.   .   .   .

> ' What is a man,
> If his chief good and market of his time
> Be but to sleep and feed ? A beast, no more.
> Sure, He that made us with such large discourse,
> Looking before and after, gave us not
> That capability and god-like reason
> To fust in us unused.'

In the first we find the dramatic setting of the words perfect, but the second raises us above all thought of the theatre
or of the footlight. *Cromwell,* a fine play though never acted,
is still full of that consciousness of dramatic power which the
highest art alone can hide. Take for instance the following

lines, when Cromwell is reproaching his son for drinking the king's health.

> ' Va, c'est un vin fatal qui trouble la raison !
> A la santé du roi tu buvais du poison !
> Ma vengeance veillait, muette, sur ton crime.
> Quoique tu sois mon fils, tu seras ma victime.
> L'arbre s'embrasera pour dévorer son fruit ! '

And Richard answers—

> ' Pour un verre de vin voilà beaucoup de bruit ! '

The love of strong antithesis is already visible, a love which was carried much further and with stronger effect in the poems of the middle period.

Though an English critic has assured us that the four or five best dramas of Victor Hugo must be looked upon as his most perfect work, we must venture to differ from this judgment. Certainly they are splendid plays, they are full of fine lines, they satisfy our dramatic instincts; but they fail to satisfy our highest ideal. Leaving them on one side, therefore, we turn again to the books which we have mentioned, to find that which may prove really satisfying to the best part of our poetic nature, though feeling that on this vast subject the critic must perforce be somewhat personal, and that he can but point to the right path and must not stop to enumerate all the flowers growing by the way-side.

But first, in order to justify our choice, we must repeat what has been said so many times before, that art should avoid mere personalities and mere personal invective. Many fine things will be ruled out of the volume of perfection because of this transgression. The verdict of time often reverses judgments, but it never gives in its adhesion to pure invective. Victor Hugo wasted much of his energy in chastising his enemies, forgetting, in spite of the good advice, as well as the trite morality, which he bestows on us, that he himself transgressed beyond forgiveness when he published his private hatreds to the literary world, a world which requires from its servants that art should be impersonal, that is an inheritance for all, and not an amusement for the spiteful. Your sin will find you out more certainly in that which you write than in anything else, for vanity, revenge, individual hatred, all these find no place in works which live, and the cup of poison mixed for another has in the end to be drunk by the author himself. Happily for us there is much of divine pity in posterity, and it reverently buries bitter curses, refusing to make them classic. Yet if ever poet fancied he had a sacred cause it was Victor Hugo when he hurled his literary lightning at Napoleon III., for it is in *Les châtiments* that Hugo's power reaches maturity. The seven books contain nine *motifs*. In the first the bandit, hidden by the fog, has taken his lamp and his knife, and approaches the bed of the sleeping Republic. Secondly, the crime is accomplished. Paris has been plunged in silent horror by the *coup d'état*. The soldiers, the generals, and the lawyers all throw themselves at the feet of the bandit. Thirdly, the man who has inherited the name of Emperor strives to throw some splendour on his own darkness by lighting his lantern at the flame of Austerlitz. Fourthly, all that is base surrounds him, cringing for favours. Fifthly, a vision of those who have died. Sixthly, the murderer's progress to the place of consecration where the Archbishop blesses him. Seventhly, the departure of those sent to Cayenne. Eighthly, the prophecy of the expiation. What will it be? Not the guillotine, for the Christ had said 'Love one another.' Then lastly comes the punishment, *i.e.*, the pillory of the poet's hatred.

We must quote a few lines of this splendid *Nox et Lux*, this palpitating poem of hatred for a debasing system, remembering that the poet prophesied long before Sedan, and that, whether at first from chance or from deep insight, he never swerved from his hatred of Napoleon 'le Petit.'

The poem addressed to the people and justly admired, begins,

> 'Partout pleurs, sanglots et cris funèbres.
> Pourquoi dors-tu dans les ténèbres ?
> Je ne veux pas que tu sois mort.
> Pourquoi dors-tu dans les ténèbres ?
> Ce n'est pas l'instant où l'on dort.'

ending with the fine refrain of,

> 'Lazare ! Lazare ! Lazare !
> Lève-toi.'

Here is the true poetic ring and no mere verse making; the effect is spontaneous, and we bow before the poet's true genius. Again,

> ' On ne peut pas vivre sans pain :
> On ne peut pas non plus vivre sans patrie.'

When the poet forbids the death of the tyrant we have this noble cry,

> ' Non, liberté, non, peuple, il ne faut pas qu'il meure.
> Le progrès, calme et fort, et toujours innocent,
> Ne sait pas ce que c'est que de verser le sang.'

The final note of hope in the poem is intensely dramatic, culminating in a fine crescendo and followed by the gradual descent—the lull after the hurricane.

> ' D'ailleurs pensons. Nos jours sont des jours d'amertume ;
> Mais quand nous étendons les bras dans cette brume
> Nous sentons une main ;
> Quand nous marchons, courbés, dans l'ombre du martyr,
> Nous entendons quelqu'un derrière nous nous dire ;
> " C'est ici le chemin." '

In the *Contemplations* the outside world is discarded, and the poet steps into an inner sanctuary, for the book has been called, ' The Memoirs of a Soul.' He first contemplates child-hood, next comes the shadow cast by love, then the soul ex-pands, and everything is viewed with new understanding. Nature teaches her many lessons, the birds, the stars, the flowers and fruits, and the ripples on the water ; then manhood arrives, duty must be faced, and truth sought for in the pro-gress of humanity.

Victor Hugo had always unbounded faith in his vocation as a teacher and a prophet, and it was because of this that those whose creed was purely ' art for art's sake,' would not reconcile themselves with the exile of Guernsey. Now he takes up the theme of social evils, and shows that the root of the evil is moral decadence. He believes sincerely in God, but, says he, ' His face is now veiled but one day the mask will fall.' In the meanwhile the ignorant and the unlearned see deeper than others into ' l'au delà,' for the man who began life as worshipper of kings, ended his career by worshipping the people. Lastly the poet takes up the theme of death, and perhaps Victor Hugo's unshaken belief in immortality did more real good than many of his mighty innuendoes against rulers and rich people.

In 'Mors,' 'Cadaver,' and 'Ce que c'est que la mort,' he shows his belief. In the first he sees a smiling angel walking close behind the reaper Death. In the second, we find a splendid idea of the joy of the dead body now regaining its freedom in the universe, and being no longer subject to man's will.

> ' Je vais me rajeunir dans la jeunesse énorme
> Du buisson, de l'eau vive et du chêne et de l'orme,
> Aux ravins, aux halliers, aux brises de la nue,
> Aux murmures profonds de la vie inconnue ! '

In the third poem the poet sums up the subject by saying, 'Ne dites pas mourir : dites naître. Croyez.'

But the *Contemplations* are not merely themes about life and death, there is a place given—and from henceforth there will be always that place at Victor Hugo's hearth—to satire. His literary enemies and those who scoff at his religious creed are scourged with words. *Réponse à un acte d'accusation* is a splendid torrent of defence against the accusations of his enemies and a description of the work he has accomplished in liberating language and poetry from its ancient chains. *Quelques mots à un autre* is a satire of the first order.

We must pass on to *Les Chansons des rues et des bois.* Here his imagination comes more into play than his passions; it is a lull in the battle. *Souvenir des vieilles guerres* and *Le Soir* are good examples, but when we come to the volume called *L'année terrible* Victor Hugo is more in his element. *Sedan* opens it. The old victories are enumerated, the old generals of the famous wars appear, and the heroes of Waterloo rise up and deliver up their swords. The book naturally falls into two parts. The first is the struggle with the foreign foe, the second is the civil war. In the first Hugo is strong as the soldier's son, and he exclaims :

> ' O morts pour mon pays, je suis votre envieux.'

And then remembering that once he wished all nationalities to be merged into one great brotherhood, he gives this explanation of his altered attitude.

' Mais l'amour devient haine en présence du mal.'

In *L'année terrible* his little grand-children flit across the
scene and throw welcome light upon the darkness.   He is
preparing for his work *L'art d'être grandpère* when he says,

> ' A chaque pas qu'il fait l'enfant derrière lui
>   Laisse plusieurs petits fantômes de lui-même.'

This beautiful idea has, we think, never been expressed before,
or at least never so well.

Then comes his cry for no vengeance on those who brought
about the civil war.

> ' De ces pleurs, de ces maux sans fin, de ces courroux
>   On entendait sortir ce chant sombre.   Aimons-nous.'

Certainly no one could hate better than the poet who, from
this time, however, is to become the preacher of love, but even
hope in this sad book is painted pale, and we close the volume
with a sigh.

Casting aside the personal, Victor Hugo sets before him in
the triple *Légende des siècles*, the epic of the centuries.   It was
to be his greatest work and it had a plan as vast as life.   God
and the devil, evil and good, were his themes, the struggle of
humanity towards divinity.   In the poem *Vision* he explains
the *motif* of his work.   He sees the wall of centuries rising out
of darkness, a chaos of human beings joining the nadir and
the zenith.   Two celestial chariots appear.   One is Fate, the
other God.   Their paths meet, there is a grand upheaval,
darkness is shaken and the centuries are broken up, but out of
the wreck one is conscious of the invisible presence of God.
We dimly perceive the ray emanating from liberty, and we
can hear the flutter of the wings of hope.

La Légende naturally begins with the origin of man ; then
follow many figures of the Old Testament.   Eve, Cain, Iblis,
Daniel, Boaz, the soul of Balaam, then Christ in His tomb.

The well known poem called *Conscience* is full of striking
symbolism and explains how the epic will be developed.   Conscience is the ray of light crossing the wall of the centuries, it
is she who shines through all the darkness, and she is here
compared to one drowned in an ocean of shame where all is

turbulence, but ever and again the drowned corpse appears, not only to such men as the Cid and Eviradnus, but also to the brute creation. Wild beasts and the horses of heroes are endowed with speech and become symbols helping to work out his great metaphor. The Archangel's sword slays Rabert, the slayer of children, for, he explains, to kill a child is to kill conscience.

' Dans l'enfant qui bégaie on entend Dieu parler.'

Further on the poet conclusively proves the triumph of good over evil, and with many symbols he marches on towards the final struggle, though death was to overtake the poet himself before he could reach the end of his great epic.

Every one has read 'Boaz asleep,' a perfect idyll full of simple grandeur. In it Victor Hugo refers to Divine goodness in these words, for the optimist in him was more and more gaining ground—

' Une immense bonté tombe du firmament.'

We cannot follow out the 'Légende,' where myths and realities are blended into a gorgeous whole. We can only indicate some of the poems to be noticed. His continual cry is 'Believe in God, the soul is immortal, and the great moral law must be kept.' His satire on the vanity of all things can be read in 'The seven wonders of the world,' but much of the 'Légende' needs close attention if we would follow out his argument, with its ever-recurring refrain of belief in man's future life.

' Et nous nous en irons vers l'étoile éternelle.'

But he does not give himself up merely to contemplation, he believes that man must ever progress, and he has thus expressed it in these very fine lines—

' Ce n'est pas de toucher le but, c'est d'être en marche,
Et cette marche, avec l'infini pour flambeau,
Sera continuée au delà du tombeau,
C'est le progrès.'

Before leaving the 'Légende' we should like to point out a poem in a lighter vein and which is as spirited a song of sea rovers as we have seen.

' En partant du golfe d'Otrante
　　　　Nous étions trente,
　　Mais, en arrivant à Cadis,
　　　　Nous étions dix.'

Also 'Chanson d' Eviradnus,' 'Le Mariage de Roland,' and
many others. Numberless lines might be quoted, but we had
better refer the reader to the original, for the more we read the
more we pause to reflect, and feel that though all the critics may
be great, Victor Hugo is greater, even if we cannot express this
fact as M. Lemaitre does, when he says, ' Let us put Victor
Hugo in his right place, that is the first rank—nothing less, but
nothing more.'

Is there not something more in these quotations?

' O triste mer, sépulcre où tout semble vivre.'

.　　.　　.　　.　　.　　.　　:　　.

' Non je ne donne pas à la mort ceux que j'aime
Je les garde, je veux le firmament pour eux
Pour vous, pour tous.'

But we must leave space for 'L'art d' être grandpère l' Here
Victor Hugo is full of tenderness and of passion. Tenderness
for grandchildren and all children, full of anger against those
who brand the new-born as criminal. Satire, idyll, and philosophy, all these can be found in this volume. Théophile Gautier
said of it, ' This book is great like Homer and simple like the
" Bibliothèque bleue." ' To him the child is ' La souveraineté
des choses innocentes.'

Perhaps there has never been such a poet of childhood as
Victor Hugo. His great love for his own children and grandchild and his power of becoming one of them, enabled him to accomplish what only a very few grown up people can do, that is,
mentally to become as a little child. Whatsoever may be their
mood he can translate their ideas. From the first opening of
their sleepy eyes and all through the livelong day, he can think
as they think, and be as delightfully positive as they are, till
nightfall comes, and tired out, they are silent in slumber.
' Jeanne asleep ' is the title of four poems in this volume, and in
each a new phase of this charming subject is presented. He sees

Paradise thrown open to sleeping children, and he hears the stars bidding them to be good.

'Jeanne au fond du sommeil médite et se compose
Je ne sais quoi de plus céleste que le ciel."

. . . .

'Il est si beau l'enfant avec son doux sourire,
Sa douce bonne-foi, sa voix qui veut tout dire,
Ses pleurs vite apaisées,
Laissant errer sa vue étonnée et ravie,
Offrant de toutes parts sa jeune âme à la vie
Et sa bouche aux baisers."

One should read the 'Sieste', and the poem on the children's visit to the *Jardin des plantes,* where 'Five-years-old' says, 'Les lions c'est les loups', and 'Six-years-old' answers, 'C'est très méchant les bêtes,' but for perfect and quiet humour we could not choose better than the poem on Jeanne when she is naughty. We see her comforted by her grandfather, who brings her some jam whilst she is in durance vile, much to the indignation of those in authority.   But jam brings Jeanne to penitence.

'Et Jeanne a dit d'une voix douce,
"Je ne toucherai plus mon nez avec mon pouce,
Je ne me ferai plus griffer par le minet."
Mais on s'est écrié—"cette enfant vous connait ;
Elle sait a quel point vous êtes faible et lâche,
Elle vous voit toujours rire quand on se fâche."'

We dare not multiply quotations.   If some have thought that a child's ideas were hardly worthy of a great poet's attention, such have failed to gather up the philosophy of life and have not understood what Victor Hugo expresses so well in his poem called 'The Pope.' 'L'enfant, c'est l'ange. Laisse-moi le bénir.' The child is the outward expression of what is best in human nature, besides being, as Wordsworth so well expressed it, "Father of the man.'

But we must close this short study of a great subject.   We have but slightly indicated what can be sought for and found in Victor Hugo's book.   After 'L'art d'être grandpère' he published in 1881 the third Légende, then 'The four winds of the spirit,' in 1882, dying two years after in 1885.   His later poems are perhaps more echoes than new notes, but they are noble echoes of the former music of the aged poet, who at 83 years old passed away when the month of May brought back the roses.

Often when a critic has spread out his carpet, meaning to sit in judgment on Victor Hugo, before long we find him like Balaam, blessing instead of cursing. Victor Hugo's themes are certainly old themes, and 'decadents' may scoff at them as at worn out creeds, for these creeds merely embody justice, love, faith, reason, beauty, liberty and the ideal. Perhaps, as in 'Plein Ciel,' these moral virtues are too indiscriminately displayed, but does humanity always rule itself so entirely by them as to find them trite? Are such themes ever worn out? The poet's own faith in God never wavered, and therefore he never ceased to fulminate against suicide, foreseeing the increase of it, to which increase we can testify, for as faith dies courage becomes weak and life's burden is too easily cast off. When death deprived the poet of his beloved daughter two months after her marriage, though prostrated by grief, he could still write these lines,—

> ' Je viens à vous, Seigneur, Père auquel il faut croire ;
> Je vous porte, apaisé
> Les morceaux de ce coeur tout plein de votre gloire,
> Que vous avez brisé .   .   .
> Dans vos cieux, au delà de la sphère des nues,
> Au fond de cet azur immobile et dormant,
> Peut-être faites-vous des choses inconnues,
> Où la douleur de l'homme entre comme élément.'

His enemies said that he saw too many visions,—so did the great Hebrew poets, whose writings are still our admiration.

Look at the force of this vision of a sower, in which three lines give us a picture full of deep thoughts.

> ' L'ombre où se mêle une rumeur
> Semble élargir jusqu'aux étoiles
> Le geste auguste du semeur.'

Again, he proved too much that the rich are bad and the poor are good. He liked the paradox, 'Le laid c'est le beau;' but if we read ' *Les Malheureux,* we see what a fine argument it is for poverty, and if it is exaggerated it is a finer exaggeration and worth more than our own plea of heredity which so often sweeps away all responsibility. More and more we shall have to be grateful to the poet for his belief in the opposite creed, and for not hurling his imprecations at the inequality of human lives, for he had a firm faith in a happier hereafter.

> ' Le monde captif, sans lois et sans règles
>   Est aux oppresseurs ;
>   Volez dans les cieux, ailes des grands aigles,
>   Esprit des penseurs ! '

Even if we could afford to despise his ' common philosophy ' there is one crown which we could not displace from his brow. This is the perfection of his style, in whatever sense we may interpret this word. ' Because Victor Hugo was a great artist in words,' says the famous critic M. Brunetière, ' some of the most hidden depths of language and thought were revealed to him.' What finer teleology and autology than his poem entitled *Abîme* when God answers all vain-glorying nature and proud humanity by this single line,

> ' Je n'aurais qu'à parler et tout serait de l'ombre ! '

It is just ten years since Victor Hugo died, and this decade suffices for us to feel the pulse of criticism, though it is not long enough for Time to make a clear distinction between what is earthly and what is heavenly in the poet's work. Victor Hugo has been no exception to the rule that the greater the man the more will he be open to fierce attack, for has it not been truly said that everybody in a crowd can throw mud and most people wish to do so ? But attack shows signs of life, so do not let us be deceived by this visible warfare, and do not let us fear to misplace our honest admiration because critics have spoken otherwise. It is now too much the fashion to think through others either for good or for evil, to criticise through critics, and to praise through connoisseurs ; often therefore all that we might gain by direct contact with an author is lost, and we are gradually bereft of power to discriminate between good and evil.

The truth is that few critics have the genius to know a great poet or a great prose writer on his first appearance ;

they like a precedent and genius has none. Jules Janin, called 'the prince of critics,' tried to kill Balzac, prophesying that his books would appear but to be forgotten: now it is Jules Janin who is nearly forgotten. It needs genius to recognise genius, so let us take our critics for what they are worth. It is not their verdict which builds up a reputation; in some mysterious manner it is that of the humble readers, for usually it is they that receive a genius gladly. Jules Janin scornfully reproached 'Paris' for reading Balzac, meaning by 'Paris' the great bulk of readers who were of no consequence. Well, Paris received Victor Hugo and applauded him though he was unlike any previous French poet. They could not criticise, they could not pick holes in him, but they knew that a great poet had been in their midst, and they honoured him gladly. He had been their mouth-piece, he had expressed what they felt, though they could not put it into words. He had understood their sins, their virtues, and their imprisoned idols, and so they rejoiced.

If we, on our side, cannot adopt all Mr. Swinburne's language, if we cannot say with him, 'Onorate l'altissimo poeta,' reserving this praise for a greater than Victor Hugo, we can at least crown him with a laurel wreath, and forgetting that at times he degraded poetry by uniting it to party hatred, remember only that at his best he soared to the gateway of heaven.

ESME STUART.

Art. III.—SUTHERLAND FOLK-LORE.

THAN Sutherland there are few Scottish counties richer in folk-tale and legendary lore, despite the fact that this remote shire is less strictly Celtic than the more southerly shires of Inverness and Argyll, both as to native population and as to language. In the days of the Vikings, this part of Scotland was the favourite 'outland' of the Scandinavians: there was a day, says Rob Donn, the Sutherland bard, when the men of Lochlin were spilt on these shores, and like manure they enriched the land they despoiled, so that to this hour the Norseman and the Gael dispute the soil in West Sutherland.

Unquestionably the natural nomenclature is everywhere mainly Celtic, except along the actual seaboard where Scandinavian suffixes and prefixes stand out like rocks among the Gaelic designations. For the most part, too, the names of the people are Celtic, though Somerled, Torcall and other Norse names are frequent, and here and there almost as common as in the Long Island itself. The commonly accepted version of the first of these names is that it comes from *Sumarlidi*, the summer-sailors, as the Vikings were called from their habit of setting forth at the first sight of summer on their predatory excursions to the Hebrides and the Sutherland and Ross coasts.

To a West Sutherlander I am indebted for a brief narrative in connection with another Norse name, Sven. He declared that the common Irish MacSweeny and the less frequent Scottish MacSween or Sweenie are variants of Sven. There was a Loch Inver man, according to him, of the name of Sween MacSween—Sven Svenson as the Norse would have it. This man died many years ago; and when he was ill he told a friend that he knew where on the Ross coast was a long lost treasure of the Norsemen, and that the secret had been handed down from generation to generation. The reason why none of the family had availed themselves of the knowledge was because of a dreadful curse which had been laid upon it. Thrice, indeed, daring spirits had ventured to put the legend to the proof, but each occasion was followed by results so terrible that sacrilegious curiosity was damped emphatically for a generation or two. The story is that each of these treasure-seekers was seized by invisible hands, whirled round and round, and then dashed to pieces on the rocks. The third was hurled over one of the cliffs of Loch Torridon—far away from the supposed site of the Norse treasure—and was dashed against them like a storm-blown bird.

It is this survival of the Scandinavian strain in place-names, human-names and in the general characteristics of the people, which makes Sutherland so especially interesting.

To the Scandinavian adventurers of old the *Sudr-eyjar*, the

South Isles, were the Fortunate Isles of the West. They knew them first in the smiling summer months or when the halcyon calms of September made them seem doubly beautiful; and moreover the summer-sailors came to them from bleak Iceland or from the even bleaker if less ice-bound Orkneys. Thus the Sudr-eyjar (particularly the Hebrides) and *Sudrland* (Sutherland) became to them the land of promise. As to those daring sea-rovers of a bygone time, so, too, is the Sutherland of to-day a Sudrland, a land of promise, to the lover of old romance, of hero-tale and folk-song, of strange half-pagan survivals and of stranger and wilder superstitions.

A century ago the mother of Rob Donn, the pride of the Reay country, would sing songs old as the tongue she spoke so sweetly, would recite stories of the heroic days when Ossian sang and Deirdrê's beauty made swords flash from sea to sea. To this day there are men and women of Sutherland whose hearts are warmed by a glow from the same wonderful past, and in whose minds still linger dreams of the time when Bran, the best-loved hound of Fionn, was buried in the district of Loth.

The place-names of Sutherland, so admirably brought together by Mr. John Mackay, yield a rich harvest to the student of folk-lore, and in not a few of them is revealed the imaginative insight of the Celt, while many others are suggestive of the oneness of his life with the life of nature. Here are some typical instances:—Cagar-feosaig, hill of the whispering wind; Ascana-greine, hill upon which the sun's rays first shine; Clais-na-creamha, hollow of the wild garlick; Dalbhain, snow-white meadow, producing abundance of daisies; Ben-chlibric, speckled mountain of strength; Monadh-stairneach, moorland of noise (of brooks); Loch-coire-na-fearna, loch of the corrie of the alder wood; Loch mo Naire, loch of my disgrace, a piece of water in Strathnaver, so called because, hard pressed, a woman of Ross had to throw therein her three pebbles efficacious in the cure of many diseases; Loch-an-fhionn-leathad, loch of the fair slope; Meall-na-h-oillte, hill of terror; Lochan-na-claidhean, lochan of the swords.

I shall not tell here of the Last of the Giants, of the Origin of Loch Ness, of the Brollachan, or any of the other Sutherland tales included in Campbell of Islay's wonderful collections. Neither shall I recount the story of Farquhar, the physician of the Reay country, of the Cailleach Mohr who dwelt on Ben Chlibric; of Modr Bbain, the witch of Assynt; or of Donald Duival and the band of little men who made the elfin bridge across the Dornoch Firth. The legends here given were gathered many years ago in Sutherland, although variants of some of them are common to other parts of Scotland, and will be familiar to folk-lorists. I am greatly indebted to Mr. John Mackay for his generous aid, and also to Mr. George Morrison, from whom I hold several of these legendary episodes.

In Sutherland, as in other parts of the Highlands, the summer sheiling and the winter *ceilidh* were two of the most potent factors in the creation and development of the love-song, in the conservation and familiarising of the folk and hero-tale. At the sheiling (*i.e.,* the hillside-croft at the summer-pasturing on the mountains) the women would sing songs while they were milking, and the old wives, and the shepherding folk in general, would narrate legends of the past, or wild tales of the Hill-witch, the Water-kelpie, and the mysterious Leannan-Sith or fairy-lover. The *ceilidh* might be described as the Winter Nights' Entertainment. Here the village historian, the bard, and the *seanachaidh*, recite and extol the heroic deeds of the clan—feuds of old time, wrongs righted or unredressed, forays, encounters, dramatic episodes by hill and glen, by moor and loch, or on the wild north seas. These songs and legends would be recited during the *ceilidh* round the ingle-nook throughout the long winter evenings, when the glow from the peat-fire fell on the face of many a brother Gael. On the hills, too, the shepherd-seanachaidh was wont to brood over the legends and traditions of his home and of his people that had passed from mouth to mouth for many generations. In this way the old legendary lore has not only survived, but often gained a new significance.

Every village and hamlet had its special house for the celebration of the *ceilidh*. Sometimes it would be one of those low, turf-built dwellings such as were to be found in Sutherland at the beginning of this century. The largest of the four rooms, built in single line, and one opening in to the other, was probably given up to the kye ; next came the ha' or sitting-room, its peat-fire smouldering on a flat stone in the centre ; the third room was subdivided for sleeping purposes, and the fourth was known as the place of the stranger, for of yore, as to-day, in the Highlands, a passing guest was ever welcome. Sometimes the *ceilidh* folk met in the kitchen of a larger house, where were several chairs and a big couch. As the stories were told, and song followed song, the man of the house would make a new creel, mend his nets against the fishing season, or wind ropes of heather or straw for his roof. Meantime the girls would be carding wool, and his woman would sit at her spinning-wheel, rising only to add peats to the fire round which the company sat.

Until recent years, many such meetings took place in the parish of Eddrachilis. This parish, lying on the north-west coast of the country, embraces some of the wildest and most desolate parts of Sutherland. On the heights of Beinn Hee, the hill of solitude, the eagle has his eyrie ; beneath, the narrow glens are the haunt of the wild deer. The people hereabouts are supposed to be descended, for the most part, from the Pictish tribes that dwelt in the straths before the Norsemen came from over the sea and drove them inland. In these days, of course, there were giants, and here is an Eddrachilis tale of one of them :—

In the valley which runs between Polin, the place of the pool, and Blairmore, the big moor, the carn-famhair may be seen to this day : great boulders of gneiss guard the entrance to the cave, and the fissures in the ground tell of the travail of the earth in past ages. Many centuries ago, before St. Ronan had set sail from Ireland towards the coast of Brittany, before Donan, the Culdee missionary, and his fifty 'muinnter' died the martyr's death on the Isle of Eigg, at the time, it is said, when the Druids performed their strange rites in the green solitudes of the forest of Reay, a giant dwelt there. Whence he had come, no man could say ; only that it was from a distant country, peopled by giants grim and mighty as himself. He was strong as the oak, and like it his strength increased with the passing years : tall he was, for his figure towered above the trees of the forest; his long hair was black, but no whit less black than the shaggy, matted beard which fell over his great chest; eyes, red with the thirst for blood which flamed therein, were almost hidden by the black eye-brows, and coarse black hair sprang from his nostrils. Save for a girdle of animal skins, he was naked; but even in time of snow, or when the deer sought shelter from the northern blasts, the tangle of hair which lay thick on his skin protected him from cold. Marks of many a bloody battle he bore, and the scars and cuts on his face made it still more hideous to look upon. His only weapon was a staff cut from the trembling poplar, of the same height as himself, and of a thickness with his thigh. This he wielded as if it were a cane. In his rough mane of hair was a tangle of aspen leaves; and one thing the Gaels of old held was that he who wore a wreath of trembling aspen leaves on his head loved not their gods; they knew, too, that the strength of such an one came from the under-world.

The giant fed upon the children of the Oldshore district. Often, as the mists crept down the mountain, he was seen to enter his cave with five or six little ones on his back. At times he feasted on the men and women, and he had been known even to carry away a Druid priest, white-robed, in the act of worship. But he liked best the tender flesh of youth, and when this was within easy reach, the elders were safe.

As day followed day, the giant grew more ravenous, and there was scarce a household that had not paid to him the tribute of a young life. Then those who dwelt between the kyles held council, and decided to march against the monster. With garlands of mountain ash and of oak to protect them from evil, and in their hands the rude weapons of the time, the men set out for the cave; but ere they were within arrow-shot of the entrance, great stones, flung by the giant as if they were pebbles, fell, killing some of the most valiant of the band, and compelling the others to retreat. The stones, rounded by the force with which they hurtled against the earth, now stud the hill above carn-famhair; on several are marks of the giant's nails graven as they slipped from his fingers. Thereafter this enemy of man grew more fierce; his devastating hand was ever at work, his wild eyes were as balls of fire in the country of Ashir. Again the

people plotted to kill him.   This second time they lay in ambush
at the mouth of his dwelling.   Long they waited for his coming,
and at last he entered through the gate of stones; then with a
shout of victory they surrounded the opening.   He must starve
was their thought, as day followed day and he did not appear.
Their watch continued.   Finally, when two moons had waxed
and waned, it was found that the giant had escaped by a low,
winding passage to an outlet a mile distant; even as they waited,
he was wreaking his vengeance on the women and the children.
The mounds which rose as he forced his way through the tortuous passage mark his course to this hour.   In vain ambassadors
with peace offerings in their hands were sent to the giant; with
a savage grin he fell upon them, and flung their bones to the
expectant folk of the clachan.

At last the great festival of the Druids drew near.   White
bulls were made ready for sacrifice; men were chosen to die the
death on the rath of the stones.   White-robed priests
chaunted strange lays to Hesus, the deity whose pulse was the
ocean-beat, whose breath was the winds of the world.   The bulls
were slain, the fair Gaels bound to the altar: all awaited the
coming of Hesus.   Instead of the god, the figure of the giant
appeared striding swiftly towards the place of sacrifice.   Every
man fled, and the giant gorged himself upon the carcasses of the
bullocks, and upon the flesh of the men on the altar.   It may
be that because of this thing the anger of Hesus was loosed, but
no man can say for sure.   Thereafter the Druids worshipped in
the groves of the oak, and when the day of sacrifice was come
again, they called with a yet louder voice to the mighty Hesus.
Then a strange thing befell.   A giant, Eoghan he was called,
came to do battle with the shaggy man of the cave.   Whence
he came none save the priests knew, and they were silent when
men questioned them.   Eoghan was not so tall as the cave-
dweller; his face and his hair were fair, and he wore a covering
woven of leaves.   No fierce light burned in his eye, but it seemed
as if the wind and the sun had beat upon his face for long.   An
oaken club, neither so long nor so stout as the poplar staff of his
adversary, was his sole weapon.   'On the morrow,' said he, as he

set foot in the country, 'on the morrow I will fight the demon of carn-famhair.'

The yellow month had passed. Every hill-side was clad in purple, and as the sun rose a soft wind, with a whisper of coming winter therein, passed over the mossy plain of Blair-Odhar—now a desert of sand—the blooms of the Canach waving their white heads as it passed.

Scarce had the sun risen over the chain of hills, when the giant of carn-famhair was seen to emerge from his rock-dwelling and stride towards the plain, brandishing his staff in the air and uttering fierce imprecations. Then Eoghan went out to meet him. Foaming with rage, the giant said: 'Hast thou come out to gaze on my strength, to minister to my wants, or dost thou await the glory of being slain by me, O thou fair man?' And Eoghan made answer: 'I come, I come, but I come not in vain, O giant. Neither to look upon thee, to serve thee, nor to be slain by thee do I come. I am here to aid the distressed. I am the servant of Compassion.' 'Bedone!' roared the giant; 'as the beasts of the forest fled at my coming, so will I drive thee from this land.' Eoghan heard the words unmoved. 'Vain boaster,' he said, 'on this field thou must die, and over thy body I will raise a hill of sand. Generations of men to come shall hear the crackling of thy bones as they walk thereon.' Then each swung his staff in the air, and their words of incantation were heard by the folk who watched. The roar of the hairy monster was as the roar of the incoming tide in the deep caverns of Cape Wrath, but Eoghan was silent and calm as the cloud-capped summit of Beinn Hee. For long it seemed as though the giant would be victorious, but at last a mighty stroke from the staff of the fair man felled him. His cries of agony rent the air, and rocks, with the strength of ages upon them, were cleft on the hill-side; his brains were spilled over the plain, and awe was in the heart of the onlookers. Eoghan went towards the Sea. As he approached, the wind broke into fury and the waves rose. Then the sand of the shore was borne in great clouds to the plain, in clouds so thick that the sun was darkened and day became as night. Thus the body of the giant was covered. Blair-Odhar became Cnoc-Odhar, and what before was a sandy shore is now a beach of shingle. The bones of the giant still crackle beneath their bed of fine sand, but Eoghan, the deliverer, has been seen no more.

The district of Assynt is overlooked by the four oldest mountains in the British Isles : Ben More, proud of his age and of his greatness ; Quinaig, the couchant lion, guarding Loch Assynt ; Canisp and Suilven whose rude heads peer over the heather-clad heights and the walls of rock that rise out of the water on the opposite side of the loch. At dawn and at sunset, and as the mists drift off the mountains, exquisite hues, like the vivid colours of dream-clouds, may be seen here ; rich gold fading through saffron to a warm half-light, or ambers too delicate to reproduce. It is, truly, a fit retreat for the 'people of old ; ' and, if, anywhere, the Celtic gods still linger hidden among the lonely places, it may well be that the land of their exile is this remote corner of Gaelic Scotland.

Formerly, and indeed until a comparatively recent date, Assynt was populous. But here, as elsewhere, 'the Sutherland evictions' cleared the ground in a tragically literal sense. Where the smoke of the croft once rose from machair and strath, may now be seen only wandering flocks of sheep, and where the laughter of children came from the bothie in the glen or the shieling upon the hill, is now to be heard only the whirr of the grouse-cock or the monotonous belling of deer.

In one of the many clachans scattered over this mountain land, Piobaire Connull was born. His name was familiar throughout the home-straths, for Connull the Piper it was who made the piobroch speak as no other man of them could do, and sweet is the sound of that voice to the Gael. In time of battle, he marched with the clan, and it was as if victory were already theirs ; when a chief was 'laid under the turf of truth,' Connull played the coronach ; and at a wedding feast none other could play save Piobaire Connull. Loved by his chief and by his people, the hero of the fair daughters of the clan, he won the heart of the fairest girl of all. Sons and daughters were born to them, and the two lived the free, blithe life of the time.

It chanced one day that the Piobaire was bidden to a marriage a short way off. It was a Thursday, and for every hour in it he played to the guests as he had never played before ; even at nightfall his pipes gladdened their hearts, for in those days the dance and song lasted long. Not until dawn did he rest, and then after a brief pause and more than one *cuachs* of drink, he went to the sports. Again, as darkness fell over the country, the skirl and drone of his pipes made the folk dance more madly than ever, made the drinking cups pass from hand to hand more swiftly. On Saturday Connull followed the young couple as they visited their friends of the clachan. The afternoon feast was heavy, and as each guest bade farewell, he quaffed the *deoch-an-doruis*, the door-drink. The Piobaire's draught was a long one, worthy of his race and of his calling, and thereafter he set out for home, marching to his favourite tune, 'I am away, I am away, I am away from Assynt !' The sound of his pipes was heard long after his figure had passed out of sight.

That night his woman waited for him by the peat-fire. At last, weary of watching, she fell asleep. Sunday passed, and still the piper did not reach home. On the morrow word of his absence was carried far and wide, and search was made for the missing man. Folk sought along the banks of the loch; the river was followed from its source among the hills to its mouth; and men peered into rocky chasms and under a hundred great boulders. But all was in vain: days and weeks passed, and Piobaire Connull was seen of no man; none heard the sound of his pipes or set eyes upon his face. 'He has gone on the way,' said some; others held he had been done to death by a rival piper, or that, weary of his own people, he had fared to the land of the stranger. But one or two, on a Friday it was, when the 'men of peace' cannot hear, murmured, 'For sure he is with the fairies; has he not played to them before?' And the lone woman he had left knew in her heart that this was a true thing.

Some time thereafter the chief was killed in a broil with a neighbouring clan, but another piper than Connull had to play the coronach when his body was laid in the earth. Many things chanced as year followed year, and at last another man took the place of the Piobaire by the side of his widow.

At this time there lived in the district of Assynt one known as Bean-Mhath Achabhan, the good wife of the fair meadow. Every woman with the 'sweet illness' upon her knew that it was she who tended them well, and brought them to the green land of joy that lies on the further side of the black passage of child-birth. She watched by the bed of peasant and chief; her gaunt figure was known alike in the croft and the castle. One night the midwife sat alone in her turf hut. Gazing at the peats, she saw token of a stranger coming for her, and she questioned whether to give him welcome by heaping more peats on the fire, or to spurn him by pouring water on his image. While she mused there was a gentle rap at her door. Opening it, she saw a little person clad in green cloth, a bow and arrow in his hands: 'Good evening, Bean-Mhath Achabhan,' was the friendly greeting of the dwarf, but the midwife knew he was a fairy of high rank. 'It is following me you will be, for my wife is in travail, and has sore need of you,' and despite a thrice-spoken refusal, the midwife at last consented. With the green girdle of the fairy over her eyes, for more than an hour she was led over hill and valley. Then she heard a sound of distant music, and the bandage was removed. She was in a grotto, brilliantly lighted, and of vast size, whose walls were gorgeously decorated. On her way to the couch of the queen she passed through the great hall. There stood a man playing the pipes, and what should the tune be but 'I am away from Assynt'; 'A, ghaoilaich! A, Phiobaire! is it you I'm seeing,' exclaimed the midwife. 'Yes, Bean-Mhath Achabhan,' said the man, and without further word he continued his playing. The shout of joy that came from the green-robed multitude when the good woman left the bed chamber of the queen filled the great palace; a host of little beings offered her thanks, and when she was ready to return, with a 'Peace be with you' to all, the Piobaire again stood in her path. 'Is it coming home with me you are, Connull, my man?' 'As soon as I will play this tune,' he re-plied. 'I was away for two nights at the marriage feast, and my word is upon giving these people a tune before I go home.' 'You have been absent many years; the chief is dead, and your woman married to another man,' Bean-Mhath Achabhan said. But the light in the piper's eyes was strange as he made answer, 'You have drunk too deep of the water of Alltan-bhan, mid-wife; when I finish my tune, it's coming I will be." As she followed the prince the sound of the pipes grew dim. She never saw the piper again.

Her guide led her, as before, blindfolded. When she thought to have reached firm ground, she drew a clew from her pocket, and, as if intent upon fastening her brogue, fixed the end to a twig by her side. Thus she hoped to discover the abode of the quiet people. Before she reached her hut, however, the thread ran out, but after a long search on the next day, she came upon the loose end and traced it to the dwarf birch whereto she had fastened it. Thereafter a council of the hill-folk was held. Now there lived in a cave on the Assynt coast, near Rhu Stoer, a hermit skilled in the black art. At cockcrow on a certain morning, this man made a circle round the fairy knoll, a staff of oak in his right hand, in his left a rowan branch. Alone on the summit of the knoll—for the people at his bidding had withdrawn, in order that his spells might work—he put the two staffs one across the other; below the point of meeting a garland of oak and rowan twigs was laid, and in the four spaces the legs and comb of a pure black cock, the mane of a black stallion, and the fins of a haddock were laid. Then the man repeated his *duanag*. No sooner had the cock crowed, than the skirl of pipes was heard on the other side of the knoll. There sat the piper Connull, with his pibroch at his side.

Frail and old was the man, and few of the clan could recognise him. He was dazed too. Not even the sight of the *tigh-dubh* * or the sound of the piobmor cheered him. After a brief while, as the darkness gathered, he was seen to leave his house. The way he took led to the hills, and since that night the piper has been seen neither on the mountain slopes nor in the valleys of Sutherland. It may be he still pipes to the green-clad inhabitants of fairyland.

Swordley, a hamlet in the parish of Farr, has been an elfin region for many ages; of the numerous sith-raths in the hamlet, four, known as *na cairn caoil*, the narrow cairns, are conspicuous objects. Around these and other cairns the little people danced; beneath them, in palaces whose gilded splendours form the subject

---

* Black house where the whiskey was distilled.

of many a ceilidh romance, they made merry as only fairies can. Within the last few years old inhabitants of Swordley have seen a ring of green-clad folk dancing on one of the conical hills in the centre of the clachan.   There now dwells at Swordley a family whose grandsire's grandsire was Adam Mòr, the miller. His mill-wheel was turned by the Swordley burn.   The little Daoine Sithe paid him many a visit, indeed at times he thought that they stole his meal as it was being ground.   Nevertheless, Adam, who was a prudent man, held his peace and said not a word to their discredit.   Time came, however, when, incensed at the repeated visits of the men of the knolls, Adam muttered, 'This thing is no longer for the enduring;' so early one morning he turned the water off the mill and went home.   When Adam Mòr returned a few hours later he saw that not one stone re- mained upon another; even to its foundations, his mill had been razed to the ground.   Thus do the men of peace treat those who seek to do them ill.

The heights of Sutherland are studded with lochs, and each has its name, Loch-na-h-ealadh, the loch of the swan, no less than great Loch Shin.   Many of these lochs were favourite haunts of the *Each-uisge*, the water-horse or kelpie.   At times he would appear as a dark, shaggy pony, or as a brindled horse with fine, glossy skin; occasionally he would take on himself the form of a man, or lie moored to the lochside as a black boat with oars in the rowlocks; nay, he has been seen to move down the centre of lochs in the guise of a boat under sail.

Loch Chrois, the loch of sorrow, which lies in a remote part of the county between Oldshore and Strathan and at the foot of Ben Chrois, has for generations been the home of a kelpie.   He has assumed various forms, and played many a belated traveller false on misty nights; but for the most part, save for the tale which follows, no crime is laid to his charge.

On a summer afternoon when silence brooded over the hills, and the waters of Loch Chrois were motionless, two lovers sat on a sand-dune at the end of the loch.   *Is milis a' burn à cup nuair ghoideas na a'*, 'sweet is the water out of the cup when stolen,' says a proverb of the Gael, and sweet to the lovers was this time because none knew of their meeting, least of all their fathers and mothers, for between the two families was a great feud. As they talked, the sun sank behind the mountain; still they sat side by side when the afterglow suffused the western sky. The silence of a summer afternoon passed into the peace of a summer evening, and dark shadows gathered in the hollows around them ere the lovers bethought them of their homes. 'The game I came out to snare is still on the wing,' the youth said; 'the kye are on their way to the homestead,' was her answer. As they spoke, their eyes lighted on a black horse which pastured beside the loch. Thinking that it belonged to the clachan whence they came, the lovers led it towards a boulder, and there sprang on its back. Hardly were they seated, than the horse headed lochwards, and when they tried to slip from his back, they found that an invisible power gripped them. Then they knew that their steed was the Each-uisge of Loch Chrois. On the further side of the water, men and women were returning from Fuaran-gearradh, the cool well, whose waters, blessed by a passing saint, cured sick folk of many diseases. To them the lovers shouted for help, but it was in vain, for already the kelpie had gained the edge of the loch. Louder than the cries of the unwilling riders, rose the wild neighing of the black horse, as with unwonted fierceness he reared and plunged into the loch. On either side of him as he fought his way to the centre, vast clouds of vapour were seen to rise from the water; and the people fled affrighted at the weird sounds that broke the stillness, and the strange sight on the loch. The bodies of the lovers were never found, and in every clachan and strath for miles around it is held that the demon carried them to the loch-depths where he dwells, there to await the call of the pibroch on the day of days.

An old woman who died at Oldshore not more than fifty years ago once saw this same kelpie. She was returning from Shinnery at the end of summer, when a thick mist fell, wrapping the valleys in gloom. Well as she knew the road, she lost her way, and the grey of the mist had become the black of the night ere she reached the edge of a loch. The boulders on its banks seemed to her as gigantic rocks, the ripple of the water as waves that beat menacingly against a shore. 'It is at Loch In-shard, the loch of the high flat lands, I will be,' thought the woman, but even as she so mused, and as she was about to set foot in the sailing boat which lay there, her eyes fell on a stone that she knew. With a prayer on her lips, she ran towards her home. It was the Each-uisge of Loch Chrois who had sought to lure her away.

Loch-na-Cloinne, in the Reay country, had its kelpie too, and an evil deed he did one day of days. A party of young Highlanders had spent many hours in the shade of the forest, exploring every remote corner, and telling tales of the wood-spirits who dwelt therein. Their path home led by the loch, in whose depths lay strange secrets of the past, and on whose surface the cloud-beauty of the moment was reflected. At the edge of the loch a horse grazed, and as its look was gentle, all the boys save one went up to stroke its sleek coat and its soft nozzle. Ere a cry could escape him, the onlooker saw the horse plunge into the water, bearing with him all his comrades. And thus it is that the loch is called Loch-na-Cloinne, the loch of the children.

But the lochs of Sutherland were the habitation of other strange creatures, the *crodh-oighre* to wit. It may be that these were cattle banned by some witch, or over which an evil spell had been cast, or perchance they were long-lived beings from another world. During the early years of this century there lived in the clachan of Swordley a woman known as Ogha Bàn, the fair-haired grandchild. She slept in a small bothie, quite alone, and though her words were fair, the folk of the strath whispered that she had dealings with the evil powers, perhaps because, as they passed the bothie, they would hear her voice raised as if in dis-putation with a visitor, when full well they knew that Ogba Bàn and no other woman or man stood therein. But there are those still living who say that at such times she did but rehearse the legends and hero-tales which, from her childhood, had been sweet to her ear and dear to her heart. Of the many tales she would tell, one was of a sister Gael who was old when Ogha Bàn had the glory of youth about her. This woman had the power to charm the crodh-oighre. 'Na-ghurra! gu'n tig Suidheag; na-ghurra! gu'n tig Buidheag; na-ghurra! gu'n tig Croman-

t-sabhaill; 's na-ghurra! gu'n tig an Odhar-Mhor, 's dar
thig sin thig mo chiodhs uile gu leir,' she would say in the
tongue which was the only one she had.   Thereat each one of
the creatures would come from the loch-depths ; she would milk
them, and they would return to their home beneath the waters.

 'The day of the black dog is coming.'   Thus runs a proverb of
the Reay country, and the legend connected therewith is this :—
Donald Tuathal, first Lord Reay, had a favourite black deer-
hound ; fierce and valiant it was, with the great sinews of its
race, and faithful too.   It chanced one autumn that the chief,
his visitors, and gillies, set out upon a deer-stalking expedition.
As they climbed from the strath to the heather-clad hill-slopes,
a thick mist fell, wrapping everything in grey obscurity.   Nevertheless the gillies, who knew each brook, morass, and crag, for
they had trodden them every day from their boyhood, led the
party upward until they reached in safety the hunting bothies.
The mist did not lift, and stalking was impossible.   Night drew
on, and the gloom became denser than before, so it was determined
to sleep in the bothie.   Food was produced, and each one of the
party, hungry with the hill-tramp, ate with relish.   Meanwhile
the dogs, among them the black hound of Donald Tuathal, lay
outstretched on the floor.   One of the strangers spoke of the
spirits of the mountains, and bade the gillies tell of them.   It
was soon after this that a lady, gaily clad, entered the hunting-
bothie.   She was blithe spoken, and the talk ran more merrily
than before.   Chancing to look towards the ground, one of the
visitors marvelled to see that in the place of a boot she had a
cloven shoe.   At the cry of terror that came from his lips, the
black hound rose, and with one leap, fell upon the intruder.
The fight which followed was long and fierce, but at last the
hound drove the woman from the bothie, albeit she had the
strength of a giant.   Without, the combat grew yet fiercer, while
within the men gazed awestruck into each others eyes.   The
howls of the dog and the cries of its opponent rang in the ears
of the men in the bothie all through that night.   At daybreak
Donald Tuathal peered through a crevice in the wall.   His noble
hound lay a few paces distant, foully done to death by a thousand
wounds.   The day of the black dog had come.

' Each donn deas mhiughach,
  Ca buidhe bus dubhach,
  Stailinn geur cruaidhach.'

' A right maned dun horse,
  A yellow, black muzzle dog,
  A sharp-pointed piece of steel.'

In the Reay country, the home of Rob Donn the singer, and many another Gaelic bard, and throughout Sutherland, this folk-saying was common. A man riding such a horse, guarded by such a dog, and having on his person such a piece of steel, was invulnerable; elf, evil spirit, or fairy could do him no hurt. One night a native of Farr, the place of the watching, fared homeward on his dun horse, beside him trotted a yellow sheep dog, and on his person he had a piece of sharp-pointed steel. The place at which he crossed the Farr Burn was remote, and the night was black. ' Ian Mhor, Mhic Mhurcaidh, Mhic Asgill. 'S crasgach t-ainmd, am beil am bior du, 's am muighean agad,' ' Big John, son of Murdoch, son of Casgill, strange is thy name. Hast thou the bright-pointed steel and the right-maned horse?' Thus was he accosted by a voice out of the dark, a voice that he knew well belonged to no man of the strath. And he made answer, ' Tha, Mhosag! tha! 's gabha thusa do chasan,' ' Yes, thou ill-favoured one, I have. Begone!' But the kelpie, for his interlocutor was no other, would not be put off; it followed the man of Farr until, with anger in his heart, he bade his faithful *busdu*, black-muzzle, attack his enemy. The obedient hound sprang upon the creature, while the traveller galloped rapidly in the direction of the clachan. Before sunrise on the morrow he set out for the field of the encounter—no other place it was than the field of Tiscarry, whereon his ancestors had driven back the Norsemen and ended their hated overlordship of the Reay country. The dog, spent with the fierceness of the contest, lay half dead on the ground, but as his master patted his head, the big eyes had a look of gladness in them. Beside the hound lay the dead kelpie, its body changed into a pulpy mass like a great jelly-fish.

Before Alexander Murray joined the 93rd Highlanders, and that was in 1800, a strange thing befell him, and he told the

story to Mr. John Mackay in 1836, as that true son of Sutherland fared from Rogarth to Golspie.

As a lad and a Highlander, Alexander Murray was wont to
spend the nights of winter first at one house, then at another,
telling tales and singing songs round the peat fire. But he was
young, and his heart was the fiery heart of the Celt. It came
about that he saw and loved a fair daughter of the strath, and
after his day's work he would walk to her home instead of to the
ceilidh. As he set out one night the snow lay thick on the
ground, and it fell silently and steadily as he continued his way;
but with his plaid round his shoulders, a stick in his hand, and
Caomhan, his faithful dog by his side, he trod onward joyously.
White dreams were his, white as the snow-flakes that fell about
him. His *leannan* gave him welcome, and more peats were
heaped on the fire. The man of the house made ropes of heather
and coiled them round his chair; his woman sat at the spinning-
wheel; and by her lover's side the girl carded wool. With a
story of the heroes of olden time from the host, and much blithe
talk and song, the hours passed merrily. Meantime a wind had
sprung up; fitful and sullen at first, it gathered force until, swift
and tumultuous, it swept down the valley with a roar as of the
tides let loose to wreak vengeance on the shores that confine them.
'The guardianship of the Almighty and of his saints be over
you,' said the girl, as she wrapped his plaid about him and opened
the door; 'the night is wild. It is careful you will be; my
heart goes with you, for sure.' And with that he went into the
night.

The snow, caught by the hurricane, was driven in thick clouds
which beat fiercely against the wayfarer and made it difficult for
him to discern the path. After strenuous battling with the wind,
he had almost gained the summit of a hill when he saw a strange
object in his course. Black it was despite the snow which covered
every other thing. 'It is an imp of darkness on some foul
errand. Forward, Caomhon!' But the dog, faithful at other
times, would not stir; instead, he cowered behind Murray as if
some ghostly presence were near. To advance was impossible;
to retreat was dangerous, for if indeed it were an evil thing, it
would rapidly overtake him; moreover, did he not grasp his oak

staff, and was he not a Gael, with the heart of his race beating strongly within him. The object in his path seemed to grow more black, its size to increase. 'It is repeating the holy commandments I will be,' and he said them word for word. Still the figure stood silent before him, oblivious of the wind and the snow. Thereafter the words of the creed were on his lips. The evil became larger than before. 'It is done, and I am lost,' murmured the lone man, but he stood facing the terror, his hand tightened round his rude weapon, his teeth firm set. Minute succeeded to minute until, on his windward side, a coating of snow many inches thick hid his plaid, and a numbness such as he had never known crept over his body. 'It is the blessed circle I must be making, in the name of the Father, the Son, and the Holy One,' and with the end of his staff he traced it on the snow-clad earth. Betwixt him and his home the black object still stood. Finally, when death stared him in the face, alike if he went on, or if he stayed to starve under the gaze of the weird visitant, the man, drawing his plaid close around him, stepped forward. 'Be it God or Devil that you are; if it is killing me you will be with your great claws or with a Highlander's dirk ; Holy Virgin take my soul in your keeping!' A blast of wind more powerful than before made him reel for an instant; the howl of it was as the wail of a lost soul. But when Alexander Murray confronted the evil, and was about to deal it a mighty blow, he found that a thistle confronted him.

FRANK RINDER.

Art. IV.—MUSIC IN OLD ENGLAND.

History of English Music. By HENRY DAVEY. London: Curwen. 1895.

The Story of British Music. Vol. I. From the earliest times to the Tudor Period. By FREDERICK J. CROWEST. London: Bentley. 1896.

Shakespeare and Music. By EDWARD W. NAYLOR. London:
Dent. 1896.

English Minstrelsie. Edited by S. BARING-GOULD. Edinburgh:
Jack.

THE story of British music as a separate growth is now,
strange as it may seem, told for the first time. Wide and
comprehensive as the scope of English literature undoubtedly is,
we have hitherto been without a book dealing specifically with
the birth and growth of English music. General histories of the
art almost rival the planets in number, but if there is one thing
for which these otherwise useful works are deserving of note it
is the scant attention which they pay to the origin and progress
of music in our 'tight little island.' The nearest approach to
anything of the kind was the late Sir Frederick Ouseley's
additions to Naumann's *History of Music,* but this attempt could
not be expected to meet the necessities of the case owing to the
circumscribed conditions under which the author wrote. Yet the
subject of England's music is thoroughly deserving of ample
treatment; and the fact that in Mr. Davey's *History* it has now
received, and in Mr. Crowest's *Story* will ultimately receive, its
due measure of recognition must be regarded as a matter of con-
gratulation on the part of professional musicians and lovers of
the art all over the country.

Mr. Davey's *History* is far and away the most valuable work
in our list, but the book has several objectionable points, and it
may be well to deal with them at once. To begin with, Mr.
Davey writes in a style which can only be characterized as slip-
shod. Certain musicians had 'the art of thriving in the world;'
Moore 'invented the down-trodden and weeping Erin;' it is
'strange that Gilbert should so persistently prevent the operas
from Continental success;' Handel was a genius, certain other
composers were 'only talents.' We read in one place that 'since
Dissent and the Low Church party began to lose their narrowness and weaken' such and such things have happened; in
another place we are told that 'musical history at this time, as
elsewhen, was a part of general history; . . . it was an age
of Wycherley, Rochester, and Aphra Behn, as of Milton, Bunyan,

Baxter, Henry More, Leighton, and Ken.' And so on. Yet Mr. Davey has the daring to say that one of Sir John Hawkins' faults as a musical historian was that he lacked literary skill!

But Mr. Davey's English is not his only weak point. There is a self-complacent boastfulness about him which has positively an irritating effect upon the reader. Macfarren defended the Puritans, but he 'could not go as far as I have done in their defence as he was unacquainted with much of the evidence I have collected.' One great point upon which he prides himself is his extraordinary discovery that 'the art of musical composition is an English invention.' This, it is only necessary to say in passing, is just as absurd as if some one were to say that the art of writing in English was invented by Chaucer. Mr. Davey, however, persists in his absurdity, reiterating his statement again and again with a dogmatic assurance which would be amusing if it were not so exasperating. Indeed this repetition of what he imagines to be 'discoveries' is one of the most obvious defects of Mr. Davey's *History.* He is wroth with Macaulay, because Macaulay, like every other writer of general history, does not stay to deal with the subject of music; and not satisfied with pointing out the circumstance once for all, he must needs repeat the statement in three or four places. He is not pleased with Burney because that learned historian 'had a singular dislike to madrigals,' and this, too, must be insisted upon on various pages. Again, there are statements throughout the book which can only be described as grossly and wildly exaggerated. As if it were not enough for a writer to declare solemnly that the English John Dunstable 'invented musical composition,' Mr. Davey must add that without the said Dunstable 'there could have been no Palestrina, no Bach, no Mozart, no Beethoven!' Evidently Mr. Baring-Gould had not read Mr. Davey when he remarked that it is one of the most characteristic features of the English people that they are ready to disparage whatever is of home growth. And what are we to think of such a statement as this? —'When a child practises a scale, when a great pianist plays a Beethoven concerto, they are repeating passages which were first used by Hugh Aston,' the said Aston being of course an Englishman. The statement, to be sure, is quite pointless as it stands, but Mr. Davey would no doubt have us infer that without Aston, as without Dunstable, we could have had no Beethoven. Mr. Davey's patriotism is indeed pathetic. Johnson said of Cave that he could not spit over his window without thinking of the *Gentleman's Magazine* : our author cannot take pen in hand without extolling some one of his countrymen for deeds of musical prowess in which nobody else would see particular cause for jubilation. The English, he declares, in one of his fits of reiteration, invented the art of musical composition, and the Germans carried it to its highest point. And yet, even his patriotism does not save him from exaggeration. In one place he asserts that 'a general history of music might after 1700 omit the compositions of Englishmen almost entirely ; ' in another he declares with a boldness which is perfectly staggering that Scott (as a poet), Keats, Byron, Wordsworth, and Shelley 'wielded no influence by their writings.' Moore's Irish melodies, we read, have had and may continue to have enormous political consequences, while the political, social and religious opinions of his immeasurably greater English contemporaries do not influence a single mind. After this the deluge, with Mr. Henry Davey and the shade of Dunstable in the ark.

Mr. Crowest's historical matter is less original, less valuable than Mr. Davey's ; but he effectually disarms criticism by admitting frankly that the ground covered by his volume is not only the most sterile in facts and material, but also the least interesting period over which his narrative, when completed, will extend. The question, however, arises whether it was worth attempting to deal with this admittedly barren period of English musical history at all. The conjectural and imaginative system does not usually commend itself to the sober historian ; and where, as in this case, there is an almost entire absence of authentic data there would seem to be nothing for it but to leave the matter in that limbo of obscurity which is alone its true safeguard. How the plan has been made to work by Mr. Crowest may be seen in a single example. This is the way in which he deals with ' Britain's first musical breathings,' to use his own phrase :

'At this earliest stage the music of our country was the carolling of birds, the monotone of bees, the fluttering of leaves, and the chirpings from the night insects. Sometimes it was the rush, at others the ripple of waters that have since swollen into our pleasant rivers. Then the groan of the wild ox and the wolf's cry clave the air; while here and there rose the human voice of gifted savages, vehement with the emotions of the giant frames which emitted it.'

There is nothing whatever to be got out of this kind of writing, unless it be a smile; and unfortunately there is far too much of this kind of writing in Mr. Crowest's volume. It is not a grave fault, of course, that our author's imagination should thus touch our risible faculties; but, on the whole, Mr. Crowest would have pleased us better if he had begun his serious history at the point where he had serious facts to set before us. The later part of his work shows that he may be fully trusted where he is able to quote his authorities, and we look forward to his succeeding volumes with the greatest interest. It is a bold undertaking on which he is engaged, and we trust he will find his reward where the musical writer is but seldom successful—in a very large body of readers.

As compared with the other arts, the rise of music in England, as indeed elsewhere, was comparatively late; for it was not until the close of the Mediæval period that it began to assert itself as an art product. It must have often occurred to the inquiring mind how music thus came to be so far behind the other arts in its rise and development. Yet the explanation is not so far off after all. As Mr. Crowest remarks, unlike the art of the poet, the sculptor, or the painter, there were no materials at hand upon which to base a tangible musical record and argument. Learning and science had first to make some headway. Music had to find its materials out of other arts, sound not being palpahle in form and materialistic in the sense that wood or stone is. Then, again, being a mathematical and theoretical art, no foundations could be laid, nor a structural form given to music until a vast amount of speculation and calculation had been propounded, worked out, tested, and reduced to rule. The deductions drawn and approved became the first basis of a formulated theoretical system. It is quite clear that such an elementary musical grammar could only come when learning and education generally had made some progress here, which was long after some of the most brilliant periods of other arts and sciences. Of course it is not to be denied that music of a kind existed in England long before any one dreamt of making it part of an art or science. Folk-songs, ballads, traditional tunes, dance tunes, indoor and outdoor music of all kinds, as Mr. Baring-Gould's collection sufficiently proves, existed in abundance; but these, together with the music of the Church, lacked one great aid—they could not be perpetuated, accurately recorded, and beyond all logically expressed. To quote Mr. Crowest:

'Whatever had been the case with the original Britons and Welsh in the matter of musical systems, nothing of the kind existed in England at the period which we are considering—that time when music, especially secular music, was an unregulated, ill-ordered, shapeless art throughout the country. There were instruments, tunes, and dance-rhythms without number, but there was no method of husbanding all this, of making it the vehicle of a reasonable art, or of using it in combination and in order, according as varying circumstances and conditions required. This vocal and instrumental material might lie to-day where it was four hundred odd years ago, save for the happy thought that overtook men's minds of moulding the art into a shape which would permit of development at the hands of those who applied themselves particularly to theory and composition.'

In this department of theory our native musicians, such as Dunstable—who has been called the father of English contrapuntists—took a leading share; but it is not our purpose in the present article to touch on technical details which are unlikely to interest the general reader. The early English School of music, so far as we have any record, was certainly inaugurated by Dunstable; but it will never do to say with Mr. Davey, that he, or any one individual, 'invented' an art like polyphony. Rather should we adopt the cautious statement of Tinctor, who remarks that 'this new art had its fount and origin among the English, of whom Dunstable was the principal.' Even this should be enough as a concession to our national conceit.

It will be impossible of course to deal here in any detail with the history of music in England; nor, in the circumstances, would such detail be expedient, even if it were possible. The most that we can do is to select a few leading themes which are likely to prove of general interest. A great deal of curious information has been got together by both our historians regarding the history and use of the organ in England. The Anglo-Saxons seem to have been acquainted with the instrument at a very early period. In the so-called Utrecht Psalter, generally ascribed to the eighth century—though Mr. Crowest unaccountably says the fifth or sixth—there is a representation of an organ played by a couple of monks ; and we know that the instrument had been introduced into the Roman Church by Pope Vitalian I. about the year 660. Vitalian's missionaries, Theodore and Adrian, are reputed to have brought the art of organ-playing to England, and this is very likely, as they were 'charged to lead the singing at the Church services, and to instruct others so to do.' Bishop Aldhelm of Sherborne (died 709), who mentions an instrument with a thousand pipes, is credited with introducing an organ into England, 'a mighty instrument with innumerable tones, blown with bellows, and enclosed in a gilded case.' William of Malmesbury chronicles the presentation by St. Dunstan of an organ to the Abbey of Malmesbury in King Edgar's reign (942-74). This instrument, as Mr. Crowest points out, is important, since it appears to have been made entirely by English workmen, who by this time had attained to such skill in their craft that they had introduced 'improvements' in the way of copper pipes for lead. In the Malmesbury instrument the pipes were of brass, no doubt with the view of obtaining a more brilliant tone. It appears to have been fabricated on the Abbey premises, perhaps under the direction of Dunstan himself, who was an expert artificer in metals. In this same century Count Elwin presented an organ to the Convent of Ramsey. On this instrument he is said to have expended the then considerable sum of £30 in copper pipes, which, 'resting with their openings in thick order on the spiral winding in the inside, and being struck on feast-days with a strong blast of bellows, emit a sweet melody and a far-resounding peal.' A most remarkable instrument, if we are to judge by the account given of it by Wulston, a Benedictine monk, who died in 963, was that built at Winchester by Bishop Elphege. Wulston declares that seventy men were required to blow it; that there were four hundred pipes and forty tongues ; twelve bellows above and fourteen below. The instrument was played by two monks, 'each of whom manages his own alphabet.' Concerning the power of the instrument, the chronicler continues thus forcibly: 'Like thunder the iron tones batter the ear, so that it may receive no sound but that alone. To such an amount does it reverberate, echoing in every direction, that everyone stops with his hands his gaping ears, being in nowise able to draw near and hear the sound which so many various combinations produce. The music is heard throughout the town, and the flying fame thereof is gone out over the whole country.' We should think so, indeed! Let us be thankful that such organs are not built in our day. Modern instruments are sometimes loud enough in all conscience, but an organ that can be heard 'throughout the town' is happily a non-existent phenomenon. No wonder that by Shakespeare's time the word 'noise' had become a synonym for music!

Although we are not altogether without details regarding these early English organs, their exact character, as well as the manner of playing them, cannot be determined with any certainty. It is, however, agreed that the keys were of such width that they could not be played in the usual way with the fingers, but had to be operated upon, like carillons, by a blow of the fist. Dom Bedos speaks of some primitive organs whose keys were five and a half inches wide! Keeping this fact in mind, it need not surprise us that the first organists were called 'organ-beaters;' and indeed a modification of that term seems to have been employed as late as the time of Purcell, who, in the records of Westminster Abbey, of which he was organist, is described as the 'organ blower.' Only one note could be sounded at a time on these early organs; nor, indeed, was more required, for harmony did not then exist; melody of the crudest kind was alone in use. The mode of supplying the wind was from the first, and long continued to be, a great difficulty with the organ-makers. For centuries the bellows remained in the most imperfect state, some twenty or more being required to supply the wind to a moderate sized instrument. Prætorius, in 1620, gives a curious representation of the twenty bellows which he found existing in the old organ in the church of St. Ægidien in Brunswick. Upon each bellows is fixed a wooden shoe; the blowers held on to a transverse bar, and each man, placing his feet in the shoes of two bellows, raised one as he lowered the other. Great ingenuity and constructive labour seem to have been bestowed upon such bellows; but a supply of wind of uniform strength could never have been obtained from them, and, as a consequence, the organ could seldom have been in tune. Our present-day organists know but very little of the troubles of their predecessors in the way of 'blowers.' It is sometimes difficult enough to get *one* blower; what must it have been when a score or more were needed!

In connection with these earlier organs, Mr. Crowest records a curious custom which throws some light upon the construction and portable character of the instruments. One church used to lend its organ to another church. Thus, in the account of St. Margaret's, Westminster, for the year 1508, we find an item— 'For bringing the organs of the Abbey into the Church and berying them home agayne, ijd.' Not an extravagant expenditure, to be sure, but money values were different in those days, and after all the 'tuppence' may have been only a porter's tip. Another entry is: '1485. To John Hewe for repairing the organ at the altar of B. V. M. in the Cathedral Church, and for carrying the same to the House of the Minorite Brethren, and for bringing back the same to the Cathedral Church, 13s. 9d.' Such instrumental aid indicates that the organs were placed in close proximity to the singers—a natural and desirable arrangement, which, as Mr. Crowest remarks, should not have been departed from. It is strange, by the way, to be reminded by Mr. Naylor that Shakespeare nowhere makes direct mention of the organ. We have that fine metaphor of the organ-pipe in 'The Tempest,' but as for the instrument itself, it is as completely ignored as the virginal, which to the young ladies of Elizabeth's time was all that the pianoforte is to the young ladies of to-day.

The treatment of the organ at the Reformation and later on by the Puritans makes a sufficiently curious chapter in the history of English music. So early as 1536 the Lower House of Convocation included ecclesiastical music and organ-playing among the eighty-four faults and abuses of religion; and although a temporary reaction set in, the nobility presently took sides with the Reformers in their eagerness to continue the spoliation which had brought them the wealth of the monasteries. The attacks on ecclesiastical music were renewed, and in 1552 the organ in St. Paul's was silenced. When Mary came to the throne, there was another brief reaction. Froude, describing Her Majesty's triumphant entry into London, tells how ' the Lords, surrounded by the shouting multitude, walked in state to St. Paul's, where the choir again sang a Te Deum, and the unused organ rolled out once more its mighty volume of music.' But Mary's reign was short, and when the Protestants who had exiled themselves at Geneva returned under Elizabeth, they at once began to press for the abolition of all ecclesiastical ' ceremonies,' the choral service being one of their special abhorences. A motion to put down ' curious singing ' and organs, which were both ranked with image worship, was made in Convocation in February, 1562-3, and was lost by only one vote. Where a Genevan disciple obtained ecclesiastical preferment, there the choral service was suppressed ; and there is extant a tract entitled, ' The Praise of Musick,' from which we learn that about 1567 ' not so few as one hundred organs were taken down and the pipes sold to make pewter dishes.' The silly outcry of the Puritans against ' playing upon organs, curious singing, and tossing about the Psalms from side to side ' was indeed one of the features of Elizabeth's reign. In 1571 they say in their Confession : ' Concerning singing of psalms, we allow of the people's joining with one voice in a plain tune, but not of tossing the psalms from one side to the other with intermingling of organs.' In 1586, again, they pray that ' all Cathedral churches may be put down where the service of God is grievously abused by piping with organs, singing, ringing, and trowling of psalms from one side of the choir to another, with the squeaking of chanting choristers disguised in white surplices.' Prynne in his *Historio-Mastyx,* published in 1633, was even more ridiculous. The music in the churches he affirmed to be not ' the noise of men, but a bleating of brute beasts : choristers bellow the tenor as it were oxen ; bark a counterpoint as it were a kennel of dogs ;

roar out a treble, as it were a sort of bulls; and grunt out a base, as it were a number of hogs.'

Such were the views of the Puritan party at this time, and such they were found to be when the Long Parliament assembled. Church music was now one of the first objects of assault. A committee of the House of Lords in 1641 recommended—' That the music used in cathedral and collegiate churches be framed with less curiosity, and that no hymns or anthems be used where ditties are framed by private men.' An attack upon cathedrals and cathedral choirs began soon after. The drunken habits of the singers, who, when leaving the cathedrals, went straight to the alehouses, were a special grievance. War was declared in the summer of 1642, and almost on the very day that the King set up his standard the soldiers ruined the organ at Canterbury Cathedral, mangling the service books, and 'bestrewing the pavement with leaves.' Cromwell wrote to the Dean of Ely, calling upon him to stop his choir-service, 'so unedifying and offensive,' and when the Dean refused, visited Ely himself and cut the service short in the middle. At Westminster Abbey the soldiers carried off the organ pipes and bartered them for beer. On the capture of Winchester a great fire was made of the choir-books, and the same was done at Norwich, apparently by the townsmen. Cromwell forbade his soldiers to injure Peterborough Cathedral, but they destroyed ' two pair of organs ' and the library, with some monuments. At Chichester the organ was hewn down with poleaxes and the choir books thrown about in derision; while at Exeter the soldiers marched along the streets blowing the pipes of the instrument they had pulled to pieces. These outrages, the result of ignorant fanaticism, were continued in legal form after the passing of the Bill for the total abolition of Episcopacy in 1643. Organs were now included with ' superstitious monuments,' and their complete removal from all churches and colleges was enjoined. This was soon effected in most cases, and when the war closed in 1646 a great and fundamental change had come over English music. It was not until the lapse of more than half a century after the Restoration that the English parish churches again began to be supplied with organs. In 1708 when Hatton published his *New View of*

London a very large number of places of worship were without them. To what an extent other cities were deficient in this particular may be gathered from Drake, who, in his *Eboracum*, published in 1733, says : 'There is now only one parish church in the whole city of York that possesses an organ, and that came from the Popish Chapel.' It is expedient to note, however, that even among the Puritans there were some who took a sensible view of the organ question. Thus, the Rev. Paul Baynes, in his commentary on the Ephesians, when remarking that the Psalms must be used to edification, speaks in this way of the Beggs of his generation : 'This doth rebuke a common practice among us who do run forth out of churches at psalms if sung with instruments—as the organ and others, comfortable and laudable—as if they were no part of God's ordinances for our good; whereas we are expressly charged by God's Spirit to praise Him both on stringed instruments and organs. If it were at a comedy, men would not lose the song and instrument or dance though played on divers pipe-instruments ; yet the wind of one pipe in the organ will blow out their zeal in the church, and them from the church.' It would thus seem that even some who did not scruple to attend the theatre could not endure an organ in the church !

Why the main body of the Puritans objected to organs, prose chanting and church music generally, is not very clear. Mr. Davey thinks the example of Calvin may have had something to do with it, and something was no doubt to be laid to the account of the personal dislike to Laud and the bishops. But it is quite as likely that the action of the Puritans arose, to some extent at least, in consequence of the revulsion arising from the glaring abuses of the old worship. Like the Scottish Reformers, too, they may have entertained the conviction that their particular view was in accordance with the teaching of the New Testament and the spirit of the Christian dispensation. In any case their reputation has suffered the penalty inflicted by posterity as a punishment for the exhibition of bigotry and intolerance in one particular direction. Mr. Davey puts himself to considerable pains in trying to remove the popular conception of those somewhat misguided enthusiasts in the matter of music.

Admitting, however—and of course Mr. Davey admits it—that the Puritans had a violent dislike to church music and that they suppressed it as far as they could, there does not seem to be any special necessity for a defence on other grounds. Some musical historians, it is true, have assumed that all music was suppressed because ecclesiastical music was. But the assumption is unfounded. It does not necessarily follow that though the Puritans disliked the cathedral service and the organ, they disliked music outside the church; and there is plenty of evidence to show that the exercise of the art in what might be called the secular walks of life was as much unquestioned then as it is now. Cromwell, Milton and Bunyan, three very diverse types of Puritan, were all enthusiastic musical amateurs in different ways. Even Prynne himself admits that 'musicke of itselfe is lawfull, usefull, and commendable ;' while another Puritan author of the period declares that ' musicke is a chearefull recreation to the minde that hath been blunted with serious meditation.' Again, Thomas Fuller in his *Worthies* says : ' Right glad I am that when music was lately shut out of our churches, on what default of hers I dare not imagine, it hath since been harbored and welcomed in the halls, parlours and chambers of the primest persons of this nation.' In short, the Puritans really did no harm to the art except in connection with the church—although, indeed, that in itself was serious enough. Why then, as Mr. Davey asks, have the Puritans been so maligned ? Mainly because the popular imagination takes a salient point and is apt to generalise from that point. The light and the shade, the modifications and the details are overlooked. The Puritans objected to music of one particular kind for one particular object ; and popular prejudice will have it that they necessarily objected to music at all times and in all places. A false notion of this kind is not readily corrected, but Mr. Davey has done all that can possibly be done towards that end, and his version of the matter assuredly claims the attention of future historians who may have to deal with the subject. At the same time it is quite impossible to defend the action of the Puritans in regard to Church music. It was worse in its effects than the doings of Knox's ' rascal multitude.'

While on the subject of Church music, it may be pointed out

that Mr. Davey is somewhat unfortunate in his treatment of the history of psalm and hymn tunes. Dr. Worgan, he tells, is 'deserving of remembrance, as his name is attached, rightly or wrongly, to the grand melody sung to the Easter Hymn.' Seeing that this 'grand melody' appeared in the *Lyra Davidica* in 1708, while Dr. Worgan was not born till 1724, the 'rightly or wrongly' can very easily be determined. Moreover, Dr. Worgan did not die in 1794, as Mr. Davey has it, but in 1790. Again, our author perpetuates the common error of supposing that the well-known hymn-tune 'Helmsley' (associated with 'Lo! He comes,') is an adaptation from a hornpipe melody sung by the notorious Ann Catley in *The Golden Pippin*. 'Musicians,' says Mr. Davey, 'have frequently denounced this tune as essentially secular, even vulgar; but all attempts to replace it have entirely failed, and it represents a part of the historical life of the Church, while it is undeniably melodious.' Now one may readily agree with the musicians that 'Helmsley' has a touch of vulgarity about it, but as to its being 'essentially secular,' it is no more so than many of the old-fashioned, ranting 'repeat' tunes that were once held in so much veneration. The fact is, that 'Helmsley' is held up to execration not because it is intrinsically bad, but because it is supposed to have been manufactured out of the aforesaid hornpipe. But the curious thing is that it was quite the other way: the hornpipe was made out of the hymn-tune! The latter was published by John Wesley in 1765, under the name of 'Olivers,' when Miss Catley was in Ireland, and long before *The Golden Pippin* was written. The first strain, however, seems to have been suggested by a popular song of the day entitled 'Guardian angel, now protect me,' and the melody of this song (adapted to the words 'Where's the mortal can resist me?') was introduced into *The Golden Pippin* in 1776. It was not in the burletta as first produced in 1773. A hornpipe constructed from the same tune appears to have been danced by Miss Catley in *The Golden Pippin*, but this was several years after the publication of the hymn tune. It is really time that this foolish notion about the origin of 'Helmsley' was corrected. In the matter of the 'Old 100th,' again, Mr. Davey is not free from errors. He tells us that, 'as the tune originally appeared, the notes at the beginning and end of each line were semibreves.' The fact is, that while the first three lines began with a semibreve, they ended with three semibreves, while the last line ended with two semibreves and a breve. A musical historian should be exact. Nor do we understand Mr. Davey when he says that in the 1556 edition of Sternhold an attempt was made 'to adapt the Genevan tune, which finally became settled in popular favour as the Old 100th.' There was no adapting: the tune appeared in practically its present form in the Marot and Beza French Psalter of 1551 (five years before Mr. Davey's date), where it was set by Bourgeois to the 134th Psalm. Its first known publication after this is in the edition of 1561. We may just add here that there is no need to throw doubts on the authorship of the Psalter attributed to Archbishop Parker. Parker's claim is proved by several circumstances, not the least being that in the preface to the 119th Psalm, consisting of sixteen rhyming lines, the first letters of each line make the acrostic —'Mattheus Parkerus.'

Regarding the musical instruments in general use among our forefathers much that is interesting might be said. The fiddle, curiously enough, was long regarded as a vulgar instrument, suitable only for minstrels and vagrants. The lute and the various members of the viol family long kept it in the background. In Elizabethan times the viol held the place that the violin holds now. It was made in three different sizes, corresponding to our modern violin, viola, and violoncello. It had six strings in place of the four now used in stringed instruments, and there were frets on the finger-board to mark out the notes. Viols were always kept in sets of six—two trebles, two tenors, and two basses—and the set was technically known as a 'chest' of viols. The musical amateur seldom failed to have a 'chest' in his house, and when his friends visited him they would play 'Fancies' in several parts, from two to the full six, according to the number of those present. About the middle of the seventeenth century the viol began to decline in favour, and by the beginning of the eighteenth century the violin had taken the place it has held ever since. It had come into general and fashionable use under the patronage of the Court of Louis XIV., and thus, as Mr. Naylor puts it, the English nation, true to their ancient habit of buying their ' doublet in Italy, round hose in France, bonnet in Germany, and behaviour everywhere,' took up the French fiddles and let their national ' chest' of viols go to the wall. Next to the viol the lute was the most popular stringed instrument. Its general shape was that of a mandoline, but about four times as big. It was used somewhat in the fashion of a guitar, and naturally it figured frequently in serenades, especially when anything had to be sung outside a lady's window. The 'Merry Monarch' was a great admirer of the instrument, and it was a favourite with all lovers in the Stuart age. Yet Dr. Burney, writing in 1776, says, 'The lute, *of which hardly the sound or shape is known at present*, was during the last two centuries the favourite instrument of every nation in Europe.' It was driven out by the spinet and harpsichord, which, as Mr. Baring Gould remarks, afforded an easy path to those musical ends which had previously been reached through the lute, only after much difficulty and labour. Thomas Mace in his ' Musick's Monument' of 1676, has a curious piece of advice about how to preserve a lute in order. ' You shall do well,' says he, ' even when you lay it by in the day time to put it into a bed that is constantly used, between the rug and the blanket; only let no person be so inconsiderate as to tumble down upon the bed whilst the lute is there, for I have known several good lutes spoilt with such a trick.' Better have provided a bed for the sole use of the instrument! In his historical sketch of English national song, Mr. Baring Gould shows very clearly how the character of early English melodies was affected by the instruments to which they were sung. There were harp and lute accompaniments to ballads, and many a ballad air seems to call out for the stringed instrument to fill up the background. Nearly all the Welsh melodies proclaim that they were composed to be chanted by a minstrel who was attended by a harpist; so do many of those belonging to the West of England. For it must not be supposed that the harp has always been associated peculiarly with Wales. It was much played in England in the seventeenth century. M. de Rochefort, who printed his travels in this country in 1672, says, 'The harp was then the most esteemed of musical instruments by the English.' Again, Carew in his Survey of Cornwall, tells how a certain family had been dispossessed of 'their estate because of their adherence to the Roman Catholic faith, and how the son ' then led a walking life with his harp to gentlemen's houses.' At this time also the harp enjoyed a considerable popularity in Scotland.

Both our historians naturally give passing attention to the bagpipe, and Mr. Baring-Gould notices it equally with Mr. Naylor. Mr. Davey identifies the instrument with the 'tympanum' found in early eleventh century manuscripts. Now in two cases where the 'tympanum' is mentioned among a list of musical instruments, mention is also made of an instrument under the name of 'corus' or 'chorus.' Mr. Davey says he cannot decide the meaning of the latter term. In this he is not singular. Tytler, in his *History of Scotland* (II., 370), faltered as to the meaning of ' chorus,' and somewhat rashly substituted for it the word ' cornu.' Pinkerton did not comprehend the word; Leyden and Ritson misinterpreted it; and the reverend author of an ' Essay on the Influence of Music in the Scottish Highlands' proposed it as a sort of enigma for the solution of the Scottish antiquary. But there is a fairly satisfactory interpretation of the word, notwithstanding; and if Mr. Davey will turn to the introduction in the Bannatyne Club edition of the Skene MS., he will find the solution of his difficulty. In Strutt's *Manners and Customs of the English* (I., plate 21, pp. 50, 109), there are certain drawings of old instruments, ' so very imperfect,' as Strutt remarks, that he fears ' their use will not be readily discovered.' Fortunately the accompanying letterpress assists us very materially. Underneath two of the drawings we find the words: ' Corus est pellis simplex cum duabus cicutis.' This inscription, as Mr. Dauney, the editor of the above-named MS., remarks, seems to give a certain degree of distinctness to representations otherwise too vague to be readily intelligible; and the result is that we see before us the outline of two figures which appear to correspond with the description. One of the figures has apparently two and the other three tubes or pipes attached. Both definition and delineation seem to indicate the simplest form of bagpipe. Further, in the Epistle to Dardanus, attributed to St. Jerome, we have the following: 'Synagogæ antiquis temporibus, *fuit chorus* quoque simplex pellis cum duobus cicutis aeriis et per primam inspiratur, secunda vocem emittit.' That is to say: 'At the Synagogue in ancient times there was also a simple species of bagpipe, being a skin (or leather bag) with two pipes, through one of which the bag was inflated, the other emitted the sound.' The words themselves give rise to no ambiguity, and only one interpretation seems possible.

But there is more precise evidence than even this as to the meaning of the word ' chorus'—evidence which we owe to the research of the late George Farquhar Graham of Edinburgh. Walafridas Strabo, a Benedictine monk, who wrote in the ninth century a Latin commentary on the Scripture, published at Paris in 1624, describes the ' chorus' as 'a single skin with two pipes.' Again, reference is made to a book printed at Lyons in 1672, which distinctly implies that the bagpipe and the ' chorus' were even then considered the same instrument. Graham cites two other instances, and adds : ' The barbarous corruptions of Latin were so frequent that there is no saying but somebody may have distorted even *corium* (a skin) into *chorus,* and this is the more likely as it is occasionally spelt *corus.*' The same interpretation of the word is given by Mainzer, who in his *Music and Education* says the bagpipe ' was called *tibia utricularis* or *chorus* (from *corium,* skin) among the Romans.' From all this it will be seen how improbable it is that the tympanum was the bagpipe, and how probable— nay, how certain—it is, on the other hand, that the ' corus' was practically identical with the present ' war note of Lochiel.' As to the history of the instrument, our authors have nothing new to tell us. Mr. Naylor is even puzzled by Shakespeare's use of the term ' woollen bagpipe' in *The Merchant of Venice.* ' What is a woollen bagpipe ? ' he asks. The obvious explanation would seem to be that the air-bag of the instrument may sometimes have been made of sheep-skin with the wool left on it. There is just a possibility, however, of the text being corrupt in this particular instance : ' wawling' would perhaps be a more suitable word. But there need be no difficulty about the phrase as it stands. Mr. Baring-Gould, we may add, is not quite courteous to the pipe. He has found an old sixteenth century figure of a goose playing the instrument, and he takes this as an evidence that the bagpipe was then falling into ridicule. Nay, he even declares that an old sow playing on this instrument for the delectation of its piglings is a not infrequent subject on perpendicular bosses to vaulting ribs! No wonder the bagpipe, as he puts it, retired to Scotland as a ' last refuge.' Only he forgets to tell us of that figure of an *angel* playing the pipe which appears on a crosier given by William of Wykeham to New College, Oxford, in 1403. William knew how to propitiate (prospectively) the Celt; Mr. Baring-Gould does not know how.

One of the most interesting of the many subsidiary questions dealt with by Mr. Davey is the origin of our National Anthem. Mr. Davey takes the view that the music is in all probability from the pen of Purcell, while the words in their present form he would assign to Henry Carey. There is, however, no evidence to support these claims. The song is said to have been given by Carey, the composer of ' Sally in our Alley,' at a dinner held in a London tavern to celebrate the capture of Portobello in 1740. This statement is made in a letter signed ' W ' which appeared in *The Gentleman's Magazine* for 1796. The writer asserts that he was present on the occasion, and we have therefore no reason to doubt that Carey really sung ' God save the King ' at the banquet. But Carey never claimed the words of the anthem ; nor is the song included in any collection of his works. He died in 1743, leaving a young family, and it was not until 1795 that a formal claim was put in for him by his son, George Saville Carey, avowedly with the object of obtaining a pension from the Government in return for his father's services in writing the loyal song. The claim was, however, unsupported by evidence, and the pension was withheld. The anthem, words and music, was printed for the first time in *Harmonia Anglicana*, undated, but generally believed to have been published in 1743 or 1744. In the absence of a date on the title-page, it is impossible to say whether ' God save the King ' was thus printed during Carey's life-time. At anyrate, it is anonymous, which it is not likely to have been if contributed by or known to be by Carey, for the latter was one of the most voluminous song-writers of the day.

But there is more than this to militate against the Carey claim. At the end of 1743 or in 1744 a concert was given by John Travers, organist of the Chapel Royal, and a unique copy of the book of words discovered some years ago contains a 'Latin chorus,' which is quite evidently intended for the tune of our National Anthem. Here is the first verse :

> O Deus optime !
> Salvum non facito
> Regem nostrum ;
> Sit læta Victoria,
> Comes et gloria,
> Salvum jam faecto,
>   Tu Dominum.

There are two stanzas, and on the opposite page there is an English version, which is, however, merely a literal translation in prose, and not the alleged Carey verses, which would almost certainly have been printed had Carey been, as claimed, the original composer in 1740. And why make a Latin version at all, if original English words were written only three years before ? Dr. Arne— who subsequently harmonised the tune for Drury Lane Theatre —when questioned on the subject, is reported to have said that it was a received opinion that the anthem was written for the Catholic Chapel of James II., and as Arne was a contemporary of Carey it is inconceivable that he should make this statement regarding a composition written in Carey's lifetime. Moreover, in one of Benjamin Victor's letters to Garrick in 1745 the song is referred to as 'the very words and music of an old anthem which was sung at St. James' Chapel when the Prince of Orange landed.' Taking all the available evidence into account, it seems, therefore, tolerably certain that 'God save the King' really had its origin in King James' Chapel in 1688, and was more than likely written by one of the clergy attached to the chapel. The adherents of the Stuart family would no doubt preserve it in their memory; and in any case it is a curious circumstance that when it burst into popularity it was as 'a loyal song' at the time

of the Scottish Rebellion of 1745. The original manuscript or a
copy of it may have been found by Travers in the Chapel Royal;
while the tune and English words probably reached Carey in a
somewhat similar manner, but independently. It is quite possible, of course, that Carey may have made his version from the
Latin of 1688; but that there were English versions or adaptations of the Latin in existence at an earlier period there would
be no difficulty in showing.

This much as to the words: what can be said regarding the
music? Mr. Davey, referring to the circumstance of the anthem
being sung at the Chapel Royal in 1688, says: 'This points to
Purcell as the composer.' Why should the circumstance point
to Purcell? He was not the only musician of the time, and the
tune of the national anthem is not such an elaborate thing that
we need to father it upon a composer of distinction. As a
matter of fact Mr. Davey has no evidence whatever to connect
the melody with Purcell. It is quite true that some of the best
of Purcell's airs are, like the national anthem, in triple measure,
but that is nothing to the point. The most plausible theory is
that which attributes at least the framework of the melody to
Dr. John Bull, King James I.'s organist. In a MS. volume of
compositions by Bull dated 1619 there appears a kind of organ
voluntary entitled simply an 'Ayre,' which is identical in rhythm
with 'God save the King,' and bears a striking resemblance to it
in the form of its melody. True, the 'Ayre' is in the minor
key, but this is of small importance seeing that other essential
elements are present. Moreover, it is quite possible that Bull
may have omitted to write in the accidentals, trusting to
musicians understanding what was required. In the MS. of
King Henry VIII.'s 'Pastime with Good Company,' now in the
British Museum, all the accidentals are omitted, and the like is
true of much of the manuscript music of the same period. But
to resume: if the National Anthem was really produced in
1688, the author of the words was likely to have been acquainted with Bull's piece, and there is nothing improbable in
the theory that it supplied the basis on which the tune of 'O
Deus optime' was founded. Dr. Bull had been dead for sixty
years, and his composition being only in MS. there would be

no scruple about using it. This, we may note, is practically the view of the matter taken by Mr. Baring-Gould. He thinks that Bull's 'Ayre' got modified into the modern scale in the mouths of the people, who were becoming unused to the old modes, and had a fancy for the new. The final shaping of the tune into the form now generally known, he would attribute to Carey. But the whole subject is one of great difficulty, and no doubt it will be debated in the future quite as much as it has been in the past.

Mr. Naylor's admirable little work is valuable not only on account of its detailed explanation of the various musical allusions in Shakespeare, but also because of its summary of the history and condition of music in Elizabethan times. It is indeed quite indispensable that the student of Shakespeare and music should have a clear idea of the social status and influence of the art in the great dramatist's day. With this, and with such explanation of the technical terms as Mr. Naylor affords, there is no reason why every reader of Shakespeare should not understand his many references to music and musical instruments in a much fuller light than the majority of readers do at present. That there is some need for a guide on the subject is only too apparent when, as Mr. Naylor points out, Schmidt's admirable Lexicon commits itself to such a misleading statement as that a virginal is a kind of small pianoforte, and when 'a very distinguished Shakespeare scholar' has described a viol as a six stringed guitar! Nor are these the worst kind of errors. Even as we write the musical journals are making merry over a droll musical blunder into which an eminent lawyer has fallen in an 'After-dinner study of Hamlet.' The learned luminary, after drawing various excellent legal parallels, proceeds to say: 'Then again it is curious that Shakespeare should not call a flute-player a flute-player. Wedded to legal matters, he salutes the musicians as the Recorders—small local judges with £40 a year.' It would indeed be curious if Shakespeare had committed such a piece of foolishness; but as a matter of fact there is hardly one of his musical references to which exception can be taken, either on the ground of fact or opinion, and in the present case he called the musicians the Recorders because they played instruments of that name.

Nor is it the layman only who needs to be instructed in regard to Shakespeare and music : there are obsolete terms which even the professional musician of to-day has some difficulty in understanding. One such term may be referred to as having been the subject of more controversy than perhaps any of the others. In 'Henry the Fifth' and elsewhere reference is made to 'broken music.' Now what was 'broken music?' Mr. Naylor's idea is that the phrase may be referred to the natural imperfection of the lute. The lute was a *pizzicato* instrument—that is to say, the strings were plucked, not played with a bow; hence the player could not do more than indicate the harmony in 'broken' pieces. Here, probably, says Mr. Naylor, is the explanation of the phrase 'broken music.' But this explanation will hardly bear examination in view of the evidence in another direction. Matthew Locke, for example, published in 1672 'Compositions for Broken and Whole Consorts.' Now we know that a set of viols was often spoken of as a 'consort;' and Mr. Chappell's explanation therefore seems feasible that when the 'consort' was imperfect—that is, when one of the players was absent, and an instrument of another kind, such as a flute, was substituted for his viol—the music was said to be 'broken.' Bacon gives some support to this view. In his essay 'Of Masques and Triumphs' he has the following passage : 'Dancing to song is a thing of great state. and pleasure. I understand it that the song be in quire, placed aloft, and accompanied with some broken music.' Again in his 'Sylva Sylvarum' the same author mentions several 'consorts of instruments' that agree well together : for example, 'the Irish harp and base-viol agree well; the recorder and stringed music agree well; organs and the voice agree well; but the virginals and the lute agree not so well.' All these and similar combinations—combinations of different instruments—seem to have been described as 'broken music.' But the term is admittedly a difficulty, and probably no satisfactory explanation of it will ever be found. The phrase 'broken time,' sometimes used in our own day, is of course easily understood.

With regard to the state of music in Shakespeare's time, both Mr. Naylor and Mr. Davey bring out clearly that if ever a country deserved to be called musical, that country was England in the sixteenth and seventeenth centuries. King and courtier, peasant and ploughman, each could 'take his part,' with each music formed a feature of the daily life; while so far from being above knowing the difference between a minim and a crotchet, a gentleman would have been ashamed not to know it. In the time of Elizabeth—who was herself a good virginal player—it was the custom for a lady's guests to sing unaccompanied music from ' parts' after supper ; and inability to take a part was liable to remark from the rest of the company. Clergymen, too, were supposed to take music as a regular branch of their education. A letter from Sir John Harrington to Prince Henry (brother of Charles I.), about Dr. John Still, Bishop of Bath and Wells in 1592, says that no one ' could be admitted to *primam tousuram* except he could first *bene le bene con bene can,* as they called it, which is, to read well, to construe well, and to sing well, in which last he hath good judgment.' The three *benes* are, of course, *le-gere, construere,* and *can-tare.* Hawkins asserts, in his *History of Music,* that all candidates for Fellowship at Trinity College, Cambridge, were supposed to be capable of taking a part in the choir service, and the statement is only a little exaggerated. The statutes provided for an examination in singing for candidates for fellowship, and ability to sing gave a candidate an advantage, in case of equality. Singing was not required of all candidates, but the subject was considered on the fourth day of the examination, along with the essay and verse composition. There is, however, plenty of evidence to show that the university gentlemen of these days thought it nothing out of the way to learn all the mysteries of counterpoint, and to solace themselves after hard reading with the practice of part-singing. Thus Anthony Wood, who was at the University in 1651, gives an exceedingly interesting account of the practice of chamber music in Oxford. He tells us that ' the gentlemen in privat meetings, which A. W. frequented, play'd three, four, and five parts, with viols, as treble-viol, tenor, counter-tenor, and bass, with an organ, virginal, or harpsichon joyn'd with them : and they esteemed a violin to be an instrument only belonging to a common Fidler, and could not endure that it should come among them, for fear of making their meetings to be vaine and fidling.' Wood went to a weekly meeting of musicians in Oxford. Amongst those whom he names as ' performing their parts' are four Fellows of New College, a Fellow of All Souls who was ' an admirable lutenist,' a certain ' Ralph Sheldon, Gent., a Roman Catholick, admired for his smooth and admirable way in playing on the viol,' and a Master of Arts of Magdalen, who had a weekly meeting at his own college. Besides the amateurs, there were eight or nine professional musicians who frequented these meetings. This was in 1656, and in 1658 Wood gives the names of over sixteen other persons with whom he used to play and sing, all of whom were Fellows of Colleges, Masters of Arts, or at least members of the University. Amongst them, it is interesting to note, was ' Thom. Ken of New College, a Junior,'—afterwards Bishop Ken, one of the seven bishops who were deprived at the Revolution—who could 'sing his part.' All the rest played either viol, organ, virginal, or harpsichord. ' These did frequent the weekly meetings, and by the help of public masters of musick, who were mixed with them, they were much improved.' Only two persons out of the thirty-two mentioned by Wood seem to have had an undesirable quality, namely, Mr. Low, organist of Christ Church, who was ' a proud man,' and 'could not endure any common musitian to come to the meeting ;' and 'Nathan. Crew, M.A., Fellow of Linc. Coll., a violinist and violist, but alwaies played out of tune.' Poor Nathan. was afterwards Bishop of Durham.

Thus we find that in the sixteenth and seventeenth centuries a practical acquaintance with music was a regular part of the education of all gentlemen of rank and the higher middle classes. Nor were the lower classes wanting in enthusiasm. A large number of passages in contemporary authors prove clearly that singing in parts, especially of 'catches,' was a common diversion with artisans and working people generally. In Delaney's *History of the Gentle Craft*, 1598, one who tried to pass as a shoemaker was branded an imposter because he could neither ' sing, sound the trumpet, play upon the flute, nor reckon up his tools in rhyme.' Even the barber kept an instrument in his shop—lute, cittern, or virginal—expressly for the amusement of waiting customers; and although the ' barber's musick' may have been 'most barbarous,' still it *was* music—of a kind. The guests in a tavern, too, were constantly being entertained with music. A pamphlet entitled *The Actor's Remonstrance*, printed in 1643, speaks as follows of the decay of music in taverns, which resulted from the closing of the theatres in 1642 : ' Our music that was held so delectable and precious [*i.e.*, in Shakespeare's time] that they (*sic*) scorned to come to a tavern under twenty shillings salary for two hours, now wander with their instruments under their cloaks into all good houses of fellowship, saluting every room where there is company with, Will you have any music, gentlemen ? ' Again, from Gosson's *Short Apologie of the Schoole of Abuse*, 1587, we find that ' London is so full of unprofitable pipers and fiddlers that a man can no sooner enter a tavern than two or three cast of them hang at his heels to give him a dance before he depart.' These men sang ballads and catches as well. They also played during dinner. Lyly says : ' Thou need no more send for a fidler to a feast than a beggar to a fair.' All this, and much more that might be quoted, leads fairly to the conclusion that the ' good old days' were, musically speaking, not so barren as they are generally supposed to have been. Where shall we now find a promiscuous company able to sing through a canon in three parts at first sight? Yet they managed as much in the public-house songs of Elizabeth's time. All these details find ample corroboration in the works of Shakespeare, and the student of the subject is under a debt of gratitude to Mr. Naylor for having brought them together within one cover, to say nothing of the lucid and generally satisfactory explanations of the dramatist's musical references which he sets before us.

Mr. Baring-Gould's *English Minstrelsie* will be a monumental work when completed ; as yet we have before us only five of the eight volumes which have been announced by the publishers.   The collection, as indeed the editor expressly tells us, must not be taken to be more than a sample of what English minstrelsy has been from the Tudor age to the end of the first half of the present century.   It differs somewhat from other collections, inasmuch as it does not confine itself exclusively to published songs by well-known composers.   It takes account of the living traditional song of the people, and all classes are represented by its melodies.   This is as it should be.   The special charm of Scottish minstrelsy consists in its being so entirely natural.   It came into existence no one quite knows how, unassociated for the most part with the names of its originators.   The great bulk of English printed song, on the other hand, was composed by accomplished musicians to words often having no relation whatever to real life, but describing the amours of Corydons and Pastorellas in an ideal and fantastical world such as never existed.   Let the English folk-music be put into association with this, and the simplicity, the genuineness, of the one at once makes an agreeable contrast to the affectation of the other.   The English labourer, as Mr. Baring-Gould remarks, is now an important factor in politics ; that he has been a factor in English music has not been recognised as it ought to have been.   If in the future there is any failing in this respect it will not be the fault of the author of 'Onward, Christian Soldiers,' who in the present work has set his hand to an undertaking that promises to be unique in its special line.

Mr. Baring-Gould is not only furnishing his collection with notes on the various songs ; he is also, as will have been gathered from previous remarks, contributing to the history of English music.   His work in this department is, to be sure, a trifle scrappy, and in some cases superficial, while it is also somewhat weak in the matter of coherence and form, to say nothing of its 'style.'   But the material is both abundant and interesting, and where it is put forward as illustrating the subject of national music, it is peculiarly valuable.   The plan has been, so far, to give an historical essay in every alternate volume, the notes to the songs being of course printed in each volume. In the first volume Mr. Baring-Gould deals with the general history of English national song. The minstrels, he thinks, originated most of the early ballad airs. These minstrels were, so to speak, the musical college of the Middle Ages. They were players on many instruments; some formed a local guild, and sat in the rood-loft of the screen dividing the chancel from the nave of the church, and accompanied divine worship with their instrumental music. Such minstrels are represented at the east end of Launceston Parish Church, carved in granite; at Beverley minster also the minstrels are represented. These primitive musicians fell out of favour in the reign of Henry VIII., and still more so in that of Elizabeth. In 1593 an Act was passed putting down the minstrels, and it was ordered that any one caught wandering from place to place with minstrelsy as his profession was to be treated as a rogue and a vagabond. The third parliament of Cromwell again smote the minstrels, not now for travelling about, but for frequenting taverns. It was enacted that any minstrel or ballad singer caught singing or making music in an ale-house, or was found to have solicited any one to hear him sing or play was to be taken before the magistrate, whipped and imprisoned. Here is a hint for those legislators who are at present agitating for the regulation of our street music! In 1642 it was gravely proposed in Parliament that, in view of the great popularity of ballads and carols, the striking deeds of Oliver Cromwell should be put into rhyme and set to be sung at Christmas in place of the carols in honour of the Nativity. The proposal however was not favoured, and nothing came of it. On December 13, 1648, there was a Provost-Marshal appointed 'with power to seize upon all ballad-singers, and to suppress stage-plays.' But the Rebellion struck and injured not merely the ballad minstrels; it affected all instrumentalists attached to theatres and churches, and led to a great migration of musicians to the Continent. The national song was, however, left untouched. As Mr. Baring-

Gould remarks, the people did not miss the scientific musicians; they had never cared for their motetts and madrigals; and if the minstrel and the fiddler were suppressed by Act of Parliament, 'no Act of Parliament could restrain the mother from singing to her babe, the milkmaid from warbling under the cow, the old ballads they loved so well to the dear old tunes that they had themselves learned in infancy.'

It was now that the opera rose to be a dominating power in altering and moulding the character of music; and in his second essay Mr. Baring-Gould shows very clearly how this branch of the art affected the English song. The first opera ever produced in England was written by Sir William Davenant, Shakespeare's godson, who liked to have it thought that he was the great dramatist's son. This was *The Siege of Rhodes*, produced in 1650. Shakespeare himself introduced songs into his plays, and other dramatists—Ben Jonson, Beaumont and Fletcher, Dekker, Middleton and Webster—did the same. These plays were the parents of the ballad-opera; for the opera as at first understood in England was no more than an increase in the number of songs and choruses introduced. In 1727 Gay wrote his famous *Beggars' Opera*, in which all the songs but two or three were set to folk-melodies born in England.. The plot of the piece is of the poorest, but it turned out an immense success, the people being 'refreshed and rejoiced to hear the old familiar notes of the English muse.' It put money in the pockets of both the author and Rich, the manager of the theatre in Lincoln's Inn Field, so that it was well said that the play had made Rich *gay* and Gay *rich!* But the *Beggars' Opera* had a further effect: it drew away the audiences from the then fashionable Italian opera, and, as the wags remarked, made that indeed what the other was in name—the beggars' opera. The enormous success of Gay's work encouraged others to follow in the same track. Over forty ballad operas appeared, and as most of these were published along with the music, they furnish us with a treasury of the folk-melodies of the English people which it is doubtful if we should otherwise have had preserved. There is another thing to be noticed which had something to do with the history of English

song. In no theatre, except the two patent houses, Drury
Lane and Covent Garden, was it lawful for actors to perform
a drama. In others only burlettas and farces were legal. To
evade the law, the performers were obliged to introduce songs,
whether appropriate to the play or not. In some cases a piano
was tinkled during the dialogue, so that the piece might escape
the condemnation of the Chancellor's Court, by being described
as a musical performance. But this necessity to evade the law
provoked musical invention and brought into notice and popularity a number of songs that might not otherwise have been
composed.

The limits of space prevent our following out this interesting
subject in further detail. When Mr. Baring-Gould's work has
been completed, we may have an opportunity of dealing with
it again. In the meantime we close with a word of congratu-
lation to the publishers of the *English Minstrelsie.* They are
producing the work in a manner which is in every way credi-
table to the literary traditions of the Scottish capital. The
music is beautifully engraved, the binding is handsome, and
the many illustrations add greatly to the value of the collection. It is a work which every lover of music, and especially
of national music, should see to having on his shelves.

J. Cuthbert Hadden.

Art. V.—THE CORONATION OF JAMES I. OF ENGLAND.*

KING James VI. of Scotland was wont while at home to
speak of his English inheritance as 'the Land of Promise,'
but when he came to take possession of it, there were many dis_
appointments. The first year of his reign, which was to have
been inaugurated by a magnificent coronation, was passed
betwixt fear of the plague, then raging in London, and the
alarm caused by the double conspiracy of the Main and the Rye

---

* From the Despatches of the Venetian Envoy.

Plot, which almost seemed a rehearsal of what afterwards made the Fifth of November so celebrated. James, though fond of pomp, was timid by nature, and curtailed the coronation. Indeed, Dr. Lingard has written in regard to this matter that 'the ceremony was hastily performed by the Archbishop of Canterbury without the usual parade.' The following account, however, from the Venetian Despatches tends to prove that this is hardly an exact statement of the case. The originals of these Despatches are preserved in the Archives at Venice, where they have remained since. Week by week they were sent home by the Envoy of the Serene Republic, read before the Senate, and then stored away to be kept jealously hidden from prying eyes. For giving us a vivid picture of the time, these *Dispacci* are unrivalled; their number is so considerable that but a very small part has, as yet, been copied, translated, or even calendared, and those of the year 1603—hitherto unpublished—with which the present article deals, were sent home by Mr. Secretary Scaramelli, who arrived in England a few weeks before the death of Queen Elizabeth, and recount many things that are worthy of note.

King James of Scotland, as is well known, owed his peaceable accession to the English throne mainly to the prudent measures concerted by Sir Robert Cecil. Before London even knew the death of Queen Elizabeth, the Privy Council, with the Lord Mayor and other persons of note, had been assembled at Whitehall, and under the guidance of Cecil, they then and there drew up and signed the Proclamation conferring the crown upon James. Cecil himself proclaimed the King at the cross in Cheapside, and very promptly the citizens testified their adhesion to the new order of things by the customary acclamations, bonfires, and ringing of bells.

However, five weeks before the death of Elizabeth, it had not seemed certain that matters would go so smoothly. Scaramelli hears that King James of Scotland, 'a melancholy, prudent, and literary' prince, has indeed from his earliest years ever aspired to succeed to the English crown, 'which hope, they say, has caused him to digest the offence of the shedding of his mother's blood; and further, with much obsequiousness and show of obedience, he has striven never to irritate the Queen against himself.' But the Venetian envoy warns the Doge that James will have two chief difficulties to overcome in making good his claims to the throne—'the one, that he, not having been born in this Kingdom, is by the law of the Realm incapacitated from wearing the crown thereof ; and the other, that the Queen of Scots, his Mother, having been beheaded for conspiracy was, as a rebel, by Parliament declared to be deprived of every right to the succession, and consequently that he, James, her son, is also for the like reason incapacitated therefrom.' Scaramelli, however, evidently thinks that James will overcome his difficulties ; the revenues of Scotland (he affirms) now amount to 400,000 crowns a year, and James has recently obtained the promise, ' with pact and oath,' from thirty thousand of his vassals to follow him south of the Solway Firth and the Tweed when occasion requires.

None the less, the five weeks which still elapsed before the death of Elizabeth, in spite of all that Cecil could do, were anxious times for King James. Scaramelli mentions in his letter of the 6th of March (24th February, O.S.) that the report had come in from Edinburgh of the suicide of a certain prisoner of State, who had thrown himself off a high tower, he having been the chief member of a conspiracy against the King, ' who, by his death remaining in ignorance of all detail of the plot, and going in terror of his life.' Even as late as three weeks before his accession to the English throne, James 'found himself, in certain wise, surrounded on all hands by fear of death from conspiracy,' and this too within his own realm of Scotland. At length, however, Queen Elizabeth expired, April 3 (March 24, O.S.), and on April 12 (2nd, O.S.) the Doge is informed that James, having received news of the death of his ' Aunt,' has written a letter to the Mayor and Common Council of the City of London, and that one hundred thousand crowns have been immediately voted for the expenses of his Majesty's journey, with four hundred thousand crowns more, to be held at his royal pleasure, against the time of the coronation. James left Edinburgh on the 5th of April, O.S., and the Despatch of the 17th (the 7th, O.S.) announced that His Majesty had come south as far as Berwick, 'the strongest place that the English have on the Tweed.' The Secretary continues that James is about to assume the title of 'King of Great Britain in order thereby to denominate the whole of the Island under one name, after the fashion of that ancient and most famous King Arthur, whose Kingdom is now in the possession of his Majesty, and is a country of seventeen hundred miles in circumference.'

A fortnight later, Thursday, May 1st (April 21st, O.S.), Scaramelli reports that Cecil had gone to *Giorch* (York), 'a city one hundred and fifty miles from London, where His Majesty is stopping for a week, in order to celebrate Easter-tide, this being the date according to the English reckoning.' Easter Sunday, O.S., fell on April 24th of that year, and the close of the Despatch announces that the Coronation is fixed for St. James' Day, the patron saint of His Majesty, 'for the which, the preparations already begun, are truly magnificent, as is the habit of such things in this country, where the people greatly love pomp and ceremony.' The Queen is to be crowned at the same time to save extra expense, so the Despatch of May 15th (5th O.S.) informs the Doge,—and many Ladies have already started for the north to pay their respects to Her Majesty, whom the King at his departure for his Land of Promise, had left safe in Scotland until it might clearly be seen what welcome would be given him by his new subjects. The welcome, however, left nothing to be desired : James reached London by May 17th (7th O.S.), and on the 22nd, Scaramelli sent off two despatches to Venice communicating the first impressions which had been made on him by a rather distant view of His Most Sacred Majesty.

'The King has been stopping four days in a Palace near the City which in old times was a Monastery of Carthusian Friars, and yesterday made his state entry into the Tower, but without passing through London. His Majesty will remain at the Tower all to-morrow, for the ceremony of taking possession of the regalia, and will thence proceed four miles further to Greenwich, a favourite pleasaunce of the late Queen. This is situated on the Thames, and thither they have ordered up the six great Ships, and the two Pinnaces that were this year put into commission and armed, by order of the late Queen, and which have hitherto been lying at the Downs near Dover ready to sail for the harrying of the Spanish coast. These vessels His Majesty wishes to see, and he will meanwhile pass the time in hunting and other amusements, proceeding also to set the royal household in order ; and further, at Greenwich, he will begin to grant audiences to the Ambassadors and Ministers of the various Princes, for the which purpose I, too, have had assigned me the next day after that on which the Ambassador of France will be received.'

This last was Monsieur de Beaumont, the new Ambassador sent by Henry IV., and whose Despatches form an important authority for the history of this epoch. Scaramelli goes on to state that ' di Beomont' (as he spells his name) is to receive six thousand crowns a year *' di ben pagata provisione '* meaning doubtless that the salary would be punctually paid. The second despatch of the same date begins with the following paragraph —

' The King had not been two hours in the Tower of London—close by and in view of which is my lodging in one of the houses of the city [*Borgo*], newly built, and fair to look at, standing in a garden laid out in the Italian fashion by a native of Lucca, formerly a merchant here—when His Majesty sent one of his Gentlemen to visit me with messages of great regard to Your Serenity and personal kindness for me, Your humble servant. This gentleman stated that the King was well informed both of my business and of me personally, that his Majesty must be held excused for not having sooner granted me an audience, but after the Ambassador of France, who had already made his demand, the King would receive me, and this, prior to receiving either the Count of Nassau, the Ambassadors of the States of Holland, or the Envoy of any other power ; further, that his Majesty desired afterwards to speak with me in private, and more fully than he would be able to do publicly.'

To all this Scaramelli returned a suitable reply : and in due course, under date of the 28th May, the Envoy, describing his first audience with James, which had taken place the day preceding, namely Tuesday, the 17th old style, writes as follows :—

' Most Serene Prince,—The King having appointed my audience for yesterday at 2 o'clock afternoon, I went down accordingly to Greenwich, and found the crowd at Court so great as to surpass what I have ever seen even at Constantinople, when that Empire is in perfect peace, and when the attendance exceeds ordinarily ten or twelve thousand persons. Such was the crush at Greenwich that the Guards, though using violence, could hardly obtain for me an entrance, even into the outer rooms through which I had to pass, filled with a great crowd of all the nobility of the realm, till at length I came to the Presence Chamber where the King himself was seated surrounded by the Council and an infinity of other Lords, who were all, so to speak, in the act of paying him their adoration. Seeing me, His Majesty rose from his chair and came forward six steps towards the middle of the room, going back one step after having made me a sign of greeting by a movement of the hands ; and here he halted, listening to me with attention, and holding his hat in his hand for some considerable time, both at the beginning and at the close of the audience. His Majesty was dressed in grey satin, perfectly plain, wearing a long cloak of black cloth which came down to his knee, lined with sarcenet. He held one arm resting in a sling of white ribbon going round his neck, for when out hunting his horse had fallen, the arm being under him ; however, the alarm of the accident has proved greater than the hurt.

' By this dress, only, the King might have been mistaken for the meanest of his courtiers, (for in this matter he displays purposely his own liking and his humility), were it not that His Majesty was wearing a collar of Diamonds, with a great Diamond in his hat, which they say is the one Don Antonio of Portugal * gave in pledge here to certain merchants for a loan of eighty thousand crowns, and which the late Queen, after his death, insisted should be given up to her for the like sum of money, although the gem is now valued at the price of about two hundred thousand crowns. As to the personal appearance, stature and complexion of His Majesty, Your Serenity will have but to recall to mind the figure of the late most Illustrious Signore Federico Nani, whose appearance, as he was some ten years before his death, might count as absolutely identical with that of the King of England,—and my memory does not serve me for ever having seen two persons more alike.'

Scaramelli then gives a summary of his speech to King James, which (he adds) was of small importance, for, after having briefly referred to the unpleasant business which had especially brought him to England, namely, the recent acts of piracy of certain English sailors,—in which business everything yet remained unsettled, the darkness awaiting ' the light of the Justice and Grace of His Majesty '—the Secretary launched forth into compliments, and rejoiced especially to be the first Venetian to congratulate His Majesty on his most rightful accession. James, in his reply, spoke in French, saying that he knew Scaramelli to

---

* Don Antonio of Portugal, better known as the Prior of Crato, was the illegitimate son of Don Luis Duke of Beja, brother of the Cardinal-King Henry. On the death of the latter in 1580, Don Antonio ineffectually laid claim to the crown of Portugal. He was defeated by the Duke of Alva, whose master, Philip II., incorporated Portugal into his dominions. Don Antonio, with a price set on his head, fled to France, and after seeking refuge in England and Holland, ultimately died in Paris, in 1595.

be well acquainted with this tongue, 'and hence (said the King) I will reply to you in that same, in order not to have recourse to interpreters, since I myself cannot speak Italian as I would wish.' James then expressed his thanks to the Senate of Venice for their congratulations, and promised his immediate attention to the matters at issue, namely, the pirates, which his 'sister, the late Queen, before her death, had been unable to settle.' Scaramelli made a short complimentary reply and took his leave, after presenting the King with a clearly-written 'memorial' of the case as touching the Venetian galleon *Venier* which the English pirates had unlawfully captured.

In May, 1603, the Queen Consort, Anne of Denmark, was still in Scotland, and Scaramelli next relates what he had learnt of the character of Her Majesty. Anne, it is well known, had some time before this secretly become a Catholic, and the Venetian despatch affords us some curious details on this and other points :—

'The Queen, whose father was, as they call it here, a *Martinist*, was brought up in the Lutheran faith, but became a Catholic since living in Scotland, through the agency of three Scotch Jesuits who had come thither, the one from Rome and the other two from Spain. In Scotland, although she attends with her husband the public services of the heretical church, she nevertheless observes certain of the Catholic rites in private, and at times can even hear Mass secretly, with the permission of the King, who loves her greatly, so that she has also obtained from him leave that her one surviving daughter, now a girl of eight, may be brought up by a Catholic lady.'

The Doge is next informed that Prince Henry, on the other hand, is brought up as a Protestant; and to insure this the King, his father, has hitherto kept him apart from his mother, leaving him, on his own departure for England, at Stirling Castle under the care of the Countess of Mar. The Despatch then relates how the Queen, being left in Edinburgh to her own devices, had recently tried to kidnap Prince Henry from Lady Mar, but failing to accomplish this purpose, had thrown herself into such a rage, striking herself so violently as not only to imperil her own life but also to deprive the King of his hopes of a third son, for the child had come into the world still-born. All this, however, and how the Earl of Mar and the Duke of Lennox were sent down to Scotland to see to the matter, may be found more fully detailed in the pages devoted to Anne of Denmark by Miss Strickland in her *Queens of England;* and, finally, what Scaramelli relates is merely hear-say report. He closes with the melancholy news that the Plague was gaining ground in London, and that an order had been issued for all dogs to be killed.

The next despatch, dated June 4th (May 25th, O.S.), speaks of the difficult question raised by the coming *Protestant* coronation as to how the rite should be solemnized, since (as Scaramelli reminds the Doge) ' former kings had all been anointed by the hands of Catholic priests and with the Roman rites, for even Edward VI. and Elizabeth, though Protestants, had, at their coronation, attended the Roman Catholic Episcopal Mass.' A postscript gives the ominous news that during this last week 22 had died of plague in 13 parishes, and the following week 32 deaths are announced from 15 infected districts. The plague continuing to gain ground (30 dead are mentioned for the seven days ending the 19th June, N.S.), the Court removes to Windsor, where the King remains and awaits the arrival of the Queen; and on July 10th (June 30th, O.S.), Scaramelli writes :—

' The Queen arrives to-day at Windsor with two hundred and fifty coaches and more than five thousand horsemen, for these during the whole length of her journey kept increasing in numbers, being intent on escorting her. Her Majesty will be received by the King and the Court with much ceremony and magnificence, and with her comes the Prince. Their Majesties will then remain at Windsor till the 3rd of August, New Style, when they will make their State entry into London together, and staying at the Tower on the 4th, will on the 5th celebrate the Coronation.'

The plague, however, the Secretary continues, is gaining ground everywhere, causing the King much anxiety, and the despatch of July 23rd (13th O.S.) announces that the state entry into London will be postponed till October, when it is hoped the plague may have diminished, and for this latter date also Parliament has been summoned. The despatch states that the Queen, though duly attending the public worship ' of the heretical Church,' is nevertheless taking into her own service as many Catholic Lords as may be; Scaramelli then concludes by thanking the Doge and Senate for letters received, as well as for the promise of 120 crowns salary a month, of which, however, he says that he will only receive 98½ in consequence of the exchange being against him to the amount of 18 per cent., on all 'white money' (*moneta blanca,* presumably silver), paid out by the most illustrious Chamberlains of the Ducal Palace. Even with the loss by the exchange, this monthly allowance comes to 1,182 crowns a year, a very fair income at the beginning of the seventeenth century, when the *scudo,* equivalent to five shillings English, had a purchasing power of at least four-fold its present value.

On July 30th (20th O.S.) a long Despatch, in cypher, relates the details of the recently discovered Plot to assassinate King James before his coronation had taken place, and to give the Crown to Arabella Stuart; but Scaramelli adds nothing to what is already known of this double conspiracy generally called the 'Main Plot' and the 'Rye,' in which Sir Walter Raleigh was implicated. Of the same date as this cypher despatch is another in which Scaramelli reports that the Court has moved from Windsor to Oatlands, and thence proceeded to Hampton Court, 'a great palace with one hundred and eighty rooms, each provided with doors and locks.' Here, after an audience with the King, who naturally could talk of nothing but the Plot, Scaramelli had proceeded to his first interview with Anne of Denmark, who also spoke to him in French (as did the King) 'for Her Majesty does not understand a single word of Italian.' This incidental detail serves to contradict the assertion of Miss Strickland, who, on the authority of Cardinal Bentivoglio, the Nuncio at Brussels, describes Anne as 'an Italian scholar.' Scaramelli pays the Queen many compliments, and when he alludes diplomatically to her being of the Catholic faith, her Majesty smiles and answers him with much graciousness.

It was probably at this interview that Scaramelli proffered his request to be allowed to see the royal children, who were at this time staying at Oatlands. The request was granted, and on Wednesday, August 6th (July 27th, O.S.), the following desscription of Prince Henry and Princess Elizabeth was penned for the edification of the Doge and Senate of the Republic. Scaramelli dates from 'Somberi,' evidently Sunbury in Middlesex, three miles above Hampton Court, whither he had recently removed from 'Eghen,' to wit Egham near Staines, the place where he and the Envoys of Lorraine and of the Netherlands had lodged, while the Court was at Windsor. He writes as follows :—

' I have recently visited the most Serene Prince and Princess at Oatlands, much to their pleasure and mine, as also to the satisfaction of the Lords their Governors, for none of the various Ministers of foreign Princes who are living in this neighbourhood have as yet either visited them or even sought so to do ; and both the King and the Queen appear to have been gratified by my insistance in requesting this permission. The Prince, who has not yet completed his tenth year, received me in the middle of his audience Chamber ; he is slender in body, high-spirited, and displayed much politeness in manner, with a gravity beyond his years, for, first taking off his hat, he bade me cover my head, and prolonged the conversation by narrating to me, through the interpreter, all his various exercises in dancing, tennis-playing, and hunting. Then the Prince himself, accompanying me down the steps, through the Palace, and up the other staircase, conducted me to the apartments of the Princess, his sister, whom we found well attended, surrounded by her Maids of Honour and her Ladies. Her Highness, standing under a canopy, received me most graciously, although she be not yet eight years of age. Both the Prince and the Princess acquainted me with their desire to learn our speech, and—as their teachers had instructed them—rendered their thanks to Your Serenity for having despatched me hither. No sooner had I taken my leave of their Highnesses, than the Governor of the Prince sent off a courier to their Majesties, with the news that the royal children had most fitly behaved, himself informing me that the Queen had expressly commanded him thus to send her word : which same I now notify to your Serenity lest I be lacking even in this small matter, rather than from any real importance that can be attached thereto.'

The account of the Coronation, which had taken place on the previous Monday, Scaramelli gives in his second despatch of this same Wednesday, August 6th (July 27th, O.S.) All that relates to the ceremony is here translated in full, for it contains many curious details not to be found elsewhere, and affords a curious picture of the Court and manners of our first Stuart King. The account of the ecclesiastical rites and vestments is also interesting, for the Puritans had not, as yet, curtailed the ritual established by Elizabeth.

'MOST SERENE PRINCE :

' The lately discovered Plot having made the King even more desirous than before of receiving the allegiance of the nobles and taking the oath at the Coronation—that affairs should thereby be brought as much as possible to a settlement—did lately issue divers orders for preventing persons coming out of London (where they are dying every week of the plague by thousands), from making their way into the Abbey during that ceremony. Further, his Majesty who had already named those of the Court who were to attend him, causing them to be given special tickets for admission, at the last moment revoked some of the orders for ensuring the complete privacy of the Corona-tion. On the last day of the month just elapsed, the King created eight Earls and four Barons, and then on [Friday] the first day of this present month their Majesties both set out from Hampton Court in two companies, each company having five hundred men of the Guard in attendance, over and above the usual number; and halting to sleep that night a mile distant from London. The next day [Saturday] passing outside London, they went straight to the royal Palace at Whitehall, which stands near the Abbey of Westminster. On Monday morning, which was St. James's Day, Old Style [25th July, the 4th of August, N.S.], their Majesties embarked on the river Thames accom-panied by the whole of the Council, and their respective Courts of Lords and Ladies in Waiting; and proceeding, landed at the ancient fane of Westminster, which, on the land side, was made impossible for the people to approach by reason of the numerous Guards posted at all the Gates of London—while as to those who went by water they must lie in peril of their lives from the crowd of boats, and from fear of falling in with plague-stricken persons come out from London. Their Majesties, as soon as they had disembarked, entered the Abbey, and the Coronation immediately began; the Procession being in such order and fashion as follows :—

' First marched twelve Heralds, in tabards, open, and painted with the arms of the four Kingdoms, after these came various companies of the merchants and officials of the City of London, followed by the Lord Mayor; all these were habited in long robes of red cloth, with broad sleeves, and the officials were some score in number. Next came two drummers and ten trumpeters sounding their instruments, then, the Officers of Justice, who were habited after the same fashion as the Officials of the City, with the Chief Justice walking behind them, wearing over his red robe a gold chain going about his shoulders, and as broad as is the Collar of the Order. These numbered about five and twenty, all marching two by two, as also did all the others.

'Sixty Knights of the Bath followed, which is an ancient Order of Knighthood, and these can only be created at the Coronation of a new Sovereign, hence of those created by the late Queen, two alone now survive.* Their habit is a tunic, reaching to the middle of the leg, with wide sleeves of purple satin; a sort of sleeve, or rather pouch attached to the belt, which, passing over the shoulder, hangs down behind, as far as the hips, after the fashion of an amice; further, they wear white plumes, but besides a plain gilt sword, with leathern belt and straps, have no other special badge.

'After these came some thirty Barons in long tunics of scarlet cloth, with mantles of scarlet over the same reaching to the ground, very fully gathered, lined with ermine, at least those parts that were visible, the sleeves hanging down; while behind, over the left shoulder, these mantles had two bands across them outside, and were also of ermine over the shoulders. Next followed the Earls, near fifteen in number, whose robes consisted of crimson velvet under-tunics reaching down only to the middle of the leg, also mantles of crimson velvet lined with ermine, having full and gathered ermine capes coming down to the hips, with cowls of crimson velvet hanging down over the said capes, somewhat like a stocking, being four fingers broad; further, they wore caps of crimson velvet, with ermine fillets and

---

* Elizabeth created eleven Knights of the Bath at her coronation, and, as a matter of fact, made no more during her reign, but the statement is, of course, incorrect that the sovereign *could* only create them at the coronation. James, for instance, besides the sixty dubbed on his coronation-day, made twelve more Knights in 1605 when Charles was created Duke of York, and twenty-five when Henry was created Prince of Wales in 1610.

small plain golden coronets, in place of bands; each peer carrying in his hand a small slight sceptre. All, whether Earl, Baron, or of other degree, went bare-headed.

'Behind these came the King, walking under a light and simple canopy, upheld by four rods, and from the summit of each rod there depended tinkling bells of silver-gilt. The King was habited as were the Earls, except that the cape was of crimson velvet lined with ermine, while the coronet round his cap was somewhat larger than theirs. Preceding his Majesty was the Regalia borne by certain Earls to wit the Crown Imperial, to be used in the coronation, carried upon a cushion by the Lord Treasurer, and after the like fashion the Sceptre, the Sword of State with its sheath, the Chalice with the Wine therein, and the Paten, also the Ducal cap set on a wand. In front of the King went the Chief Herald or the King of Arms, who acted as master of the ceremonies, wearing a plain coronet without the cap, a mantle of crimson satin reaching to the knees, and, over this, the coat of arms emblazoned with the quarterings of the four Kingdoms. Following the King were the Gentlemen of the Court, in coats to the knee of crimson velvet; further, one hundred and fifty halberdiers, the usual Royal Guard, in their crimson liveries, but these were that day new, having gold embroideries, rich above the ordinary, covering both back and front; then about thirty Gentlemen Pensioners, in coats of red silk reaching to the knee, some of whom carried halberds, the staves being covered with velvet. Immediately behind the King walked the Queen under a canopy similar to that of His Majesty, wearing a long crimson robe lined with ermine, having wide sleeves without any ornament, and a simple girdle, her hair hanging loose over the shoulders, confined by a plain gold coronet. Preceding the Queen were the Countesses in robes of crimson velvet, lined with ermine without ornament; but the Peeresses had their hair braided up, and each wore a small coronet.

'The King on entering the Abbey found the clergy already standing at the door to await him, all fully robed in Chasuble and Cope (these vestments being after the Roman pattern), and they accompanied his Majesty up to the Choir, where the King, ascending the dais covered with red cloth, between the Choir and the High Altar, took his seat on the Chair of State, as likewise did the Queen. Their two Chairs were similar one to the other, set apart with a distance in between them of about seven feet, and both turned towards the aforesaid Altar,—if, indeed, one may call " Altar " what was merely an ordinary and moveable table. The King being thus seated, the Archbishop of Canterbury, between the Lord High Admiral and the Lord Treasurer, with the King of Arms preceding him, advanced before the people, and the King of Arms called aloud three times in the English tongue,* " Hear ye ! Hear ye ! Hear ye l " on which the Archbishop read out of a book certain words to the effect That should there be any who held King James the Sixth of Scotland, but First of England, to be no lawful King of England, he should straightway declare it, for hereafter such a one would come to be a traitor, seeing that he, the Archbishop, was about to bestow on King James aforesaid the Insignia of the Kingdom, it being the general hope of all men that his Majesty would defend and govern well his people, who therefore prayed unto God to grant him a long life. Thereupon, and after the Archbishop had thus spoken, the people all shouted for joy.

‘ This part of the ceremony being accomplished, the King and the Queen went up to the altar, where they knelt at two faldstools, and for a space of time made their prayers to God ; after which, again seating themselves, they listened to the sermon preached by one of the Bishops. The sermon being ended, the Archbishop read the Gospel from the Book which lay on the altar, and afterwards gave the same to the King to kiss. Then the King, being disrobed by his Earls, and standing up in doublet and hose of white sarcenet, he having unlaced the front part of the said doublet, knelt before the altar, when the Archbishop immediately anointed his Majesty in various places on the bare skin, having taken the holy oil from an ampulla which stood upon the altar in a basin covered with a white cloth. On this altar also stood the regalia which had been carried before the

---

* Doubtless ‘ Oyes, Oyes, Oyes,’ pronounced *English* fashion.

King, to wit, the crown and sceptre, as also the chalice and paten. It is said this holy oil was consecrated in ancient days, and that it was found in the same place where the crown, likewise consecrated, was kept; further, that with this same oil Edward VI. and Elizabeth were annointed, although they both were Protestants, as is also this present King. Then after his Majesty's head had been wiped with a white cloth, the King was re-habited, but in other robes; of these, namely, there was the long coat of crimson velvet, lined with white, reaching down to the middle of his leg, having sleeves not very wide, over this came a royal tunic fashioned like a deacon's cassock, with the garter, sword, and collar of the Order, his Majesty wearing over all a mantle of purple brocade without pleats, like a cope.

'Robed after this fashion, the King was conducted to his seat on the royal Throne of red brocade, that stood in the middle of the space between the dais and the Altar, facing the people. Then the Archbishop coming forward, took the Crown from the Altar, carrying it to the King, and placed it on his head. The King having thus been crowned, was conducted by the Archbishop to the Altar, where the latter read some words from a book, giving this same book to his Majesty, who, laying his hand thereon, took the Oath. Then one of the Earls, taking the Sword of State from the Altar, drew it from the scabbard, and carried it thenceforward, always drawn, before the King, who took his seat again on the Throne above mentioned, while the Archbishop, bringing the Sceptre and the Wand of gold, placed the Sceptre in the right hand of the King, and the Wand in his left. The Sceptre is about two palms in length, with the Orb at the one end, surmounted by the Cross; the Wand is of a length to reach the ground, with the Orb at the top surrounded by a Crown.

'When all these ceremonies had been duly accomplished, the Archbishop, assisted by the Lord High Admiral and the Lord Treasurer, who both had taken a special part in all that has been above described, accompanied by the Earls and Barons, led the King (his crown being upheld by two bishops) to the Dais, where his Majesty took his seat on the Throne, raised on steps, forming an octagon base about eight feet in diameter. The King being thus

enthroned, the Earls advanced, and having previously put on
their caps, took the Oath of Allegiance thus covered, then again
uncovered ; following them the Barons did the same, but these
bare-headed. After the Oath of Allegiance had been taken in
this wise, the Earls first, next the Councillors and the Barons,
one by one, went up and kissed the King's hands, with the following ceremony : namely, each advancing bowed at the foot of
the throne, went up the steps and knelt on a cushion of red
brocade ; next each kissing his own right hand laid it upon the
King's crown, which some also touched with their lips ; the King
then extended his hand, and this each of the Peers kissed.
Among the rest was the Earl of Pembroke, a graceful youth,
who is much with the King, and he, being very fond of joking,
in addition kissed his Majesty on the face ; whereupon the King
began to laugh, and gave him a good slap. While this obeisance
was taking place, the King of Arms advancing between the Lord
High Admiral and the Lord Chancellor, as before, called three
times upon the people to give ear, and the Chancellor, speaking
in a loud voice, declared to them that His Majesty was indeed
their rightful King and supreme Lord, being now anointed and
crowned : and, when he had finished speaking thus, the people
once again shouted for joy.

' This being ended, the Archbishop with the assistance only of
the Lord High Admiral and the Lord Chancellor, proceeded to
crown the Queen with the Crown Imperial, and gave her a
Sceptre and a Wand of gold like those which the King carried ;
then, with no further ceremony, they led her up to the Dais and
seated her on a Throne raised upon steps similar to that occupied
by the King, in a line with the same, but of smaller size, and
standing some eight feet distant therefrom ; for it should have
been said that up to this moment her Majesty had remained
seated in her private chair near the altar, taking no part in
aught that was going on. The King then went up to the altar
and kneeling in his fald stool received the communion at the
hands of the Archbishop, with the Bread and the Wine that had
been carried before him in the chalice aforesaid ; but the Queen
did not receive the Communion, and did not indeed move from
her Throne.

'The Coronation was now ended, and the King withdrew to certain rooms behind the altar, as likewise did the Queen, and here the King exchanged his crown for one of lesser weight, while the Queen taking off her red robes exchanged these for a black dress. Then their Majesties, after having taken some refreshment, came forth again, and the procession returned in the same order as it had come; the King and the Queen going on board a great barge, magnificently decked out, which carried their Majesties for a long space, in full view of the people, in a triumphant procession down the river to the City; whence they finally returned to dine at the Royal Palace [of Whitehall] already mentioned. Here all have remained until this evening [Wednesday] when the King and Queen, the Court and the Council have departed, and have now gone back to Hampton Court.'

The conduct of Queen Anne, in refusing the Protestant Communion, naturally caused much scandal; but the Government, both now and later, consistently ignored the fact of her having joined the Church of Rome; for Anne, though at times obstinate, was of too frivolous and pleasure-loving a nature to have any desire for the glories of martyrdom. Her tempers and her vagaries are often mentioned in succeeding Despatches, but this account of the Coronation may be fitly brought to its close with a paragraph, that Scaramelli thought important enough to warrant its being put in cypher when forwarding his next communication to the Doge, under date of August 13th (the 3rd O.S.) that is to say on the following Wednesday.

'On the date of the Coronation, the King had urged the Queen most strenuously to partake of the Communion with him at the Abbey, according to the Protestant rite, and further, the chaplains of the Archbishop, that 'same morning, had done their uttermost to persuade the Queen thereto. (For otherwise, as it was justly said, her Majesty must seem to live, and in fact must live, without Religion : for she could never be permitted to practise any other religion than that which had been established by Law, and which is now preached throughout the Kingdom.) However, her Majesty placidly answered " No " two or three times to all their remonstrances, and after this refused to add another word.'

James, on this occasion, evidently did not press the matter, and showed much good sense in not being more obstinate than

the Queen. Of Court functions in England, however, Scaramelli had reported the last, for before the end of the year 1603 he
was superseded by the arrival of the Ambassadors-Extraordinary
—the Most Illustrious Pietro Duodo and the Most Illustrious
Nicolo Molin sent by the Doge to congratulate the King on his
accession, and thereupon to renew full diplomatic relations between the Serene Republic and the Court of St. James.   The
two Ambassadors had their first audience of the King in the last
days of November ; and Secretary Scaramelli, being recalled,
travelled in January 1604 *via* Calais to Brussels, next transacted
some business for the Republic at the Hague and Utrecht, from
thence going direct to Venice, reaching home again after an
absence in the north of a little over a year.

GUY LE STRANGE.

ART. VI.—ST. MARK'S INDEBTEDNESS TO ST. MATTHEW.

MY object is to prove that S. Mark is generally posterior to
S. Matthew. There is, of course, nothing really novel in
such a view—S. Mark's posteriority was long ago proclaimed at
Tübingen—but since the days of Tübingen, advocates of the
opposite view have had a complete ascendancy. As a summary of the present situation, we may conveniently turn to the
article on the ' Gospels' in the new edition of Smith's *Bible Dictionary*. Dr. Sanday, the author of it, declares that the greater
originality of S. Mark is, if not an assured result of criticism
is rapidly becoming so ; but he is obliged to recognise that
the claim 'cannot be made without reserve ;' and he follows
with a tentative conclusion that 'there are distinct layers in
our present S. Mark, one layer (commonly called "ur-Marcus")
that is earlier than our S. Matthew, and another (" deutero-
Marcus ") that is later.'
    The present situation is obviously far from satisfactory ; for
' ur-Marcus ' and ' deutero-Marcus ' have been in stock for a
considerable period, and the difficulty of separating them is

just as much a difficulty now as it was forty years ago.
Matters appear to be at a dead lock. No one has ever succeeded in distinguishing the two layers solidly, or in discovering any internal signs of duality in S. Mark which correspond
with the variation of aspect towards S. Matthew, or in sub-
tracting from S. Matthew any considerable amount of the
matter common to S. Mark without leaving the remainder of
S. Matthew unmanageable. Besides, it has never been more
than an assumption, one of several explanations possible, that
the dual aspect of S. Mark towards S. Matthew is an index of
duality of source. The only essential difference in the situation to-day from what it was forty years ago is the formidable
increase of S. Mark's supporters—it is apparently their number
that convinces Dr. Sanday of S. Mark's approaching triumph—
but the significance of this increase may easily be over-rated.
The doctrine of S. Mark's originality, it so happens, has appealed
to a diversity of interests; and that Westcott, Abbot, and
Renan, should have coincided in advocating S. Mark's claims
is a phenomenon which loses in effect when we discover that
the reasons for their preference are, to a great extent, inter-
necine.

One of the chief differences between S. Matthew and S.
Mark is the distinctly un-Judaic character of the latter. It is
a difference of which advocates of S. Mark's priority have
scarcely realized the full import; for that a Gospel prepared
for Gentiles should afterwards have been altered to suit Jews,
is almost inconceivable. True that some of the most Judaic
features in S. Matthew occur in passages altogether peculiar
to that Gospel, and may perhaps be derived from quite another
source than the sections paralleled in S. Mark, but the sections
paralleled in S. Mark contain too many for this avenue of
escape to remain open very long. On one side or the other
there must have been deliberate alteration of the text.

In reporting the cure of the withered hand our Second
Evangelist omits all mention of 'the Law,' and in place of the
rabbinical rule about sheep fallen into pits, he gives us the
general principle as to saving life or killing. He again omits
all mention of 'the Law' in reporting the lawyer's question.

'Some say thou art Elijah,'—he omits 'and others, Jeremiah;' 'that your flight be not in the winter,'—he·omits 'nor on a Sabbath;' 'the abomination of desolation,'—he omits 'spoken of by Daniel;' 'no sign given you,'—he omits 'save the sign of Jonah.'

The omission last mentioned is especially interesting, for the reference to Jonah is one of those things that occur in the First Gospel twice (Matt. xii. 39; xvi. 4), and in the eyes of many critics these doublets are evidence of the combination of two distinct documents. In any case the fact of the double occurrence renders it very unlikely that 'save the sign of Jonah' is a post-addition. Similar remarks apply to S. Mark's omission of the twice quoted passage, 'mercy not sacrifice' (Matt. ix. 13; xii. 7).

Notice again S. Mark's omission of the prophecy quoted in Matt. xiii. 14, 15. Surely we find a relic of this prophecy in Mk. iv. 12,—'That they may not perceive, lest haply they should turn again and it should be forgiven them.' The quotation being from the lips of our Lord Himself it seems, *prima facie*, far likelier that the shorter form in S. Mark is an abbreviation than that the longer form in S. Matthew is an expansion.

In his report of the rich ruler's enquiry, S. Mark omits the chiliastic promise 'In the regeneration ye shall sit on twelve thrones judging the twelve tribes'—an omission which makes the subsequent request of James and John for the two chief thrones sudden and abrupt. In the brief denunciation of Scribes and Pharisees (Mk. xii. 38-40, contrast Matt. xxiii.) his introductory phrase ἐν τῇ διδαχῇ αὐτοῦ ἔλεγε, 'said in the course of teaching,' is suggestive of his knowing more that it was to his purpose to report. By omitting Christ's declaration about the need of fulfilling all legal righteousness he leaves Him undistinguished from the penitents who come 'confessing their sins.' By omitting 'then shall appear the sign of the Son of man in heaven: and then shall all the tribes of the earth mourn' he leaves the subsequent ὄψονται ('Then shall they see') without a subject.

Still more significant is his treatment of the Syro-Phœnician narrative. He omits the first repulse and Christ's declaration of being sent only to 'the lost sheep of the house of Israel' (Matt. xv. 24) ; and thus plunging in *medias res* he leaves the woman's abject attitude unaccounted for, and also, to some extent, Christ's commendation. But especially notice the statement with which he replaces the matter omitted,—'Jesus entered into a house, and would have no man know it, and he could not be hid ;' for here the narratives in S. Matthew and S. Mark are running too parallel for independent information to be reasonably expected, and while it is obviously impossible to derive S. Matthew's description from S. Mark's, the reverse process is easy. S. Mark's new detail looks like an excuse for, and explanation of what he does not relate : the request of the disciples, 'Send her away for she crieth after us,' being interpreted as a desire to avoid publicity, not a reflection on the woman's Gentile birth, it would seem natural that her second approach should be timed when the privacy of a house afforded the opportunity needed.

If it be admitted that our Second Evangelist had Matt. xv. 21-28 in his hands, then it seems probable that he also had the analogous passage in Matt. x. 5, 6, 'Go not into any way of the Gentiles: go rather to the lost sheep of the house of Israel.'

Before quitting the subject of the un-Judaism of our Second Evangelist, attention is due to his constant explanation of Jewish customs and softening down of Jewish terminology. We are informed that John's disciples and the Pharisees were in the habit of fasting; that the first day of unleavened bread was that on which the Passover must be slain; that amongst Jews it was of traditional obligation to rinse the hands before eating and after marketing. (In passing, notice what an awkward repetition this gloss about rinsing necessitates,—'had seen that some of His disciples ate with defiled hands;' 'Why do they eat with defiled hand ?'). 'Syro-Phœnician' takes the place of 'Canaanite;' 'healed' is twice explained by 'taught;' 'long robes' replace the large fringes and broad phylacteries of Matt. xxiii. 5 ; and for the oriental metaphor of bearing the shoes is substituted 'unloose the latchet.' Such differences between S. Matthew and S. Mark are of course merely superficial, but cumulatively they have force.

In fine, the un-Judaism of S. Mark is consistent, systematic and eminently artificial.

A comparison of the Eschatology of S. Mark and S. Matthew reveals some significant differences which tell strongly for the priority of S. Matthew.

In Matt. x. 23 Christ promises that the Messianic reign shall commence before His disciples have visited all the cities of Israel, but just at this point the replica in Mk. xiii. 9-13 stops short. It is conceivable of course that this verse is a post-addition; but its peculiarly Judaic character, its close con-nexion with what precedes (*cf.* 'To the lost sheep of Israel'), and the fact that it completes the parallel to Matt. xxiv. 14-19 render the idea of post-addition exceedingly improbable.

In Matt. xvi. 28, Christ declares that 'some stand here which shall in no wise taste of death till they see the Son of man coming in his kingdom.' But in Mk. ix. 1, 'in no wise taste of death till they shall see the kingdom of God come with power.' The original idea was surely of the *personal* advent, for it is of His coming with the angels that Christ has just spoken, and of rendering to every man according to his works. Does not the interpretation in an *impersonal* sense,—'some standing here shall see my gospel triumph'—indicate a time when the ex-pectation that Christ would return during the lifetime of His immediate followers was already disappointed?

So again with regard to the great final charge in Matt. xxiv. We are told that 'this gospel shall be preached to all the nations; and then shall the end come.' The οὖν in the next verse, ('When therefore ye see') makes the setting up of the great abomination a sign of the beginning of the end. And, further on, the darkening of the sun and the appearance of the Son of man on the clouds of heaven follow the desolation of Jerusalem εὐθέως,—'*immediately* after the tribulation of those days.' But in Mk. xiii. these prophecies appear with such differ-ence as to suggest that a difficult interval after the destruction of Jerusalem has already elapsed. 'The gospel must first be preached to all nations' repeats the Second Evangelist, but without telling us that when missionaries to all nations have gone forth, 'then shall the end come.' The setting up of the great abomination is introduced by '$\delta\epsilon$' instead of $o\tilde{v}\nu$. And the advent of Christ follows the destruction of Jerusalem indefinitely,—'In those days after that tribulation.'

It is perhaps worth noticing too that instead of S. Matthew's 'standing in the holy place' we have in Mk. xiii. 'standing where it ought not.' The variation may be merely due to S. Mark's un-Judaic design, but it may also be due to the fact that the flight to Pella was not occasioned by the setting up of any idol in the Temple itself. The general expectation of an idol in the Temple was never realized, and expounders of prophecy appear to have been thrown back on the Roman eagles that encircled Jerusalem (*cf.* Luke xxi. 20).

The glosses and expansions which occur in the second Gospel may next be noticed :—

In S. Matthew.	In S. Mark.
'Preached saying, Repent.'	'Preached a baptism of repentance unto remission of sins.'
'Came into Galilee saying, Repent.'	'Repent and believe in the Gospel.'
'For my sake.'	'For my sake and the Gospel's' (twice).
'How hardly they that have riches.'	Qualified, 'That trust in riches.'
'Shall receive a hundredfold and inherit eternal life.'	Precluding Chiliastic interpretation, 'A hundredfold now in this time with persecution, and in the world to come eternal life.'
'Destroy this temple and build it in three days.'	'This temple made with hands, and in three days build another made without hands.'
'The poor ye have always with you.'	'Always with you, and whensoever ye will ye can do them good.'
'If I send them away fasting, they will faint by the way.'	'Will faint by the way, for some of them come from afar.'
'Many publicans and sinners sat down with Jesus.'	'Sat down with Jesus, for there were many and they followed him.'
'He prayed, Father, let this cup pass from me."'	With explanation, 'He prayed that the hour might pass from him, saying.'
'Father, if it be possible.'	Lest the Divine power should seem to be limited, 'Father, all things are possible unto thee.'

'Drink ye all.'	'And they all drank.'
'His leprosy was cleansed.'	'Straightway the leprosy departed from him, and he was made clean.'
Ambiguously, 'A renowned prisoner' ἐπίσημος.	Renowned, but for his crimes, 'lying bound with them that had made insurrection, men who had committed murder.'
'The other Mary,' 'James,' 'the sons of Zebedee,' 'Simon of Cyrene.'	With specification, 'Mary of Joses,' 'James the Less,' 'James and John, the sons of Zebedee,' 'the father of Alexander and Rufus.'
'Whosoever shall put away his wife.'	Further providing for a contingency impossible under the Jewish Law, but common enough in Greece and Rome, 'And if she herself shall put away her husband.'
'The disciples had indignation, saying, To what purpose is this waste.'	Softened, 'There were *some* that had indignation.'
'Then come the disciples of John, saying, Why do we fast, and thy disciples not?'	Acquitting John's disciples, 'They come and say, Why do John's disciples?'
Pilate immediately grants the body to Joseph.	He only grants it after obtaining a certificate of death from the centurion. Our second Evangelist refutes the cavil that Christ merely revived from a swoon.
'Μηδὲ ῥάβδον μηδὲ ὑποδήματα.'	Mitigated, 'Εἰ μὴ ῥάβδον μόνον, ἀλλὰ ὑποδεδεμένους σανδάλια.'

Notice in this case the two awkward ruptures of construction that the alteration involves—'He charged them that they should not take—but shod with sandals—and do not put on two coats.' In S. Matthew, Herod said, 'This is John the Baptist. He is risen,'—in S. Mark, 'Herod said John the Baptist is risen. But others said, It is Elijah. And others, It is a prophet even as one of the prophets. But Herod said, John whom I beheaded, he is risen.' The extra matter in S. Mark looks very like a slavishly-conceived justification for the opinions held about Christ which the disciples are presently to report. And notice the awkward repetition of Herod's opinion which this intercalation necessitates. In S. Matthew, Herod desires to kill John, but fears the people, for all account him a prophet. In S. Mark, it is Herodias who desires to kill, and

Herod's respect for John that prevents. The discrepancy is pronounced, but the two Gospels at this point are running too parallel to allow our taking refuge in the hypothesis of independent traditions. We are obliged then to infer the existence behind both Gospels of a text susceptible of either interpretation; but while to arrive at it we have only to alter the text of S. Matthew slightly, (*e.g.*, καὶ ἤθελεν αὐτὸν ἀποκτεῖναι καὶ ἐφοβήθη ὅτι πάντες ὡς προφήτην αὐτὸν εἶχον) we are obliged in the case of S. Mark to dispense with several extra details which are thus shown to be secondary—'She set herself against him,' 'He kept him safe,' 'He was perplexed and heard him gladly.'

Again, it is surely a sign of posteriority that the Second Evangelist should twice excuse the apostles' attitude—'For they wist not what to say;' should supply the moral to be drawn from the Draught of Meats, 'This he spake making all meats clean;' should explain the Gadarene demoniac's ejaculation, 'What have I to do with thee' by adding, 'For Jesus had said, Come forth, thou unclean spirit;' should give motive for Christ's *touching* the leper, 'Being moved with compassion;' should think it necessary to explain Herod's relationship to Herodias 'for he had married her;' should extenuate 'they left their father in the ship,' by adding, 'with the hired servants;' should account for Christ taking the Twelve apart (Matt. xx. 17) by explaining that the rest of the company were in a state of panic; should qualify the harshness of 'It is not meet to take the children's bread,' by prefacing 'Let the children be fed first;' should illustrate 'straightway ye shall find' by making the disciples in very fact find the ass in a gateway, and should represent the contingency provided for 'if any man say aught' as actually arising; should illustrate 'Go into the city to such a man' by adding a note for identification; should account for the sternness of 'Behind me Satan' by representing the prediction of the Passion as uttered παῤῥησία, and Peter as remonstrating in the presence of the disciples; (There are awkward consequences here, for our Second Evangelist, requiring some enlargement of audience for the utterances that follow, avails himself of 'the multitude,' forgetful that Christ is in retirement at Cæsarea Philippi). Again, those statements in Mark iv., 10, 33, 34, that Christ was 'alone' when questioned about the sower, and explained all things to the disciples 'privately,' are they not due to a mistaken interpretation of Matt. xiii.?—for at the close of day Christ is still sitting in the boat in the presence of the multitudes; and the notion of His selecting an audience frustrates the invitation 'He that hath ears to hear, let him hear,' and also the reproach 'They close their ears.'

Our consideration of the longer text in S. Mark now brings us up facing that elaboration of detail which S. Mark's champions never weary of appealing to as infallible proof of originality and eye-witness. There are, however, as Strauss pointed out, good grounds for a view quite contrary. What an extraordinary conception of S. Matthew we are driven to by the hypothesis that the precise vivid details of S. Mark are original! For these details are absent from S. Matthew one and all, and if the Matthaean narratives are to be derived from those in S. Mark, the conclusion is inevitable that the author of the former was unprecise, unpicturesque deliberately! Again, on the hypothesis that the precise vivid details are not the outcome of determined artistic design, but a natural result of eye-witness, how strangely they sometimes occur. The first, in an utterance of the Baptist's, ' κύψας;' the second, 'with the wild beasts,' belonging to a time when Christ was alone. From the exactitude of 'even to the half of My kingdom' are we to infer that the artless eye-witness was actually present at Herod's banquet? As a rule, the sequence of events is definitely noted ('on that day,' 'straightway after'), and gestures and emotions are continually reported ('looking round,' 'frowning,' 'embracing,' 'sighing'), but let anyone consult his own memory as to events a few years back. How often can he really assign events to a day, to an hour? How often can he recall the exact expression on a person's lips, the direction of his eyes, the tone of his voice? No; in any case we are forced to infer a certain self-consciousness and a deliberate artistic design on the part of the Second Evangelist.

The Second Evangelist's details are often purely ornamental, rather awkwardly distracting attention from the main idea, and quite dispensable. Such are his statements that the blind man threw off his garment when he rose, and that his father's name was Timæus; that there were four men carrying the paralytic's mattress, one at each corner; that the cock crowed twice before Peter remembered; that the feeding multitudes arranged themselves in groups, and that the grass on which they sat was green; that the angel of the sepulchre sat on the right side; that it was in the stern of the boat, on the cushion, that Christ lay asleep; that a child whom Christ raised was exactly twelve years old, and that her father's name was Jaïrus; that the number of rabid swine was two thousand; that the sum requisite for the purchase of loaves was two hundred pence, and the market value of the precious ointment three hundred.

How few of these details really require any special knowledge! How many are suggested by or might be inferred from the briefer narrative in S. Matthew! Anyone might conclude for himself that when Peter was recognised he was exposed to some artificial light; that when the disciples arrived in port 'they moored to the shore'; and that Herod's birthday guests, whose good opinion he valued, were 'his lords, the chiliarchs, and the chief men of Galilee.' The legion of possessed swine would naturally suggest the idea that the demoniac's possession was multiple. The fact that in Matt., xxi. 19, the withering of the fig tree takes place 'immediately,' might well lead to a commentatorial notice that the foliage appeared drooping on the day subsequent; and that such is the relationship of Mk., xi. 11-23, to Matt., xxi. 19, is proved by the fact that this desideration of a second day for the curse to take outward effect, leaves our Lord on the first day of his arrival in Jerusalem with nothing whatever to do except περιβλέπεσθαι (one of our Second Evangelist's mannerisms), and also involves an awkward repetition of the evening retirement to Bethany (Mk., xi. 11, 19). Consider the frequently trivial character of these details. It is a rule in biography that later biographers employ what the earlier disdain. Crumbs are swept up only when the feast is finished.

Consider, too, the tendency to emphasize the marvellous. With the phenomena of the apocryphal gospels before our eyes, it ought surely to be reckoned a sign of decadence that our Second Evangelist dilates so exuberantly on the Gadarene's ferocity and the epileptic's paroxysm. And sometimes the new details do not seem conceived quite in the character of the narratives to which they are added. ' The time of figs was not yet' explains the tree's barrenness, but is inharmonious with Christ's expectation of finding fruit. After the very vigorous expulsion of the money-changers, it is said ' He would not suffer that any man should carry a vessel through the temple'; a remark which awkwardly separates the money-changers from Christ's address to them. It is strange to hear that ' He wanted to pass them by' after ' seeing them distressed He came to them walking on the sea;' strange that the demoniac about to cry out against interference 'ran ' to meet Christ; strange, and from its needless exactitude, grating, ' And they had only one loaf' after ' They had forgotten to take bread.'

Finally, we come to that point, so emphasized by Strauss, that the new details, though in some cases bizarre enough to give us confidence that they were not invented, are, in others, of a character incompatible with their being first-hand. It may well have been that a paralytic was let down by cords from a roof, let down into an ordinary central court-yard, but the Second Evangelist makes the bearers actually dig through and break up solid tiling, notwithstanding that the people were underneath. In the case of the pricing of the loaves and of the precious ointment, is there not something untrue to nature in making the disciples so ready with their figures? Did onlookers in Gadara really occupy themselves in ascertaining the exact number of swine that perished?

All the characteristics above noted in S. Mark's elaboration of detail are especially conspicuous in the Jaïrus history. Let us consider the extra items separately. Firstly. Why should the hemorrhagic woman come behind and touch? Because Christ was thronged suggests our Second Evangelist. But the crowd has had no opportunity to gather, for Christ has only just disembarked from Gadara (a difficulty underlined by our Third Evangelist's transparent device of keeping a previous crowd waiting on the shore, Luke viii. 40). Further, Christ's address to the woman is rendered ineffectual by the awkward interval of thronging which separates it from her cure. Secondly. Notice the exuberance, 'begging and praying;' 'fearing and trembling;' also the nervous explanations of motive, 'Perceiving that the power from Him had gone forth,' 'Overhearing the word which was spoken,' 'Feeling in her body that she was healed;' and the replacement of the oriental 'flute-players' by the elucidatory paraphrase, 'many weeping and wailing.' Thirdly. Does not the First Evangelist's statement that the hemorrhage was of twelve years' standing imply its incurability? It is mere embellishment then, when the Second Evangelist adds, 'And she had suffered many things of many physicians, and spent all she had, and was nothing bettered, but rather made worse.' Fourthly. The ruler's amazingly trustful request—as reported in Matt. ix.—that Christ will come and work such an unprecedented wonder as raising the dead is one that to a later writer, straining after verisimilitude, would naturally seem to require some shading off. That this is our Second Evangelist's motive in at first representing the child as merely sick is shown by Christ's speech to Jaïrus, when death has actually supervened, 'Fear not, only believe.' Fifthly. 'Talitha Cumi.' It is a thing to be felt, not argued about, that it was a later generation that required here and elsewhere the actual wonder-words, but it may be observed that in another case where the Second Evangelist, as against the First, supplies an Aramaic expression, viz., 'Boanerges,' Mk. iii. 17, the remarkable disturbance occasioned in the construction extrudes it as unoriginal. Sixthly. 'He charged them (Jaïrus and his wife) that they should say nothing to any one.' But Christ was accompanied by a great crowd let us remember, when He started for Jaïrus's house. The message of the child's death was publicly delivered; and He found the house full of mourners. What possibility was there of secrecy? Where the prohibition comes from will appear presently. Sufficient here to notice that it is entirely out of keeping with its context. Thus the Jaïrus history of Mk. v. seems to stand in the same relation to the correspondent section of Matt. ix. as a developed picture to an original sketch. Though thrice as long, it contains few features really new. But magnifying these new features to the utmost, still we have no more reason to assume that the author was independent than to infer from the ordinary un-canonical details of a sacred picture that the artist had any exceptional source of information.

S. Matthew is twice corrected in S. Mark. Firstly, we find S. Mark singularizing the pairs of Matt. viii., ix., xx., two blind men near the house of Jairus,* two Gadarene demoniacs, two blind men at Jericho. It is generally supposed, in fact no other reasonable explanation has ever been suggested, that the duplication in Matt. viii., ix., xx., is a harmonist's device for reconciling conflicting traditions: and, at any rate in the case of the cures at Gadara and Jericho, it is certain that neither of these conflicting traditions can possibly have been derived from S. Mark, since all and everything predicated in S. Matthew of the two Gadarene demoniacs, the two blind men at Jericho, is predicated in S. Mark of the single Gadarene demoniac, the single blind man at Jericho. It may be also noticed that the Second Evangelist's definite personal des-criptions of the Gadarene and of the blind man at Jericho would preclude subsequent duplication. Thus, although in singularizing the pairs of Matt. viii., ix., xx., the Second Evan-gelist seems to stand on superior ground to the First, the form of his narrative shows that he singularized with the narrative of the pairs before his eyes. Secondly, we find S. Mark de-liberately improving on the introduction to the charge 'By Beelzebub' Matt. ix. 27-34; xii. 22-24. With regard to this introduction, everything in S. Matthew is in the greatest con-fusion. In ix. 27-34 we have the pair of blind men, already

---

* It seems reasonable to identify the miracle at Bethsaida Mk. viii. 22-26 with that in Matt. ix., considering how rarely the Second Gospel omits any *incident* of the First. Besides, there is resemblance as to the privacy of the occasion, the manual action, the injunction of secrecy, and the modulation of the cure.

mentioned, and a dumb man (v.r. 'and deaf'); and in xii. 22-24, evidently a doublet to the above, a man blind and dumb (v.r. 'and deaf').* In S. Mark on the other hand we have clear definite descriptions of a deaf mute in Decapolis Mk. vii. 32-37, and, as said before, of a blind man at Bethsaida: but neither of these narratives corresponds in position to the blind-deaf-dumb cures of S. Matthew, and their place as introduction to the charge 'by Beelzebub' is taken by 'His friends went out to lay hold on him for they said, He is mad.' Let us examine these new passages separately.

The cure of the deaf mute in Decapolis, standing where it does, is demonstrably a foreign intrusion, for (a) It eats away a necessary preface to the congregation of the 4000 : *cf.* Matt. xv, 29-31. How abruptly the 4000 appear in Mk. viii. 1! They have already been with Christ three days! (b) A surviving fragment of the Matthæan preface, 'He doeth all things well' Mk. vii. 37, requires for its justification some wider proof of power than a single cure : *cf.* Matt. xv. 30, 31. (c) The appearance of *two* multitudes Mk. vii. 33; viii. 1, which the private withdrawal for the mute's cure involves is awkward in the extreme, (d) and so is the 'they' in verse 37, for Christ and the mute are alone. But though the Decapolis miracle is not at all of a piece with its context, it is easy to perceive the attraction which that context presented, viz., the reference Matt. xv. 31 to 'the dumb speaking.' Similarly with regard to the miracle at Bethsaida, a context seems to have been suggested by 'Having eyes, see ye not;' and though in this case there is nothing actually resentful in the context, for the miracle stands isolated, yet it is so obviously from the same pen as the miracle in Decapolis that the two narratives must

---

* 'And two blind men followed. . . . And there was brought to him a dumb man. And the dumb spake : and the multitudes marvelled, saying, It was never so seen in Israel. But the Pharisees said, By the prince of the devils casteth he out devils,' Matt. ix. 27-34.

'There was brought to him one blind and dumb : and the dumb spake and saw. And the multitudes were amazed, and said, Is this the son of David? But the Pharisees said, This man doth not cast out devils, but by Beelzebub the prince of the devils,' Matt. xii. 22-24.

be extruded together.   It may be added that both are shown
to be editorial by the fact of their being entirely couched in
the *general* style of the Second Gospel, the style common to
all parts indifferently.*

And now let us look back on the decapitated Beelzebub
section in Mk. iii.   That new and independent-looking introduction, ὅτι ἐξέστη 'they said, He is mad,' so impressive at first
sight on account of its startling crudeness, is it new and independent in reality?   Turning to the parallel passage in the
First Gospel we find that there the multitudes ἐξίσταντο (the
only instance of ἐξίσταναι in S. Matthew), and the coincidence
between the two Gospels cannot reasonably be set aside as
fortuitous.   Possibly it is the multitude, not Christ, that ought
to be supplied as the subject of ἐξέστη, a supposition rendered
likelier by the fact that mention has just been made of frenzied
concourse.   But the text at this particular point is in great
confusion, and there is much in favour of the *Codex Bezæ* and
the old Latin 'ἔλεγον γὰρ ὅτι ἐξίσταται αὐτούς,' 'exentiat eos.'   Which-
ever explanation be correct, one thing is clear, that the ὅτι ἐξέστη
of Mk. iii. 21 is not independent of Matt. xii. 22-24.

Thus, by many considerations, we are brought to a conclusion which the doublet, Matt. ix. 27-34; xii. 22-24, by itself
renders inevitable.   For it is obvious that the introduction to
the Beelzebub section given in Matt. ix.; xii. and that given
in S. Mark are, as literary devices, antagonistic; and the coincidence between the two Matthæan introductions, (both
narratives stating that Christ cured blindness and dumbness,
that the multitudes were amazed, and that their amazement
provoked the Pharisaic charge, 'By Beelzebub,') precludes
any reasonable suspicion of unoriginality in S. Matthew.

Let us turn now to the injunction of secrecy, Mk. v. 43.   In
Matt. ix., Christ raises the daughter of Jaïrus, and then heals
two blind men—'and he strictly charged them (ἐνεβριμήθη) say-

---

* Notice the forcible phraseology and the exactitude of detail,—the
medium employed in both cases, the Syriac wonder-word, the graduation
of the blind man's recovery, and the report of Christ's gestures and emotions.

ing, See that no man know it. But they went forth, and spread abroad his fame (διεφήμισαν) in all that land.' As the two blind men are omitted in the Second Gospel (see above), it results that the injunction of secrecy is left applying to the persons mentioned just previously, viz., to Jaïrus and his wife—'He charged them much that no man should know this' Mk. v. 43. Now it may be answered that the addition of an injunction of secrecy to the longer account of the raising of Jaïrus's daughter in S. Mark is independent of the injunction to the blind men, and that here we have only a curious coincidence. But the absolute impropriety of the injunction as delivered apropos of the raising of Jaïrus's daughter, a case in which secrecy was absolutely impossible (see above), stands in the way of such an escape. Again, this view of the matter is confirmed by the evidence of language. The combination of the words 'ἐμβριμᾶσθαι' and 'διαφημίζειν' is peculiar to the passage in point and to Mk. i. 43, 45—'He *strictly charged* him (the leper), See thou say nothing to any man. But he went out and began to *spread abroad* the matter.' Things being so, it seems that in Matt. ix. 31. we have no mere editorial addition, but that behind both the First Gospel and the Second, there was a document which contained matter peculiar to each. If the injunction of secrecy in Mk. v. 43, be admitted as a veritable relic of the cure of the two blind men, then once more we have occasion to recognise the priority of S. Matthew's pairs to the narratives of single cures in S. Mark; for, the doubleness being evidently systematic, the cure of these two blind men cannot but come from the same hand as the double cures at Gadara and Jericho. Once more we have occasion to recognise the priority of the three simple narratives of Matt. viii., ix. xx., to the ornate narratives in S. Mark with all their picturesque details. And if in these three cases the priority of S. Matthew be admitted, then it must be admitted also in the case of the other miracles simply recounted in S. Matthew, embellished in S. Mark, *e.g.*, in the case of the cure of the epileptic (Matt. xvi. 14-20, Mk. ix. 14-29). Thus the arguments for the posteriority of S. Mark overlap, confirming and re-confirming one another.

It is always difficult for one writer to abbreviate another's work quite successfully. Subjoined are certain reasons for inferring that the frequent abruptness, forcedness, and inconsequentiality of the Second Gospel are due to abbreviation and excision. Champions of S. Mark's originality generally explain this abruptness by adducing a very late tradition [*] that S. Mark made hasty notes of S. Peter's discourses—an explanation which breaks down entirely when worked out in detail. For (a), the instances of abruptness, as will appear presently, are not at all of a superficial or irregular character, such as one might expect in a reporter's note-book, but are uniform and often intricate; (b), the Second Gospel, far from being a haphazard collection of notes, exhibits both in substance and style unmistakable tokens of art and design. No, it is in the fuller Matthaean text that the explanation of S. Mark's abruptness is to be found. The apostolic mission (Mk., vi. 7-13) lacks occasion; we require the shepherdless multitudes of Matt., ix. 36. The prohibition against any viaticum appears unmotived in the absence of 'For the labourer is worthy of his hire.' That reference to the inhospitality of Sodom (unsuited to our un-Judaic Evangelist's Gentile audience), its omission leaves us with the impotent climax! —'Shake off the dust for a testimony.' The centurion's sudden exclamation, 'Surely this man was the Son of God,' requires phenomena like the earthquake and opening of the tombs to justify it, for of the rending of the veil the centurion would of course know nothing. The 4000 appear quite unexpectedly in the absence of any prefatory statement like Matt., xv. 29-31. 'But one of them that stood by smote the servant of the high priest' stands isolated and without literary motive, whereas in S. Matthew it forms a natural introduction to Christ's utterance about the legions of angels and drawing the sword. 'He will send His angels to gather His elect' is surely no fitting climax to the eschatology of Mk. xiii., but leads us to expect a higher note such as is struck in Matt. xxv., 'Then shall he sit on the throne of His glory.' On

---

[*] Reported by S. Jerome.

artistic grounds it seems impossible that the skeleton account of the Temptation (Mk. i. 12, 13) should be original; and the ministration of angels, in the absence of any allusion to fasting and hunger, is left unexplained. Christ's suddenly reproachful address to the disciples, ' O faithless generation,' explicable enough in S. Matthew, where the disciples' failure to cure the epileptic is due to their want of faith,* stands without point in S. Mark, where the failure is attributed to other causes than faithlessness. The extreme awkwardness of ' After two days was the passover: and the chief priests sought,' appears due to the Evangelist's incorporating Matt., xxvi. 2 (' Ye know that after two days the passover cometh ') into the narrative.† Such a climax as Peter's confession seems to require some commendatory reply to emphasize it, and without such reply the severe rebuke ensuing is left unbalanced. (By the way, notice the close correspondence between commendation and rebuke in Matt. xvi.—'Art a rock,' 'art an offence;' 'revealed to thee by God,' 'savourest of men'). How disappointing, ' He entered into Jerusalem into the Temple' (Mk., xi. 11), not followed by any incident whatever.‡ How superfluous 'And they came to Capernaum. And when He was in the house,' etc., Mk., ix. 33; for the incident subsequent, the contention ' Who greatest?' is not one that requires any localization; whereas when we turn to S. Matthew we find that there the

---

* ' If ye had faith as a grain of mustard seed,' perhaps omitted by our Second Evangelist because another authority provided him with the text elsewhere (see Mk., xi. 23).

† It is difficult to imagine the reverse process, an Evangelist's putting part of the narrative into a speech of Christ's.

‡ In S. Matthew this entry is followed by the expulsion of the money-changers, and the introduction into the Temple of ' the blind and the lame ;' but the extra day desiderated in the Second Gospel (see above) attracts the money-changers, and the introduction of the blind and the lame,' significant merely as pointing a contrast between David and the Son of David (cf. 2 Samuel, v. 6-8), would have been inharmonious with the Second Evangelist's un-Judaic design.

Apropos of the excision of ' the blind and the lame,' compare Matt., xxi. 15, 16, with Mk. xi. 18. The latter might be derived from the former, but the former could scarcely be derived from the latter.

mention of Capernaum and the house are thoroughly appropriate, prefacing as they do the demand on S. Peter for the didrachma—a demand which would naturally have been made in Capernaum where Peter's house was situated.

Mk. iii. 7-20 is in some respects one of the most important passages in S. Mark. That remarkable abruptness and forcedness, which has before been noticed, here reaches a climax. How strangely and suddenly the scene shifts,—' He spake that a boat should wait on Him,' ' He goeth up into the mountain,' ' He cometh into a house.' The ascent of the mountain is surely but inadequately accounted for by the mere intention to appoint Apostles. How strange that Christ should be said to appoint Twelve with the object of conferring on a future occasion the functions for which He appointed them!* Is there not some strain observable in ' He calleth unto him whom he would *himself*, and they went unto him?' Why the awkward repetition of πλῆθος in verses 7, 8? ' A multitude from Galilee followed him. And from Judea and from Jerusalem and beyond Jordan a multitude hearing what great things he did, came to him.' ' Hearing what great things '—but none have been recorded at this particular juncture.

But all these peculiar phenomena receive explanation when we consider Mk. iii. 7-19 in connection with the correspondent verses in the preface to the Sermon on the Mount (Matt. iv. 23, v. 1). There the congregation of the multitude from Galilee and the remoter districts follows naturally on a great circuit during which Christ ' healed all manner of disease : and the report of him went forth into all Syria :' but separated as it is from that circuit in our Second Gospel (*cf.* Mk. i. 39), the ' πλῆθος ' ' πλῆθος ' becomes necessary, the distinction that is to say between a multitude of Galileans who *followed* from a particular town, and a multitude from the remoter districts who ' hearing what great things he did,' *came*. Again, considering the preface to the sermon *en bloc*, we can see that the coming of the

---

* ' He appointed twelve *that he might* send them forth to preach, and to have authority to cast out devils,' Mk. iii. 14, 15. ' He called the twelve, and began to send them forth, and he gave them authority over the unclean spirits,' Mk. vi. 7.

disciples to Christ in Matt. v. 1, forms a clear doublet to their coming in Matt. ix. 35, 36; x. 1; * and thus we obtain adequate motive for the nervously awkward gloss above noted in Mk. iii. 14, 15, 'that he might (presently) send them forth,' etc. Further, considering the combination in Mark. iii. 12 of 'His disciples came unto him' (Matt. v. 1) with 'He called unto him his twelve disciples' (Matt. x. 1), we find adequate motive for that other nervously awkward gloss, that the disciples who came to Christ were ' whom he would himself.' Again, the close connection observable in Matt. iv. 23, v. 1, between circuit and multitude and disciples forbidding any doubt that the arrangement there is original, it follows that Mk. iii. 13-19, interrupting the narrative so sadly, is a section out of place. Once having broken the continuity of his narrative by inserting this mountain section our Second Evangelist was obliged to pick up the thread from the point where it was broken; and hence we are told 'He cometh into a house' and ' The multitude cometh together again.' Thus it appears that the peculiarities of Mk. iii. 7-20, far from evidencing originality, constitute on the contrary a striking exhibition of elaborate mechanism. Other peculiarities pointing in the same direction are noticed elsewhere. And the importance of the passage is still further increased when we consider that Matt. iv. 24, v. 1, thus fragmentarily repeated in S. Mark, is the preface to the Sermon on the Mount, and presumably involves some portion of the Sermon itself. †

---

* ' Jesus went about in all Galilee, teaching in their synagogues, and preaching the gospel of the kingdom, and healing all manner of disease and all manner of sickness. And seeing the multitudes, he went up into the mountain : and his disciples came unto him,' Matt. iv. 23, v. 1.

' Jesus went about all the cities and villages, teaching in their synagogues, and preaching the gospel of the kingdom, and healing all manner of disease and all manner of sickness. And seeing the multitudes, he was moved with compassion for them. And he called unto him his twelve disciples,' Matt. ix. 35, x. 1.

† S. Mark omitted the Sermon perhaps because it presupposes the Law, —'Ye have heard how it was said by them of old time.' It may be noticed too that he was otherwise supplied with several of the important utterances (Mk. iv. 21 ; ix. 43-50 ; x. 11, 12 ; xi. 25, 26 ; xii. 40). But

In conclusion, there are many other points, illustrative of S. Mark's posteriority, on which I should like to have dwelt; for example—

> The fact that in S. Mark the apostolic charge is given an immediate character (contrast Matt. xiv. 12, 13, with Mk. vi. 29, 30), and that a portion, unsuitable under the altered circumstances, is transposed—(Mk. xiii. 5-13, Matt. x. 16-23; The fact that several of the Matthæan parables which S. Mark omits are connected by phraseology with matters that he repeats, and that on one notable occasion the omission is marked by 'With many such parables spake he unto them'; The fact that the angels' speech (Mk. xvi. 1-8), appears to involve a position *outside* the sepulchre;

> The fact that in Mk. i. 1, and elsewhere we have re-echoes of S. Matthew's redactorial matter, and, contrariwise, that none of the general, presumably redactorial, peculiarities of S. Mark are reproduced in S. Matthew;

> Finally, the fact that in substance and style S. Mark is one and whole in a sense in which S. Matthew is far from being, and, consequently, that the removal of any portion causes the whole work to fall in pieces—the unity of its design becoming a fatal measure of its unoriginality.

These and other points I hope soon to deal with in book form, making it my object to trace S. Mark's indebtedness to the extent of not leaving sufficient material or room enough for an 'ur Marcus.' The present article is only a reconnaissance, undertaken with further operations in view, but I submit that it contains proof that the indebtedness of S. Mark has been vastly under-rated,—that priority to S. Matthew is not the rule but the exception.

F. P. Badham.

---

in this and similar cases we must beware of exaggerating the difficulty of omission. S. Mark's elaboration of miracle shows that his view of the relative importance of things was not the same as ours. Above all it must be borne in mind that we do not know to what extent he intended to supersede previous documents.

Art. VII.—THE POETRY OF THE SKALDS.

THE Old Northern poets were liberal in praise, and they have not lacked pens to commend them : they were sometimes bitter in satire, and they have not escaped the contempt of others. Two quotations will give in brief compass the attitudes of their admirers and detractors. The one is :—

'Such an inspired and improvised poetizing occurs nowhere else in history. Compare but the northern poets—and they were all improvisers— with the lamentable poetastery of the Roman emperors which Suetonius quotes, or with the Emperor Hadrian's verse-making, among which the disgusting "animula vagula blandula" is known to all.'*

The other runs :—

'If we make a distinction between Eddaic and Skaldic poetry, "grand and sublime" are epithets quite inapplicable to the latter, by far the greater part of which is mere bombast, "tumid and obscure" enough to be utterly worthless.'†

There are reasons for both of these opinions, and it may be worth while to make some attempt to disentangle them. The Old North has so much poetry in its history, that one is loath to dismiss its poets as the Muse's charlatans. To judge them aright, some account must be taken of their own aims and poetic ideals ; and if their work is to be presented in a tongue not their own, this must be done in forms which do not entirely omit all that they considered essential to it.

The common conception of a skald seems to be that of a poetic berserk, who hurled himself into the midst of battle, shouting rude snatches of alliterative verse to cheer the hearts of his fellow-warriors. The picture is not unnatural, but is nevertheless incorrect. It has, however, the merit of being a shade nearer reality than the belief that the skalds were the authors of the sagas. No doubt Snorri and Sturla were good skalds, but that is not what is meant by the belief.

The skald is primarily neither fighter nor historian, but a *poet*, and this is all that his name in itself implies. In respect of worldly position, he might be either king or cottar, earl or hench-

---

* Benedict Gröndal.   † J. A. Blackwell.

man, so long as he had in him the gift of verse. The shepherd
who lay on the old poet's grave-mound, and wrestled in vain with
the making of verse, until the dead man came by night and
helped him, became, we are told, 'a great skald,' and made his
fortune at the courts of foreign princes. So the most untravelled
Icelander might be a skald, though he had never seen the face
of king or earl, and never wielded sword and shield, nor seen
more glorious fray than a dispute over a horse-fight or the right
of pasture. No doubt, if he were a good skald, this home-glory
would not content him. It was a stirring time in those days,
when 'the cankers of a calm world and long peace' were unknown. But his travels would only confirm the title, and not
confer it. If his verses found favour with the king or earl whom
he chose to visit, he might become retainer and court-poet, and
follow his lord both in peace and war, but all this was only the
external glory of his profession. The skald was not the battle-
bard of Celtic custom (the precursor of the bagpipes and their
bitter rival in the seventeenth century), though his own verses,
or his recitation of older poems, might help at times to stir the
courage of his comrades. When Thormod made the valley above
Stikla-stead ring at daybreak with the lines of the old Bjarka-
mál, he only did it by request for King Olaf's entertainment,
and the saga adds that the host was delighted with his idea.
King Olaf also wished to have his skalds safe inside the shield-
burg. 'You shall stay here,' he said, 'and see all that is done,
and it will be no carried tale then, for you yourselves shall tell of
it, and make verses on it.' The skalds then agreed with each
other that it would be a good thing to make some memorial verses
on the events about to happen. So each of them composed a
single verse, which was immediately got by heart by the men who
stood round about them.

It is probably from a few instances like these that the conception of the wild fighting skald has been derived. Mallet, for
example, states of Earl Hákon's skalds that 'they each sang an
ode to animate the soldiers before they engaged' with the Jóms-
víkings. Some verses certainly did pass on that occasion, but
they bear no analogy to Mac Vurich's *brosnachadh catha* at Har-
law, or to any institution of the kind. It may also be suspected

that Ragnar Lodbrók's death-song has helped the common view a little. There is indeed no lack of battle-rage in *Kráku-mál*, but 'many speak of Wallace who never bent his bow,' and the author of the poem was not with Ragnar in the serpent-pit.

The name of skald, then, whatever its various applications may be, means in itself no more than 'poet,' one skilled in the art of verse-making. Its origin is uncertain, none of the derivations that have been proposed being quite satisfactory.[*] Dr. Gudbrand Vigfusson inclines to the belief that the original sense was a bad one, denoting a composer of satirical or libellous verse. There are certain facts which lend some support to this theory, but there is against it the strong objection that language does not tend to improve the meaning of such words, and the word is commonly used in a good sense. Even the compound *skaldskapr*, or skaldship, which in legal language denoted 'a libel,' is also current with the honourable meaning of 'poetry,' especially in its formal aspect.

The formal side is indeed, as we shall see, the safest from which to approach the poetry of the skalds, if we use the name in its technical sense,—the sense in which it commonly meets us in the sagas. The skald in the tenth, and still more in the succeeding centuries, was above all an artist in language. His poetry consisted in the expression quite as much as in the matter of his verse, and the tendency was for the former to overgrow the latter. 'The rude strains that were jingled out on the skaldic lyre,' is no more applicable to the verse of Sighvat and Arnorr than to the odes of English laureates. There may be differences of opinion as to the interest or poetic value of their work, but the form is perfect of its kind, and as far from 'rude' as any verse could well be. On the other hand, when we read that Kormak's verses 'were equally devoid of true poetic genius as

---

[*] Most improbable (or rather impossible) is that which derives it from the Old Irish *scélide*, a story-teller. Even if the word should not more correctly be written *scélaighe*, the Norsemen could never have heard it so pronounced as to give it the form *skald*. In modern usage the word is written *skáld*, and pronounced almost like the English *scowled*, but the vowel was originally short. The plural has the same form as the singular, the gender being *neuter*.

those of the other *verse-smithiers* . . . who, in that rude age, hammered out their rhapsodical ideas into the form of alliterative metre,' the criticism is more to the point, though none the less capable of being disputed.

The forms of Old Northern verse were numerous enough, as may be seen at length in Snorri's treatise *(Hátta-tal),*—for the Icelanders wrote metrical treatises as well as the Irish, though they did not divide the metres into 'common,' 'uncommon,' and 'unknown!' In dealing with skaldic verse, however, we have practically only one metre to consider,—that which goes by the name of *drótt-kvætt.** The earliest specimens of this belong to the poets of Harald Fairhair, and throughout the tenth century the metre is steadily ousting all others; in the eleventh and twelfth it is all-prevailing. The name indicates that the poems composed in this metre were intended for recitation before the king and his *drótt* (O.E. *dryht*), or household. It was thus the commonest metre for the *drápa,* or laudatory poem, in which the skald celebrated the exploits of the king or earl to whom he attached himself, or whose favour he was desirous to gain. The name of 'court-metre' is thus appropriate enough, but it had another and no less important use. It was the constant sonnet-metre of the improvising skald, in which he expressed some feeling of the moment, or summed up some personal exploit. The limitations of space gave no great room for poetry, perhaps, but the lines were easily remembered; they served as a perpetual register of the fact which caused them, and they formed an essential part in the telling of many a tale. On such verses the saga-writer often had to depend, and numerous incidents were no doubt only remembered because of their connection with the poet's words. If these single verses lack the complex symmetry and majestic swing of the regular *drápa,* they contain much of what is most poetic in the work of the skalds. A solitary verse is sometimes the expression of the most striking moment in the life of an individual. The author of it may not be reckoned among the famous skalds, but his single sonnet had enough in it

---

* The substitution of *v* for *u* in the English word *quite* will give the pronunciation of *kvætt*.

to keep his name alive to after-times: When Hallstein, son of
Thengil the voyager, returned from Norway to his home in the
north of Iceland, and learned that his father was dead, he made
these lines :—

> ' Droops the Headland,
> Dead is Thengil ;
> Long hills lightly
> Laugh to Hallstein.'

The simplicity of this is something rare among the verses of the
skalds, to whom intricacies of metre and of diction were very
dear.

The first essential of a regular *dróttkvætt* verse is that it shall
consist of eight lines, each of three accents, and commonly of
six syllables. This at once distinguishes the Scandinavian alliterative verse from the Anglo-Saxon and Old German, where
no such division into stanzas is observed. That the skalds considered the verse to consist of eight lines is manifest from several
passages in the sagas, to say nothing of the treatises on metre;
and it is very unfortunate that in the *Corpus Poeticum Boreale*
the arrangement of printing the stanza in four long lines was
adopted. It is not only contrary to universal practice, but has no
advantages to recommend it.

Alliteration, of course, is necessary; no Icelandic poetry can be
without it, from the earliest times to the present day. When this
type of verse was first introduced, probably no more than the
above requirements were necessary, but even in the earliest specimens the additional ornament of assonance is present. This
feature is lacking in the older and shorter measures employed in
the lays of the Edda, and its adoption has been attributed to
Celtic influence. We are here on very doubtful ground indeed.
Chronicles assure us that Scandinavian contact with Ireland began in 795 A.D., and for a long time the relations were exclusively hostile. The poet Bragi must have flourished previous to
850 A.D., as Dr. Finnur Jónsson has lately taken the trouble to
establish. In Bragi's verse we find the beginnings of this system
of assonance, so characteristic of the Skaldic verse. Whether
these dates will allow us to assume, with Whitley Stokes, that
assonance was adopted from the Irish metre *rinnard,* is a very

doubtful point. The rules for the composition of *rinnard* are by no means the rules observed in *dróttkvæt*, and the imitation is at best very problematical.

The general effect of Bragi's verse, as distinct from its more elaborate successor, may be sufficiently illustrated by two later examples. The one is taken from the verses composed by Torf-Einarr, the Orkney Earl, and the other belongs to Egil the son of Skallagrim, or at least is assigned to him in the saga. Einarr had avenged the death of his father Rögnvald, and thus comments on the way in which his brothers had neglected their plain duty in the matter.

> ' Neither Hrolf's nor Hrollaug's
> Hand I see outsending
> Flight of shafts on foemen,
> Father's death avenging :
> And this eve, while eager
> Arms we bear, uncaring
> Thorir, thane in Mæri,
> Thinks of naught but drinking.'

This verse, besides the strict alliteration required,[*] shows full assonance in some of its lines (*bear, care; think, drink*), and imperfect in others (*hand, send; Thorir, Mæri*), being rather more complete in this respect than the original, which has only imperfect ones. Nor is the second assonant syllable always found at the end of the line, as in the above. Egil's verse, which follows, shows it in a position not uncommon in this early type. Egil, in his seventh year, had lodged an axe in the head of one of his playfellows, which made his admiring mother declare that there was good viking stuff in him, and that he must get a warship when he was old enough. Then Egil, says the saga, made this verse :—

> ' Mother mine has bidden
> For myself to purchase
> Vessel fast in floating—
> Fare abroad with vikings :

---

[*] The second line of each couplet shows the alliterative letter in its first accented word. The same letter begins two words in the preceding line. Thus—

> ' Rögnvald's *F*all is *F*airly
> (*F*ate is just) requited.'

High in stern upstanding
Steer unfearing onward ;
Hold me then to haven,
Hew both shield and wielder.'

Here the only assonances are in the sixth and eighth lines, and in the former the rhyming syllables are *steer, fear*, both in the first half of the line. A good deal of spurious verse of this early type was manufactured in the 13th and 14th centuries for insertion in the mythical sagas. The death-song of Lodbrók is one of these productions, marked also by showing a verse of ten lines instead of eight.

What distinguishes the finished *dróttkvætt* verse from this, is that in it the assonances are subject to as strict rule as the alliteration. The first line of each couplet has a half rhyme (*skothending*), while the second line has a full one (*adal-hending*). The last accented syllable in each line supplies one of the rhymes, the other must be in the first half of the line. For all these varieties there are technical names, which we here 'willingly pretermit.' Carrying these rules into English verse, the stanza assumes the form of the two specimens given below. A remarkable feature of the metre is the use of parenthetic clauses, which have been retained exactly as placed in the originals.

The first stanza is a rendering of a verse by Sighvat Thordarson on the loss sustained by him in the death of King Olaf the saint, and perhaps contains an echo of Hallstein's verse in the mention of smiling hills. He was restless at home, says the saga, and went out one day, and said :—

' All, me seemed, were smiling
Softly Norway's lofty
(Far I sailed a-faring)
Fells, while Olaf held them :
Now, me seems, their summits
(Sorrows mark me) darken
(Sore I missed my master
Mild) with tempest wildest.'

The second is a somewhat free translation of one of Kári's verses in Njáls saga. Kári could not sleep by night for thinking of the burning of Njál and his sons, and when questioned by Asgrim, answered him in these terms :—

'Long nights through I linger,
Lord of the elm-bow corded !
(Keen regrets for kindred
Keep me waking) sleepless,
Since grim foes, with glancing
Gleam of firebrands streaming,
(Full is my thought, with fretting
Fraught) burned Njál in Autumn.'

These samples will show in what fetters the skald's poetic fancies bestirred themselves ' in the quick forge and working-house of thought.' Yet it is not incredible that long practice might enable him to produce them with greater ease than their form would suggest. Of Sighvat we are told that in ordinary conversation he was slow and stiff, while his verses came as smoothly and quickly as other men's talk.

Sponte sua carmen numeros veniebat ad aptos,
Et quod tentabat dicere, versus erat.

If we accept the evidence of the sagas, a great number of these occasional verses were extemporized, or at least made with very little premeditation, and in many cases this might be true enough. The saga of Harald Hardrádi presents us with an interesting picture of the king, his poet, and a fisherman, rivalling each other in producing verses after a special model. During the contest the king objects to his poet's metre. ' Hear, poet Thjódólf,' said he ; 'you said *gröm : skömm*. That's a false quantity. If you had said *hrömm : skömm*, the quantity would have been right, though that makes no sense. You have made many better verses.' Of equal interest in this connection are the verses made by King Harald just before the battle of Stamford Bridge. He first made one in a very simple old metre, and then withdrew it. ' That verse we recited just now is not well made,' said he, ' and we shall make another and better one '—the better one being a strict *dróttkvætt*-stanza. There can be little doubt that by ' better' the king meant ' more skaldlike,' that is, in finer metre. Earl Rögnvald of Orkney was a ready improviser in this metre, as may be read at length in the Orkneyinga Saga, which also tells of the task set by him to an Icelander, Oddi the little. ' Make you a verse,' said the earl, ' about what that man is doing on the tent there, and have *your* verse ready by the time I have finished reciting *mine*, and don't use any words in your verse that I use in mine.' These and other instances, such as Hallfred's 'sword' verse, show that the skald was expected to express himself with readiness even under additional difficulties.

But if a single verse in this metre was not such a difficult task, to compose a drápa of twenty, thirty or even sixty stanzas was something for the skald to be proud of. Einarr Skúlason's poem on King Olaf, which he recited before the kings and archbishop at Nidaros in 1152 A.D., extends to 71 stanzas of *dróttkvætt*, and its composition could have been no light task. While other metres were not seldom employed for this class of poem, no other was so general a favourite. Some poets attempted variations on it by dropping a syllable in the line, but the result is not a pleasing one. It is very different when the line is lengthened by a foot, resulting in the metre *hrynhend*, the best specimens of which are the poems of Arnorr and Sturla. Of Arnorr's poem King Harald Hardrádi declared that it would be repeated so long as the Northern lands were inhabited. Probably the earliest specimen is the fragment of a poem composed by a Hebridean Christian, when the ship he was sailing in encountered some tremendous waves in the Greenland seas, about the year 986. The *stef*, or burden, of the poem is preserved in *Landnámabók*, and makes up half a verse.

> ' Mildest judge, that monks upholdest,
> Make my path amidst the breakers ;
> Highest might, in heaven that sittest,
> Hand me safe through all my wand'ring.'

It might have tasked the worthy Egil to save his bald pate and wolfish eyebrows at York, if he had tried to compose his ' Head-ransom ' in any of these metres. `He chose the rarer but simpler device of end-rhymes, and set out thus in praise of Earl Eirik.

> ' O'er waves I went
> To westward bent,
> With Odin's art
> In eager heart ;
> Drew out my oak
> When ice upbroke,

XXVIII.   23

And launched along
With load of song.'

This was in 936 A.D., before the use of *dróttkvætt* had become
so inevitable as it was at a later period. When Gunnlaug in
1002 treated Earl Sigtrygg at Dublin to a poem in the same
metre, he was no doubt influenced by the example of Egil, in
whose district he had grown up. Only twelve lines are
preserved, besides the *stef* or burden (which is ' With flesh he
feeds The Fury's steeds,' *i.e.*, the wolves) :—

' I know right well
Whose worth I tell ;
Of Kvaran's kind
His kingly mind.

To me he'll lend
(He loves to spend :
The bard is bold)
His brightest gold.
Did ere his ear
Another hear
His fame rehearse
In finer verse.'

One can hardly believe that this kind of thing cost Gunnlaug
much racking of brains.   Perhaps he thought it good enough for
Earl Sigtrygg, who was evidently unaccustomed to hear his
praises from a skald.   When the recitation was ended, he called
his treasurer to him, and said, ' How shall I reward the poem ? '
' What do you think yourself ? ' asked the treasurer.   ' How
would it do, if I gave him two merchant vessels ? ' asked the
king, as the saga styles him.   ' That's too much,' said the
treasurer ; ' other kings give such things as swords or gold rings
in return for a poem.'   Sigtrygg, thus advised, rewarded Gunnlaug with articles of dress and a gold ring.   The story makes
one speculate whether Earl Sigtrygg was ever berhymed by Irish
bards, as his father Olaf Cuaran seems to have been in the lines,

' Olaf, that's over
The eastern outflow
Of Erin the ancient,*
The dear king of Dublin, etc.'

---

* ' Prince of the eastern ford of meadowy Erin ' is the literal rendering,
i.e., King of Ath-Cliath, or Dublin.

These are lines which certainly have a kind of Northern ring about them, and make us wish to know more about the personal relations of Gall and Gael in tenth-century Ireland.

To return to the *drápa*, there are various technicalities connected with its arrangement, division into parts, insertion of the burden, and so on, which need not be more minutely considered. They could hardly have added much to the difficulty of composing it, though they may have made it more hard to understand when it was recited. In this we come to the real crux of skaldic poetry, over which so many have stumbled. The hardest of Greek choruses is not more difficult to unravel than some of these complicated verses, though if but one-tenth of the labour that has been spent on Greek choruses had been given to the Old Northern poetry, the difficulties would have been much fewer by this time. To a considerable extent they have been due to manuscript corruptions, and to imperfect acquaintance with the poetic vocabulary and rules of the verse. Comparison and wise conjecture have already done much to remove these initial bars to the study of skaldic verse, and there is now no lack of reliable material on which to work. In no long time we may expect to see the whole of the Old Northern poetry in as satisfactory a form as that of Greece and Rome.

The point that remains is that of the boy with the alphabet,— is it worth while going through so much to learn so little? A verse of eight lines is apt, when analysed and translated, to dwindle down to some dozen words of very ordinary import, in which no poetry whatever is discernible. 'Translating the Gaelic word for word is what spoils it,' and it is probably a false method of translation that has ruined the reputation of the skalds as poets. The elocutionist who insists that verse is to be read as prose leaves no reason for writing in verse at all; and what *operae pretium* is the skald to have for his alliterations and his assonances, if his work is to be judged by its value in unregenerate prose? The reader of the bald abstracts in the *Corpus poeticum boreale* may well be excused for seeing neither beauty nor poetry in what is there presented to him, but who would estimate a chorus of Aristophanes by its value even in the best translation? The translation ought to guide us back to the original, and not take its place.

It was not metre, however, but mythology, combined with their views of poetic diction, that made the skalds both diffuse and obscure. The *kenning*, or device to avoid calling a spade a spade, or anything else by its own name,* is the distinctive mark of all their verse; and Gröndal is right in saying that it is ' the eternal theme which lies at the bottom of these complaints that so little is to be made out of the poetry when one has got to understand it.' It is, no doubt, extremely annoying to the beginner to find that some two lines of sonorous words, mainly perfect strangers to him, mean no more than ' man,' or ' woman,' or ' ship ; ' and there is ample excuse for his saying in his haste that the whole of skaldic verse is vanity. He is not likely to appreciate the enthusiasm of Gröndal, who maintains that the kennings are the glory and beauty of the poetry,—' the magic veil which the poet casts over the idea. There is such an enchantment over all this poetry, that we become enchanted ourselves, and do not know up from down. These are the dragons of fabulous colours and forms which lie outside Beauty's enchanted castle, and when one has overcome them, they themselves become Beauty, the true poetical idea.'

We must plead guilty in the matter of the kennings, and we shall probably take the true view of them, if we remember that the skald was, above all, an artist in language and an authority on myths. In his verses he desired to display both of these accomplishments, and it is a feature by no means confined to Northern literature if in the end the style overpowered the matter. Skaldic poetry is not simple and easy to understand; simply because it was never meant to be. If Thucydides wrote darkly ἵνα μὴ πᾶσιν εἴη βατὸς ἀλλὰ τοῖς λίαν σοφοῖς, as Marcellinus assures us, so also the skald composed with the fear of his fellows before his eyes. When the poetic aspirant, fresh from the wilds of Ice-

---

* A *kenning* is a phrase like ' storm of the sword's edges '=battle ; ' wound-snake '=sword ; ' wound-snake's wielder '=warrior. The kennings for ' man ' in Gröndal's *Clavis Poetica* extend to 33 closely printed columns, probably some 2000 in all.

land, thrust himself into the king's hall in Norway, and asked leave to recite his panegyric, he knew that among his hearers would be the king's own skalds, ready to comment on any want of knowledge or want of skill he might display. Elaboration of allusion, of language, and of metre, was the standard that all aimed at. When Gunnlaug recited his poem to the Swedish King Olaf, the latter asked Hrafn for his opinion of it. 'It is a high-sounding poem,' said he, 'but coarse and somewhat stiff, as Gunnlaug's own nature is.' Then Hrafn recited his own poem, and Gunnlaug criticised it. 'It is a pretty poem,' he said, 'as Hrafn himself is in appearance, but it has little show about it; and why,' he added, 'did you make only a *flokk* about the king? Did you not think him worth a *drápa?*'

In reading the verses of the skalds, whether the single sonnets or the long poems, the question suggests itself, whether it is possible that they could have been clearly understood by those who heard them for the first time. The elaborate kennings, the parenthetical clauses, the insertion of parts of the burden in separate verses,*—all this must have laid a heavy tax on the attention of the hearers even although the style of poetry was familiar to them. This is shown by the fact that a modern Icelander finds the verses unintelligible without study, though every word may be familiar to him, and in reading the sagas aloud, the verses are nearly always omitted as conveying no meaning to the audience. It is perhaps going too far to say that they were 'conundrums' to the poet's contemporaries, but in the sagas themselves indications are not wanting that the meaning was sometimes difficult to follow. When Thorleif made bold to repeat his satire to its object, Earl Hákon, the latter was at first under the impression that there was praise in every verse. This may have been an exceptional piece of cleverness on the part of Thorleif, but one is inclined to think that various other poems could not have yielded a very distinct impression at their first hearing. The probability is that only when the verses were got by heart, did the meaning of each word and line become perfectly

---

* As in Hallar-Stein's *Rekstefja*, where it requires the last lines of three verses to make up the whole *stef*.

clear. This was certainly the case with much of the Old Irish verse, in which wisdom was intentionally darkened by obscurity of expression. An oral literature is not necessarily a simple one, as we are sometimes inclined to think. It may be suspected that not seldom the unprofessional hearer of a *drápa* was in the position of the King of Greece, when Brian, the son of Tuireann, made his covert request for the famous pigskin. 'That is a good poem,' said the King, 'only I do not understand a word of its meaning.'

Even a skald might at times be imposed on in this way, if we are to give credit to the amusing anecdote of Sneglu-Halli, told in the saga of Harald Hardrádi. Halli was in England, and when all his preparations to sail for Norway were complete, he went to Court and recited a poem to the English King. When the recitation was ended, the King asked a skald who was with him, what the merits of the poem might be. The skald answered that it was well done, whereupon the King asked Halli to stay there and let it be learned by others. 'That may not be,' said Halli, 'I am all ready to depart, and can make no stay here.' 'Then,' said the King, 'your reward for the poem will be in accordance with the satisfaction we have out of it. Sit down there, and I shall make them pour silver over your head, and you shall have what sticks in your hair.' Halli went outside first, got his hair smeared with tar, and made it stick out as much as possible, so that it caught a fair amount of the King's silver. But as for the poem, says the saga, it was all nonsense, made up as he went along.

We shall, therefore, in all likelihood be doing no injustice to the skalds if we judge their work to a great extent, though not entirely, from the formal side. Of its excellence in this respect there can be little question, considering the difficulties of the form. Lucilius, with his two hundred verses an hour *stans pede in uno*, had a slight task compared with the Old Northern poet. But the skald had an ample reward when his poem was completed. In the hall of some mighty king or earl, hung with shields and swords, and filled with famous warriors, he would pour forth his well-conned poem, with the ring of battle in every line, till the listeners seemed again to hear the clang of blades and crash of shields from some hard-fought fray, in which they themselves had borne a manly part. This was a glory well worthy the poet's pains, and shield or sword or good gold-ring were a sure addition to his treasures. It needs no understanding of their meaning to feel the effect of the sounding lines of Hallfred or Sighvat, Arnorr or Sturla; and it is not the poet's fault if the effect he aimed at is lost, when the wreathed folds of his verse are shaken out into plain prose.

It would be a mistake, however, to suppose that there is only form and nothing more in the verse of the skalds. They are not to be talked of all in one breath; some were true poets, and others were mere versifiers, as in any other literature of the same extent. It must also be borne in mind that many of the separate verses in the sagas are of very doubtful authenticity. The saga-editors of the 12th and 13th centuries did not hesitate to put verses of their own manufacture into the mouths of their heroes. Such, for instance, are the verses in Grettis Saga, which need not be laid to the outlaw's charge. That such verses should have much poetic value is hardly to be expected. But where the verses are genuine, there is often true poetry in the thought which underlies the skald's artificial expression, and it only requires a thorough acquaintance with his language, and some sympathy with his conception of the poetic ideal, to discover a real beauty in his work. To translate it adequately is difficult, often well-nigh impossible, because the kennings are not available in a modern rendering, and in them lies the poetic adornment of the thought. Whatever be the value of his verses, it is doing the skald an injustice to translate them into prose, or even into ordinary English verse. This is a task which the English translators of sagas have not come out of as well as could be wished, probably from an indisposition to give the necessary time to it. One can well understand that a translator of Heimskringla, for instance, should feel impatient at the even flow of Snorri's prose being broken up by these polished boulders of verse. They can hardly be thrown aside, but they are to be got round as easily and as quickly as possible, and a rough rendering into English rhyme enables the translator to go on again with the prose narrative. This is scarcely fair treatment either of the skald or of Snorri, who relied on the verses for his facts, and inserted them to adorn his tale. If full justice is not to be done to the technique of the verses, it would be much better to omit them altogether. To render them worthily it would be necessary either to practice the writing of *dróttkvætt* in English—which would be no impossible feat—or to adopt some equally complex metre more in accordance with the spirit of English rhythms. The kennings, no doubt, would have to be largely abandoned. Their allusions are too recondite for the general reader, and the want of variety in English inflections would render them awkward to handle. Some natural expansion of the poet's thought might be required to fill their place, but this need not altogether spoil the faithfulness of the rendering.

Only when this method of translation is properly carried out will English readers have any opportunity of forming a fair judgment of the quality of skaldic verse. Their opinion then would probably be, that the truth lay very much between the two views with which we started. The verses are scarcely to be called 'inspired,' and 'grand and sublime' are not the natural adjectives for them; but they have an accuracy of form that removes them from any charge of being 'rude,' nor are they always 'tumid and obscure enough to be utterly worthless.' They have no mean value in many respects—artistic, poetic, linguistic and historical, but perhaps no one is likely to find much enjoyment in them, who is not thoroughly versed in the language and learning of the skalds themselves.

W. A. CRAIGIE.

ART. VIII.—A LIBERAL EDUCATION: THE FUNCTION OF A UNIVERSITY.

An Address delivered before the University of Edinburgh at the Graduation Ceremony, 11th April, 1896.

THE Universities of Scotland have lately passed through a series of changes probably wider and more searching than have ever befallen similar institutions within the same space of time. It was natural, therefore, that many of my recent predecessors in this place should have found matter for their discourses in the revolution, by which they themselves were so closely affected. My chair, on the other hand, is one of the products of the Universities Commission, and it would be a sort of impiety on my part, even if I possessed the necessary knowledge, to criticise the system which gave me birth.

But avoiding particular remarks, which would be out of place, and setting aside personal considerations, which it is always easier to do where one acknowledges a benefit than where one conceives an injury, I may be permitted to congratulate the University on the general scope and direction of the recent change. It is a reform imbued with a large and tolerant, a progressive and hopeful spirit. Without obstructing the ancient and time-honoured avenues of learning, the Commission has opened up new roads to distinction, and sanctioned new methods of stimulating mental activity. By enlarging the curriculum, it has not only recognised studies hitherto ignored or discouraged; it has also implicitly adopted the view that the method of education is even more important than the subject, that it matters less what you learn than how you learn it. It has, in fact, brought the University one long step nearer to the ideal towards which all Universities should strive—the ideal of a liberal education.

In these days of commercial schools and technical instruction, it may almost seem retrogressive to point to liberal education as the supreme end of academic effort. And yet I am inclined to maintain the paradox, that it is just in these latter days that we are grasping, more closely than before, not only the true nature of liberal education, but also the fact that a University is its proper home. But first, what is a liberal education? Let us define it as a mental, moral, and physical training, which aims uniquely at the elevation of the mental, moral, and physical man. This, indeed, is liberal education in its fullest sense: it is moral and physical as well as mental: but, as the function of a University is primarily intellectual, and as the distinctive marks of a liberal education are to be found on its intellectual side, to that side I shall naturally confine myself.

The first, then, of these marks is a negative one. A liberal education fits a man for no special pursuit; it turns him out a master of no single craft. On the contrary, it makes a boast of that characteristic which, in the eyes of Cato the elder, was the reproach of Greek philosophy. Its very essence, if we regard it from the utilitarian point of view, is its inutility; for it is in the fact that it has no professional aim, that its liberality consists. Professional education, however excellent in its own way, inevitably partakes, in a greater or less degree, of what the Greeks called, τὸ βάναυσον, the mechanical. As it becomes practical, it ceases to be liberal. Hence it was that the medieval schools distinguished the three great faculties of Divinity, Law, and Medicine, from the seven Liberal Arts. But let me not be misunderstood. There is nothing more ennobling than the earnest and enlightened pursuit of those great professions in which year by year the flower of our youth enlists—the professions of the Church and the Bar, of Medicine and Education. The special instruction which fits a student for these professions is energising in the highest degree: it stimulates mental activity and holds aloft the lamp of learning; but, in so far as it is limited or specialised in its aim, in so far as it conduces to success and distinction in a certain walk of life, it is not liberal. It would be well, if it were possible, that all those who enter on those special courses of study could pass first through the wider fields of a really liberal education. I do not say that professional education is better or worse than liberal: I am not concerned to argue this point: all I say is, that it is not the same. It may no doubt be urged that the utility of a liberal education is only less apparent because it is more general, more diffused. But its defenders had better resign the claim to utility. Nothing is gained by confusing different things.

From this primary difference there follows a second. Inasmuch as liberal education aims at the improvement of the whole man, irrespective of any special vocation, it is naturally universal in its intellectual range. It is free, unrestricted, liberal, not only in its object, but in its scope. It takes all knowledge for its province. All subjects of human enquiry are open to it, so they fulfil one condition—the condition, namely, that they shall be capable of scientific treatment. I do not mean to say that a man shall not claim to be liberally educated till he have mastered all the sciences. Whatever universality of knowledge an Aristotle or a Bacon may have attained to, in the days of Aristotle or of Bacon, such universality is no longer attainable by the most gifted of men, much less by the average University student. What I mean is, that it is essential for a place of liberal education that it shall exclude no worthy branch of human knowledge : that all manner of studies shall be open to the student, who has a right to find in a University competent direction in any subject which he may desire to know.

This was not, I need hardly say, the old idea of a University : it was not the principle which governed the great schools of the Middle Ages, whence our modern Universities have sprung. The ancient University of Salerno was simply a school of medicine : the University of Bologna was a school of law : yet they were none the less Universities in the medieval sense. We are all of us aware that the title University had no original connection with universality of learning ; it was simply a collective title for the whole body of teachers and students : but it is inseparably and rightly connected with the idea of universality in the present day. It is in this sense that a University has been well defined by a great teacher as ' a school of knowledge of every kind, consisting of teachers and learners from every quarter.' So we may have schools of theology, schools of medicine, schools of agriculture, but it is the University which contains them all.

This universality at which we now aim leads me on to another distinctive mark of a liberal education. As it is unlimited in its range, as it has no specific professional object, what is the unity that binds it together? It is to be found in its method and its aim—an aim and method inseparably connected—the scientific pursuit of knowledge for its own sake. I use the phrase, ' for its own sake,' because it expresses the independence which I insist on ; but it must not obscure the fact that the advancement of the student, and not the advancement of knowledge, must be the supreme aim of a place of education. A University is indeed, or ought to be, not only a place of education, but a place of learning and research. I would even maintain that, whatever elementary teachers may do, no holder of an academic chair can duly instruct and stimulate his pupils, unless he enlarge and re-invigorate his own mind by frequent voyages into the unexplored or less-known regions of the science which he is called to teach. This, however, is by the way. It is with education, not with research, that we are just now concerned. Regarding our academic duties from the educational point of view, we subordinate research to education, and say that it is essential to liberal education to pursue knowledge for its own sake.

But the scientific nature of this pursuit introduces the limitation of which I spoke just now—the limitation, namely, that the subjects studied in a University must be capable of rational treatment. They must be food not merely for the perceptions or the memory, but for the intellect. In other words, they must belong rather to the field of science than to that of knowledge. It is not the acquisition of knowledge, but the processes of reason which educate the mind. Knowledge, we are often told, is power; but science, which is reasoned knowledge, is powerful in a tenfold degree. For knowledge is applicable only to particulars, but a scientific education—I use science in no narrow sense—gives a general capacity and flexibility to the intellect. And this scientific training is at its best when it is both wide and independent; when, as the Greeks put it, the mind follows whithersoever the λόγος leads, with no ulterior motive beyond the discovery of truth. This kind of intellectual pursuit is, indeed, essentially Greek : the stimulus to pure research is one of the greatest of our debts to Hellas. It is also the main business of a University, whose highest function, as John Henry Newman has said, is ' to educate the mind to reason well in all matters, to reach out to truth and grasp it.'

Yes, to reach out to truth and grasp it, to desire truth and to become capable of finding and holding it—that is indeed the highest aim of a liberal education and of University life. And this is where the moral effect of a University training comes in : here the moral and intellectual influences converge. The Church may inculcate morality by precept, the home may induce it by practice and example, the law may enforce it by legal sanctions, but it is for the University to found it upon an intellectual basis. Have we not been told, by the Greeks again, that virtue is knowledge—in other words, that intelligent virtue is the stoutest, the most enduring virtue? It is not the primary duty of a University to teach morality : its direct influence is principally intellectual ; but its indirect ethical effect can hardly be over-estimated. For, on the one hand, this bold and independent search for truth stimulates and sustains the higher morality by the qualities which it calls into play, by the devotion to an ideal aim, by the abnegation of self ; while, on the other hand, it facilitates the discovery of that rational basis of ethical conduct which is demanded by the reasonable man.

But it is not only the art of reasoning well, not only the desire for truth, which a liberal education should confer. There is also something further, something which is not reason nor science nor knowledge, but rather is connected with these as effect with cause. It is a habit of mind, which, for want of a better name, we call culture. I am half afraid to employ the word, so abused has it been, so tainted, one may almost say, by the neighbourhood of priggishness and pedantry. And yet surely it is a most estimable quality of mind which is produced by a liberal education, working on a generous and fruitful soil. 'Reading,' says Bacon, 'maketh a full man,' but reflection must be added to make culture. Culture is not fullness : at all events it is not repletion. It is rather an attitude or habit of mind, comparable to the effect of good society on manners and deportment, or to the bodily results produced by a sufficiency of good food and plenty of wholesome exercise under the open sky.

The mind that has habitually fed upon what is worthiest in science and literature acquires a combined firmness and sensitiveness, a grasp and subtlety, a decision and a delicacy of touch, which are the mental equivalents of vigorous bodily health. Such a mind gaius confidence, for in its stores of information it possesses a touchstone, a standard by which to judge new things. But at the same time it is humble and cautious, for it has proved its own weakness, and has found how difficult it is to see into the heart of things. It is not lavish of its praise, for it is aware how few reputations stand the test of time; but it is tolerant, for it knows that a great many average men go to make one genius. It is this thoughtful mental habit, this candid and dispassionate outlook, which we associate with culture in its true sense. The furniture of the cultivated mind is not facts, not what we call learning, but rather the ideas which are the deposit of facts well pondered: its peculiar characteristic is that mental courtesy and polish which springs from intimacy with the great works of the intellect in all time. This is the ripest fruit of a liberal education: a University is the garden where it ought most easily to grow. I am far from saying that it infallibly ripens in a University, or that it ripens nowhere else. All I say is that it is in a University, and by means of a liberal education, that it has the best chance of coming to maturity.

There are yet two other aspects of University life which contribute to the liberality of its influence. One of these is its cosmopolitanism, its social universality. A University is, as I said just now, not only a place of universal learning, but a body of teachers and learners from every quarter. It is a microcosm, a little world, open to every comer. Here we find a larger choice of friends than we have ever had before, larger probably than we are ever like to have again. And we rank our friends, our prophets, our heroes, by a liberal, an unconventional standard. It is in one sense a democratic, in another sense an aristocratic society, to which we belong. It is aristocratic in that it discards the pretence of equality, that it falls willingly into line behind its recognised leaders: it is democratic in that those leaders bear sway according to what is in their heads and hearts, not in proportion to the money in their pockets or the clothes they wear upon their backs. Such leadership is open to all: here we have, as nowhere else, the *carrière ouverte aux talents.*

Here, too, we pass beyond the bounds of our parish, our

school, our religious circle, our native town, even our native country, into a wider field, which knows, or at least may know, no limits save the great world. We rub shoulders with men from across the Border, from across the seas, from the furthest ends of the earth. We do not come to love our country less, but to appreciate other countries at a truer rating. We do not grow less patriotic, but we learn that patriotism need not be provincial.

And this brings me to the last of those elevating and liberalising influences exercised by a University, to which I call your attention to-day—the influence of site, of beautiful and stimulating environment. We leave our homes: we exchange what in general must be petty or common-place surroundings for new scenes, a wider range of view, noble buildings and historic memories. The influence which these things bring to bear should at once deepen the feeling for our native land, and relieve it from ignorant and narrow prejudice. Such an influence is in itself a liberal education, and it is one to which we in this ancient seat of learning owe a peculiar debt. Other famous places of education may trace their origin to a more remote antiquity, and in the midst of their gardens and their palaces may enjoy a more opulent repose. But in no other academic spot is the *genius loci* at once so original and so inspiring: in no other are the beauties of nature and the adornments of art so effectively intertwined: in no other are we so forcibly reminded at every turn of a great and historic past. Nowhere else does the routine of academic life so readily draw inspiration from the infinite field of national history, from the vital associations of popular romance and song. Yet at the same time the towering monuments of ancient glory look down in this city upon no dead or decaying present. The busy tide of human life, the rush of industry and traffic still sways to and fro in the streets where Douglases and Hamiltons strove for power or revenge; it hums and bustles over the stones where Knox lies buried, under the walls whence Montrose stepped bravely forth to death, past the haunts which Scott and Stevenson knew and loved so well.

In no other place of education are these two influences so harmoniously blended : in no other is the ancient so subtly and so equally fused with the modern, the living with the dead. Fortunate, indeed, are you who are now going forth into the world, bearing with you, among all the other liberal influences of academic life, the potent and, let me hope, enduring memory of those scenes and conditions among which you have spent your happiest and most fruitful years. They should be to you no slight source of inspiration in after-life. The roll of fame appointed for the *alumni* of this great University is not yet full : in it there is always room : see that some of you at least repay the debt you owe to your *Alma Mater* by adding to her glory ; see that you set up fresh examples to be followed by the generations of Edinburgh students that are yet to come.

G. W. PROTHERO.

ART. IX.—JOURNALISM FROM THE INTERIOR.

LORD ROSEBERY may not be the greatest of living men of affairs, but he has certainly no rival in the art of playfully hinting what many other men are thinking seriously, and of humming to himself, and by way of rehearsal as it were, a tune which is certain in time to become a national favourite. He never did this more effectually than when in June of the present year, he took advantage of the opportunity afforded him by the opening of a public library in London, to make some remarks on 'the dying out of independent thinking' and 'the growth of intellectual apathy' in the country, and to associate both with the present-day triumphs of journalistic enterprise. He did not deny the fact or the extent of that enterprise. Nobody, of course, can. It is one of the greatest feats of allied money and brains in modern days. But what he contended was that the newspaper, being so much in evidence, was accepted too implicitly and absolutely as a dictator, in public opinion, and that the amplitude of details which it supplies upon every subject it treats of, destroys the intellectual vitality of its readers. Lord Rosebery's remarks were much, and in the main unfavourably, commented upon at the time they were delivered, and it is, of course, easy to say that no reader of a newspaper need accept its guidance unless he is so minded. At the same time, these remarks, from their very originality, are calculated to lead to a reconsideration, on the part of the public, of the very remarkable industrial, social, political, and possibly ethical questions involved in the power of the press.

There is no doubt whatever as to the sentiment which prevails in circles outside of journalism as to the magnitude of that power, and the rapidity of its rise. Mr. Gladstone is still the most eloquent expositor of popular opinions upon certain familiar subjects, and he was quite in his vein when, in a letter to a correspondent who had sent him a copy of the *Times* a hundred years old he recently wrote 'The mustard seed of the press has, indeed, grown into a tree that overshadows the earth.' Possibly the press suggests to many minds a mustard blister rather than mustard seed. But the image will be generally accepted as a manifestation of the mark-of-exclamation order of the wonder with which the uninitiated public regard the rapid development of a power which, being exercised anonymously, has all the curious fascination that is associated with mystery. Lord Rosebery, perhaps, because he is a younger man, and more of a humourist than Mr. Gladstone, is not content to hold up his hands in wonder at and admiration of this portent. He is audacious enough to hint that the influence exerted by this modern Veiled Prophet of Mokanna is not all for good, even that from the purely intellectual point of view it may be positively demoralising. He almost hints that there is a good deal of humbug about the Prophet, Veil and all, but especially the Veil. One could conceive him, were he to get behind the scenes, revelling in the part of the incendiary Pancks, and, with infinite gusto, shearing the flowing locks, tearing off the spectacles, and crushing the imposing hat, which constituted nine-tenths of the patriarchal benignity and coercive authority of the autocrat of Bleeding Heart Alley.

XXVIII.   24

Were the Press conducted on the principles not of capitalism
but of co-operation, were it disciplined as a modern Trade
Union or even an old Trade Guild is disciplined, it could—so
much is plain even to the outsider—be converted with ease
into the most influential Secret Society the world has ever
seen.   As things are, it has its agents in every corner of
the globe, who are quite as eager and enthusiastic as ever
were the members of the Society of Jesus, though for more
sordid reasons.   Were the unscrupulousness which is perhaps
not quite fairly associated with modern financial operations
when conducted on a sufficiently large scale, imported into
journalistic management, that might very well become the
embodiment in modern literature of the 'Napoleonic idea'
looked at from the Craigenputtoch standpoint as colossal
selfishness in the individual and buccaneering aggression on
the part of the nation.   There is no saying what mischief
might not be done by powerfully written but utterly and intentionally misleading leading articles based upon cooked
news.   It may be said that no such danger will ever occur in
such a country as Great Britain, the distinguishing note of
whose public life is probity.   This is insisted upon in what is
perhaps the latest paper on journalism by a journalist—
'The Power of the British Press,' by Mr. H. W. Lucy.   Mr.
Lucy undoubtedly deserves to be heard upon this subject.
He has had, he himself confesses, a very large experience in
all the departments of newspaper work that are with comprehensive vagueness described as 'editorial.'   He is, above all
things, a journalist pure and simple.   He is not a man of
letters who occasionally dabbles in journalism, but a journalist
who occasionally dabbles in literature.   After dwelling upon the
melancholy case of the luckless French millionaire, M. Lebaudy,
—'this hopeless inheritor of millions of francs made in the
sugar business having been drawn by conscription, half a
dozen newspapers fastened upon him like wasps on the oozing
joints of the paternal sugar vats,—he proceeds to lay down
these views as being of the kind that are beyond dispute.

'An English newspaper may be lacking in all the qualities that go to
make a daily or a weekly news-sheet acceptable.   But the poorest in

condition is free from taint of deliberate black-mailing. There are occasionally hints current in financial circles of newspapers launched with the design of preying upon company promoters. But the mere suspicion of such a design attached to a newspaper in London or any provincial centre of financial activity is sufficient to defeat the purpose of its proprietors. Its good word is not worth buying, nor is its hostility to be feared. It may be accepted as an unassailable axiom in respect of the English press that the higher is the standing of a newspaper, the wider the range of its influence, the more unapproachable it is by those who come with money bribes in their hands. . . Probably the worst thing an English Prime Minister, desiring to further a particular line of policy, could do would be to send a message to the editor of the so-called ministerial organ, instructing him or even inviting him, to adopt a stated line of argument or assertion. . . . The power of the press in England is mainly based on conviction of its honesty of purpose, and the cleanness of the hands of those who conduct and contribute to it.' Finally, ' the power of the press in England might become even dangerously autocratic but for a lack of cohesion. If there existed amongst newspapers any organization akin to Trade Unions the British newspapers might rule the roost. Unfortunately (perhaps fortunately) every paper, whether daily or weekly, stands aloof from its contemporaries, or comes in contact with them only for the purposes of a scolding match. The idea in every British newspaper office, small or large, is, that the sheet it turns out is, if not literally the only one printed that morning, the only one worthy of notice. This curious delusion is carried to such lengths that, for fear of breaking the spell, no well regulated morning paper will mention another by name. If temptation to show how foolish or unreliable a neighbour has been prove irresistible, it is loftily alluded to as " a contemporary." '

This is a very fair statement of the present position of the British press, regarded from the standpoint of good-natured optimism. Mr. Lucy, though he writes from the inside, is tolerably contented with things as they are. And yet it will be seen that even in his eyes our press is in a position of unstable equilibrium. It is based on British ' character' which may change, and it is allied with an inefficiency of organization which might be altered for the better or, as Mr. Lucy evidently prefers to believe, for the worse. He says roundly : ' If there existed among British newspapers any organization akin to Trades Unions, the British newspapers might rule the roost.' But why should there not be such an organization ? Trades Unions cannot be said to be ' un-English ; ' on the contrary they flourish on British soil better than they do anywhere else. The

relations between capital and labour in the 'working-class'
field are regulated by them.   The spirit of Trade Unionism, if
not its modern organization, dominates the leading professions.
It will take generations, if not centuries, of Trade Union congresses to make any trade in the United Kingom such a powerful corporation as any one of the Inns of Court is at the present
moment. Working printers have a Trade Union, and one which
is not only powerful but aggressive. How comes it that working journalists have nothing of the kind?   There is indeed an
organization of newspaper men, called the Institute of Journalists, with a charter and branches all over the Kingdom, and
which holds an annual conference in the autumn.   But it is
expressly debarred by its own charter from becoming a Trade
Union. As a matter of fact, capitalists, in the persons of newspaper proprietors, are the most important persons in it.   No
doubt the Institute does real good as a Friendly Society.   Its
annual conference, also, appears to be a very agreeable picnic,
like the annual meetings of most congresses. The Institute
may be a temporary obstacle in the way of the creation of a
journalistic Trade Union ; it will certainly not hasten that possibly undesirable consummation.

But this talk of the formation of a Trade Union among newspapers or among newspaper men raises the whole question of
the relations between an important daily journal, which is
the only one worth considering in this connection, and the
public on one side and its employés on the other.   Such
a paper is now-a-days essentially, though not absolutely,
a commercial concern, and one involving the expenditure
of an enormous amount of money, and therefore requiring
the backing of an enormous amount of capital.   Thus it
was recently computed that the starting of a new daily
paper in Scotland to compete, after an inevitable loss of
time and money, with the journals firmly established, would
mean an outlay of £500,000.   When it is borne in mind
that but a hundredth part of that sum was required only about
half a century ago to start in Edinburgh a political journal
which in the course of ten years became the leading organ
there, the marvellous growth of the influence of capital in

newspaper production may at once be realised. According to many thinkers on economical questions, the great struggle of the future will be not between capital and labour but between capital and co-operation. Considering the triumphs which of late years have been achieved by co-operation in the commercial and industrial fields, it might be rash to say that a great newspaper governed by and managed on co-operative principles may not be started and successfully carried on. It is safe to say, however, that such an enterprise does not come within the ken of co-operative dreamers or the range of probability.

For one thing, the very inception of such an enterprise would involve a complete and precipitate revolution in newspaper management and *personnel*. Leaving out of consideration the commercial aspect of journalism—although in a sense that is the most important of all—let us contemplate a daily newspaper from the employer and employed points of view. It involves the most effectual subordination of labour to capital that the world possesses at the present moment. In any other large mercantile undertaking—a railway company, a bank, a limited liability brewery—some employée, a General Manager, an Agent, a Secretary, is known and accessible by name to the public. Even a drapery or ironmongery firm advertises that our Mr. Blank has returned from Paris or Berlin with the latest special trade ideas or fashions. But, as a matter of etiquette, no person actually engaged on a newspaper is known to be so by its customers and patrons. On its last page the information is vouchsafed that it is printed and published by, say Messrs. John Smith & Co. They employ a gentleman called 'the Editor,' for their business announcements generally include some such statements as that 'All Letters are to be addressed to the Editor,' and that 'The Editor does not undertake, under any circumstances, to return rejected Manuscripts.' 'The Editor' has of course the natural human ties of ordinary men, and so a particular Thomas Jones or Edward Brown is known not only to his colleagues and subordinates, but to a circle of friends and acquaintances, as being 'the Editor.' He may, in answer to a letter addressed to 'The Editor,' sign himself Thomas Jones, and so take off the mask which conceals his face. In these days of 'personal' journalism, one often sees a paragraph announcing—probably quite inaccurately—that a particular person who is named is editor, or sub-editor of, or contributor to a particular journal. All this, however, is quite irregular, and out of keeping alike with the conditions and with the traditions of anonymous journalism. The legendary perhaps, rather than the real, John Thaddeus Delane, who for many years edited the *Times*, was the incarnation of impersonal journalism. According to gossip, which has no doubt some backing of fact, Delane declined to accord personal interviews to official personages, however high in their own hierarchy, not to speak of their own estimation—foreign princes, and even Scottish Lord Provosts—that called at the *Times* building and asked to see him by name. Mr. Delane, however, made one great, and indeed fatal mistake in his editorial career. He allowed himself to be drawn into a personal controversy by Mr. Cobden over a question in which the policy of the *Times*, and therefore of the company that publishes that newspaper was involved. He withdrew himself from the shelter of anonymity when it was personally unnecessary, and officially improper for him to do so. What was perhaps even worse, he came off second best in the dispute. This was the exception, however, that proved the excellence of the *Times*' rule of anonymity.

It is a tolerably open journalistic secret that 'the Editor' has under and associated with him a staff of officials, the size of which varies with the importance of the paper. These include leader-writers, whose business is to present in more or less literary form the opinions which the journal holds on political, ecclesiastical, social, and other questions; reporters, who attend local meetings, and, speaking generally, see that their newspaper gives an adequate record of the events in its district; and sub-editors, who prepare for publication the enormous amount of telegraphic and other intelligence which is sent by news-agencies and correspondents all over the country, and indeed all over the world. As a matter of fact, a newspaper office is as much a business establishment and is conducted on as strictly business principles, as a bank or manufactory, or a large shop. It is not quite on all fours with these other business establishments, however, in that unity and solidarity of interest which are the bases for a Trade Union. There is not for example that plain ascent to the top of the tree that there is, say, in a bank—where clerk may become cashier, and cashier become agent, in due hierarchical order. There is no such ascent in a newspaper. A reporter may develop into a sub-editor, and a leader-writer may become an editor. But as things are now-a-days a reporter or a sub-editor is not at all likely to become a leader-writer. The reason is obvious. A man may be a good shorthand writer, or may have considerable faculty for preparing news for a paper, and yet have no decided opinions on any subject under the sun, or even the capacity for giving expression to the opinions of others. There is no real community of professional interest between the editor and the leader-writer on the one hand and the sub-editor and the reporter on the other. The creation therefore of a genuine Trade Union feeling in 'the editorial department' of a large daily newspaper is a virtual impossibility. One can quite understand reporters or sub-editors uniting for the purpose of raising the rates of remuneration for their special labours. That work is if not quite mechanical, devoid of partisanship. In other words, there is nothing in professional etiquette or honour at all events to prevent a reporter who has a salary of £100 on a Liberal newspaper from leaving his post for another worth £150 a year on a Unionist journal. He has nothing to do with the opinions of others. His business is simply to record accurately, impartially, and at the rate of so many words a minute, what a speaker says. What is true of the reporter, or of the man who records events himself, is true of the sub-editor, or of the man who prepares for publication records of news that have been sent in from the outside for publication. The positions of the editor and the leader writer are somewhat different. They hold their positions largely because their opinions are in agreement with those held by the proprietors of the newspaper in whose employ they are. No doubt it is open to a contributor to a newspaper, as it is to any other man, to change his opinions, and to leave a concern in the prosperity of which he has, therefore, ceased to have an interest. But for the editor of a Liberal journal to become the conductor of a Unionist organ simply because he is offered £200 more of salary would be regarded—and rightly regarded —as a piece of mercenary cynicism, if not of political blackguardism. His professional, political, and personal reputation would, in all probability, be irremediably ruined.

Should, therefore, an attempt be made in the profession of journalism, to establish a trade organisation of labour with a view to checkmating or controlling capital, it may be assumed that two at least of the foremost orders in the hierarchy of that labour would be excluded from it. An editor or a leader-writer might, adequate temptation having been offered, exchange from one newspaper into another of the same persuasion. But journalistic Trade Unionism based on, or even associated with partisanism is an impossibility. No doubt the conductors and proprietors of newspapers have private methods of discovering the sort of men that will suit them. The profession of journalism, like every other, has its freemasonry, which allows of, and, indeed, encourages the secret deed of kindness. Above all things, a very capable man cannot be prevented, even by the restraints of anonymity, from asserting himself, and making himself known to a circle interested beyond the newspaper with which he is connected. At the same time a trade which is composed of men arranged in grades that have virtually nothing in common, and between which there can be nothing savouring of *esprit de corps*, cannot organise itself to any effectual purpose. It is, and must be, at the mercy of capital. That so placed it has remained so pure, so free from even the taint of bribery, is a very high testimony to the worth of the British character on which Mr. Lucy so much relies.

Is journalism, looked at as in a sense a department of literature, upon the decline? The *Spectator* has recently answered this question in the affirmative, and the conductors of that journal deserve to be heard with the respect which is due to men of very long experience and highly honoured in their profession. The statement may seem a remarkable one to make in view of the extraordinary growth of ordinary newspapers as news-agencies even within the past few years. They were never such complete records of contemporary history as they are at the present moment. Yet, in spite of their very perfection as historical records, their literary quality,—certainly the literary quality of the leading articles in which opinion is expressed upon current events—is said to be on the decline. It can hardly be otherwise. The public demand not only that the events of a day be recorded for their advantage on the following morning, but that they be commented upon at the same time. At all events the conductors of newspapers believe so, and that comes to the same thing. It follows, as a matter of course, that this comment must be hurriedly prepared. And then the old law of literature undoubtedly holds good, that what is easily written is easily read ; or rather it is not read at all by men who have any conception of what constitutes either style in letters or weight in opinion. The wisest editors seem to be quite aware of this. They are trying to abolish the long leading article dealing with some political event of the previous day or night which for many a year was regarded as being quite as essential a feature of the morning paper as the ante-breakfast tub is of the ordinary Briton's life. And they are substituting for the long leaders numbers of what in the fearful, wonderful, and nowise literary slang of the profession are known as 'leaderettes'—short paragraphs containing intelligent chat on Lord Salisbury's 'incisive speech' upon the Eastern Question, Lord Kelvin's 'thoughtful paper upon the Röntgen Rays,' or 'the latest triumph of the vigilance of Scotland Yard.' This is better because honester work than the long leading article written against time, and notable simply as a feat of sentence-spinning within a certain number of minutes. But it is not satisfactory, as every journalist who is true to his ideals must admit. In the first place it is impossible for a writer thus situated to be literary, at least in any true sense of the word. He has no scope in a paragraph. He cannot work out the ideas he has—or ought to have —in a few abrupt sentences. Writing for and against time he cannot even try to write for eternity, which ought to be the aim of all literature. Colour and light—such things journalism taboos and must taboo. Leading is equally out of the question. A public writer may be as good a man and as able a thinker on political questions as the Foreign Minister or ex-Premier whom he criticises of an evening, but he has not the advantages of his opponent (or fellow-partisan), even if they are on an equality as regards experience and ability. The politician has time to get up the case he presents to the public, the journalist has not. No doubt after twenty-four hours' reflection the journalist may have something to say worth putting in print, but he will be behind the fair, and will find himself hopelessly distanced in the race for the public head, or heart, by his rival. Besides, in twenty-four hours a new sensation may appear which will call for the critic's attention and comment, to the exclusion of its predecessor.

It is the consciousness of this weakness which is leading the more astute and far-seeing conductors of newspapers into certain new developments, which the general public will have to watch with care and even with anxiety. One of these has been brought into striking relief by the Armenian 'atrocities' agitation. The massacres in Constantinople 'under the very eyes of diplomacy and journalism,' sent a thrill of horror throughout the country. But they occurred in the holiday season, in what one of the most ardent of British sympathisers with Armenia mournfully termed 'the desolation of September.' The ordinary leaders of public opinion, such as the front-bench politicians, were off duty, and seemed reluctant to leave their summer recreations—which, under ordinary circumstances no one grudges them—to take a part in great public meetings. Then a daily morning newspaper in London, which has during the past few years distinguished itself by its fearless and almost feverish sensationalism, rushed to the front and summoned the nation to arms against the Turk. Fiercely, and almost rudely, repudiating the generally recognised leaders of the party with which it is associated, and more particularly Lord Rosebery, it called upon 'the people' and the party to 'march' without leaders. Whether this journal acted rightly or wrongly in making this appeal, whether the special policy in connection with the Armenian problem which it advocated is a dangerous or a safe one, need not be discussed. But what it did was, to use the expressive slang of the day, ' good business.' Its name was in all mouths ; its articles led to its correspondence columns being flooded with suggestions. It may be doubted if any newspaper even performed so successfully the feat, through the pen of its leader-writer, of playing off its own bat, as did the *Daily Chronicle* on this occasion. Its example, having been so successful, cannot fail to be catching. For playing off one's own bat, chimes in with the self-respect which is to be found in the breast of the anonymous journalist as of every other man. It is better, or at least ever so much pleasanter, to write out one's thoughts upon a particular question, than simply to mince down or repeat the thoughts of Mr. Balfour or Lord Salisbury upon the subject, which must be what the writing late at night or early in the morning of an article upon a speech comes in effect to.

This tendency will grow unless, of course, it is checked by some other influence which is not apparent at the present moment. It may be doubted whether the growth of the tendency will be beneficial either to journalism or to the public, which is but too apt, as Lord Rosebery has noted, to take not only its reading but its thinking from the newspaper or newspapers it reads. It will and must have the effect of making newspaper articles effective pieces of declamation rather than of reasoning. The first business of a newspaper is to sell— and to sell it must tell. And a telling effect is produced much more easily by an appeal to emotion in the shape of a sustained strain of rhetoric than by an appeal to reason in the form of a detailed but cold piece of argumentation. A league of journalists would find it a much less difficult task to persuade the country to undertake a great war than to pass a complicated Local Government Bill. An anonymous journalist, anxious to impress his personality upon the country or upon the district in which he performs his work, will seek to become not so much a preacher or a pleader, as a tribune or a demagogue.

There is another feature in what is called the New Journalism which must contribute to the decline of the ordinary newspaper from the ordinary literary point of view.   This is the development of the 'interview'—an institution borrowed from the go-ahead but not specially dignified journalism of the United States.   The development of the 'interview' means the growth of the expert at the expense of the ordinary newspaper man.   When Dr. Nansen returns from his expedition in search of the North Pole, or Sir Henry Irving announces his intention of venturing on a new Shakespearian production, the enterprising editor sends a reporter to interview the hero of the new sensation.   Or, if it is impossible to get at principals, who, owing to their importance, or perhaps their self-importance, may object to be 'drawn,' the interviewer gets at some other or outside authority, some other Arctic explorer than Nansen, some actor who has, or fancies he has, a right to criticise even the manager of the Lyceum.   The enterprising editor is right.   The man who reads his morning paper after breakfast, or in the train when travelling between his suburban house and his city office, and who is almost invariably in a hurry, prefers to have the judgment of a known rather than of an unknown man upon the phenomenon of the day.   He reads the 'interview,' and lets the unsigned article of the anonymous leader-writer severely alone.   That once admired person, 'the all-round journalist,' who was believed to be capable of treating any subject, at any moment, from Shakespeare to the Rand Gold Mines, is being jostled out of his old and commanding position.   There is no room for Captain Shandon in a modern newspaper office.   Jack Bludyer has gone; and the old but rather sloppy omniscience of the Admirable Crichton of the leading columns will soon go too.   As newspapers become larger and specialism develops, something like an ideal newspaper may be produced—one written entirely by experts.

This ideal is in the future, however.   It may never be realised.   For the bulk of writing for daily newspapers has of necessity to be done at a very late hour.   The man who commences his work at nine or ten o'clock at night labours under unhealthy conditions and cuts himself adrift from the ordinary pleasures of domesticity. Abandon all hopes of longevity all ye who enter here, might with truth, though not perhaps with propriety, be written above the doors of most newspaper offices. It may be questioned if genuine experts in politics, literature, science, and art, could be tempted by such inducements as the proprietors even of very wealthy newspapers can offer to leave their firesides night after night, if at all events they could command a market elsewhere. Second-rate writers and thinkers, more or less of the all-round type, though no doubt quite conscientious, must for many years to come perform the regular work of ordinary newspapers. It is, no doubt, to the haste and consequent perfunctoriness with which daily newspaper thinking and writing have to be done, that we have to attribute the increasing demand for weekly newspapers and monthly magazines of the more serious order. If a man has a week or a month to mature his ideas in, he will certainly be able to give weightier and more artistic expression to them, than when he has to write on the spur of the moment. And so a sort of quasi-hierarchy is emerging in periodical literature. The monthly magazine gives materials if not a cue to the weekly newspaper; the weekly newspaper gives a cue, and less frequently materials, to the daily journal. This quasi-hierarchical arrangement is not without its uses. The monthly magazine and the weekly newspaper between them keep in check the demagogues or tribunes of the daily journals. It is through the three between them that 'the common-sense of most keeps a fretful realm in awe,' and secures it peace with dulness.

In one of the few greatly daring moods in which Mr. John Morley has shaken his fist in the face of British Philistinism, he described the newspaper press as a great engine for keeping thought and discussion on a low level. There is in this description quite as much truth as is to be found in most statements whose vitality depends upon their literary form. Mr. Morley did not take any account of one of the reasons why discussion and thought are kept on a low level—the men who do the thinking and discussion in the newspapers are themselves kept on a low level. To use a fine Disraelian distinction, journalism is very greatly respected, but journalists are very little regarded. Of newspapers everybody speaks with bated breath; newspaper men nobody knows. The *Times*, it has been declared, has oftener plunged the nation into war, or prevented it from being plunged, than any statesman even of the highest rank. Yet the leader-writers who, as a matter of fact performed these feats, have died unwept, unhonoured, and unsung. It was either Mr. Tremaine Bertie, or Mr. Bertie Tremaine, who said that personal progress was most effectually marked by the dinner invitations one receives. In this respect journalism is the least honoured of all the professions; strictly speaking, it is not a profession at all. It will be admitted that a first-class reporter performs an important duty to Society; yet whoever met such a man 'in Society?' A leader-writer may mould a mighty state's or a large vestry's decrees; a dramatic critic or a reviewer may make or damn a literary reputation; yet a young clergyman, lawyer, or doctor is of almost infinitely greater regard and influence than leader-writer, critic, or reviewer. An editor may be and frequently is asked to social functions; but he is asked not as Mr. So-and-so and for his personal qualities, but as the conductor of a particular journal. In nine cases out of ten virtue is the moderately successful journalist's sole reward—virtue and a salary as large as that of a second-class clerk in a Government office or a large mercantile establishment.

It may be said that this social ostracism, or negative ostracism in the shape of ignoring, is due to the conditions under which the work of journalism is performed. The bulk of it is done anonymously. How is it possible for 'Society' to ask to its functions men whose names it does not know, whose names in a sense it ought not to know? Again, journalists are as a rule at their busiest at night, when other men make a business of pleasure. For a newspaper man, therefore, to make a practice of dining-out would mean that he must make a habit of neglecting his duties at the only time when they can properly be performed. Besides this, journalists are almost forced to shirk entertainments which, owing to their comparatively limited means, they cannot return. A successful newspaper being supposed, largely on account of the mystery associated with it, to have a great amount of power in various departments of human activity and adventure—politics, commerce, literature, art, the drama—it has become the interest of a very great number of people to 'get at' or 'nobble' it. And incomparably the easiest and most swiftly effectual way of accomplishing this result is to show some social attention to a contributor to or official in the newspaper who from the character of his connection with it may, if he chooses, say a good word for a new novel, a new play, a new mining syndicate, or even a new political leader. A journalist who wishes to preserve his purity and independence, and to do his duty by his journal with an easy conscience, resents efforts to 'get at' him, and declines invitations to social entertainments, the real object of which is obviously to influence that journal through him.

All this is true. But it only emphasizes the fact that journalists are and must be under existing newspaper conditions, a class apart. It may be said that they may form a society among themselves like artists or men of letters. But this they can do to a limited extent, and that nowhere but in London. Besides, as has already been seen, they cannot form a solid class. The reporter or the sub-editor, the man who obtains or arranges the news, has no natural sympathy with the leader - writer, or the editor, or the critic, the man who criticises a speech, or thinks out a policy, or judges a modern book by the classics of the past. The two men may be friends, but they are not drawn into friendship by community of professional interests like painters or novelists, doctors or lawyers. Not having the freedom of other professional men, they have not the social or personal power. From their anonymity and their inability to form trade combinations among themselves and to make genuine and profitable friendships among the members of other classes, they are more completely at the mercy of the capitalist than any other labouring men.

All this involves no disparagement of the moneyed people who either individually or in companies run, and must run, large newspapers. They are neither better nor worse than the men who run other businesses. Having paid the piper they have a right to call the tune, and even to dismiss the piper at a month's notice, no outsider daring to interfere. Moreover, the public hear very few complaints of cruelty or injustice by the literary employees of newspapers against their capitalist employers. The very fact that every newspaper's hand is against every other's, and that it is engaged in labour the value and profit of which depend largely upon the secrecy with which it is performed, often brings about a sort of freemasonry or even family feeling in a newspaper office—a feeling which is cherished by employers quite as much as by employees. Life is a lottery at the best; and the man who is the servant of a newspaper publishing company, conducted on the admirable business principles preached and practised by the Cheeryble Brothers, might lead as happy a life as he would under any other conditions. At the same time the finger of capital is always on his shoulder, even although its touch be caressingly, not patronisingly, slight and tender. The journalist, therefore, and more particularly the journalist who tries conscientiously to perform his duty to his employers, cannot possibly write with the vigour which is associated with or springs from absolute freedom. He must always be thinking of his employer's interests, and endeavouring to reproduce not what he himself thinks, but what they would say were they in his place. The ideal of the ordinary journalist, unless he be an editor with an absolutely free hand — which is, speaking generally, an absolute impossibility — is very much that of the confidential clerk writing to dictation. He produces so much 'copy' within a certain time, and at the rate of so many guineas a week. But the production of so much 'copy' does not mean the production of so much thinking or of so much literature. It means in many cases quite the reverse. The large and increasing employment of capital in newspaper production confers many advantages upon the public. Above all things, it ensures a very large, and, thanks to competition, a marvellously accurate supply of news. Journals were never such complete daily histories of the world as they are at the present moment. After all, it is the first business of a newspaper to give news; the public ought to do for themselves the bulk of the thinking which such news suggests. The reporter, not the sophist or party disputant, is the mainstay of a daily journal; that is inevitable. But it also involves the dominance of the reporter's ideal—the production of so much up-to-date 'copy' within a certain limited time—in the departments of the journal that are concerned with thought, politics, and criticism. The ordinary writer sets himself, quite unconsciously perhaps, to write out what he imagines his proprietors, as represented by his editor, would wish to be said. His is not and cannot be the feeling of the ambitious literary aspirant whose bread depends upon his originality, or who, being above all things an artist, takes a supreme delight in giving the best literary form to his ideas. The inclination of successful capitalist journalism is, and must be, to substitute caution for brilliancy alike in thought and in expression. And if the public, as Lord Rosebery appears to believe, takes its thinking as well as its news from daily papers, no wonder that public discussion tends all round to become tame even to monotony. If dulness, relieved by occasional bursts of demagogism, is the journalist's ideal, and if the public take their views from him simply because he is every day in evidence, the outlook for an Empire which is, in the last resort, governed by argumentation, is neither very bright nor very reassuring.

Thus far, then, the evolution of the newspaper and the application of capital to its production have brought us. But it might be rash to add, at least in a pessimistic vein, 'and no further.' Newspaper enterprise must, like every other, be governed by public demand. Undoubtedly there is a demand for 'smartness,' above all things else in literature. That demand has revolutionised monthly magazines, and it threatens to revolutionise weekly newspapers. Within the last few years, moreover, there has been an extraordinary development of evening newspapers, not only in London but in the provinces; so much so, that prophecies are freely made that the evening newspaper will supersede its morning rival or collaborator, as the leading power in daily journalism. Be that as it may, the strength of an evening

newspaper depends in the first instance on the amount and
variety of its news, and in the second on the literary piquancy
of the comments upon that news.   If the evening newspaper
ever becomes in any formidable sense, the rival of its morning
contemporary, the latter must betake itself to some of the
weapons of the aggressor.   Already, as has been noted, the
more far-seeing conductors of newspapers are anticipating
the future, by introducing articles on special subjects by
experts more and more freely into their columns.   There will,
in time, be a demand for vigour of thought and artistic expression.   There is, no doubt, abundance of capital at the
back of the great newspapers to command these if it were
only a question of money.   But the artist and the
thinker demand something more.   They wish, in the gratifi-
cation of a natural ambition, to make a personal impression
upon the public; and in the interests of truth artistic and
other, they desire to be and to feel independent.   There is at
least a faint glimmer of hope that their wishes may be gratified.   It is a growing tendency with large daily newspapers to
become less and less the organs of parties and interests, and to
become more and more the forums for the free and full discussion of public questions.   What is to prevent the proprietors of
journals from paying able men to say what they think?   As has
been already said it is what tells that sells, and a journalist must
of necessity write in a more telling manner when he says what
he personally thinks.   It has been pointed out that there is no
sound trade reason why the men who have in newspapers to do
the procuring and arranging of news—reporters and sub-
editors—should not form a Union or Guild to secure advance
of salary or improvement in position.   Critics and other writers
are not so situated.   But is there any good reason why they
should not move in the direction of the abolition of that
anonymity, which stands in the way of their personal recognition at the hands of the general public?   It is at least possible
that, owing to the rapidity of the rate at which newspaper
development proceeds, they would be met half-way by their
employers.   At all events, there seems no hope for the
genuine inclusion of journalists among the professions, by any
other method.

SUMMARIES OF FOREIGN REVIEWS.

GERMANY.

THEOLOGISCHE STUDIEN UND KRITIKEN (No. 4, 1896).—
Dr. Hermann L. Strack, Professor of Old Testament Exegesis
and Semitic Languages at Berlin University, has the first place
in this number with a short article, in which he discusses the
literary relationship of the book of Job to the book of Proverbs,
or rather to the first nine chapters of the latter work. The
question may be called a vexed one. While scholars like Ewald
and Ed. Riehm regarded Job as of earlier date than that section
of the Proverbs, others, as Kuenen and Cheyne, assign the
priority to Proverbs. It is generally admitted that the author of
one of them was influenced by the work of the other ; and the
point of dispute is which was earliest in point of date. Professor
Strack has hitherto held and advocated the priority of Proverbs
i.-ix., but a more thorough and minute study of both writings has
led him to reverse that opinion, and he here marshals the evidence
or considerations which have brought him to this conviction as to
their relative age. Herr Pfarrer Brochert of Goeddeckenrode
raises the question as to the original significance of the Divine
Name Jahve Sabaoth. The various meanings attached to it by
exegetes are here carefully considered, that Sabaoth, *e.g.*, meant
originally the armies of Israel, and that the title was given to
God as the God of war ; (2) that Sabaoth did not refer to the
armies of Israel but to the stars, the heavenly hosts, or to the
elements and forces of Nature, and was applied to God because
He was regarded as the God, or Lord, of the Universe ; and (3)
that Sabaoth denoted the angels, those who formed the court of
the Eternal in heaven, and were the messengers of His will. All
these views are discussed here with critical minuteness, and the
arguments by which their advocates have defended their positions
are judicially weighed. Dr. Strack favours the last of these
opinions, and presents a series of weighty considerations that tell
in its favour.—Herr Pastor Köppel, of Manker, furnishes a
lengthy dissertation on ' Inspiration and Authority,' which he
sub-titles, ' Eine biblische Studie mit Streitlichtern auf die
Gegenwart.' There is, he says, a cry rising ever louder and
louder on every side of us, from the family, from the State, from
the Church, for some well-defined and indisputable authority on
which to rest these institutions. Especially emphatic is this cry
in connection with the Church. The need of an unimpeachable

authority here is imperatively felt to inspire her members, and nerve them with an unflinching courage in their offensive and defensive work. The early Christians felt they had such an authority, and it was because of their invincible faith in it that they laboured with such zeal as they manifested, and accomplished so much as they did. And what was the authority on which they rested, which they offered to others, and before which the thousands of their converts humbly bowed? It was none other than Jesus Christ Himself. Herr Köppel here takes us away back to the infancy of the Church, and asks us to observe the confidence and courage of the first Christian preachers, and see on what they based their confidence. It was not on the inspiration of the written word. It was on Christ, and on Him only. Christianity was to them not a matter of doctrine; it was to them a matter of life. That life came—could only come—through a living person. It came through Jesus the Christ. The life might be fed by doctrines, but it could not be generated by them. To all the first Christian missionaries Christ was the one subject of their preaching. He was 'im Tode der Versöhner, in Leben der Herr.' So Herr Köppel maintains that the one hope of the Christian Church to-day lies in the replacing of Jesus Christ into His true position in Christian preaching, in Christian thought, and in Christian life.—Professor Blatz follows with a short study on Luke's account of the institution of the Lord's Supper; Dr. Nestle has a couple of pages on $\tau \acute{e}\lambda\epsilon\iota os = o\iota\kappa\tau\acute{\iota}\rho\mu\omega\nu$; and Professor Hoffman closes the series with a brief 'Ethical Study' titled, 'Es geschah in guter Absicht.'—Dr. F. Haupt revi∘∘ two recent works on the Epistle of James. The one is Professor Spitta's book, and the other is Dr. Wandel's.

RUSSIA.

The seventh year of the VOPROSI, No. 2, begins with a paper on Herder's 'Philosophy of History.' The author, Mr. Gerye, begins by telling us that to understand History is to make a science out of accumulated chronological data. The idea of progress or of advancing movement in a given direction is necessary. This idea was carried into history in the eighteenth century, and it was precisely in that age that the philosophy of history became born! The idea was wrought out rationally, and because from the beginning it had a purely rationalistic tendency, the aim of History was admitted to be progress in enlightenment. But against this understanding of History a huge protest was raised, founded upon a doubt as to the advantages of enlightenment or civilization. The conception of enlightenment or civilization was opposed to the conception of happiness, the conception of which was founded on the idea of an approximation to Nature. In order to emphasize this idea of progress in History, it was necessary to take the conception of it more broadly and to comprehend it in relation to the whole of humanity, not merely to the civilized part. The youthful development of Herder, like that of Bekkaria, falls together with the celebrated idea of Rousseau. Herder became acquainted with him when a student in Königsberg, at the lectures of Kant, who was then remarkably interested in the author of ' Emile.' But the more serious and deeper culture which Herder enjoyed as compared with Rousseau, enabled him to stand high above the historical pessimism of Rousseau and lifted him above the idea of a contradiction between Nature and Culture. The poetical gift of Herder manifested itself not only in independent creation, but to a great extent in the singularly living apprehension of all that was truly poetical in Nature, as also in the productions of man. The poetical gift often controlled the scientific in Herder, filled up the gaps of his knowledge, and gave him a possibility of divining the truth. Subsequently, the author points out that Herder in his early views found himself under the influence of Leibnitz, whose Monadology was reflected in his views of nature. To the author of the Monadology, the world consisted in unending phases of individual forces according to his different degrees of knowledge, from the most confused to the most enlightened and comprehensive. Herder appropriated this view—his conception of Nature dissolved into an aggregate of living, individual forces, acting on the organism, and substantially forming this organism by means of the attraction and assimilation of the necessary particles of matter. Herder added to his view, however, another, also borrowed by him from Leibnitz, that of uninterrupted development, and then the world of living forces was transformed for him into a world created and completed by means of the progressive movement and development of these forces from the lowest to the highest forms. The historical principle was carried into Nature, and the completed structure of the world was transformed into an eternally creative process! The philosophical thought of Herder, however, did not remain at Leibnitz's point of view. In proportion, as he became acquainted with Spinoza, he gave way to the influence of that powerful spirit, and as he went more deeply into the views of Nature held by Spinoza, and his conceptions of physical processes, the philosophy of Spinoza presented itself to him as the true key to the structure of the world!—Mr. D. G. Obolenskie completes, in the second paper, his views of the 'Autonomy of Man in its progress and various stadia.' As, however, he conjoins man and the lower animals, the result is a confusion which renders his ideas on the subject very difficult of presentation. We have the following *resumé* of the 'Stadia of Autonomy,' which have been dealt with in the preceding parts of this article :—(1), The mechanical or physical ; (2), Vegetative stadia ; (3), Subjective, or physical stadia (animalia) ; (4), Such as alterohonorative ; (5), Ego-honorative ; (6), Synthetical. Each of the following includes in itself all the preceding.—The article following upon this, which is also a continuation from the preceding number, is by Prince Serge N. Teubetskoi, and is designated the 'Grounds of Idealism.' The author proceeds to notice the history of various abstract foundations of Idealism — in such terms as *being, substance, cause, action,* and *reaction;* and he maintains that the concrete idea of action and reaction presupposes the conception of cause, that the conception of essence or substance is found in the relation of action and reaction, and that the conception of the conditioned relatively supposes the idea of the unconditioned or *the being out of all relation.* But each of these conceptions, taken separately, abstractly considered, is shown to be invalid, as has already often been shown by sceptics and critics. Before all, mutual action without cause and *substantiality* indicates a logical unthinkableness which constitutes the inner contradiction of all 'phenomenism.' The conception of substance, taken in and for itself, indicates a completely abstract non-content, including in itself an inner contradiction, under which laboured all human thought, beginning with preSocratic times and reaching up to the days of Locke and Kant. The writer proceeds to deal with other of these abstract conceptions in the same negative fashion. As these general conceptions or abstract conceptions are pretty much concerned or have very much to do with the 'grounds of Idealism,' it is clear that the author's critique is of a somewhat negative or destructive character as regards 'Idealism' as a philosophical doctrine. There is, however, to be a continuation of the article.—The next article is 'On the Conception of Soul or the Data of Inner Experience.' This is a paper read by the author, M. L. Lopatin, one of the co-editors of the journal, at a meeting of the Moscow Psychological Society. It takes the form of an enquiry into the question whether beyond the phenomena of the soul there be any substance save psychical phenomena. What is the soul in itself on the ground of experience, whether as the bearer of the spiritual process or *substratum* apart from the bodily and animal life ? On this question, says the author, the metaphysician will be interested, but it is not the business of the psychologist. Perhaps there is no spiritual substance, and the only things existent are the purely psychical phenomena, as matters of occurrence following one another in order according to uniform laws, and forming by their course what we call the spirit. Perhaps we must admit the relation of these to each other in the spiritual, as follows: there are no phenomena without substance, as there is no substance without its properties, conditions, and action, the nature of substance is expressed in the laws and properties of its phenomena; and, on the contrary, it is impossible to speak of the nature of a substance that is not revealed by phenomena. In other words, substance is not *transcendent* but *immanent* in its phenomena. Every phenomena in its original activity is the very substance in the given peculiar moment of its being. The author pursues the subject through five sections in his paper. At the end he posits the unity of consciousness as bound up with the consciousness of the reality of *time* as transcendental facts of our inner experience. To these transcendental facts he adds another, the consciousness of our activity, which is closely connected with the two first, for if we in fact receive the substance of our spirits, we ought also to receive immediately their activity. Activity is the actual property of our consciousness which it is not possible to deny.—Professor Grote closes the leading papers of the journal with an obituary notice of M. N. N. Strachoff, in which he sketches the characteristics of his philosophical views. ' A man many-sided and widely cultivated, a deep and powerful thinker, a remarkable psychologue and aesthete, firm in his convictions, never fearing to grapple with prevailing views in science and literature when he thought them wrong. As a writer he was clear in style, weighty in matter, powerful in utterance and in the logical concatenation of his views. As a thinker he belonged to the left wing of the followers of Hegel, keen and accurate in logical analysis. Such was the man who has now left us after forty years of activity. Perhaps the most important of his many writings were *The World as a Whole, The Fundamental Conceptions of Psychology and Physiology*, both of which went to second editions.—The number contains the usual critical and bibliographical notices, and records of the work of the Moscow Psychological Society.

ROOSKAHYAH MYSL.—*Russian Opinion*—(April, May, June, July, and August).—Of complete tales in these five numbers we have—1, ' A House with an Attic,' a story of an artist, by A. P. Tchekoff; 2, ' Trifles of Foreign Literature,' short tales from the French, by A. A. and N. K.; 3, 'Sakhar Stepanitch,' a tale of prison life, by N. Ya. Mourinoff; 4, 'The Love of Henriques' (Lyouboff Enrikesa) by Bret Harte, translated from the English by G.; 5, 'The Black Sea Siren,' by K. M. Stanyoukovitch; 6, 'A Ravisher,' by Fr. Dana, translated from *Harper's Monthly Magazine* by K. B.; 7, 'How the People Marry,' a tale of Siberian manners, by K. Nosiloff; and 8, 'Klyatva' (an oath, a vow, a curse), by J. G. Roni, translated from the French by M. N. R.—The incomplete tales comprise —1, three further instalments and conclusion of 'A Drama behind the Scene,' by V. I. Nemirovitch-Dantchenka; 2, conclusion in two instalments of 'A Tragic Idyll,' a Monte Carlo romance by Paul Bourget, translated from the French by M. N. R.; 3, commencement in three instalments of 'Serge Shoumoff,' a domestic tale by N. I. Timkofski; 4, commencement in two instalments of 'Pasteli,' by Yana Lahdy, translated from the Polish by V. M. Lavroff (editor of *Rooskahyah Mysl*); and 5, a first moiety of 'Lyalka,' from 'Tales of Reality,' by V. I. Nemirovitch-Dautchenka.—Poetry is sparely represented by three contributions of V. Golikoff, three of K. D. Balmont, and one each of N. Nikolaeff and V. Poltavtseff. —General literature furnishes us with—1, 'An Introduction to the Study of Housing Questions,' by V. V. Svyatlofski; 2, 'On the working of Peasant Councils in the Government of Kalouga, under V. A. Artsimovitch,'* by P. N. Obninski; 3, conclusion of M. N. Remezoff's 'Judea and Rome,' pictures of the ancient world; 4, 'On Economic Materialism,' by V. A. Goltseff; 5, 'Outlines of Provincial Life,' five additional essays by I. I. Ivanyoukoff; 6, 'On the last Historical Romance of Senkevitch'—*Quo Vadis?* now complete, and published in separate form, nearly 800 pages for 1 rouble 50 kopeks (about 3s. 1½d.)—a review by M—na; 7, 'Macbeth,' by George Brandess, translated from the Danish by V. M. S.; 8, 'On the History of Contemporary Georgian Literature' of Prince Vakhtang Vakhtangovitch, by A. A. Khakhanoff; 9, 'The Swedish War of 1788-90,' from new data in the French archives, by A. Brikner; 10, 'Outlines of general Biology,' a review of 'La structure du protoplasma et les théories sur l'hérédité et les grands problèmes de la biologie générale' of Yves Delage, by M. G.; 11, 'Observations on Literature,' by O. T. B; 12, 'Contemporary Madagascar,' by M. Venyoukoff; 13, 'Popular Education in the Government of Saratoff,' by N. Th. Kazanski; 14, 'The Peasantry of Hungary until the Reforms of Joseph II.,' by E. V. Tarle; 15, 'Robert Burns,' by Ivan Ivanoff, a paper in two instalments, of especial interest

* From 1861 to 1863.

to Scotsmen; 16, 'Assyrian exorcisms, and Russian popular conjurations,' by V. Millar; 17, 'John Milton,' by M. Sh., another strong proof of the interest taken by Russians in our literary celebrities; 18, 'Traces in History of the enlightenment of Western Europe,' by V. V. Ivanofski; 19, 'The Poesy of Yve Guyau, and his world-contemplative philosophy,' by Sophia Kavos-Dekhterevoi; 20, 'Pictures of Contemporary Manners,' by K. M. Stanyoukovitch; and other papers.— 'Home Review,' deals as usual with Russian current events, but all are dwarfed by the Coronation at Moscow, a ceremony of which we could say much, the present writer being privileged to assist thereat within the sacred walls of the Cathedral.—'The Foreign Review,' by V. A. Goltseff, embraces the whole of the exciting events which have occupied the attention of the world during the last few months.—'Contemporary Art,' has abundant material with which to deal in consequence of the national fetes, and, while doing justice to the musical and theatrical efforts, finds opportunity of discussing pictorial art also.—'The Bibliographic Division,' occupying 245 pages, gives short notices of 184 works, original and translated.

ITALY.

LA NUOVA 'ANTOLOGIA (July 1).—E. Masi, reviewing Zola's *Rome*, denies that it is a work of art, though containing several powerful and beautiful passages. Zola tells some plain truths about modern Italy, though his judgments are tinged with old and new French prejudices. His intention in the whole book is decidedly benevolent, and this fact has, more than any defect in the book, brought upon the author's head the furious criticism of those French writers who cannot bear to hear of any possible fraternity between France and Italy.— Madame Jessie White Mario commences the first instalment of her personal enquiry into the penitental system and establishments of Italy, describing the prisons on the island of Favignano.—G. Monaldi in a · paper on the late Italian tragedian, Ernesto Rossi, says that since his death and the retirement of Salvini, there remains on Italian boards no worthy interpreter of Shakspeare's characters. This may be doubted, because Giovanni Emanuel still lives and acts, and Salvini's son, Gustav, a rising artist, is acquiring fame, and may some day step into his father's shoes.—O. Grandi's novel, 'The Cloud,' and Boglietti's 'Socialism in England' are continued. —C. del Lungo writes an essay on Goethe as a man of science.—(July 16)—One of the principal articles in this number is by Signor Cottran on the 'Crisis in the City of Naples,' examining the causes and results of the city's bad municipal administration, the railway and operative questions, the isolation of Naples, and its too evident neglect by the Italian government.—Professor Villari devotes a long article to the late Mrs. Salis Schwabe, whose benevolent career attained its chief success in the institute she established in Naples. Among the facts stated, it may be called to memory that Mrs. Schwabe obtained the first subscription for her purpose from Jenny Lind, to the amount of one thousand pounds. The first school under Mrs. Schwabe was founded in 1862. The present large institution is in a flourishing condition, and Professor Villari insists that it is the duty of the Italian Government and of the School Committee to faithfully carry out all the late founder's intentions and ideas.—A. Chiapelli continues his paper on 'Philosophy and Socialism,' evidently resulting from his diligent study of German authors.—In that portion of the paper on the luxury of Isabella d' Este, entitled 'Jewels and Gems,' the authors give many curious descriptions of the ornaments worn by the above lady. The article bristles with dates and quotations in quaint Italian.—P. Scoy contributes a pleasant paper on 'Voices of the Summer Night,' in which he describes the cries and noises made by many insects.—(August 1st). The most important papers in this number are by Professor Villari on the 'Straw-plaiters of Tuscany' and one on last year's situation in the East by L. Nocentini.—C. Caressai has a great deal of information to give about religious corporations; and the story, 'The Cloud,' is concluded. So also are the remarks on Italian enterprise in Africa by G. G.—(August 16th). A. Luzio begins a discussion on Giuseppe Acerbi and the 'Italian Library.'— P. Sabatier contributes a portion omitted in his 'Life of St. Francis,' which he is now able to complete from having discovered at Florence, Assisi and Rome, documents throwing light on the famous 'indulgence' called the '*Perdono di Assisi.*' —F. Raccoppi gives an account of the constitution of Utah.— A new story, 'Elena,' is commenced by the novelist who has adopted the pseudonym of 'Tristam Shandy.'—L. R. Bricchetti contributes a political article on Tripoli.—A. Paoli commences a paper on the bankruptcy of science at the time of Galileo, concluded in a following number.—F. de Simone Brouwer gives a full description of the newly excavated House of the Vettii at Pompei.—(September 1st). R. Bonfalini writes on Candia. He does not think its situation such as to break the conservative union of the European Powers, but considers the Oriental question in general full of the possibility of great surprises, capable of producing the destruction of the Ottoman Empire at any moment, and concludes his article by saying that Italy ought to be prepared to take the part imposed upon her by her interests and her cizilization.—Under the title of 'Archduke Luigi Salvatore and the fable of Majorca,' Signor Mantegazza gives an account of an interview he had at Spezia with a gentleman calling himself L. Neudorf, owner of the yacht 'Nixe,' who afterwards turned out to be the son of the last grand duke of Tuscany. Signor Mantegazza then tells the story of the Prince's Voyages.—E. Catellani contributes a thoughtful article on the institution of international law.—A. G. Barrili gives the story of A. G. Briguole and his family under the title of 'A plunge into the seventeenth century.'—A. Lauria sends an interesting article on Neapolitan songs and parodies, which in old times were most original, and which even now are produced in quantities with much of the old spirit.—(Sept. 16.) E. Masi contributes a paper on the late Signor E. Nencione, who was a veteran reviewer on the staff of this magezine, but in consequence of a two year's illness his last contribution to its pages dates as far back as 1894. He was one of the principal introducers into Italy of English literature, beginning with Browning. The famous Italian novelist, Gabriel d'Annunzio, said of him that he did not merely explain and comment on foreign poets but, himself a poet, he entered into the inmost thought and soul of the men he translated and criticized, and knew how to communicate their ideas to Italians.—V. Grossi has a long and instructive article about the Italian colony at Sao Paulo in Brazil. The chapters on the Luxury of Isabella d'Este, describe this time the furniture of palaces, etc.—'Tristam Shandy's' novel, 'Ellena,' is concluded.—Follows the second part of 'The penitentiary system in Italy.'—F. Ponetti reviews Chearim's recent studies in Shakspeare.

RASSEGNA NAZIONALE (July 1st).—G. Morando has a paper on an 'Unknown Critic' of Rosmini.—V. di Giovanni describes the old memoirs of the Monastery of S. Maria del Bosco, and the corrections of the text by Tasso.—R. Mazzei studies the social question from the spiritual point of view, inquiring whether the supernatural has any efficacy in solving the important problems of life. He concludes that in order to mitigate present evils, it will be necessary once more to take the Gospel for our codex.—R. Corniani deplores the publicity of criminal trials, which he says are a school of crime open to all comers, and most dangerous to the young, whom it is the duty of society to protect from all influences that can injure their morals.—The number closes with a paper on the Italian Conservative party, by A. d'Arzago, and one on Pierre de Nolhac's Study of Italian literature.—(July 16th.)—P. Giacosa writes on various ancient and modern facts and notions concerning poisons.—Professor De Giorgi has an interesting paper on the 'Cathedral of Nardo,' referring to recent studies and discoveries.—X.X.X. publishes a dissertation on the fundamental questions of Catholicism and Protestantism.—M. J. de J. describes the lagoons of Venice and the port of the Lido, from a practical point of view.—P. L. D. G. has much to say on religious instruction in schools. The other portions of the number are continuations of previous papers.— (August 1st.)—A pleasant story by Elvira, entitled 'Diplomacy and Love,' varies the generally grave character of this review.— It is followed by the first part of an unsigned paper on the 'Written and Spoken Word,' which is concluded in a following number.—Some translations from Juvenal, a paper by C. Rossi on the logic of abstaining from voting, on the part of the Italian clericals, and various continuations complete the number.— (August 16th.)—The deputy Signor Ricci continues his considerations on decentralization.—R. Farrini sends a paper on the Röntgen rays;—L. Biagi gives an account of the poems of G. B. Faguili, which were inspired by a long residence in Poland.— There is another instalment of the campaign of Prince Eugene, by P. Tea, and a paper by Senator Rossi on Sunday rest.— (Sept. 1st.)—The most interesting paper in this number is one on Leopardi's 'Ideal of Woman,' which the writer says he vainly sought on earth and was compelled to hope for in heaven.—The other articles are continuations, except one on Pope Gregory and the Sienese, compiled from original state documents kept in Siena.—(Sept. 16th.)—E. Cenni, in a long paper on the only remedy for the evils of the times, finds it in religion, that is to say, the Roman Catholic religion.—The paper on Pope Gregory is concluded; and that on the 'Spoken Word' continued.— Guido Fortebraccio dedicates an appreciative article to the late distinguished Italian critic, E. Nencione.

REFORMA SOCIALE (July 10).—'Socialism and Pessimism.' by A. Chiappelli.—'Culture and the Development of the Masses in Great Britain,' by Professor Geddes.—'Peasants and Pellagra,' by Professor Sitta.—'The Problem of Strikes,' by C. Garibaldi.—'The New Chain,' by Professor Contento.—'Urgent Judicial Reforms,' by L. Mortara.—'Labour Accidents before the Chamber of Deputies,' by G. Fusinato.—(July 25, August 10, 25).—'Urgent Judicial Reforms' by L. Mortara.'—'Is the Social Organism a Super-organism?' by L. de Lilienfeld.— 'The Labour Question in Portugal,' by J. T. de Medeiros.'— 'The Florence Congress,' by A. Labriola.—'An Arab Sociologist of the 14th Century,' by G. Ferrero.—'The Actual Phase of the Question of Tithes,' by Ulisse Papa.—'The Reform of Taxes on Rents,' by R. Della Volta.

LA CULTURA (July 1, 15) contain reviews of following works—Lewis's 'Some Pages of the Four Gospels,' by J. Guidi.—Bertraux's 'Question de morale et d'éducation,' by F. Tocco.—Clarette's 'The Painter Zuccano and his Residence in Piemonte,' by C. Manfrone.—Ricci's 'Dante Alighieri. An Apostolic Roman Catholic,' by B. Labanca.—Robinson's 'Euthaliana,' by J. Guidi. Park's 'Manual of Object Lessons,' by G. Fraccaroli, etc.—(Aug. 1, 15).—Labriola's 'Historic Materialism.'—Fornelli's 'Recent Attempts at University Reform in Italy.'—E. di Sant Artemo's 'The Man Napoleon.'—Adolf Schulten's 'The Roman Proprietors.'—E. Legouvé's 'Moral History of Woman.'—Dupanloup's 'The Studious Woman.'—L. Auzoletti's 'Woman in Christian Progress.'—Percy Gardner and Frank Byron Jevons's 'Manual of Greek Antiquities.'—H. A. Holden's 'The Oeconomicus of Xenophon.'—N. Vaccalluzzo's 'Galileo: Literary Man and Poet.'—U. Valcarenghi's 'The Apostles.'—'G. Flamengo's 'Contemporaneous Social Protectionism.'

GIORNALE DEGLI ECONOMISTI (August).—'Some obscure points in Demography.'—'Valuation of Taxes.'—'The Wool Production and Important Data.'

NATURA ED ARTE (August).—'Antonio Rosmini.'—'Emérita Augusta.'—'Bacon's New Atlantis.'—'The Saporetti Tunnel.'—'Sigismond Castrome.'—'Diano.'—'Monleveigine.'—'Historic Curiosities.'—'An Excursion to Mantua.'—'The Thirtieth Exhibition of Fine Arts at Naples.'—'The Epiphany at the Great St. Bernard.'—'The Eastern Drama.'—'Antonio Dal Zotto.'—'Italian Literature.'—'The Sailor.'—'Carducci's Military Poetry.'—'At the Fort of Ampola.'

ARCHIVIO STORICO DELLE PROVINCE NAPOLITANE (Year 21, Numbers 1 and 2,) contains:—'Clement VI. and Johanna I. of Naples,' by F. Cerasoli.—'The Patto di Arechi and the Terziatori,' by G. Rocioppi.—Then follow various short historic papers, by B. Capasso and other learned writers.

LA VITA ITALIANA (August).—'The Dissolution of Parliament.'—'Giuseppe Tartini.'—'Paul Bourget's Last Romance.'—'Symbolism.'—'Claudio Loreneso at Rome.'—'What is not in the "Memoirs" of Casanova.'—'Diary of the Siege of Adigiat.'—'Italians Abroad.'—'The Echo of a Mythic Night,' by G. Pascoli.—'In a Chapelle Ardente.'—'Authors' Originality.'—'Contemporaneous Crime.'—'The Tower of Silence.'

GIORNALE DANTESCO (Year 4, No. 3.)—'Dante and Franceser de Bamberino,' by G. Melodia.—'Dante and Shakspeare,' by L. Mascetta, who shows that Shakspeare not only knew Italian but loved its musical and limpid energy; that he was even acquainted with different Italian dialects, and that he freely borrowed or imitated thoughts and verses from Dante, Ariosto, Petrarch, Tasso, and others.—(No. 4).—'The Virgilian Letters and the Defence of Dante,' by A. Torre.—'Guido Guinizelli and his Poetical Reform,' by A. Bongiovanni.—'The Interpretation of Verses 8-9 in Dante's Inferno,' by R. Murari.—'Quotations from Dante in some Foreign Writings,' by P. Bellezza. The writer shows many misprints and misapprehensions in various English authors.

L'ECONOMISTA (August 28th) contains: 'The Financial Balance for 1896-97.'—The 'Memorandum' of the Sicilian Socialists.'—'Strikes in Italy in 1894.—'The Economical Condition of Crete.'—'Mining Industry at Cagliari.'—'The Finances of the United States.'—(Sept. 13) contains: 'The Sardinian Emigration.'—'Italian Agricultural Co-operation.'—'The Wine Harvest of 1895,' etc.

LA RIFORMA SOCIALE (Sept. 10) contains: 'The Hedonistic Problem in Financial Science,' by Professor Puviani.—'Social and Economical Condition of the Workmen of a Suburb of Turin,' by G. Lombroso.—'Social Finance in Italy,' by A. Geisser, etc., etc.

EMPORIUM (July) contains: 'Dante Gabriel Rossetti.'—'Max Nordau.'—'The German Army.'—'The Poets of the Caucasus.'—'Professor Laskowski and his Anatomical Preparations.'—'The Legend of the Wandering Jew.'—'The Triennial Exhibition at Turin.'—'The Tiara of Olbia.'—etc.—(August).—Continuation of 'Dante Gabriel Rossetti.'—'The great Capitals: Washington.'—'The Wandering Jew.'—'Andrée's Voyage to the North Pole.'—'Dr. Maragliana and the Tuberculosis Serum.' —German Exhibitions in 1896.—etc.

IL PENSIERO ITALIANO (July, August).—'The Slav Colonies in Greece.'—'Taine and the Origin of Psychological Criticism.' —'The Character of the Social Phenomenon and the Individuality of Socialism.'—'The Spirit of the German Language.'— 'The Sentimentalism of a Poet.'—etc.

RIVISTA ITALIANA DI FILOSOFIA—(July, August).—'The Biological Aspect of Conduct according to Spencer.'—'Normal and Morbid Facts in Psychology.'—'Organic Education.'— 'Neo-Criticism apropos of a New Edition.'—Reports, etc.

FRANCE.

REVUE DES DEUX MONDES—(July, August, September).— 'Une Vie de Savant,' which is contributed by M. George Guéroult, and is amongst the most noticeable of the articles in either of the July numbers, is a most able sketch of the career of the German scientist, Hermann von Helmholtz. Not only does the writer show a thorough knowledge of his subject, in the lucid summary which he gives of Helmholtz's labours and their results; but he displays a spirit far above all national jealousies and prejudices, in the praise which he bestows upon the man of whom he says that he is one of those who have shed the brightest light on the most obscure points of science, and who have either realised or suggested the most interesting discoveries. —In ' La Gauche Féministe et le Mariage,' M. Arvède Barine, sets forth the views on marriage held by the most advanced section of those who have taken it upon themselves to claim for women absolutely equality with men.—'The Story of an African Farm,' ' A Yellow Aster,' ' Discords,' ' Dr. Janet of Harley Street,' ' A Superfluous Woman,' ' The Woman who Did,' and, above all, ' Jude the Obscure,' being, so to speak, the text-books used by the essayist, English readers will not find anything that is very new to them in her article; it cannot, however, fail to interest them for the brilliant qualities of style, and for the critical acumen which characterize it.—' Le Gouvernement de la Défense Nationale,' of which the concluding instalment appears in the number bearing date of the 15th of July, is a vigorous criticism, if not actually an impeachment, of the men who undertook to hold out against Germany after the fall of the Second Empire. It admits their patriotism, but it censures their errors with unsparing severity, and blames them for having given the invaders the very pretext which they wanted for continuing the struggle.—' Wordsworth's works, admirably rich, ample, and profound as they are, are too often wanting in that perfection of form which—to mention only one of his countrymen—has ensured the success of Byron. Perhaps, taking him altogether, the author of *Don Juan* is less truly a poet than the author of *The Excursion;* but, it is none the less true that Byron has been translated, imitated, plagiarised, throughout the whole of Europe; whilst, on the contrary, Wordsworth's doctrine, like the form of his work, retains a purely 'exoteric' character. He tried to be, and often succeeded in being, a great artist; he tried to be more than this, and he succeeded in being a thinker. But, his poetical realism is of so peculiar a nature, that the indelible stamp of the national spirit appears in every page; and his ardent optimism, besides being a rather artificial production, is manifestly opposed to the current of the continental ideas of his time.' Such, in substance, is the judgment which M. Joseph Texte passes on Wordsworth, in the very thoughtful and well-balanced article which he devotes to him, and in which he more particularly endeavours to account for the comparative indifference which, outside his own country, has hitherto been the poet's fate. At the same time, he seems to look forward to a closer sympathy with him, and almost ventures to prophesy that the Europe of the 20th century will give him that admiration which the 19th refused him.—In continuation of the series of studies which he is devoting to Swedish fiction, M. de Heidenstam devotes an article to the novelist Strindberg. Whilst recognising and fully doing justice to his eminent qualities, he is severe upon the bitter, combative, pessimistic and captious spirit which disfigures some of his work.—The article which Th. Bentzon—or the lady who bears the masculine pseudonym—devotes to Miss Mary Wilkins, the New-England novelist, and author of ' A Humble Romance,' ' A Far Away Melody,' ' A New England Nun,' and ' Pembroke,' is less a criticism than a summary, at times, indeed, a translation. It is, however, a most interesting production, and succeeds in conveying a very vivid idea both of the writer's manner and matter.—In the same number, the first of the two for August, M. Pierre Leroy-Beaulieu, contrasts the present condition of society and social institutions in Australia, with those of the mother country. Amongst the colonials, he finds a higher standard of life, and a more thoroughly democratic spirit, and above all, a nearer approach to that equality between the sexes, which has not yet gone very far beyond the theoretical stage in the old world.—In the mid-monthly number, M. de Heidenstam concludes his Swedish studies with a cursory analysis of the works of Mme. Leffler, of Geijerstam, of Levertin, and of Vernier de Heidenstam. The article is interesting, but rather cursory, and scarcely up to the standard of the earlier instalments —a peculiarity which may, however, be as much due to the lesser importance of the novelists here dealt with as to the writer's treatment of them.—As pure literature and criticism, there is nothing in any one of the six numbers for the quarter that is more deserving of notice than the article which M. René Doumic devotes to the brothers Goncourt. Even he has seldom been more caustic and uncompromising than he here shows himself in his treatment of the leaders of the ' naturalist' school.— In the September numbers a further instalment of M. Rod's essay on ' Goethe' is the most important contribution. Of lighter articles, that by M. René Doumic on ' The Statues of

Paris,' and that by M. Talmeyr on 'The Age of Posters,' are the most readable.

REVUE CELTIQUE (Avril-Juillet, 1896).—In this double number, the first place is given to a somewhat brief article by M. L. Duvau with the title 'Les poètes de cour irlandais et scandinaves,' in which he sets forth the theory maintained by Professor Bugge in his recent 'Bidrag til den ældste Skaldedigt-nings Historie,' that the Court Poetry of the Norsemen is of Irish origin. M. Duvau accepts the theory, but fails to notice the arguments which have been advanced against it by Finnar Jonsson and others.—Dr. Whitlev Stokes continues his articles on the 'Annals of Tigernach.' He gives the corresponding dates in the Annals of Ulster, the Chronicon Scotorum, the Four Masters, the Annals of Loch Cé, and the Annals of Inisfallen. The annalists seldom agree in their dates, but the amount of error in each case is seldom of importance. Many of the qua-trains cited by Tigernach are corrupt, and the versions here given of them are only tentative. As usual, explanatory notes are added by Dr. Stokes.—M. A. le Braz follows with a number of Gwerzion Breiz-izel, and accompanies them with a version in French.—M. Chr. Sarauw discusses the verb *fil*. 'This verb *fil* (*fail, feil, fel*),' he remarks, 'is, in the older monuments, used only as what seems to be the 3rd. sg. pres. of an impersonal verb, meaning "*il y a*." Nouns and pronouns, when connected with it, are put in the accusative. The latter circumstance seems to show that *fil* did not originally mean "to be."' He concludes that the forms *fel* and *feil* and *fil* are used indiscriminately, for the indicative as well as for the conjunctive, in relative as well as in non-relative sentences, and that the word is an impera-tive from the root *Val*, 'to see.'—Under the title, 'Le Poème de Torna-Eices sur le Cimetière de Croghan,' the learned editor of the *Revue* discusses the list of names contained in these verses, attributed to Torna, surnamed Eices or the Learned. They profess to be the names of individuals who were buried in the burying-ground of Rath Croghan, in the parish of Kilkorkey, Roscommon. Some of the names M. D'Arbois de Jubainville points out are those of purely mythological individuals, such as Midir, the three kings, Mac Cuill, Mac Cecht, Mac Grene, and their wives, Erin, Fotla, and Banba. The others he believes belong to the legendary history of Ireland.—The 'Chronique' and 'Périodiques' are as usual full of news and notes interesting to Celtic students; the former noticing, among other matters, the new edition of the *Annals of Clonmacnoise* and Mr. Mac-bain's *Gaelic Dictionary*.

XXVIII. 26

REVUE PHILOSOPHIQUE (August, 1896).—Dr. Dumas concludes his studies on 'Joy and Sorrow,' dealing here with the phenomena of moral sorrow, and in conclusion defending Lange's vaso-motor theory of the emotions.—Abbé Jules Martin, in his 'Metaphysic and Science,' maintains that science is simply a development of the instinctive knowledge of the world, which is possessed even by uncivilized man. It gives a knowledge of the connection of phenomena; it can discover the *how*, but never the *why*, of things. For this we must look to metaphysic, and to talk of a scientific philosophy or psychology, or the illusions of metaphysic, is simply to multiply fine phrases.—M. Dauriac finishes his 'Studies of the Psychology of the Musician.' He draws attention to the difference between persons who simply find music pleasing and those who understand it.—Among the books noticed are Rehmke's *Psychology*, which demands a metaphysical basis for the science, in opposition to the psycho-physical school, and a French translation of Miss Martineau's *Positive Philosophy of Comte.'*—(September, 1896).—M. A. Lalande, in his 'De la Fatalité,' indicates the various forces other than the conscious will which determine human action. Man knows himself for a free and reasoning agent, but as his experience increases he becomes conscious of other forces, blind and unreasoning, which influence his actions. The writer classes these as fatality of circumstances, physiological fatality—for instance, incurable or hereditary diseases—and fatality of character. The victory rests with these—' Things will better than men, for they never for a moment cease to will with inflexible constancy'—and men must either cut the confused knot like Brutus, change their desires like Epictetus, since the world's course cannot be altered, or bear to see themselves the victims of fate, like Ivan Ilyitch.—M. J. Saury discusses blindness due to cortical lesions in the brain, and its bearing on psychology.— M. Tannery has an interesting paper on the 'Final Period of Greek Philosophy,' in the course of which he shows that the closing of the Athenian school was not due to intolerance, but formed part of a plan for reorganising the teaching of law. Justinian wished to concentrate this in the capital, Berytus, and Alexandria, and thus secure uniformity, and probably find a better use for funds which were being expended on a number of small and decaying schools.—Both numbers contain the usual reviews and summaries.

REVUE DES RELIGIONS (No. 3, 1896).—M. the Abbé A. Loisy takes up again here the subject of the Babylonian Creation Tablets, and offers some corrections on his translation of the tablets which he gave five years ago in this *Revue.* Discoveries made since then, and progress made by Assyriologists in the mastery of the language, render it necessary to revise already the translations then given, and some of the conclusions drawn from them. He deals also here with the structure and parallelism of the poem.—M. Castonnet des Fosses continues and concludes his very interesting and instructive series of papers on ' Japan, from the religious point of view.' He tells us here the story of the introduction of Christianity into Japan in the sixteenth century, and of its early successes there ; also of what led to its loss of official or Court favour, and finally to its prohibition and practical extinction. In 1549 a young Jap, who had fled his country, and landed at Goa, a Portugese settlement on the Indian coast, south of Bombay, came under Catholic influence, and was baptized. He represented to the Portugese there the advantages to be got by opening trade with Japan, and the likelihood of converting his countrymen to Christianity. An expedition was fitted out, and several priests of the Society of Jesus accompanied it. Both merchants and priests were well received. Japanese ports were opened to Portugese vessels and a ready market was found for the merchandise offered. Churches and religious houses of different kinds were speedily founded in many centres. The rapid success of the Jesuit Fathers soon gave occasion, however, for alarm on the part of the native priests, and also of the civil authorities. Their success too unduly elated the priests of the Catholic Church, and made them arrogant in their treatment of native officials and of native customs. They studiously violated the sacred laws of official etiquette. One offence of this kind given to a chief dignitary of the State formed the turning point of Christian propagandism in Japan. At once severe measures were taken against all converts to the new faith, and against all who were of Portugese blood. They were now represented as the enemies of the country, and were ordered to quit it at once, and for ever. ˙ A violent persecution was instituted against all professing the Christian Faith. All its institutions and churches were suppressed, and to profess the Faith was punishable with death. M. C. des Fosses asserts, however, that it was not altogether extinguished, but continued to be secretly held and practised by a considerable number of the population. When religious toleration was again proclaimed in 1858, and Christian missions set to work there, Christians were found, and much success consequently attended these first missions. M. C. des Fosses laments that the Japan of to-day is not so ready to welcome the Gospel as it was in the sixteenth century. ' The minds of the people are now honey-combed with free-thought.'

'The people are becoming engrossed with philosophical speculations of an agnostic or atheistic character.' Still there are
50,000 Catholics, with 92 missionaries and 22 native priests at
work there. There is an Archbishop over the Church, and there
are three bishops. There are schools, hospitals, and various other
organizations under Papal authority. There are several Protestant missions, too, chiefly of the Methodist Church. The Protestants number about 20,000 ; they are, however, sadly divided
among themselves, and do not look on each other with a friendly
eye. Our author does not regard the future prospects of the
Roman Church with a very hopeful spirit. It will be, he thinks,
at best, the Church of a small minority. But of the Protestant
missions he has just as little hope. The native religions, it is
true, are discredited ; but the Christian dogmas do not appeal to
a people so given over, as the modern Japs are, to crass materialism and worldliness. The recent military successes of the
Japanese arms have fired the populace with a fever of self-
conceit, and national vanity, which is likely to lead to a growing
dislike to the presence of foreigners, and to extravagant measures
being again taken against them.—The Abbé Loisy carries over
to these pages the continuance of a work on the Synoptic
Gospels, which has been appearing in the columns of *L'Enseign-
ment Biblique.*' It opens here with Section XLV., but no indi-
dication is given, by prefatory or footnote, of the object the
author has in view in his treatise. It would seem, judging from
what is here given of it, that he is comparing the Synoptic
Gospels with a view of constructing from them a consecutive
Life of Jesus. The Second Gospel forms for him evidently the
norm by which to judge of the others. The others are supple-
mentary to it.

REVUE DE L'HISTOIRE DES RELIGIONS (No. 3, 1896).—M.
Louis Leger has the first place here with another of his studies
in Slav Mythology. But here he takes us back, not as in former
studies to that mythology itself, but to the sources of what
knowledge of it we may yet obtain. 'Les sources de la Myth-
ologie Slav,' is the title of this paper, or series of papers; for
only the first part of the study is given here. The sources are
numerous enough, it seems; but none of them, nor all of them
together, are sufficient to enable us to form a complete idea of it.
We learn from them something of the deities worshipped, and
something of the cult that was paid them ; but beyond that, and
some of the superstitions cherished by the people as a whole, we
have little or no information. And besides, the sources while
numerous, are not always trustworthy, if indeed any are so. We

have no contemporary writings; only the debris of some monuments and sculptures, together with some snatches of songs and popular tales. These latter, however, have all passed through the hands of Christian editors filled with a holy horror of the Paganism therein revealed. M. Leger gives a list of the sources that may be exploited, and selecting the most important of them gives account of them, and summarizes the nature of their contribution to our knowledge of Slav Mythology. He divides them into classes or groups, and overtakes here two of these classes, showing what light they shed on his subject.—M. F. Macler continues and concludes his series of papers on the Apocryphal Apocalypses of Daniel. Here he takes up first the Armenian Apocalypse. Three MSS. of it are known, and each has been made the subject of minute study by Continental scholars. This Apocalypse bears the title of the Seventh Vision of Daniel, because the Armenian Book of Daniel is divided into six Visions. The character of the Apocalypse is noted, and scholars' opinions are weighed, and a translation of it follows. Next the Greek Apocalypse is dealt with in the same way by M. L. Macler. The history of the text is given, and opinion regarding it is weighed in the same critical scales, and then the translation is added. The commentary on these Apocalypses is intended chiefly to help us to apprehend their meaning and importance by placing us in a position to see them in the light of the period in which they were composed, and of the circumstances that called them into being; as also to enable us to identify the persons intended to be veiled under the historic personages whose names are given them in these writings. M. Macler, too, is careful to bring out the great value of these writings to the historian and the Bible student.—M. Maurice Zeitlin furnishes a very interesting and instructive paper on 'Les divinités féminines du Capitole.' The cult practised in the temple of the Capitol, he reminds us, was addressed principally to Jupiter Optimus Maximus. Along, however, with him were associated two female deities. These were Juno and Minerva. Together they formed a divine Triad, and stood, so to speak, at the head of the Roman pantheon. The Triad was evidently a favourite figure with the Eastern religions. We find it in high favour in India, in Persia, in Egypt, in Greece, as well as in Rome. In India we have Brahma, Siva, and Vishnu; in Persia we have Ahuramazda, Anahita, and Mithra; in Egypt we have Osiris, Isis, and Hor, at Abydos; Ammon, Mouth, and Khousou at Thebes; Ptah, Sukot, Imhotpou at Memphis; Zeus, Poseidon and Hades; and again Demeter, Dionysos and Iaccos, in Greece. The peculiarity of the Roman Triad was the association of two female divinities with one male. This combination is not explained, as in other cases, by genealogical myths. So M. Zeitlin sets himself here to find out the reason for this singular combination. He discusses first, however, the origin of the cult that was practised in the temple of the Capitol. Passing then to the divinities worshipped there, he reminds us that neither Jupiter nor Juno are proper or personal names. The names are common nouns denoting merely god and goddess. Juno = Juvino, the feminine of Jovis. What denotes her personality is the epithet Lucina, or Quiritis, or Lanuvina, or Coelestis. These are all different Junos, different persons, different goddesses. It was the place where they were worshipped that gave them their distinctive character. In the Roman religion, as contra-distinguished from the Greek, the female deities were peculiarly the object of worship on the part of the women, while the male were paid homage to by the men. As Jupiter was the protector of the latter, so Juno was the protector of the former. And she came gradually to be the representative of all the divine personages in the female pantheon. Minerva represented the Etruscan, or foreign, elements in the State, and was their protector, as Juno was that of the purely Roman, or native element. Combined, the three were the guardians of the whole populace, and the recipients of the State worship, in the State temple, *par excellence*, the Capitol.

REVUE DE L'HISTOIRE DES RELIGIONS (No. 4, 1896).—M. A. Foucher, the head of a scientific mission to India, has sent recently to the Academie des Inscriptions et Belles Lettres squeezes and photographs of the Chinese inscriptions that were discovered some years ago in the Buddhist temple at Buddha-Gaya. Two or three of them have occupied the attention of Chinese scholars, and translations of them have been offered, which, however, have been only tentative for the most part, as the decipherment has been extremely difficult owing to the smallness and faultiness of the texts or inscriptions themselves. These new squeezes and photographs have induced M. Chavannes to venture, in co-operation with M. Foucher, a new examination and translation of them, and he gives us here the results of his patient and learned labours.—M. L. Knappert follows with an article on Christianity and Paganism in the ecclesiastical history of the Venerable Bede, 'Le Christianisme et le Paganisme dans l'Histoire ecclésiastique de Bède le Vénérable.' He first calls attention to the caution necessary to be observed in the study of the writers to whom we owe what knowledge is now possible of the Celtic and Teutonic Paganism. These writers were either Christian missionaries or converts from Paganism. In the eyes of the former, the beliefs and practices of the people to whom they preached the Gospel were all inventions of the Evil One, and were not worthy of notice. The converts from Paganism were not one whit behind their spiritual fathers in their abhorrence of their old faiths and rites. It is only incidentally, therefore, that they ever mention any details regarding them, and their accounts of them are coloured by their scorn for and loathing of them. They could not describe without exaggerating. With their ideas of the pit from which they had been mercifully delivered, it was not possible for them to be just in their allusions to it, or accurate in their descriptions of it. M. Chavannes, has devoted, nevertheless, a very considerable amount of time and patience to the study of these works, and some of the fruits of his researches have appeared from time to time in the pages of the *Theologish Tijdschrift.* Here he takes up Bede's *Historia Ecclesiastica Gentis Anglorum,* and endeavours to bring out what light it sheds on the Paganism of Bede's compatriots and contemporaries, and on the nature of the Christianity that was taught to them. In doing this, he leaves Bede's work to speak as much as possible for itself.—The book reviews are numerous in both these numbers, as are also the shorter notices of less important works.—The summaries of periodicals and the ' Chronique ' are comprehensive and valuable.

REVUE DES ETUDES JUIVES (No. 1, 1896).—In the number of this *Revue,* which was issued last year, shortly after the death of M. Joseph Derenbourg, we were promised a fuller account than was then given of the life and literary work of that distinguished and venerable scholar. He died on July 29, at the ripe age of 84. In the number referred to there was but a brief announcement of his death, and an expression of the regret with which the announcement of his loss was made, and would be received by all who knew him or were acquainted with his writings. This was followed by some of the addresses which were delivered at the grave, on the occasion of his funeral, by representatives of several learned societies of which he had been a revered member. The promise made at that time M. W. Bacher here worthily fulfils. He outlines for us in this number the history of the man, the scholar, and the writer. M. Derenbourg's life was seemingly an uneventful one, so far as its scenic side was concerned. He took little or no part in the public affairs of his time. He was from first to last a student. His passion was to learn, and his life's work to impart to others the ripest and surest fruits of his researches. He was constantly absorbed in a variety of literary problems that were likely to suggest themselves only to a scholar whose training and tastes led him into regions visited but by a few rare spirits now and then.   He was an Arabic scholar of the first rank, was deeply versed in Talmudic lore, and every branch of Jewish literature had for him an irresistible attraction.   In the course of his long and fruitful life he rescued from the unmerited oblivion into which they were falling the works of several Arabic writers, patiently copying the texts from decaying MSS., collating them, wherever they were to be found, with a care that may be described as loving, and furnishing translations of those he thought likely to prove helpful to a wider circle than that familiar with the original tongue.   M. Bacher details these labours, following them in chronological order, interweaving here and there the incidents as they occurred of Derenbourg's social and literary career.   M. Bacher speaks in glowing terms of his friend's high talents, of his lofty aims, of his genial disposition, unassuming manners, and patient industry, and of the sterling and lasting value of his work.—M. S. Krauss, in 'Encore un mot sur la fête de Hanoucca,' returns to the controversy between him and M. Israel Levi as to the period in which the part which women take in the celebration of the feast took its origin.—M. Krauss dates it from the institution of the feast itself, after the death of Antiochus Epiphanes.   M. Levi contends for a much later date, viz., the Roman period.   M. Levi contends that there is no trustworthy evidence that the Syrians or Greeks under Antiochus ever sought to impose on Jewish women the *jus primæ noctis;* it was under the Roman rule that that form of persecution took its rise.   In a note appended to M. Krauss's article here by M. Levi, the latter refuses to continue the controversy, saying he has submitted the evidence for his view of the matter, and he now leaves the reader to decide for himself as to the point in dispute.—M. L. Bank continues his ' Etudes Talmudiques,' discussing here 'une Agada provenant de l'entourage du Resch Galoute Houna bar Nathan.'—M. S. Mendelssohn seeks to define the exact meaning of 'scheel,' 'scheelta,' and ' scheeltot,' in Talmudic writers.—M. I. Levi furnishes an article entitled ' Clement VII. et les Juifs du Comtat Venaissin.'   The policy of the Popes, he says, has never with respect to the Jews been consistent.   Now they have favoured them, and now harrassed them.   This has been the case not only with different Popes, but sometimes with one and the same Pope.   M. Levi produces the evidence that this was the case under the rule of Clement VII.—M. M. Kayserling briefly describes the Jewish community in Amsterdam, which was formed chiefly of Marranes of Spain and Portugal, and prints, as an appendix, a little work by one of them, a literary history, or rather, 'a history of Jewish literature,' which he regards as of considerable merit.—M. A. Danon gives a 'Recueil de romances judée-espagnoles chantées en Turquie.'—Of the minor articles we may note M. Jastrow's 'Les Juifs et les Jeux Olympiques.'—In the 'Bibliographie' there is a lengthy notice of Mr. A. Neubauer's recent work, *Anecdota Oxoniensis: Mediæval Jewish Chronicles and Chronological Notes, edited from Printed Books and Manuscripts.*

REVUE DES ETUDES JUIVES (No. 2, 1896).—'Les dix-huit Bénédictions et les Psaumes de Salomon,' is the subject of the first article here. It is from the pen of M. Israel Levi. The eighteen Benedictions, or the 'Schemoné-Esré,' have naturally excited the interest, and exercised the wit of many Jewish scholars. Their origin and history are veiled in some obscurity, and several attempts have been made to lift the veil. That they were not all written at one time, or by one author, is admitted by all who have studied them. But as to when they were composed and under what circumstances, there is little agreement. M. Levi is of opinion that the so called Psalms of Solomon shed considerable light on the problem. Though we have these Psalms only in Greek there is no doubt that they were written first in the Hebrew. Their special value lies in this, that they are dated with a precision which leaves nothing to be desired, and are characterised by a unity of spirit which is perfect. They form, therefore, one of the most important documents we have for getting at the ideas which were cherished by the Jews on religious matters in the century prior to the Christian era. The spirit which breathes through them is that of the Pharasaic party of that century, and they furnish a complete commentary on the Schemoné-Esré. The very same ideas are reflected in both, the same tendencies are manifest, and the same state of mind is seen throughout them. The resemblance enters even into their phraseology, so much so that each paragraph of the Schemoné-Esré has its pendent and parallel in these Psalms. M. Levi shows this by a wealth of quotations, and seems to prove his point completely. The Psalms and the Benedictions belong to that century;—the majority of the Benedictions preceding the Psalms, but both composed by the same party, reflecting the same thoughts, and breathing the same hopes and desires.—M. A. Buchler gives the first instalment of a paper in which he proposes to examine the sources from which Josephus drew the data of Bks. XII. and XIII. of his Antiquities. That he made use of the first Book of the Maccabees is admitted by everybody, and by most scholars that he was dependent for many of his statements on one or more non-Jewish works. But what was it, or what were they? MM. Bloch and Nussbaum regard his narratives concerning Syria as having been inspired by Posidonius of Apamea, and by Polybius, whose work Posidonius continued. Destinon maintains that Josephus did not make use of their works directly, but found their histories incorporated in a Jewihs work, and that he merely added some details, not very accurate for the most part, and easily distinguished from the rest. M. Buchler proceeds to examine minutely the incidents narrated by Josephus *seriatim* in the hope of showing both how the history has been composed, and what sources were made use of by Josephus.—M. D. Gaubart enters into an elaborate examination of the question of the authorship of the Tractate, ' Kelim.'—M. D. Kaufmann furnishes a historical paper, of considerable interest and showing much minute research, entitled ' Contributions à l'histoire des Juifs de Corfou.'—M. Jules Bauer writes on ' Les Juifs de la principauté d'Orange,' and gives as an appendix the documents from which he has taken his information.—M. G. A. Kohut contributes an article on ' Les victimes de l'Inquisition á Lisbonne á la fin du XVIIe siècle ; ' and M. A. Danon continues his ' Recueil de romances judéo-espagnoles chantées en Turquie.'

REVUE SEMITIQUE D'EPIGRAPHIE ET D'HISTOIRE ANCIENNE (No. 3, 1896.)—The section of Genesis covered by M. Halevy in this number is from chapter xxxii. 3 to xxxvii. 1. It embraces the history of Jacob from his leaving Mount Gilead on to the death of his father Isaac at Hebron, and the *Toledoth*, or Generations, of Esau, and the list of kings of Edom. An outline summary of the story contained in the section is first given, and then the Hebrew text is examined, and some of the details are commented on, as they seem to demand it. No emendations of the text are seemingly here called for, or offered, that are of much importance. But every point is nevertheless carefully noticed. The masculine form of the numeral *one, e.g.,* in xxxii. 8—one company—is recommended, as it is in the Samaritan Version, because *machaneh*, ' camp,' is in reality masculine. *Vav* is substitued for *yod* in Peniel, for reasons given, and so becomes Penuel. Horites, in the text where it appears, it is maintained, does not mean, as is generally held, ' dwellers in caves,' ' Troglodytes, but ' free-men.' Its root, M. Halevy asserts, is not *chur*, ' hollow,' but *chor*, ' white,' ' noble.' Again, the verb in xxxiii. 15, ' he kissed him,' which so perplexed some of the rabbins of old, M. Halevy regards as correct, but he would place it after ' embraced him.' The exegetical notes are often interesting. Why, *e.g.,* did the angel at Penuel refuse to give his name to

Jacob? M. Halevy answers that, previous to the Greek Period the angels, in Israelitic belief, had no names. They were regarded as only the temporary agents of Jahvé. During the Greek Period, however, they came to be looked upon as old Pagan deities relegated to their proper places, and a kind of worship was paid to them. They then came to bear personal names. Daniel gives us the names of two. The book of Enoch names several. The Sadducees alone retained the old Biblical idea as to the ephemeral and anonymous nature of angels. There are other points here touched on which will greatly interest all readers of these notes. The chief interest, however, of these papers centres in M. Halevy's defence of the unity of the text of Genesis; that it is not a conglomerate, as critics of the Modern School maintain, but is essentially the work of one author, mistakes of copyists and the alterations of would be wise editors being admitted. Dillmann's arguments in favour of the attribution of this and that verse, or clause, or section, to this or that writer, are those which M. Halevy here chiefly examines and sets himself to refute. His explanations of the difficulties which have perplexed the Modern Critics are always at least plausible, and deserve, as they are sure to receive, the respectful attention of those interested in these questions. The Psalms dealt with in the second part of these 'Recherches Bibliques' are Psalms lviii. to lxv., inclusive. The text of each is minutely examined, and corrections suggested where they are thought to be necessary. All the difficulties that present themselves to the scholarly reader are discussed, and what light can be thrown on them by our improved acquaintance with the Semitic tongues and Semitic customs, etc., is given. A new translation of each Psalm is furnished according to the improved text offered by our author. M. Halevy continues next his transcription and translation of the cuneiform text, the first part of which was given in last number of this *Revue.* It is accompanied with a series of very valuable notes, chiefly philological. Dr. J. B. Chabot furnishes a series of 'notes on some points in connection with the history of Syriac literature.' M. Halevy gives us another learned study on 'Traces of Indian and Parsi influence in Abyssinia.'—M. E. Blochet deals with the 'Arabisation of Persian Words.'—M. J. Perruchon continues his 'Notes pour l'histoire d'Ethiopie.'—M. Halevy extracts from the *Journal officiel de la République française* of March 25. M. Mispoulet's *compte rendu* of M. Clermont Ganneau's paper read before the Academie des Inscriptions, on March 13, and makes some observations on it. They are also of a philological nature. He furnishes, too, a short study, titled 'Israel dans une inscription égyptienne,' and the 'Bibliographie.'

REVUE PHILOSOPHIQUE (October, 1896).—M. Egger resumes his consideration of the 'Self of the Dying,' which he first discussed in the January number. He examines several criticisms and communications which he has received since then. The principal conclusion at which he arrives is that a conviction that death is at hand is essential to evoke the rapid survey of events observed in cases of drowning, etc., or the succinct and characteristic 'last words' recorded in so many instances.—M. H. Lachelier treats of the 'Logical Formula of Inductive Reasoning.' Induction designates 'a complex aggregate of processes by which the scientist on the one hand discovers the hypothetical causal laws to which he endeavours to reduce empirical laws, and on the other verifies the consequences which logically result from these hypothetical laws. But none of these processes can constitute a new form of reasoning. Scientific certainty, in fine, is always obtained deductively.'—Professor Lombroso in ' The Instinct of Preservation in Children,' shows how this instinct dominates their whole physical, mental, and moral activity. All their peculiarities are due to the desire to avoid effort.—The remaining pages are occupied with a very full account of the International Psychological Congress, and book-reviews.

SPAIN.

LA ESPAÑA MODERNA (August, September, and October, 1896).—In the first of these numbers Juan Ochoa begins a new story entitled ' Los Señores de Hermida.' It is continued in the number for September, and ends in the October number.— The Marquess de Valmai contributes two interesting papers under the title ' An unknown Historical Painter.' The artist referred to was Don José de Méndez, who devoted himself to his art and cared little for popular fame. The articles contain a list, though incomplete of his works. Interspersed through the articles is a number of interesting remarks respecting the art of the present, and the estimation in which it is held by the public.—Among· the most attractive contents of these numbers are three papers contributed by ' An Old Soldier,' in which he relates his experiences in war. His adventures were not always pleasant, and he has many particulars to give respecting the Spanish wars on the African continent and elsewhere, and as to the way in which Spanish armies, and some other matters in Spain, are managed.—José Echegaray begins a story in the August number with the title ' Recuerdos.'—The translation of Wolf's work on the Poetry of the Spanish Romances is continued in all the numbers.—The ' Crónica Internacional ' in the September number is contributed

by E. Castelar, who takes for his text Li Hung Chang's visit to
Europe, and discourses pleasantly about the Chinese and their
ways.—The same writer contributes the Crónica to the October
number, and deals in it with a variety of topics; among others,
with the Czar's visit to Paris, closure in the British Parliament,
recent land legislation for Ireland, the Armenian question, and
' Sir Balfour,' under which designation we recognize the present
leader of the House of Commons, to whom Senor Castellar pays
several high compliments.—The last number contains an interesting and informing article from the pen of Ernesto López on
' Matrimony in the Middle Class.'—As usual there are numerous
translations.

HOLLAND.

DE GIDS.—A large space of the August and September
numbers is occupied by a translation of George Meredith's
Amazing Marriage, the intention being to introduce this novelist who is little known by the Dutch public.—(Aug.)—' From
Canton,' an impressionist sketch, by Henri Borel, portrays
scenes in that city and on its river.—An admirable analysis of
the Mimes of Herodas, accompanied by translations of several
of them, the Schoolmaster; Women in the temple of Asklepios;
The two female Friends; The Shoemaker, is the work of N. J.
Singels, who also traces the origin and history of this species
of composition.—' A Freethinker of the Sixteenth Century,' by
Max Rooses, gives a fascinating account of the life of Christoffel
Plantijn, a printer. A few years ago in the Leiden Library
Drs. Nippold and Tiele discovered records about Plantijn in
the manuscript chronicles of the ' Family of Love,' a small
sect of the time. From these it appeared that Plantijn, although commissioned by Philip II. to bring out the famous
Polyglot Bible, and though his trade was chiefly printing
missals and breviaries for the Catholic Church, yet secretly belonged to an Anabaptist sect, and was in close and constant
correspondence with Hendrik Niclaes, and printed for him *The
Mirror of Righteousness*, and other smaller works. This was
before 1555. Plantijn stood high in favour with such diverse
people as William of Orange, the Archduke Matthias, Alençon
and Philip II. While ostensibly he was, till his death, in 1589,
the great Catholic printer favoured by the Pope and King, and
ever increasing his large business, his inner life was entirely
out of sympathy with his public repute. His close friend was
Barrefelt, a sort of anarchist of a peaceful and mystic type,
only a working man, the untaught author of nebulous dreams,
and head of a sect which forbade all formal worship, and
sought in spirituality and self-denial union with God. Plantijn,

with his clear head and sound understanding combined, strangely enough, a tendency to mysticism, and was so devoted to Barrefelt that he translated and at the same time improved his books and printed them. Much to the amazement of his Catholic friends he migrated in 1583 to Leiden and became printer to that heretical university, but again when Parma conquered Antwerp he returned to his business there and died apparently a good Catholic. All along he kept his inner life and thought free, and was on the side of tolerance pursuing his way to use his own watchword 'Labore et constantia.' Though very rich he lived simply, and in the best sense religiously, for there is nothing in his life or writings that shows him in the least demoralised by the strange contradiction of his inner and outward life. On the contrary in all respects, except this, which he must in some way have justified to himself, his life was a pattern of humanity, charity, and integrity.—Another strange inner life, but of modern date, is unfolded in G. A. E. Cort's paper on the Norwegian novelist 'Arne Garborg,' whose life and works are reviewed. Rejecting every optimistic system he is a pessimist who fully recognises that human life thoroughly protests against pessimism, so that he is almost persuaded to accept the optimist view of life if he could honestly do so. His strangely weird and vivid pictures of humble life are illustrated by quotations.—(September)— 'Egidius and the Stranger,' by W. G. van Nonhuys, is a sort of mystic dialogue full of the poetry of life and death, the stars and moonlight, but rather wanting in perspicuousness.— An article 'Netherland and the Convention of Bern' endeavours to rouse Dutch authors, publishers, and booksellers to take steps along with other countries for protecting their own interests which it seems they have been backward in doing.—'The Hongi-Expeditions' treats of various expeditions to the Moluccas from early times onwards.—(October)—Marcellus Emants gives in 'A Day in Benares' a vivid and lifelike picture of that teeming city, as well as some instructive side glances at its religious life.—'Perfide Albion' consists of notes of English character by L. Simon, a resident in our country. The English he divides into two types constantly acting and reacting on each other. The one is characterised by devotion to physical force, independence, manifested in the uncultivated as hardness and cruelty, hence the enormous number of convictions for wife-beating, cruelty to children, etc. In the cultivated this type shows itself in self-sufficiency, self-esteem, hence their fitness to go out into the world as adventurers caring for nobody's interests but their own. This too is the High Church aristocratic type. The other type is the nervous, sentimental, easily and lightly moved, but, when moved, fanatical, as on such subjects as slavery, drink traffic, vivisection, but this type has also its good side manifested in extreme self-sacrifice. In religion the Nonconformists and wilder sects like the Salvation Army are examples. In art, England, so long far behind the continental nations, has only reached mediocrity. Its best productions are to be found in the architecture of country mansions and in black and white. Art and music are taken up passionately, but only as a hobby or fashion, and in real merit the Scotch and Irish are first. Democracy is not in England hostile to aristocracy; it is its stay, hence the phenomenon of democratic conservatism. The occurrences in South Africa are taken up to show how Imperial England is decadent and may possibly soon go to pieces. —'Lodewyk van Deyssel' and his collected essays and other pieces forms the subject of a lightly written and amusing article by J. M. Acket. It is as a *litterateur* and critic that Van Deyssel is famous—a sort of Dutch Carlyle, sardonic, a creator of phrases, and with a prophetic vein piercing to the heart of things disregarding conventionalities, and a devoted admirer of Zola.—Next follows 'John Burns,' socialist and organiser of unskilled labour, by Tex.—A charmingly written paper by H. Pyttersen Iz, 'A Queen,' gives the story of Désireé Clary, wife of Bernadotte, King of Sweden.—'The Ideas of Karl Lamprecht' is a review not too favourable of that Leipzig professor's views on how to write history and on how he has written it in his *History of Germany* so far as it goes.

GREECE.

JOURNAL OF THE HISTORICAL AND ETHNOLOGICAL SOCIETY OF GREECE (Vol. V., Pt. 17, June, 1896).—The k. Sp. P. Lambros publishes a number of MSS. The first is a sixteenth century version of Aesop by George Aitôlos from an Athos MS., interesting both for the study of the fables, and of the development of the language.—The next is the didactic poem of Alexios Komnenos (Spaneas), of which other MSS. have been published. One of the present versions, from the Docheiarian Monastery on Athos, is given in a corrected form, the other, a fragment from the Iberian Monastery is so full of errors that it has been thought worth while to give it as it stands. The k. Lambros also publishes a lease of the fourteenth century from a Paris MS. Symeon, a monk of the Monastery of St. Kontostephanos, under Monemvasia, lets a parcel of ground to two farmers for three years, which they are to occupy and crop for that time. At harvest time they are to retain two-thirds of the produce, and pay the other to the monastery. The monastery is to give them four monzouria of corn and six measures of wine for the first, but not for the remaining years, except in the event of war, in which case it will receive one-half of the produce.—The k. Dassarêtos discusses the situation of Koritsa, which he assignes to Epeiros and not to Macedonia as some recent geographers have done.

DENMARK.

YEAR-BOOK FOR OLD NORTHERN ARCHÆOLOGY AND HISTORY (Vol. XI., Part 2, 1896).—In this part are two articles, both of some historical value. The first, by Kr. Kaalund, of the Copenhagen University Library, deals with the authorship of the *Profectio Danorum in terram sanctam*, 'A history of a Danish Crusade in the year 1191-92.' The work existed only in one MS., found at Lübeck by J. Kirchmann about 1620, and now lost. The author's name is not given, but Dr. Kaalund makes out a good case for assigning it to the monk Theodoric, author of the *Historia Norvegiæ*. The two treatises were found in the same MS. (where they were appended to a copy of Josephus), both of them display an acquaintance with Norse rather than with Danish forms of words and names, and the style in the two works has many points of resemblance, so that a common authorship is a very natural supposition.—The article by P. Lauridsen on 'Old Danish Villages,' is an extremely suggestive study of a somewhat difficult subject. The old village life in Denmark was broken up about a century ago, and the accounts preserved of its original forms are not at all satisfactory. The author deals only with the older villages, which are distinguished from later formations by their endings (inge, by, sted, etc., over against rup, röd, bolt, etc.) Among these older settlements he distinguishes three classes, the closed or round village, the long village, and the single-line village, whose form is determined by its situation. A number of plans, showing these different types, make the author's views very clear and convincing. Of especial interest is his treatment of the common pasture, and his explanation of the mysterious 'forta,' spoken of in old Swedish and Danish law. To the student of agrarian history and economics the whole article ought to be very interesting and instructive.

SWITZERLAND.

BIBLIOTHÈQUE UNIVERSELLE ET REVUE SUISSE (July, August, September).—Merely mentioning M. Numa Droz's 'Geneva and Zurich,' which, being a comparison between the Swiss exhibitions of 1883 and of 1896, is not of very general interest, we come to a contribution which will appeal to most readers. It is entitled 'Under the Walls of Plevna,' and is based on the letters of Sergius Botkine, who accompanied Alexander II. as his private physician. These letters go far towards explaining how it happened that the Russians were kept in check for some six months by a comparatively insignificant fortress. There were in the Russian army too many people who thought of nothing but turning the war to their own pecuniary profit. In the Turco-Russian campaign corruption reached even more fearful proportions than during the Crimean War; and to that must be ascribed the failure of the Russian army the last time it faced an adversary whom the Powers of Europe are too accustomed to look upon as of no account.—The 'Irish Idylls' of Miss Jane Barlow are reviewed and summarised in an interesting article by M. Aug. Glardon. He describes the author as being an exponent of 'photographic realism.' She writes, he says, with absolute simplicity, noting, by preference those slight and insignificant details which, when taken together, convey the impression of reality. The art of contrasts, of antitheses, of vigorous contrasts between light and shade, in short, the art of 'effects,' is unknown to her. All conventionality has disappeared to give place to a conscientious search after truth.—In both the July and the August numbers M. Maurice Muret gives an account of Slatin Pasha's captivity with the Mahdi. The article is most interesting, but, being based on Slatin's own work, 'Fire and Sword in the Soudan,' cannot, of course, lay claim to originality.—'The Causes of a Great War,' that is, of the Franco-German War, are set forth by M. Edmond Rossier in the numbers for August and September. In his opinion, the events which took place in July, 1870, did not *cause* the war, but were only the *occasion* of it. The war, he says, was the result of the whole political evolution of Prussia and of France since 1860, and even prior to that date. To justify this assertion he enters into a detailed exposition of the condition of both countries prior to the fateful candidature of Prince Leopold of Hohenzollern.—The impotency of the European powers, which M. Ed. Talichet discusses, refers, it scarcely needs to be said, to their Armenian policy. The author not only censures them vigorously, but also shows them how they may bring the Sultan to his senses. That is, by confiscating Crete at once, and threatening to lay hands on further slices of territory whenever there is a renewal of atrocities.—The September number opens with an article in which M. Michel Delines begins an account of the three great reforms introduced by the Emperor Alexander II. of Russia—the emancipation of the serfs, the abolition of corporal

404 *Summaries of Foreign Reviews.*

punishment, and the institution of the jury.—'Cleg Kelly,' by S. R. Crockett, supplies M. Glardon with material for a very readable essay, of which the chief point is a comparison between the Scottish Arab and Victor Hugo's Gavroche—an honour of which some may think the Edinburgh urchin was scarcely worthy.

ICELAND.

EIMREIDIN (Vol. II., 1896).—The success of this new periodical has induced the editor to issue three parts of it this year in place of two, and all three are quite up to the level of the earlier ones. The contents are very varied, and include a number of interesting items of prose and verse. Among the more serious articles may be mentioned the long dissertation by the editor, Dr. Valtýr Gudmundsson, on the political relations of Iceland and Denmark; 'The old Parliament in the Isle of Man,' and 'Bismarck on Iceland,' by Jón Stefánson—'Life in Copenhagen' (continued), by Jón Jónsson, giving glimpses of the University and the Elections.—'Peat and Coal' (continued), by Hegli Pjetursson.—'Potato Disease,' by Hegli Jónsson.—'Fowling in the Vestmannaeyar' (with an illustration), by Thorstein Jónsson,—and 'Goethe and Schiller,' by Steingrím Thorsteinsson. Even the new photography is described and illustrated in a short article. In light literature are two original stories, 'Sigrun,' by Gudmund Fridjónsson, a pathetic tale of servant life in Iceland, and 'The Bridge,' by Einar Hjörleifsson, a well written story, with a moral attached to it, viz., the necessity for increasing the means of communication in the country.—'Old Gunnhild,' is a translation from L. Dilling by the editor.—A good part of the poetry in the volume consists of translations, but there are also original verses by Steingrim Thorsteinsson and Valdimar Briem, and the continuation of a longer poem (a love-tale) by Thorstein Erlingsson.—The translations from the Norse poets Wergeland and Welhaven, by Matthias Jochumsson, are executed with his usual skill, and no less successful are the renderings of Goethe's 'Bride of Córinth' and 'Elf-king,' by Steingrim Thorsteinsson. *Eimreidin* is evidently supplying a felt want among the reading public of Iceland, and is a remarkable product for so small a nation.

AMERICA.

THE AMERICAN HISTORICAL REVIEW (July.)—Cast on the lines of the 'English Historical,' this review is making a place for itself, and contributing, so far excellently, to the elucidation of problems connected with the History of the United States of

America. Under the title ' Hotman and the " Franco-Gallia," '
W. H. M. Baird contributes an article bearing on the Huguenot
movement in France. The particular point to which attention
is called is the attitude of the French Protestants to the doctrine
of passive obedience, with special reference to the opinions of
the jurist, F. Hotman, as set forth in his work, *Franco-Gallia.*
Mr. Baird, it need hardly be said, differs widely in his estimate
of that work from Viceron, by whom it was condemned as unworthy of a French jurisconsult.—Mr. Melville M. Bigelow continues his valuable and interesting articles on the Bohun wills.—
Over the signature of Mr. C. F. Adams we have a graphic
description of the Long Island campaign in 1776, a campaign in
which, ' in spite of what historians have since asserted,' remarks
the author, Washington's ' prestige at the time was greatly diminished, and his control of the situation imperilled.'—In an article
on President Witherspoon Mr. M. Coit Tyler gives a biographical sketch of this great Scotsman who, landing in America after
he had passed middle-life, managed to raise himself to the President's chair.—The last article in the number is by Mr. J. S.
Murdock on the ' First National Nominating Convention.'—
Under the section of Documents are the draft of an address of
the Continental Congress to the people of the United States,
1776; papers connected with the surrender of Fort Charlotte,
Mobile, 1780; and a letter of John Page to Madison, 1801.—
Among the books reviewed are Mahaffy's *Empire of the
Ptolemies,* Harrisse's *John and Sebastian Cabot,* Seeley's *Growth
of British Policy,* Sayce's *Egypt of the Hebrews and Herodotus,*
and the third volume of Wylie's *England under Henry IV.*

QUARTERLY JOURNAL OF ECONOMICS.—In the July number
of this journal, which issues from the Harvard University, is a
notable article by Mr. W. J. Ashley, the Professor of Economics there, and well known on this side of the Atlantic through
his two admirable volumes on *Economic History and Theory.*
The article we refer to is on ' The Beginnings of Town Life
in the Middle Ages.' What mediæval town life was when
fully developed, say in the fifteenth century, is, as the author
observes, very evident; but the two questions, whence did
towns acquire their characteristic constitutions and their characteristic population? are, as he further observes, among the
most obscure and perplexing. Professor Ashley has no new
theory of his own to propound; his aim in the article is simply
expository. Passing by the older literature, he takes the
theories which have been propounded during the present
decade by M. Jacques Flach in the section ' La Commune
Urbaine' in his *Origines de l'Ancienne France;* by Dr. Willi

Varger in his three articles entitled 'Zur Entstehung der deutschen Stadtverfassung.' contributed to Conrad's *Jahrbücher* in
1893-94-95 ; by M. H. Pirenne in three articles which appeared
in the *Revue Historique*, 1893 and 1895, on 'L'Origine des
Constitutions Urbaines ; ' and by Dr. F. Keutgen in his ' Unter-
suchungen über den Ursprung der deutschen Stadtverfassung.'
These theories Professor Ashley analyses in a most lucid and
attractive way, pointing out in passing their differences, and
interspersing notes of criticism. Speaking of von Below, he
observes that it is one of his chief services 'that he has
impressed upon us the necessity of separating the question of
the forces which led to constitutional change—one often of
economic history—from the question of the structure and
derivation of the constitutional forms themselves, which is one
of legal or constitutional history.' 'But,' he adds, 'we must
go further and distinguish provisionally between the *town*
(Stadt, ville) as a legal conception and the *town* as an economic
conception. Usually the two meet. What was economically
a town was, as a rule, legally (or constitutionally) a town. But
it was not necessarily nor universally so. And the discussion
on both issues really turns, in large measure, on a question of
definition. What shall we agree to call a 'town' economically?
what constitutionally? Until we have come to some common
understanding on these points, there is always the danger of
arguing in a circle.'

CONTEMPORARY LITERATURE.

Studies Subsidiary to the Works of Bishop Butler. By the Right Hon. W. E. GLADSTONE. Oxford: At the Clarendon Press. 1896.

This volume of Essays, some of which have, in part, seen the light before, was necessary in order to complete the presentation of Mr. Gladstone's Studies on Bishop Butler and his works. It is questionable whether the writings of any other English theological author have ever been subjected to so careful a scrutiny. Certainly those of Bishop Butler, notwithstanding the number and ability of his editors, have never before been so acutely analysed or expounded or defended with such elaborate care or with such manifest skill. Mr. Gladstone's edition of the *Analogy* and Sermons may almost be called definitive and will doubtless hold its own as the standard edition for many a day, while his Essays Subsidiary are likely to take a permanent place in the theological literature of the country, and to become an abiding source of assistance to all serious students of Butler and to all who wish to appreciate to the full the value of his work. The 'Studies' are divided into two classes, entitled respectively 'Butler' and 'Subsidiary.' Among the first we have essays on Butler's method, on his Censors, on his mental qualities, on various points of his positive teaching, and on his theology, celebrity and influence. The essays under the second division are mainly taken up with discussions in connection with the doctrine of the life hereafter. Others of them are devoted to discussions on Necessity or Determinism, Theology, Miracles and Probability as the guide to life. The main point insisted upon throughout is the enduring character of Butler's argument. The direct value of the argument of the *Analogy*, Mr. Gladstone maintains, is, notwithstanding the lapse of time, unabated, and is not likely to be abated as the years run on. But great as is the value of Butler's argument in his largest work, the value of his method is, in the estimation of Mr. Gladstone, greater still. Its principal and distinguishing feature is that it is an inductive method. 'Butler was a collector of facts and a reasoner upon them.' He 'chose for his whole argument the sure and immovable basis of human experience, from his earliest tracings of natural government, up to his final development of the scheme of revealed religion.' In this, Mr. Gladstone finds the probable explanation of the *Analogy's* success. 'It is probable,' he says, 'that this great feature of Butler's method supplies the explanation of the singular fact, that a work, rarely presenting to us the graces of style, not produced in connection with any academic institution or learned class, singularly difficult to master from the nature of the subject, and running directly counter to the fashionable currents of opinion, should at once have taken hold upon the educated mind of the country, and should, as will appear from the language of Hume, very rapidly have acquired for its author a high position in the literary and philosophic world.' Among other features exhibited by Butler's method which are pointed out are the author's habit of self-suppression, the frank and often surprising concessions which he makes to his opponents, and the powerful tendency of his method 'to create in his reader a certain habit of mind which is usually far from common, and which at the present day, and amidst the present tendencies, both of the average and even of the more active mind, may justly be termed rare.' This mental habit Mr. Gladstone describes as that 'which, in all questions lying within the scope of Butler's arguments, suits and adapts itself with gradually increasing precision to the degree of evidence adapted to the subject-matter; where that is much, thankfully rejoices in the abundance; where it is scanty, recognises the absolute duty of accepting the limitation; backed by the consciousness that, in each and every case, it is sufficient.' 'The student of Butler,' he further remarks, 'will, unless it be his own fault, learn candour in all its breadth, and not to tamper with the truth; will neither grudge admissions nor fret under even cumbrous reserves.' And to know what kinds and degrees of evidence to expect or to ask in matters of belief and conduct, and to be in possession of an habitual presence of mind built upon that knowledge is, in Mr. Gladstone's view, the master gift which the works of Butler are calculated to impart. Dealing with the indeterminate, Mr. Gladstone recommends the study of Butler's method to those in whose pursuits the indeterminate largely prevails, and especially to the politician, inasmuch as of all sciences politics is that which, according to Lord Bacon, is most deeply immersed in matter, or as Mr. Gladstone phrases it 'most closely kneaded up with human action.' 'Undoubtedly,' he says, 'if my counsel were asked, I should advise the intending politician, if of masculine and serious mind, to give to Butler's works, and especially to the *Analogy*, a high place among the apparatus of his mental training.' Reverting in words which are not without a pathetic interest, to Butler's argument, Mr. Gladstone maintains that it was probably greater than Butler himself was aware, and that he has accomplished more by it than he engaged to do. The chapter bearing the title 'The Censors of Bishop Butler,' is perhaps the most attractive, as it is the most obviously skilful in the volume. Mr. Gladstone is here on his own ground as a dialectician and disposes of the allegations which have been brought against Butler's arguments with ease. The Censors with whose opinions he chiefly deals, are Mr. Bagehot, Miss Hennell, Mr. Leslie Stephen, Mr. Matthew Arnold. At less length he refers to those of Professor Maurice, Dr. Mark Pattison and Goldwin Smith. Incidentally he drops the remark, the truth of which most mature students of Butler will feel, that 'there is no preparation for a satisfactory study of Butler so good as to have been widely conversant with the disappointing character of human affairs,' and adds, 'with touching simplicity he [Butler] says: "Indeed the unsatisfactory nature of the evidence, with which we are obliged to take up, in the daily course of life, is scarce to be expressed."' In the section dealing with Miss Hennel's opinion on Butler's argument, Mr. Gladstone refers to the reported remark of Mr. Pitt on the *Analogy*, to the effect that it suggested more doubts than it solved, and after examining all that can be said in favour of its authenticity, comes to the conclusion that it is not, as it stands, entitled to credit. Here, however, it is altogether impossible to refer to the numerous points of interest in this very exceptional volume. There is not a chapter or a section in it which is not of much more than ordinary value, and which will not amply repay the most careful study. Among the chapters which may be specially pointed out are those under the titles 'Comparison with the Ancients,' 'Points of his positive Teaching,' 'Celebrity and Influence,' 'A Future Life,' 'Probability as the Guide of Life,' all of which have their own peculiar values and are often marked by passages of great eloquence.

ΧΡΙΣΤΙΑΝΙΚΗ ΑΓΙΟΓΡΑΦΙΑ ΤΩΝ ΕΝΝΕΑ ΠΡΩΤΩΝ ΑΙΩΝΩΝ. *(Christian Sacred Art of the first Nine Centuries, 1-842, or from the Beginning of Christianity to the Restoration of the Sacred Images.)* By GEORGE LAMBAKES, Licentiate in Theology, etc. Athens. 1896.

In this work the author, who is a director of the Museum of Christian Archæology and Lecturer on the same subject in the National University at Athens, sketches the growth and decline of Byzantine art. He begins with the purely symbolic forms of the catacombs, of which he gives a very complete catalogue, and shows how these were afterwards combined in symbolic representations of sacred events, which in turn gave way to pictorial ones. The purely classical character which these works exhibit gradually vanished in the second period, from Constantine to Justinian, yet even in the mosaics of S. Sophia the antique spirit is still manifest. With this period too, Christian forms, our Lord, the Theotokos, the Archangel, S. Demetrios, S. George, and others, in some hundred different types are figured on the coins of the empire. Christian art thus attained a definite national form : but it had entered on a path of decline. A spirit of formalism had already manifested itself. Kedrênos records how about 463 A.D. a certain artist who presumed to represent Jesus under the form of Zeus had his hand withered. Similar stories are recorded by other writers. The insistence on accepted forms, which gave rise to these traditions —no doubt closely connected with the theological troubles of the time—became more disastrous than ever for art when the Iconoclast struggle began in the eighth century. This part of the k. Lambakês' work is mainly occupied with a discussion of the question of images, a list of passages of Scripture symbolised in art, and the traditional descriptions of Our Lord's and the Theotokos' appearance. The triumph of the Image-worshippers was the death-knell of Byzantine art ; which was henceforth made subservient to the dogma and teaching of the church. At Mount Athos, which is now its seat, there is no scope for originality. The artists there simply follow slavishly the directions of the *Ermêneia Zôgraphôn* or *Painters' Instructor.* In a compass of less than a hundred pages the author gives an excellent view of his subject. His lists should be exceedingly valuable. Among the very numerous references to Western writers on Christian Art, we notice none to Lethaby and Swainson's work in the pages devoted to the church of S. Sophia.

Schopenhauer's System in its Philosophical Significance. By WILLIAM CALDWELL, D.Sc., Professor of Moral Philosophy in Northwestern University, U.S.A. Edinburgh and London : William Blackwood & Sons. 1896.

It may very well be an open question whether the time for a final treatise on Schopenhauer has yet arrived, but there can be little doubt that need existed for a systematic account of his philosophy in English. Previous writers have confined themselves to translations, to fugitive essays, to Schopenhauer's life, or to aspects of his system in their connection with similar thought in previous ages and other civilizations. Some of them have certainly presented their reflections with a brilliancy and literary finish to which Professor Caldwell can lay no claim. But his purpose is different, and in supplying a complete analysis of the protagonist of pessimism in his relation to previous and subsequent philosophers, in his ethical, artistic, metaphysical, and religious doctrines, he has laid all students under heavy obligation. The striking feature of the book is the steady balance that it holds, or tries to hold, between adulation of Schopenhauer and that supreme contempt with which many affect to treat him. Professor Caldwell falls into the error of being too lenient towards the subject of his theme, but at the same time, he fully realizes Schopenhauer's importance, and strives, with large measure of success, to estimate his legacy. The extreme care he has bestowed is everywhere evident ;

indeed, he sometimes fails to see the wood for the trees, so numerous are the considerations which varied views culled from Schopenhauer's writings, systematic and occasional, compel him to pursue.   The best parts of the volume are to be found in the chapters on the 'Bondage of Man' and Schopenhauer's 'Moral Philosophy.'   The conclusions which Professor Caldwell draws throughout respecting the importance of Will as an element in a philosophical system are also interesting, and in the present state of speculative questions, should attract attention.   It can easily be predicted who will welcome them, and who will serve them with derision.   But whatever these varied judgments may be, no one will fail to allow that Professor Caldwell has produced a judicial work on a subject to which impartial study has hitherto been rather foreign ; one, further, that cannot but serve to lead students into an unworked field, and to supply them with valuable hints towards fresh lines of inquiry.

Ireland. 1494-1868. With Introductory Chapters. By WILLIAM O'CONNOR MORRIS. Cambridge: At the University Press. 1896.

This volume of the 'Cambridge Historical Series,' which is being issued under the editorship of Professor Prothero, is admirably adapted to enable the reader to follow the general course of Irish history from its earliest beginnings down to the year 1868, when, as Mr. O'Connor Morris remarks, ' Mr. Gladstone entered upon that path of reform for Ireland which he has ever since followed wherever it has led.'   The book lays no claim to original research.   For his facts Mr. O'Connor Morris has gone to the best and most reliable printed authorities of which there is now fortunately no lack.   These he has studied with care, and apparently, as far as possible, without prejudice, intent solely on ascertaining their real significance, and the result is a volume which, though necessarily, on account of limitation of space, brief and wanting in detail, will be welcomed as eminently fair and impartial.   Mr. O'Connor Morris is known as a strong Unionist, and here and there his narrative is slightly tinged with politics ; but even so, his volume is none the less valuable as an introduction to Irish history, whether for the general reader who merely wishes to know what its main outlines have been, or for the student preparing to enter upon a more detailed study of the subject.   The first two chapters are introductory.   In the first, Mr. O'Connor Morris touches lightly upon the mythical history of Ireland and then proceeds to sketch the condition of the country down to the coming of the English.   The sketch is by no means exaggerated. If anything, it falls a little below rather than exceeds what may be said of the Ireland of the period.   Still, general views of this period are apt to become unintentionally misleading.   The disparity between the civilisation of the cloister and of the people and the absence of altogether trustworthy records as to the actual condition of the latter leave the subject in considerable obscurity.   The civilisation of the cloisters, however, does not seem, at least during the first half of the period, to have permeated the people to any great extent.   The Danish invasion is dismissed in a single paragraph.   'The invaders,' says Mr. Morris, 'did not blend with the native race ; the Irish scarcely show no trace of Danish blood.'   Coming from one so well acquainted with Ireland as our author, these statements are interesting in the face of the contention of Professor Bugge that most of the Court poetry of the Norseman is largely due to Irish influence.   The second chapter deals with the Norman Conquest, and though merely introductory may be taken as one of the most important in the volume.   The same, indeed, may be said of the first.   Neither can be passed over.   Both show what, so to say, the raw material of Ireland was, while the latter is instructive as describing the beginning of evils—the seed-time during which the seed was sown which afterwards, in various ways, sprung up and proved more or less the cause of Ireland's sorrows. With his third chapter Mr. O'Connor Morris fairly launches upon his subject. The chief figures in it are, of course, Poynings and Kildare. Poyning's measures are aptly likened to those of one of the great Viceroy's in the early days of British rule in India. While Henry VII.'s Irish policy is regarded as weak, that of his son is regarded as judicious and attended with promising results. Elizabeth's treatment of Ireland Mr. O'Connor Morris is disposed to some extent to excuse. 'All that is worst,' he says, speaking of this period, 'had its parallel in contemporary event. If rebellion in Ireland was mercilessly crushed and the island was strewn with ashes and blood, Alva did the very same things in the Netherlands and was more pitiless than Sussex and Mountjoy. . . . The sixteenth century, in fact, was an age of violence, when Christendom was torn in pieces in a deadly strife ; and Ireland had but a share in the conflict.' The good as well as the evil of Stafford's administration is pointed out. To Cromwell's conquest but brief space is given. 'The fanaticism of his men' it is said, 'was no doubt quickened by the prospect of a rich spoil of Irish land.' Of Cromwell himself, we read, 'he had always shown himself to be a great soldier, if humanity shudders at Wexford and Drogheda.' Coming down to later times, Mr. O'Connor Morris sketches briefly, but with sufficient fulness for his purpose, the policy of Pitt and the rebellion by which the partial carrying out of it was preceded. He admits the use of bribery and corruption for the purpose of securing the Union, and agrees with Mr. Lecky that Pitt's policy would have been more successful had it been carried out as he originally conceived it. The story which our author has to tell is, as need hardly be said, distressful. The perpetual feuds, so characteristic of Irish history, are of course alluded to, as well as the part which race hatred and personal ambition have played in the history of the country, but Mr. O'Connor Morris is more intent on showing the influence they have had on the general trend of affairs than in describing them in detail. Here and there he indulges in speculations as to what might have been ; but his main theme is constantly kept before the reader, even at the expense of an occasional repetition. Here and there the work suffers from overmuch condensation and would gain in impressiveness by expansion.

Annals of Garelochside: being an Account Historical and Topographical of the Parishes of Row, Rosneath, and Cardross. By W. E. MAUGHAN. Illustrated. Paisley and London : Alex. Gardner. 1896.

Some time ago we had the pleasure of noticing in the pages of this *Review* Mr. Maughan's *Rosneath : As it was and is,* and spoke of it as one of the best local histories with which we were acquainted. In his present volume Mr. Maughan has surpassed himself, and produced a work fuller, more graphic, and in every respect superior to his earlier performance. He has evidently gone further afield in his search for information, and besides consulting aged inhabitants of the district, and using his own faculties of observation, he has made use of a large amount of printed material, and apparently spared no effort to make his *Annals* of one of the most beautiful districts of Scotland as complete as possible. The use of the word 'Annals' on the title-page may perhaps prove somewhat misleading. Certainly it does not sufficiently indicate the richness of the contents it covers. For the work contains not merely the annals of the picturesque and romantic country along the shores of the Gareloch, but a vast deal more in the shape of statistics, family and clan history, biography, manners and customs, and other matters pertaining to human life during several centuries. Mr. Maughan's plan is to give in the first place a general description of the county of Dumbarton, and then to describe the three parishes of Row, Rosneath, and Cardross, each of which is notable, though in a different way, in the history of Scotland. In dealing with the county Mr. Maughan gives many details respecting the life and pursuits of its inhabitants during this and earlier centuries, and furnishes many interesting particulars respecting their occupations and industries, the social habits of the landowners and peasantry, and the many changes that have occurred in the ownership of different estates, as also respecting the geological formation of the district, its fauna and flora and other products. Family histories receive, as might be expected, a large share of Mr. Maughan's attention in the other chapters of his volume. In the section devoted to the parish of Row we have summaries of the histories of the Lennox and Colquhoun families, and excellent sketches of Henry Bell, of steamboat fame, and of Robert Napier of West Shandon, the engine builder. Mr. Maughan's account in the same section of the Rev. John M'Leod Campbell is brief, but sufficient. He has wisely abstained from adventuring upon the controversy which Mr. Campbell's preaching gave rise to, and has confined himself to a bare narrative of the facts. The famous battle of Glenfruin is, of course, noticed, and the slaughter of the Colquhouns and the barbarities perpetrated by the Macgregors are described with sufficient fulness. To the town of Helensburgh, so named after Helen, a grand-daughter of John, Earl of Sutherland, and wife of Sir James Colquhoun, its founder, considerable space is devoted. It was founded, it would appear, in 1777, and could then boast of only a single row of humble thatched or red-tiled cottages running along the shore where what is now known as Clyde Street stands, and for twenty years made but very slow, if any progress. The tide of prosperity set in to it in 1795, since when it has gone on increasing till it now numbers a population of over ten thousand, and claims with one or two other places on the Clyde to be the 'Brighton' of Scotland. Mr. Maughan's new chapters on Rosneath are an improvement on those of his previous volume. The same topics are necessarily treated, but their treatment is fuller. In the section on the parish of Cardross among other family histories, that of the Smolletts is sketched. Mr. Maughan has made good use of the parochial records of each parish, and has much to say about their ministers. The district is less rich in archæological remains than in historical and biographical associations. Mr. Maughan does not omit to notice how the ornithology of the district has been impoverished during recent years. Among the most notable habits of past generations in the districts was that of smuggling. As an indication of the social condition of the people at the time, he mentions that in a parish of about 2000 souls there were no fewer than thirty places for the sale of intoxicating liquors, most of which, if not the whole, had never paid duty. The volume is filled with interesting and instructive matter. Several awkward slips occur in it, and the index is neither full nor always correct.

Memorials—Part 1.—Family and Personal, 1766-1865. By ROUNDELL PALMER, EARL OF SELBORNE. 2 vols. London and New York: Macmillan & Co. 1896.

Public feeling cannot but be gratified that the intention long cherished by the late Lord Selborne to commit to writing, with a view to its subsequent publication, some account of his personal history, private and public, was, at the instance of his daughter, Lady Sophia M. Palmer, by whom these volumes have been . carefully edited, successfully attempted while there was yet time for its completion. The present volumes are but an instalment, and covering only what was practically but the first half of their author's career, they deal, as might be expected, for the most part with his private and family life. Some part of his public career is narrated, but the greater portion of the narrative of that is yet to come, and will doubtless prove of not less, if not of more, interest than the more important passages in it, which are related here. The hand of Lord Selborne is everywhere apparent in the volumes, and that calm, restrained, and judicial temper which formed so large a feature in his character, is manifest on every one of their pages. Not less manifest is his intense moral earnestness, which at times becomes exceedingly impressive, and though always restrained, reveals a depth and fervour of religious feeling which, for some reason or other, is seldom associated or expected with great legal attainments. The prevailing tone of the volumes, indeed, is somewhat sombre. The style is grave and stately, unrelieved by a single flash of humour—an element which seems to have been altogether wanting in the author's character. All the same the narrative is far from unattractive. Both the character and position of its author invest it with an exceptional interest, and few 'Memorials' will be read with equal pleasure and instruction. The future Lord High Chancellor of England came, on his father's side, of an old Yorkshire family, and was not very distantly connected with the famous Dr. Samuel Horsley, successively Bishop of St. Davids, Rochester, and St. Asaph, distinguished as a mathematician and editor of Newton's works, but best known, perhaps, through his controversy with Priestley. Yorkshire was also the native country of his mother, a daughter of Richard Roundell of Gledstone, in the parish of East Marton, situated in the district of the West Riding of Yorkshire which is known as Craven. A college friendship brought the Palmers and Roundells together, and in 1810 W. J. Palmer, who was then rector of Mixbury in Oxfordshire, to which he had been presented by his uncle, the Bishop of Rochester, married Dorothea Richardson Roundell. Roundell Palmer, born Nov. 27, 1812, was the second son of the marriage. At first he was educated at home along with his elder brother, William. In 1823 the two were sent to Rugby, then under Dr. Wooll. After remaining two years Roundell was sent to Winchester, while his elder brother remained at Rugby a year longer. Leaving Winchester, of which we have a minute description, and for which he always entertained a profound affection, Roundell Palmer was sent to join his brother at Oxford, and matriculated as a Commoner at Christ Church in the spring of 1830, but gaining an open scholarship at Trinity, after the long vacation he began residence there. At Trinity he met with several of his schoolfellows, and became intimate with Charles Wordsworth, Thomas Legh Claughton, and John Thomas. Others with whom he formed friendships 'to be dissolved only by death' were Nutcombe Oxenham and George Kettiby Richards. The 'Union' was then in its zenith. 'William Ewart Gladstone,' he says, 'was President. He was a student of Christ Church, prince of the Etonians of his time, and at the head of the literary society of his " house." He must have been then in the third year of his University course. He had been a frequent speaker at the " Union " since the beginning of 1830, always on the Tory side, but attached to the memory of Canning and opposed to the Duke of Wellington and his government.' Speaking of the meetings at the Union in May, 1831, during the crisis of the first Reform Bill, he says :—' We had a three nights' debate on a motion of want of confidence in Lord Grey's Ministry, to which Gladstone moved and carried by ninety-four to thirty-eight, this rider :—" That the Ministry has unwisely introduced and most unscrupulously forwarded, a measure, which threatens not only to change the form of Government, but ultimately to break up the very foundations of social order, as well as eventually to forward the views of those who are pursuing this project throughout the civilised world." ' The speech Mr. Gladstone delivered in support of this proposition is said to have been one of ' extraordinary power and eloquence.' George A. Denison, ' the redoubted Archdeacon,' then fellow of Oriel and a Liberal according to Mr. Mozley's *Reminiscences*, prophesied, from the nature of the arguments, that the speaker was on the high road to Liberalism. Lord Selborne somewhat caustically remarks upon the speech, that it ' might perhaps have been repeated without change of a word by those who dissented from his own Irish measure of 1886.' Beyond the hereditary Toryism of his family Lord Selborne when he went up to Oxford, had no politics ; but in the company of Cardwell, Lowe, and Tait, he began to interest himself in them on the Conservative side. He became a member of the short-lived ' Rambler' Club, and with the rest of its members ran the risk of expulsion from the Union. To the *Oxford University Magazine*, which was started under the editorship of Wall in 1834 and lived on till the summer of the following year, he was a frequent contributor. He confirms what has frequently been said as to the prophecy contained in the poem entitled ' Seaton Beach,' published by a dissenting minister of Seaton while he and four or five others, among whom was Tait afterwards Archbishop, were residing there as a reading party. In 1834 he obtained a fellowship in Magdalen, and for some time acted as tutor to Lord Maidstone. Two years prior to this, his mother's health had begun to fail, and from that illness he says, ' I date the awakening within me of higher and more lasting spiritual aspirations than I had known before.' From the last of his undergraduate years (1834) he traces the beginning of his interest in public affairs. At the time Oxford was the centre of political emotion, owing to the death of Lord Grenville, the Chancellor, and the opposition, in which Mr. Gladstone took a prominent part, to the election of the Duke of Wellington as his successor. Leaving Oxford Mr. Palmer took up his legal studies at Lincoln's Inn, and was called to the Bar in 1837. Though keeping up his interest in Oxford and all that concerned it, he was not drawn into the Tractarian movement. Most of his spare time was devoted to writing articles for the *Times*, to which he became a regular contributor, and to reading. Among other authors he made the acquaintance at this time with the writings of Carlyle, ' but not,' as he says, ' to become one of his worshippers.' ' The style, even of his *French Revolution*,' he goes on to say, ' unlike anything that I had before read, was too much like chopped straw to satisfy my taste, notwithstanding the passages of splendid pictorial and dramatic power which relieved and lighted it up all the more vividly, perhaps, on account of the spasmodic sententiousness of his general manner. Nor was I able to discover in him any light for the formation or direction of positive, as well as negative, moral judgments. My nature was not so constituted as to be satisfied with mere iconoclasm (though I allow the reasonableness of destroying idols), nor with the substitution of an idolatry of strength for spiritual forms of belief and Christian morality.' Well connected and having brought with him a high reputation, business soon began to come in to the young barrister, and before long his success at the Chancery Bar was assured. Among his contemporaries were Campbell, Pollock, Follett and Rolfe, Bethell and Turner, John Romilly, and W. Page Wood. In 1847 he was returned in the Liberal interest for Plymouth, and in the same year married Lady Laura Waldegrave. From this year the life of the author becomes more and more mixed up with public affairs, and the interest of the *Memorials* deepens. To follow the *Memorials* further here is impossible. We hope to return to the volumes when those which are to follow are published. In the meantime it must be said that the reader will form a far from inadequate conception of the contents of the two volumes now issued if he supposes that the author has confined his attention simply to a narration of the story of his own life. Chapters of considerable length are devoted to his relatives and friends, and to various subjects, literary and ecclesiastical. The Jerusalem bishopric is treated of at great length as is also the career of William Palmer, the author's eldest brother, while not the least valuable among the chapters of the first volume are those bearing upon the 'Oxford Movement.'

A Cameronian Apostle. Being some Account of John Macmillan of Balmaghie. By the Rev. H. M. B. REID, B.D. Illustrated. Paisley and London: Alex. Gardner. 1896.

Mr. Reid has exercised a praiseworthy industry in searching out and presenting in a readable way all that appears to be known about one who is perhaps the most famous of his predecessors in the ministry of the parish of Balmaghie. Outside Scotland, and perhaps outside the small denomination known as the Cameronians, Macmillan, who is here designated the Apostle of the Cameronians, is now in all probability remembered by few. The part which he played was not a great one ; still, he has left his mark upon religious Scotland, and his biography, as here told by Mr. Reid, is worth perusing for the not inconsiderable light which it throws not only upon the history of a religious denomination, but also upon the ecclesiastical affairs of Scotland during the first half of the eighteenth century. According to all accounts John Macmillan, afterwards minister of Balmaghie, was born in the parish of Minnigaff, in Kirkcudbrightshire, in 1669. There is some doubt as to the parish in which he was born, and even as to the exact year. His parents belonged to the strictest party of the Covenanters, and were members of what was known as the United Societies, whose principles were separation from all Presbyterians who accepted the Indulgencies or in any way held communion with the Indulged, and separation from the State. Every member of the Societies were forbidden to appear in a court of law, and was prohibited from having any dealings of any kind, either personally or through an agent, with any of the existing powers, either of Church or State. In his early days Macmillan must have had large experience of the 'hill-meetings,' and most of his acquaintances at the time must have been numbered among the 'Hill Folks.' Among his relatives was Macmillan of Caldow, a Covenanting preacher, and Mr. Reid is probably right when he says : 'The very blood in his veins was Covenanting blood.' For a number of years Macmillan seems to have been engaged in farm labour, but in 1695, when he was probably about 26 years of age, he matriculated in the University of Edinburgh, and graduated there in 1697. For some reason or other, he then entered the Divinity Hall of the Established Church, and so gave great offence to the 'Godly Remnant.' Among his fellow-students in Divinity was Thomas Boston, author of the once widely-read *Fourfold State.* On the conclusion of his studies, Macmillan returned to Kirkcudbrightshire, where he received an appointment as chaplain or tutor in the family of the Laird of Broughton. In 1700 he was licensed to preach the Gospel, and in April of the following year was chosen minister of Balmaghie, and was shortly afterwards settled in charge of the parish. For a time all went well with him, though his ordination had not taken place without a certain amount of distrust on the part of some of the members of the Presbytery, foremost among whom was Cameron, minister of Kirkcudbright, brother of Richard Cameron who was slain at Airdmoss. The fact is that Macmillan's separatist tendencies clung to him, and Cameron was probably not far wrong when he called him a 'born separatist.' Still, as a minister and pastor, there is every reason to believe that he was in every way exemplary. He continued in the quiet and indefatigable discharge of his duties until the beginning of 1703, when the Privy Council sent down an order for all ministers to 'swear Allegiance and subscribe the Assurance to Queen Anne's Government.' This was the beginning of troubles. Macmillan protested against the evils in the Church, and refused to take the oath. Negotiations were tried on the part of the Presbytery, but in vain. Macmillan was deposed, but though deposed, continued for twenty years to occupy the manse and glebe, and in possession of the church. In the end, however, he found a home among the United Societies, and became the founder of the denomination known both as the Cameronians and the Macmillanites, most of the congregations of which were, some years ago, joined to the Free Church. Such is an outline of Macmillan's life. Mr. Reid, however, has filled in the sketch with many picturesque details. By Macmillan's time the troopers had ceased to be used against the Covenanters. Still, Mr. Reid has several times to tell how the Sheriff came to Balmaghie to eject Macmillan and take possession of the church and its appurtenances, and how on each occasion he was prevented either by armed men or crowds of women. He has much to tell also of the religious habits of the time, and of the way in which the ecclesiastical courts of the period did their business. Altogether, there is much in his volume both to attract and to repay the reader.

Deux manières d'ecrire l'histoire. Par H. D'ARBOIS DE JUBAINVILLE. Paris: E. Bouillon. 1896.

Celtic philology has apparently so very little connection with the methods writers of history may choose to adopt in the composition of their works, that one is at first sight not a little surprised to see the name of M. D'Arbois de Jubainville on the title-page of this volume as its author. On the other hand, the learned Professor of Celtic at the College of France is a man of such consummate energy, and his activities are so many-sided, that it is almost impossible to say in what line of literary authorship one may not find him. And, after all, from the study of Celtic literature and philology to the methods of historical writers, is not so far a cry as one might at first suppose. The histories of France, Ireland, and Scotland, at least in their early periods, cannot now be adequately written without a very considerable acquaintance with Celtic literature and Celtic philology, while as to the methods of writing history there is no reason whatever why a Professor of Celtic should not equally well with any other learned Professor, be quite as competent as any one else to deliver a sound opinion upon them. The little volume before us has been suggested by the perusal of M. Julien Havet's *Questions Mérovingiennes* and the works of M. Fustel de Coulanges, particularly of his *La Cité Antique* and his *Histoire des institutions politiques de l'ancienne France, La Monarchie franque.* This perusal has convinced M. D'Arbois de Jubainville that M. Fustel de Coulanges has attached far too little importance to the arguments and discoveries of M. J. Havet in respect to many of the charters and documents which have hitherto been assigned to the period of the Merovingians. And this again has set him thinking about the two methods of writing history. One of these he terms the *a priori* and the other the *a posteriori.* As samples of the two, he takes Bossuet's celebrated *Discourse* and Tillemont's *History of St. Louis,* and then proceeds to show that in his work, *La Cité Antique,* M. Fustel de Coulanges follows precisely the same method as Bossuet, basing his narrative not on a careful induction from facts, but writing from a preconception, and selecting and using such facts only as support or corroborate it. In the second half of the volume, M. D'Arbois de Jubainville criticises very keenly a number of statements advanced by M. Fustel de Coulanges in the second of his volumes named above, and cites against them the testimony of the original records. The volume, though small, is of manifold interest. Here and there the author diverges into politics. In the preface he gives an account of his family and of his own position in regard to politics. Scattered through the volume are references to English history, as well as to such writers as Guizot, Thierry, and Sir Walter Scott. Though controverting many of M. Fustel de Coulanges' positions, M. D'Arbois de Jubainville pays a high tribute to his learning and character.

Études sur le droit celtique. Par H. D'ARBOIS DE JUBAINVILLE, avec la collaboration de PAUL COLLINET. Tome Second. Paris : Albert Fontemoing. 1895.

With the assistance of M. Collinet, M. D'Arbois de Jubainville here completes for the present his learned studies on the ancient laws of Ireland. This, the second volume he has devoted to the subject, forms one of the series which has now for some time been appearing under the general title *Cours de littérature celtique,* and of which he is the editor. It divides itself into two parts which form the third and fourth of the whole work. In the first we have a translation of the first section of the treatise contained in the Senchus Mor, dealing with the law of seizure, together with an elaborate commentary, philological and explanatory, upon it ; and in the second the original text of the same forty-eight articles of the Senchus Mor, as corrected by Dr. Whitley Stokes, accompanied by an interlinear and word for word translation. The volume in fact contains two translations of this part of the text of the ancient laws. The first, however, is regarded by its author as for the most part tentative, being in many places more paraphrastic than literal. The second is followed by an elaborate glossarial index which has been prepared by the skilful hand of M. Collinet. By the student it will be found exceedingly useful. M. Collinet has called to his aid all the resources of Celtic philology, and has thus placed the student in a position to check the freer translation given in the earlier part of the volume. M. D'Arbois de Jubainville's commentary is, as it is almost unnecessary to say, highly instructive, and goes far to justify the renderings he has given to what is confessedly a difficult text. The indices which have been prepared for the volumes are, in addition to M. Collinet's, eleven in number, and like that are remarkably elaborate, and deserve to stand as models to be followed.

A Primer of Burns. By WILLIAM A. CRAIGIE, B.A., Assistant and Lecturer in the University of St. Andrews. Methuen & Co. 1896.

This little book is not the least noteworthy of the many contributions which this year has added to the literature of Burns. As the title implies, it is meant as an introduction to the study of the poet. Its aim is not to present any theory of Burns, but simply to take up his work as it stands and point out its characteristics and its worth as poetry. Perhaps this is the service which Burns most needs at the present time. It is becoming harder and harder to look on him fairly and judge him as we might judge any other poet. We are in danger of feeling that we might lose our admiration if we examined too closely into his actual work. Mr. Craigie has tried to show us that Burns can speak for himself. The book deals successively with the life, the poems, the songs, and the letters of Burns. A chapter, not the least valuable, is added on the language. Mr. Craigie has been best known hitherto as an expert in Scottish language. He might have been tempted to give a disproportionate treatment to this aspect of his subject, but has wisely limited himself to this short and admirably lucid chapter. At the end of the book there is a bibliography, brought down to the present year. In dealing with the life Mr. Craigie does not write either as an advocate or a judge. His method is simply to recount the facts as they happened, without apology or criticism. This treatment may not be ethical enough for some readers, but we do not think that anything is lost by it. Most of us are getting tired of contemplating Burns under the moral dissecting knife. Mr. Craigie proceeds to examine the poems in the light reflected on them by the life. He takes up the principal poems one by one, and gives a few lines of explanation and criticism upon them. The result, however, is no mere catalogue, but a clear, connected story of how Burns gradually attained to mastery in his art and gave expression to his genius on its varied sides. In this section there is much to be said about Burns's obligations to the Scottish poets before him. These obligations have often been over-rated, and Mr. Craigie has done good service in examining into the matter thoroughly and disposing of it once for all. 'If it is unjust to Ramsay and Fergusson,' he says, in summing up, ' to ignore their share in the making of Burns,—an injustice that he was never guilty of,—it is equally unfair to suggest that his reputation is any way stolen from theirs. No borrowing of ideas will ever explain why Burns is an English classic in a way that the others can never be. Here it is that Homer borrows from Virgil; the broad original mind from the narrow and more artificial.' From the poems Mr. Craigie passes to the songs. This section is perhaps the most suggestive and valuable in the book. There is nothing that tests so well the real insight of a critic, his sympathy with what is most intimate and essential in poetry, as his power of analysing a song. Mr. Craigie has done this for Burns with remarkable delicacy and success. He holds that in the songs we have the ripest and most individual expression of Burns's genius. 'His poems,' he says, ' raised him from the obscurity of his native parish and gave him a place in the literature of Britain. His songs have entitled him to rank among the great poets of the world.' We cannot leave Mr. Craigie's book with any other words than those of unqualified praise. In a small compass he has said all that needs to be said in order to put a reader in the way of understanding Burns, and of enjoying him with a true critical feeling of his peculiar worth as a poet. We rise from the book with a new sense that Burns can take care of his own fame. When all deductions have been made, and he is judged, as he must be judged in the end, on his own inalienable merits, he is still one of the poets for all time. In making us feel this in his *Primer*, Mr. Craigie has done the truest service to our poet.

The Scenery of Switzerland and the Causes to which it is due. By the Right Hon. Sir JOHN LUBBOCK, Bart., M.P., D.C.L., etc. London and New York: Macmillan & Co. 1896.

Readers who take up this volume with the expectation of finding in it glowing descriptions of scenery in Switzerland will be disappointed ; but he who wishes to learn how the scenery of Switzerland has come to be what it is, and to know something of the causes to which it is due, will find it both interesting and instructive. The book is written throughout from the point of view of science, and tries, with the aid of the most recent scientific theories, to explain the many interesting problems which the physical geography of the country presents. After an introductory chapter on the geology of Switzerland, in which it is pointed out that the principal axis of the Alps follows a curved line from the Maritime Alps towards the north-east, by Mont Blanc, Monte Rosa, and St. Gotthard, to the mountains overlooking the Engadine, and the prevailing rocks are described, another follows on the origin of mountains, in which the non-geological reader will find much to entertain and instruct him. In the next chapter the author fairly enters upon his subject, and begins with an elaborate description of the mountains of Switzerland. Subsequent chapters deal with the snow-fields and glaciers of the country, describing the formation and movements of the latter, their present and former extension. The erosive action of water, the agencies at work in the formation of valleys and the effects which weathering, climate, and the character and inclination of the rocks have upon scenery, are described. The difficult problems presented by the Swiss and Italian lakes are discussed and many interesting particulars both as to the formation of their beds and the colour of their waters are pointed out. In the remaining chapters Sir John Lubbock turns his attention to the various districts of the country, such as the Jura district, the Central plain, the Outer Alps, the district around Mont Blanc, the Rhine Valley, the Valais and the Bernese Oberland, the Ticino and Engadine, and enters into an elaborate account of their geological structure. The work takes in the whole of the surface of Switzerland and forms an admirable introduction to the geology of the country. It is supplied with a map and bibliography but lacks an index.

The Poetical Works of William Wordsworth. Edited by William Knight. Vol. VII. London and New York : Macmillan & Co. 1896.

This volume of Professor Knight's edition of Wordsworth contains t' ɔ poems written during the years 1821-34. Among them are some of the best known of the poet's verses. The volume opens, of course, with the long series of Ecclesiastical Sonnets. To these the editor has added a considerable number of useful notes, though from the list of Cambridge Platonists given on page 76 the name of Benjamin Whichcote, the chief of the School, to whom Smith and the rest owed, for the most part, their inspiration, is, strangely enough, omitted. Among the other pieces written during the same decade as the series just mentioned are ' The Skylark,' ' To the Cuckoo,' ' Incident in Bruges.' ' The Power of Sound,' ' Humanity,' 'The Egyptian Maid.' The second year of the following decade brings us to the group of poems written during a tour in Scotland and on the English border in the autumn of 1831, and published in 1835 in the volume entitled *Yarrow Revisited and Other Poems.* Following these is a number of pieces originally issued in the same volume, such as the poems suggested during a tour in the Western Highlands and Islands during the summer of 1833, ' Devotional Incitements,' written in 1832, the ' Labourer's Noonday Hymn,' and ' The Redbreast.' The volume gives evidence of great care in the editing, and the edition bids fair to be the best yet issued.

The Poetical Works of Robert Burns, with Notes, Glossary, Index to first Lines, and Chronological List. Edited by J. Logie Robertson, M.A. London and New York : Henry Frowde. 1896.

The Poetical Works of Lord Byron. Same Publisher.

These two volumes belong to the Oxford Series of the Poets, now in course of publication by Mr. Henry Frowde. Among recent editions of his works the ' Oxford Burns ' will take a high place both on account of the form in which it is issued and the cheapness of its popular edition, and not less on the careful manner in which it has been edited. The pieces are divided into two classes : Poems, Epistles, etc., and Songs and Ballads ; and these again are arranged, not according to their chronology, but according to the order of their popularity, which, as Mr. Robertson observes, ' pretty well corresponds with the order of merit.' The text has been carefully collated, and that reading has been adopted which, in the editor's judgment, seemed the best. The notes which are given at the end of the volume are brief, but sufficient for the ordinary reader, while now and again they show to some extent what was the source of Burns's inspiration, and his indebtedness to contemporary poets. In addition to a carefully compiled glossary an index to the first lines and a chronological index are given. The work is published in three forms : one on ordinary paper, another on the Oxford India paper, and the third on the same paper, but in bold type, in three dainty little volumes with case. Of minature editions this last is the prince. Nothing like it has appeared.—Byron's works are published in the same sizes and on the same paper. No editor's name is attached to the edition, but the text is that of Mr. Murray's edition of 1867, and containing the copyright matter of that edition, is, like it, complete.

Reminiscences of Walt Whitman, with Extracts from his Letters and Remarks on his Writings. By WILLIAM SLOANE KENNEDY. Paisley and London : Alex. Gardner. 1896.

Among admirers of Walt Whitman and his poetry this little volume, like most others that contain information about him, is sure to meet with a cordial welcome. It cannot be said that it contains anything of great importance either in connection with the poet or his poetry, yet it contains a number of personal details as also of particulars regarding his works which, as they serve to give a fuller idea of his methods and habits those who esteem his writings will be glad to become acquainted with. Mr. Kennedy seems for some time to have been on intimate terms with the poet, and to have had frequent intercourse with him both by correspondence and personally. In the first of the three sections into which his volume is divided he records the impressions made upon him by his visits to the poet from the year 1880 up to the time of his death, together with similar reminiscences communicated to him by others, or extracted from various publications. The insight which these afford into the private life of Whitman is, as may readily be inferred, very considerable. Among the fullest and most interesting of the last kind are those written by Colonel Scovel and a Mr. Johnson, both of whom, besides describing the poet and his dwelling, give a number of pieces of information respecting the publication of his works. In this section Mr. Kennedy prints a number of letters and post-cards received by him from Whitman during the years 1881-91. Some of them are very slight, consisting of but a few words, of no particular importance, while others of them run to considerable length. In the second section of his volume Mr. Kennedy designates Whitman 'the evangelist of the human heart, the poet of universal humanity,' and proceeds to discuss what seem to him the characteristics and merits of his poetry. The last section is taken up with an essay on Whitman's style of writing, and an attempt to justify his rejection of the ordinary forms of versification. Mr. Kennedy is full of his subject, and, as need hardly be said, writes in a somewhat exalted vein.

Sir George Tressady. By Mrs. HUMPHREY WARD. London: Smith, Elder & Co. 1896.

This is unquestionably a very clever performance, and a book which will be widely read and admired. It is characterized by most, if not by all, of the excellencies of its author's previous productions, and will possibly increase the estimation in which she is already held as a writer and novelist. Whether it will live or add to her permanent fame, are questions it is at present impossible to answer. There are passages in it which are at least equal, and probably superior, to anything she has yet written. At the same time it is scarcely possible to give the work one's unqualified admiration. There are points about it which tell decidedly against it. The conversations have a general tendency to become tedious. Instead of contributing to the development of the plot, they as often as not retard it. The feeling grows upon one that those who take part in them have a fatal fluency of speech and are possessed by an inappeasible desire to hear themselves speak. As for the individuals to whom we are introduced, most of them are little if anything better than lay figures. The exceptions are the principal characters, and even here the delineation is wanting in fulness. With the exception of Lord Maxwell, Marcella's husband, who is mostly in the background though constantly hovering about the story, they are all very intense, very decided, and, to a certain extent, very explicit ; all the same nothing is seen of them save that particular side of their life which it is necessary for them to show for the development of the story. Those luminous touches by which the great masters of fiction show that the character with which they are dealing have another or higher or deeper life than that which they are directly depicting, are here for the most part wanting. The hero of the story is Sir George Tressady, a Mercian landowner and coal master ; but whether intentionally or not, the apparent aim of the story is the glorification of Marcella and her Socialism. Discussions on Socialism and its theories are all very well in their way, but one may have too much of them. Socialism, again, may certainly be introduced into fiction without violating any of its canons ; but the real subject of fiction is not the passing fashions of opinion or of Society, but that which is eternal in human nature, and of that, while there is much in it which is superficial and temporary, there is extremely little in *Sir George Tressady*. Letty, who subsequently marries Sir George Tressady, is pretty nearly a social adventuress. Her chief desire is to get into London Society to be admired and enjoy herself. She has no liking for politics, falls into questionable company, and, though living with her husband, becomes estranged from him. Sir George, on the other hand, comes under the influence of Marcella, becomes converted to her theories, throws over his political leader at a critical moment, is infatuated about Marcella and estranged from his wife. The main interest of the story lies in the fortunes of 'the Bill' which is to realise some of Marcella's reforms, Sir George's passion for Marcella, the estrangement between him and his wife, and the attempts made to bring about a reconciliation. The plot betrays no facility of invention. It is a kind of plot which is greatly in use and apparently in great favour. All the same it is high time that for the sake of art, if not for the sake of something higher, some other were tried. There is nothing heroic in falling in love with another man's wife ; nor is there anything womanly, or anything that a man would like his daughters to admire in a married woman taking up with questionable characters and preferring their company to her husband's or her home. Of course the terrible domestic infelicities which usually follow are depicted ; but art has other methods of teaching and is more concerned, and always has been, except in its periods of decadence, in revealing the charms of goodness than in giving prominence to wickedness. Sir George Tressady has excellent points about him, but his character is unformed. It is in process of formation, but Mrs. Ward makes the mistake of killing him off before her story is completed, and while the reconciliation between him and his wife is apparently being brought about. If Letty is the real heroine of the story and is to appear again, made wise by her terrible experience, an excuse for the termination may be found ; otherwise, the ending is most unsatisfactory. The mission by which Sir George meets with his death was, to say the least, foolhardy ; but perhaps that is the way intense people act. Marcella is, of course, so far as her character is revealed in the story, all that can be desired, whatever may be thought of her theories, and forms a good contrast to Letty as well as to her mother-in-law, the dowager Lady Tressady. Towards the close Letty gives evidence of having something at least of a higher and better nature than she exhibited during the first months of her marriage, but the sudden ending of the story, leaves one in doubt as to the truth of the evidence. Yet after all, it must be admitted that, like the rest of Mrs. Humphrey Ward's work, *Sir George Tressady* is, in spite of its defects, a remarkable piece of literary workmanship. It wants the notes of greatness, but it is far beyond the work of the ordinary novelist.

The Murder of Delicia. By MARIE CORELLI. London : Skeffington & Co. 1896.

The preface to this book has evidently been written with the intention that it should be read, and it deserves to be read. Some things in it are true ; one or two strike us as almost amusing. Miss Corelli has come across that brilliant set of people who imagine that women have no brains or that if they have they must necessarily be ugly or 'unsexed' or both, and has made up her mind to have her say about them. The inanity of their notion deserves to be exposed, but is it worth while to be angry with them, or to take the trouble of writing a dozen or more pages in denouncing the silly chatterers who entertain it. Most people who know the world would say it is not. No amount of writing will silence them or put sense into them. Miss Corelli has also come across a number of men who live on their wives' brains and do not hesitate to squander the earnings they have never won, upon their own whims and caprices, and sometimes upon their vices. That such creatures exist there can be no doubt. Some might say their number is increasing ; but it is doubtful, exceedingly doubtful, we should say, that their number is such, or that the temper of men in general is such, as to justify the sweeping assertion of the following sentence : 'To put it bluntly and plainly a great majority of men of the present day want women to keep them.' There may be a large number in a certain class, or they may form a class, and a pretty numerous class by themselves, but that does not warrant the assertion that 'the great majority of men' in the present want women to keep them. The complaint is usually the other way. It may be, however, that Miss Corelli has made a discovery ; but whether or not, and without denying the truth of the assertion, we should require before accepting it as an article of belief grounds more relevant than any produced either in the preface or in the body of the volume. Our respect for Miss Corelli as a novelist is much greater than it is for her as an inductive philosopher. The *Murder of Delicia* is beyond question a powerful story. It has all the enthusiasm and skill and straightforwardness and hard-hitting at social vices which is characteristic of most of her other stories. The subject of it will have been gathered from what we have said. Delicia is a novelist, highly popular, and making immense sums of money by her books. She is neither ugly nor ' unsexed,' but charming in appearance, and altogether a beautiful type of womanhood. She is also a good business woman, prompt to act, and withal sagacious and prudent. She meets with Carlyon, afterwards Lord Carlyon, an ex-officer of the Guards, and is married to him. The only thing he has to recommend him is his form and good-looks. ' Beauty' Carlyon he was wont to be called. For the rest he is vain, ignorant, and stupid, and has not a couple of ideas in his head. Half of what she makes by her books Delicia pays into his bank account. In return he pays her little attention, becomes enamoured of La Marina, *alias* Miss de Gascon, but known to her father in Eastcheap as ' my gal, Jewlia Muggins,' a favourite ballet-dancer, coarse, and fond of champagne, able to touch her nose with her toe, and capable of other artistic effects of a similar kind, yet not without a touch of rough honesty about her. Upon her Carlyon squanders his wife's earnings. Hints are dropped to Delicia of what he is about, but they are resented. Her love for him is of the thoroughly ideal sort, and she will hear nothing against him. At last, while purchasing a birthday present for him, she is accidentally undeceived in a jeweller's shop. Then comes the end. She is killed by his ingratitude, leaves £40,000 for the poor, and ' Beauty' Carlyon £250 a year. The story of all this is wonderfully well told, the characters live, the plot is managed with skill, and some of the scenes are intensely dramatic. The difficulty all through the story, however, is to understand how Delicia ever came to have so intense an affection for so poor a specimen of humanity as 'Beauty' Carlyon proves himself to be. Of course there is the fable of Cupid's blindness. But we can scarcely imagine that one so well versed in human nature as we are forced to suppose Delicia to have been, and withal so practical, notwithstanding her idealism, could fail to see through so shallow an individual, who has, besides, nothing whatever in common with her. She is thoroughly cultured, open eyed and swift to understand other matters, and yet she gives herself away to a man whose only recommendation is his physical form, and whose inanity one would have thought would have been repellent to her. There is, as it seems to us, a want of consistency in her character and doings in connection with him. When the proofs of his ingratitude are before her, she is a changed being, and one wonders how her better sense could have been so completely set aside as to allow of her marrying him. At bottom Carlyon is a fool, and is perfectly consistent throughout the story. All the same, one would be sorry to think that ' the majority of the men of the present day ' are like him.

SHORT NOTICES.

A Most Provoking Girl (Oliphant Anderson), by Margaret Moyes Black, though by no means sensational, is, to say the least, a very readable story. The locality of it is the East of Scotland, probably between Arbroath and Montrose. The plot is simple, but effective and worked out with care. Among the individuals to whom we are introduced is the inevitable minister, but fortunately there is no villain. The story for the most part is of simple Scottish life, and several touching scenes occur. But why call the heroine ' A most provoking girl ? ' Considering her character and early training she must at times have felt very bitterly provoked by the things she had to endure and the restraints put upon her.

My Bagdad (T. Fisher Unwin) by Elliott Dickson, begins with visions and ends with visions. The story between them—a well-told story of Scottish life—might have stood alone, and would have been better without these somewhat fantastical impedimenta. In the final vision the author proclaims the immortality of his book.

The Carrisford Tablets (Elliot Stock) by John Wilson, M.A., professes to be a translation of a number of Cuneiform tablets discovered at Carrisford recording the voyages and adventures of Simran, a Babylonian commissioned some 1300 years before our era to make inquiries respecting the tin mines in the South of England. Mr. Wilson has read widely for the materials for his story and gives a graphic account of what life may be supposed to have been at the remote period of Simran's adventures both in the East and in the South of Britain. Simran's adventures are numerous and often exciting ; and Mr. Wilson's account of them is instructive as well as entertaining.

The Christian Inheritance (Burns & Oates) is a volume of sermons by the Bishop of Newport. Most of them appear to have been preached on special occasions. Among them is the remarkable discourse which the author delivered at Cardiff during the meetings of the British Association for the Advancement of Science there in 1891, and which at the time of its delivery attracted considerable attention. Similar in tone and character to this are most of the sermons, particularly the two singularly eloquent discourses on Revelation and Mystery. A vein of controversy, in the present perhaps more than in most periods unavoidable in preaching, runs throughout the volume. Bishop Hedley appears to be quite as much a philosopher as a theologian. At anyrate, he is quite aware of the antagonism there is between the philosophy of the day and Catholic theology, and seeks to vindicate the latter by a series of well chosen and forcible arguments. Not the least remarkable characteristic of these sermons is their eloquence. There are passages in them of great brilliancy, which, if well delivered, must have been profoundly impressive.

In a Far Country (Alex. Gardner) is a volume of sermons on the Parable of the Prodigal Son by the Rev. Thomas Cook, M.A., minister of Levern. If their burden of thought is somewhat slight, the language in which Mr. Cook expresses himself in them is at least picturesque, if not eloquent. He has certainly seized the main thoughts of the parable, but beyond expanding them and applying them in the ordinary way he has not gone. The exhortation, ' Place your ear against your own heart,' is somewhat difficult to obey.

In his ' Modern Reader's Bible ' Dr. Moulton has now placed the Book of *Deuteronomy* (Macmillan & Co.), which he claims as affording a specially clear illustration of the principles of treatment underlying the series. As the reader will remember, Dr. Moulton's aim is to treat each book of the Bible simply as literature, and altogether apart from theological questions, religious dogma, and historic criticism, in the belief that the masterpieces of literature carry within themselves sufficient light for their own interpretation, and that they can be best enjoyed when studied by their own light alone. In his introduction Dr. Moulton emphasizes this belief, and then proceeds to analyse the book, pointing out its literary excellencies.

The text is divided into four orations, followed by the Song of Moses and the last words of the Lawgiver. As usual the volume concludes with an adequate amount of notes.

An Archæological Survey of the United Kingdom (MacLehose). This scholarly and in every way admirable address was delivered by Dr. D. Murray at the opening of the last session of the Archæological Society of Glasgow, as its President. It is a temperate but strong plea for the institution by the government of an archæological survey of the United Kingdom with a view not merely to the enumeration of the ancient monuments scattered over the country, but also to their protection and preservation. The plea is opportune, and the work might without difficulty be started and carried on at the present moment, if not in England and Ireland, in Scotland at least, where the government is busy with the revision of the Ordinance Survey. The expense of that revision would, no doubt, be increased, but surely the work deserves to be done, and to be done at once. Dr. Murray gives an account of what is being done in other countries in this direction, and the marvel is that so little has been done in this.

Messrs. Macmillan have completed the issue of their new edition of the late Mr. J. R. Green's *History of the English People* by sending out the eighth volume. It covers the period from the outbreak of the American War of Independence to the Peace of 1815, and contains an index to the whole work of a very full and complete kind. As we have more than once remarked, this edition of Mr. Green's great work belongs to the publishers' 'Eversley Series.' Like all the other works in that series, it is handsomely printed on excellent paper. The very moderate price at which it is issued ought to secure for it an abundance of readers.

In their 'Famous Scots Series,' Messrs. Oliphant, Anderson, & Ferrier have included the *Balladists* by John Geddie. The 'Balladists' are known by their works if not by their names; still, they scarcely come under what is usually understood by the phrase 'Famous Scots.' However, be that as it may, Mr. Geddie shows a considerable acquaintance with the ballad literature of the country, and has written an essay about it which to many will be pleasant and instructive reading.

The Condition of Working Women (Elliot Stock) is a joint production. The two names which appear on the title-page are Jessie Boucherett and Helen Blackburn. Other writers also have had a hand in the writing of the volume. Their work may be commended. It is written with great clearness, and, brief as it is, it is full of information and sound sense. The authors point out very distinctly the hardships which have been inflicted upon numbers of working women by recent Acts of Parliament, and advocate the cause of the sufferers with tack and judgment.

Lightning Source UK Ltd.
Milton Keynes UK
UKHW012237110219
337137UK00006B/1082/P